Lecture Notes in Artificial Intelligence   991

Subseries of Lecture Notes in Computer Science
Edited by J. G. Carbonell and J. Siekmann

Lecture Notes in Computer Science

Edited by G. Goos, J. Hartmanis and J. van Leeuwen

Springer
Berlin
Heidelberg
New York
Barcelona
Budapest
Hong Kong
London
Milan
Paris
Santa Clara
Singapore
Tokyo

Jacques Wainer
Ariadne Carvalho (Eds.)

Advances in Artificial Intelligence

12th Brazilian Symposium on Artificial Intelligence
SBIA '95, Campinas, Brazil, October 10 -12, 1995
Proceedings

 Springer

Series Editors

Jaime G. Carbonell, Carnegie Mellon University, USA

Jörg Siekmann, University of Saarland, DFKI, Germany

Volume Editors

Jacques Wainer
Ariadne Carvalho
Cidade Universitária - Barão Geraldo, UNICAMP - IMECC/DCC
Caixa Postal 6065, 13081-970 Campinas - SP, Brasil

Cataloging-in-Publication Data applied for

Die Deutsche Bibliothek - CIP-Einheitsaufnahme

Advances in artificial intelligence : proceedings / 12th Brazilian
Symposium on Artificial Intelligence, SBIA '95, Campinas,
Brazil, October 11 - 13, 1995. Jacques Wainer ; Ariadne Carvalho
(ed.). - Berlin ; Heidelberg ; New York ; Barcelona ; Budapest ;
Hong Kong ; London ; Milan ; Paris ; Tokyo : Springer, 1995
  (Lecture notes in computer science ; 991 : Lecture notes in artificial
  intelligence)
  ISBN 3-540-60436-7
NE: Wainer, Jacques [Hrsg.]; Brazilian Symposium on Artificial
  Intelligence <12, 1995, Campinas, São Paulo>; GT

CR Subject Classification (1991): I.2

ISBN 3-540-60436-7 Springer-Verlag Berlin Heidelberg New York

© Springer-Verlag Berlin Heidelberg 1995
Printed in Germany

Typesetting: Camera ready by author
SPIN 10485781   06/3142 – 5 4 3 2 1 0   Printed on acid-free paper

Preface

The Brazilian Symposium on Artificial Intelligence (SBIA) was first conceived as a gathering of Brazilian researchers, students and practitioners of AI. At the X SBIA, the Brazilian AI community realized it was mature enough to collaborate and compete with the international community. The XI SBIA adopted English as the official language, announced the conference in international forums and invited leading names of the AI community as members of the program committee.

At this XII SBIA we hope to be moving forward in the direction of making SBIA an important and truly international conference by: 1) expanding the number of international members of the program committee; 2) adopting reviewing procedures used in the best AI conferences, such as blind reviewing and discussion among reviewers; and 3) publishing the proceedings through a well known and respected publishing house.

We received 57 papers, 30 of them from abroad, distributed as follows: Portugal 8, France 6, Argentina 5, US 3, Canada 2, UK 2, and Spain, Germany, The Netherlands and India 1 each.

We would like to thank the program committee members for the difficult task of reviewing and commenting on the submitted papers. We would also like to thank SBC, FAPESP, CNPq, CAPES and IBM-Brazil for supporting the realization of the SBIA, and Springer-Verlag for publishing the proceedings of the conference.

Campinas, October 1995

Jacques Wainer
Ariadne Carvalho

Program Committee Members

Carlos Alchourron (Argentina)
Guilherme Bittencourt (Brazil)
Helder Coelho (Portugal)
Yves Demazeau (France)
Gerhard Fischer (US)
Peter Gardenfors (Sweeden)
Hector Geffner (Venezuela)
Soundar Kumara (US)
José Gabriel P. Lopes (Portugal)
Maria Carolina Monard (Brazil)
Eugenio Oliveira (Portugal)
Donia Scott (UK)
Clarisse S. De Souza (Brazil)
Tarcisio Pequeno (Brazil)
José Armando Valente (Brazil)
Rosa Viccari (Brazil)
Jacques Wainer (Brazil) **Chair**

Local Organization Committee Members

Ariadne Carvalho (UNICAMP) **Chair**
Beatriz M. Daltrini (UNICAMP)
Eduardo Kerr (TELEBRAS)
Fernando Gomide (UNICAMP)
Flávio Soares Correa da Silva (USP)
Heloisa Vieira da Rocha (UNICAMP)
Maria Cecilia C. Baranauskas (UNICAMP)
Ricardo Dahab (UNICAMP)

Reviewers

Contents

Invited papers

Rethinking and Reinventing Artificial Intelligence from the
Perspective of Human-Centered Computational Artifacts 1
Gerhard Fischer

Automatic Documentation Generation: Including Examples 12
Cécile L. Paris

Market Oriented Programming (Abstract) 26
Michael P. Wellman

Knowledge Representation and Automated Reasoning

Belief Increasing in SKL Model Frames 28
Matías Alvarado, Gustavo Núñez

Sensivity of Combination Schemes under
Conflicting Conditions and a New Method 39
A. V. Joshi, S. C. Sahasrabudhe, K. Shankar

Two Conditional Logics for Defeasible Inference:
A Comparison Preliminary Version 49
Verónica Becher

Underlying Semantics for the Assessment of Reiter's
Solution to the Frame Problem 59
Tania Bedrax-Weiss, Leopoldo E. Bertossi

Modeling Intentions with Extended Logic Programming 69
Michael da Costa Móra, José Gabriel Lopes, Helder Coelho

Labelled Theorem Proving for Substructural Logics 79
Claudia M. G. M. Oliveira

Labelled Abduction 91
Nicia Cristina Rocha Riccio, Ruy J. G. B. de Queiroz

PROMAL: Programming in Modal Action Logic 101
Odinaldo Rodrigues, Mario Benevides

A Goal Directed Reasoning for Semi-Normal Default Theories 112
Gerson Zaverucha, Sheila R.M. Veloso

Tutoring Systems

Towards New Learning Strategies in Intelligent Tutoring Systems 121
Esma Aïmeur, Claude Frasson, Carmen Alexe

Modeling the Influence of Non-Changing Quantities 131
Bert Bredeweg, Kees de Koning, Cis Schut

Mathema: A Learning Environment Based on a
Multi-Agent Architecture 141
Evandro de Barros Costa, Manoel A. Lopes, Edilson Ferneda

A General Model of Dialogue Interpretation for
Concept Tutoring Systems 151
Alexandre I. Direne

Machine Learning

Knowledge Based Clustering of Partially Characterized Objects 161
Manuel L. Campagnolo, Helder Coelho, Jorge H. Capelo

Constructing the Extensional Representation of an
Intentional Domain Theory in Inductive Logic Programming 171
M.C. Nicoletti, M.C. Monard

A Generic Algorithm for Learning Rules with Hierarchical Exceptions 181
Tobias Scheffer

Neural Networks

A Neural Model for the Visual Attention Phenomena 191
Luís Alfredo V. de Carvalho, Valéria L. Roitman

Learning Rare Categories in Backpropagation 201
Lucila Ohno-Machado, Mark A. Musen

An Automatic Adaptative Neurocomputing Algorithm for
Time Series Prediction 210
Emmanuel Passos, Romildo Valente

Distributed AI

A Computational Approach to Situation Theory Based on
Logic Programming to Design Cognitive Agents 219
Milton Corrêa, Sueli Mendes

Measuring Agreeement and Harmony in Multi-Agent Societies:
A First Approach 232
Flávio M. de Oliveira

Detecting the Opportunities of Learning from the
Interactions in a Society of Organizations 242
Marcos A. H. Shmeil, Eugenio Oliveira

Exploiting Social Reasoning to Enhance Adaptation in
Open Multi-Agent Systems 253
Jaime Simão Sichman, Yves Demazeau

Knowledge Acquisition and Knowledge Bases

A System for Aiding Discovery: Mechanisms for Knowledge Generation ... 262
Edilson Ferneda, Mário E. de Souza e Silva, Hélio de Menezes Silva

On a Composite Formalism and Approach to Presenting the
Knowledge Content of a Relational Database 272
M. M. Fonkam

Method for Knowledge Acquisition from Multiple Experts 283
Sofiane Labidi, Mohamed Mohsen Gammoudi

A Conceptual Model for a Knowledge Base Homogeneously
Stored in a Database Environment 293
Emmanuel Passos, Alberto Sade Jr., Cícero Garcez, Asterio Tanaka

Natural Language Processing

A Hierarchical Description of the Portuguese Verb 300
Paul McFetridge, Aline Villavicencio

Talisman: A Multi-Agent System for Natural Language Processing 310
Marie-Hélène Stefanini, Yves Demazeau

Part-of-Speech Tagging for Portuguese Texts 321
Aline Villavicencio, Nuno M.C. Marques
José Gabriel P. Lopes, Fabio Villavicencio

Quantification and Cognitive Constraints in Natural
Language Understanding 331
Walid S. Saba, Jean-Pierre Corriveau

Table of Contents — Posters

Interlocking Multi-Agent and Blackboard Architectures 371
Bernhard Kipper
DCS, University of Saarbrücken, Germany

A Model Theory for Paraconsistent Logic Programming 377
Carlos Viegas Damásio and Luís Moniz Pereira
CRIA, and DCS, Universidade Nova de Lisboa, Portugal

Promoting Software Reuse Through Explicit Knowledge
Representation 387
Carmen Fernandez-Chamizo, Pedro A. Gonzalez-Calero and
Mercedes Gomez-Albarran
Universidad Complutense, Spain

Efficient Learning in Multi-Layered Perceptron Using the
Grow-And-Learn Algorithm 397
Gildas Cherruel, Bassel Solaiman and Yvon Autret
Univ. de Bretagne Occidentale, and TNI, and ENSTB, France

An Non-Diffident Combinatorial Optimization Algorithm 403
Gilles Trombettoni and Bertrand Neveu
INRIA-CERMICS, France

Modelling Diagnosis Systems with Logic Programming 409
Iara Mora, José Alferes
CRIA, U. Nova de Lisboa, and DM, U. Evora, Portugal

Agreement: A Logical Approach to Approximate Reasoning 419
Luís Custodio and Carlos Pinto-Ferreira
ISR, Technical University of Lisbon, Portugal

**Constructing Extensions by Resolving a System of Linear
Equations** 429
Messaoudi Nadia
Université Aix-Marseille II, France

**Presenting Significant Information in Expert System
Explanation** 435
Michael Wolverton
Daresbury Rutherford Appleton Laboratory, UK

**A Cognitive Model of Problem Solving with Incomplete
Information** 441
Nathalie Chaignaud
LIPN, Université Paris-Nord, France

Filtering Software Specifications Written In Natural Language ... 447
Núria Castell and Angels Hernandez
Universitat Politécnica de Catalunya, Spain

Parsimonious Diagnosis in SNePS 157
Pedro A. Matos and João P. Martins
DEM, Technical University of Lisbon, Portugal

Syntactic and Semantic Filtering in a Chart Parser 465
Sayan Bhattacharyya, Steven L. Lytinen
University of Michigan, and DePaul University, USA

GA Approach to solving Multiple Vehicle Routing Problem 173
Slavko Krajcar, Davor Skrlec, Branko Pribicevic and Snjezana Blagajac
Faculty of Electrical Eng. and Computing, Croatia

**Multilevel Refinement Planning in an Interval-Based Temporal
Logic** 483
Werner Stephan and Susanne Biundo
German Research Center for AI Germany

Rethinking and Reinventing Artificial Intelligence from the Perspective of Human-Centered Computational Artifacts

Gerhard Fischer

Center for LifeLong Learning and Design (L^{3}D)
Department of Computer Science and Institute of Cognitive Science
University of Colorado at Boulder

Abstract. Many research efforts in Artificial Intelligence (AI) have focused on replacing rather than augmenting and empowering human beings. We have developed human-computer collaboration environments to demonstrate the power and the possibilities of Intelligence Augmentation (IA) with human-centered computational artifacts.

A focus on IA instead of AI requires different conceptual frameworks and different systems. Our theory is centered around shared representations of context and intent for understanding, mixed-initiative dialogs, management of trouble, and integration of working and learning. Our system building efforts exploit the unique properties of computational media rather than mimicking human capabilities. We have developed (i) specific system architectures including a multifaceted architecture characterizing the components of design environments, and a process architecture for the evolutionary development of such environments, (ii) specific modules such as critiquing systems, and (iii) a variety of design environments for specific application domains.

1. IA: The New Look of AI

Traditionally, the most widely understood goal of Artificial Intelligence has been to understand and build autonomous, intelligent thinking machines. We believe with a number of other researchers that a more important goal is to understand and build interactive knowledge media or collaborative problem solving environments. The idea of human augmentation, beginning with Engelbart (Engelbart and English 1968) has been elaborated in the last 25 years (e.g., (Stefik 1986; Hill 1989; Fischer 1990; Bobrow 1991; Norman 1993; Terveen 1995) and is gaining widespread acceptance as the dominant research paradigm for AI.

In collaborative problem solving systems, users and the system share the problem solving and decision making and different role distributions may be chosen depending on the user' goals, the user's knowledge and the task domain. Any collaborative systems raises two important questions:

- What part of the responsibility has to be exercised by human beings?
- How do we organize things so that the humans can communicate effectively with the computational system?

Collaborative systems can be differentiated from autonomous systems (such as expert systems) along the following dimensions:

- a partial understanding and knowledge of complex task domains is acceptable,
- two agents can achieve more than one, especially by exploiting the asymmetry between agents,
- breakdowns are not as detrimental, especially if the system provides resources for dealing with the unexpected,
- background assumptions do not need to be fully articulated beforehand, but can be incrementally articulated,
- semi-formal system architectures are appropriate, and
- humans enjoy "doing" and "deciding" by being involved in the process.

Collaborative problem-solving approaches do not deny the power of automation (Billings 1991), but they focus our concerns on the "right kind of automation" including interaction mechanisms designed for humans rather than for programs.

2. Requirements for Collaborative Problem Solving Systems

Beyond Intelligent, Deaf, Blind and Paraplegic Agents. Bobrow (Bobrow 1991) has characterized the prevalent style of building AI systems as follows: *"a human agent will formulate the problem in a previously defined language understandable to the computational environment including background knowledge which will then use logical reasoning to achieve the desired goal."* This isolation assumption has led to a deemphasis of collaborative systems' dimensions such as communication, coordination and integration.

Beyond User Interfaces. Effective human-computer collaboration is more than creating attractive displays on a computer screen: it requires providing the computer with a considerable body of knowledge about a task domain, about users and about communication processes. Computational environments need to support *human problem-domain communication* (Fischer and Lemke 1988) by modeling the basic abstractions of a domain (as pursued in efforts in domain modeling) thereby giving designers the feeling that they interact with a domain rather than with low-level computer abstractions. Domain-orientation allows humans to take both the content and context of a problem into account, whereas the strength of formal representations is their independence of specific domains to make domain-independent reasoning methods applicable (Norman 1993).

Mixed-Initiative Dialogs. Despite the fact that communication capabilities such as mixed-initiative dialogs (Carbonell 1970) have been found crucial for intelligent systems, the progress to achieve them has been rather modest. Collaborative systems must support information volunteering by the users as well as by the system. Real users are not just data entry clerks (a role which they are left with in many expert systems), but they must be able to volunteer information (Fischer and Stevens 1991) and integrate new knowledge. On the other hand, humans often learn by receiving answers to questions which they have never posed or which they were unable to pose. Information access techniques must be complemented by information volunteering techniques in which the systems provides information which is relevant to the task at hand (Nakakoji and Fischer 1995).

Shared Understanding. Collaboration is a process in which two or more agents work together to achieve shared goals. In human-centered approaches, these goals originate from the humans, not from the computational artifact. This sets our approaches apart from expert systems and intelligent tutoring systems which are based on system-driven architectures. In our research, a shared understanding is achieved through the domain orientation, the construction and the specification of an artifact(Fischer, Nakakoji et al. 1993).

3. Examples of Human-Centered Computational Artifacts

Domain-Oriented Design Environments. Domain-oriented design environments (DODEs) support collaboration between (1) all stakeholders in a design process and (2) between stakeholders and computational environments. They serve as model for the design of collaborative systems by exploring and supporting different relationships and task responsibilities between humans and computers. Within human-computer collaboration, they are grounded within the complementary approach rather than the emulation or replacement approach by exploiting the strengths and the weaknesses of human and computational agents. They are semi-formal systems that integrate object-oriented hierarchies of domain objects, rule-based critiquing systems, case-based catalog components, and argumentative hypermedia systems. They do limited reasoning and interpretations, trigger breakdowns, deliver information, and support the exploration of the rationale behind the artifact.

By representing models of specific domains, DODEs provide a shared context and ground design with representations supporting mutual education and understanding by all stakeholders. In our research, *DODEs* have emerged as systems serving the integration of working, learning, and collaborating by modeling problem domains. They (1) allow users to focus on their tasks (and not just on the interface), (2) increase the usefulness without sacrificing usability, (3) facilitate human problem-domain interaction, and (4) support short-term and indirect, long-term collaboration. In the context of these research efforts, we have explored topics such as design by composition, design by modification, the integration of problem framing and problem solving, the use of critics to increase the back-talk of situations, and the reconceptualization of breakdowns as sources for creativity.

Critiquing. The critiquing approach (Fischer, Lemke et al. 1991) is an effective way to use computational knowledge bases to aid users in their work and to support learning on demand. In many design situations, artifacts do not speak for themselves. To address this problem, we augmented our environments with computational critics identifying breakdowns, which might have remained unnoticed without them. These breakdowns provide learning opportunities for designers by supporting them to reframe problems, to attempt alternative design solutions, and to explore relevant background knowledge. Critics in design environments "look over the shoulder" of users as they perform tasks in computational environments and signal breakdowns and offer critiques from time to time. Critics compute their advice by using domain knowledge to examine the actions users perform (e.g., information spaces visited) and the products they create (e.g., constructions and specifications). In critiquing, humans select (partial) goals and communicate some of them to the system, attempt to achieve these goals, and retain control of the interactions. Critics detect potential problems and provide information relevant to the identified problems. Users evaluate the critiques and decide how to respond.

Examples of Design Environments. Over the last ten years, we have developed design environments in several domains, including kitchen design (Nakakoji and Fischer 1995), computer network design (Fischer, Grudin et al. 1992) and voice dialog design (Repenning and Sumner 1992). The Voice Dialog Design Environment (VDDE) illustrates our conceptual framework. Voice dialog interfaces consist of a series of voice prompted menus. Users press buttons on a telephone keypad and the system responds with appropriate voice instructions. Current interface design techniques for voice dialog systems are based on flow charts. It is difficult for designers, customers and end-users (representing the different stakeholders, each suffering from their symmetry of ignorance) of these systems to anticipate what the (audio) interaction will sound by simply looking at a static visual diagram. To experience breakdowns, simulations are needed which can serve as representations for mutual understanding by allowing designers, customers and end-users "experience" the actual audio interface. The VDDE allows domain designers to create graphic specifications. The behavior of the design can be simulated at any time. Design simulation consists of a visual trace of the execution path combined with audio feedback of all prompts and messages encountered. The designer can activate different rule sets for critiquing and determine with the critiquing parameter the "intrusiveness" of the critics. VDDE is implemented in Agentsheets and Hypercard using AppleEvents for the communication between the two systems.

With our prototypical developments, we were able to demonstrate the following learning and collaboration possibilities provided by DODES:

- the creation of a mutual understanding between stakeholders through an external representation of the artifact in a form understandable to all of them,

- the domain-orientation enhances the conversation with the materials of a design situation,

- simulations let stakeholders experience behavior and see the consequences of their assumptions,

- critiquing signals violation of rules and controversial design decisions, and

- argumentation provides the argument behind rules and artifacts to empower designers to disagree.

A Process Model for DODES. Our process model (Fischer, McCall et al. 1994) for continual development of design environments from an initial seed through iterations of growth and reseeding is illustrated in Figure 1:

- the *seeding* process, in which domain designers and environment developers work together to instantiate a domain-oriented design environment seeded with domain knowledge.

- the *evolutionary growth* process, in which domain designers add information to the seed as they use it to create design artifacts.

- the *reseeding* process, in which environment developers help domain designers to reorganize and reformulate information so it can be reused to support future design tasks.

During seeding, environment developers and domain designers collaborate to create a design environment seed. During evolutionary growth, domain designers create artifacts that add new domain knowledge to the seed. In the reseeding phase, environment developers again collaborate with domain designers to organize, formalize, and generalize new knowledge.

The top half shows how DODEs are created through a collaboration between the environment developers and domain designers. The bottom half shows the use of a DODE in the creation of an individual artifact through a collaboration between domain designers and clients. The use of a DODE contributes to its evolution; i.e., new knowledge, developed in the context of an individual project, is incorporated into the evolving design environment.

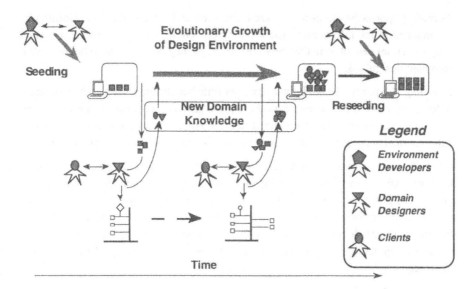

Figure 1: The "Seeding - Evolutionary Growth - Reseeding (SER)" Model:
A Process Model for the Development and Evolution of DODES

The Seeding Process. A seed is built by customizing the domain-independent design environment architecture to a particular domain through a process of knowledge construction. Although the goal is to construct as much knowledge as possible during seed-building, for complex and changing domains complete coverage is not possible. Therefore, the seed is explicitly designed to capture design knowledge during use (Girgensohn 1992).

Domain designers must participate in the seeding process because they have the expertise to determine when a seed can support their work practice. Rather than expecting designers to articulate precise and complete system requirements prior to seed building, we view seed building as knowledge construction (in which knowledge structures and access methods are collaboratively designed and built) rather than as knowledge acquisition (in which knowledge is transferred from an expert to a knowledge engineer and finally expressed in formal rules and procedures). New seed requirements are elicited by constructing and evaluating domain-oriented knowledge structures.

Evolutionary Growth Through Use. During the use phase, each design task has the potential to add to the knowledge contained in the system. New construction kit parts and rules are required to support design in rapidly changing domains. Issue-based information in the seed can also be augmented by each design task as alternative approaches to problems are discovered and recorded. The information accumulated in the information space during this phase is mostly informal because designers either cannot formalize new knowledge or they do not want to be distracted from their design task.

Reseeding. Acquiring design knowledge is of little benefit unless it can be delivered to designers when it is relevant. Periodically, the growing information space must be structured, generalized, and formalized in a reseeding process, which increases the computational support the system is able to provide to designers (Shipman 1993).

The task of reseeding involves environment developers working with domain designers. After a period of use, the information space can be a jumble of annotations, partial designs, and discussions mixed in with the original seed and any modifications performed by the domain designers. To make this information useful, the environment developers work with the domain designers in a process of organizing, generalizing, and formalizing the new information and updating the initial seed.

4. Impact

Knowledge Acquisition versus Domain Construction. Domain-oriented systems offer many potential benefits for users such as more intuitive interfaces, better task support, and knowledge-based assistance. A key challenge for system developers constructing domain-oriented systems is determining what the current domain is and what the future domain should be; i.e. what entities should the system embody and how should they be represented. Determining an appropriate domain model is challenging because domains are not static entities that objectively exist, but instead they are dynamic entities that are constructed over time by a community of practice. New software development models and new computational tools are needed that support these communities to create initial models of the domain and to evolve these models over time to meet changing needs and practices.

The domain modeling approach assumes there exists a common conceptual model of the domain shared by all practitioners and the problem is simply to identify what this model is and codify it. This approach falls into the category of first generation design methods that assume a strict separation between design, use, and implementation phases. In the design phase, these approaches try to identify the domain model through knowledge acquisition practices such as interviewing selected domain experts. As such, these approaches do not acknowledge the situated (Suchman 1987) and tacit (Polanyi 1966) nature of professional expertise. In the implementation phase, these approaches adopt an engineering perspective in that they emphasize domain model representations rooted in computational formalisms rather than representations rooted in work practices. The result is domain models that cannot be inspected or modified by domain practitioners to reflect changing work practices.

The domain construction approach address these shortcomings by explicitly acknowledging that shared domain models do not de facto exist but instead are socially constructed over time by communities of practice. As such, this approach emphasizes the prominent role that domain practitioners must play in constructing an initial model of the domain rooted in work practices and evolving this model over time to suit their changing needs. Computational tools and new models of software development are needed that enable domain practitioners to fully participate in the design and evolution of their domain-oriented system.

The predominant activity in designing complex systems is the participants teaching and instructing each other (Greenbaum and Kyng 1991). Complex problems require more knowledge than any single person possesses, making communication and collaboration among all the involved stakeholders a necessity. Domain designers understand the practice and environment developers know the technology. None of these carriers of knowledge can guarantee that their knowledge is superior or more complete compared to other people's knowledge. The goal of the seeding process is to activate as much knowledge from as many stakeholders as possible taking into account that system requirements are not so much analytically specified as they are collaboratively evolved through an iterative process of consultation between all stakeholders. This iterative process of consultation requires representations (such as prototypes, mock-ups, sketches, scenarios, or use situations that can be experienced) which are intelligible and can serve as "objects-to-think-with" for all involved stakeholders.

This iterative process is important to support the interrelationship between problem framing and problem solving documented by many design methodologists (Schoen 1983). They argue convincingly that (1) one cannot gather information meaningfully unless one has understood the problem, but one cannot understand the problem without information about it; and (2) professional practice has at least as much to do with defining a problem as with solving a problem. New requirements emerge during development because they cannot be identified until portions of the system have been designed or implemented. The conceptual structures underlying complex software systems are too complicated to be specified accurately in advance, and too complex to be built faultlessly. Specification and implementation have to co-evolve, requiring the owners of the problems to be present in the development.

Supporting Work Practices. The development and evolution (see Figure 1) of computational artifacts requires the collaboration between system developers and domain practitioners raising the following issues:

(1) What software development methodologies are best suited to support the process of system developers and domain practitioners engaging in collaborative domain construction and evolution?

(2) What tools are needed to assist ongoing developer-practitioner communication during system development and extension?

(3) What system architectures are required for developers to create domain-oriented systems in an iterative, yet resource-efficient manner?

(4) What mechanisms can these architectures provide to support domain practitioners to incrementally enrich their tools with computationally interpretable design languages without developer support?

Integrating Working and Learning. Critiquing naturally offers learning opportunities to users. A critic offers alternative perspectives on what a user has done by pointing out potential problems, suggesting additional relevant information to consider, and making reasonable guesses to fill in low-level details. Critiquing brings not just the immediate benefit of improving the current product, but it exposes users to new knowledge.

Critiquing is one way to support learning on demand (Fischer 1991)— learning is contextualized to the task at hand. Critiquing provides support for users who are engaged in understanding, formulating and solving their own problems, rather than solving the problems which the system posed (this is a fundamental difference which sets our approaches apart from intelligent tutoring systems).

Using systems for real work will lead to situations in which the system lacks the knowledge and understanding for a specific problem. End-user modifiability support is needed to allow users to integrate their knowledge into the system (causing the evolutionary growth as illustrated in Figure 1).

Mimicking versus Complementing. Human-computer collaboration can be conceptualized and operationalized from two different perspectives (Terveen 1995):

(1) the *human emulation* approach where the basic assumption is to endow computers with human-like abilities (such as natural language, speech, etc.), and

(2) the *human complementary* approach which exploits the asymmetric abilities of humans and computers and tries to identify the most desirable and most adequate role distributions between humans and computational environments (Billings 1991).

Our work is grounded in the complementary approach. We have explored (depending on the task, the interest and the people involved) different styles of collaboration.

5. Conclusions

The challenge for AI is to augment and empower human intelligence by creating collaborative support systems in which humans can concentrate on the tasks which they can do best. We need systems that are convivial, domain-oriented, open, evolvable and provide a shared understanding for mutual learning and mutual understanding of all stakeholders involved.

Acknowledgments. The author would like to thank the members of the Center for Lifelong Learning and Design at the University of Colorado who have made major contributions to the conceptual framework and systems described in this paper. The research was supported by (1) the National Science Foundation, Grant RED-9253425, (2) the ARPA HCI program, Grant N66001-94-C-6038, (3) Nynex, Science and Technology Center, (4) Software Research Associates (SRA), and (5) PFU.

References

Billings, C. E. (1991). Human-Centered Aircraft Automation: A Concept and Guidelines. NASA Ames Research Center, NASA Technical Memorandum, No. 103885. Moffett Field, CA,

Bobrow, D. G. (1991). Dimensions of Interaction. AI Magazine. 64-80.

Carbonell, J. R. (1970). Mixed-Initiative Man-Computer Instructional Dialogues. BBN Report No. 1971.

Engelbart, D. C. and W. K. English (1968). A Research Center for Augmenting Human Intellect. Proceedings of the AFIPS Fall Joint Computer Conference. Washington, D.C., The Thompson Book Company. 395-410.

Fischer, G. (1991). Supporting Learning on Demand with Design Environments. Proceedings of the International Conference on the Learning Sciences 1991 (Evanston, IL). Charlottesville, VA, Association for the Advancement of Computing in Education. 165-172.

Fischer, G., J. Grudin, et al. (1992). Supporting Indirect, Collaborative Design with Integrated Knowledge-Based Design Environments. Human Computer Interaction, Special Issue on Computer Supported Cooperative Work. 281-314.

Fischer, G. and A. C. Lemke (1988). Construction Kits and Design Environments: Steps Toward Human Problem-Domain Communication. Human-Computer Interaction. 179-222.

Fischer, G., A. C. Lemke, et al. (1991). The Role of Critiquing in Cooperative Problem Solving. ACM Transactions on Information Systems. 123-151.

Fischer, G., R. McCall, et al. (1994). Seeding, Evolutionary Growth and Reseeding: Supporting Incremental Development of Design Environments. Human Factors in Computing Systems, CHI'94 Conference Proceedings (Boston, MA). 292-298.

Fischer, G., K. Nakakoji, et al. (1993). Facilitating Collaborative Design through Representations of Context and Intent. Proceedings of AAAI-93 Workshop, AI in Collaborative Design (Washington DC). 293-312.

Fischer, G. and C. Stevens (1991). Information Access in Complex, Poorly Structured Information Spaces. Human Factors in Computing Systems, CHI'91 Conference Proceedings (New Orleans, LA). New York, 63-70.

Girgensohn, A. (1992). End-User Modifiability in Knowledge-Based Design Environments. Ph.D. Dissertation, TechReport CU-CS-595-92. University of Colorado. Boulder, CO.

Greenbaum, J. and M. Kyng (1991). Design at Work: Cooperative Design of Computer Systems. Hillsdale, NJ, Lawrence Erlbaum Associates.

Nakakoji, K. and G. Fischer (1995). Intertwining Knowledge Delivery and Elicitation: A Process Model for Human-Computer Collaboration in Design. Knowledge-Based Systems Journal. Vol. 8, Issue 2-3, 1995. 94-104

Norman, D. A. (1993). Things That Make Us Smart. Reading, MA, Addison-Wesley Publishing Company.

Polanyi, M. (1966). The Tacit Dimension. Garden City, NY, Doubleday.

Repenning, A. and T. Sumner (1992). Using Agentsheets to Create a Voice Dialog Design Environment. Proceedings of the 1992 ACM/SIGAPP Symposium on Applied Computing. ACM Press. 1199-1207.

Schoen, D. A. (1983). The Reflective Practitioner: How Professionals Think in Action. New York, Basic Books.

Shipman, F. (1993). Supporting Knowledge-Base Evolution with Incremental Formalization. Ph.D. Dissertation, TechReport CU-CS-658-93. University of Colorado. Boulder, CO.

Suchman, L. A. (1987). Plans and Situated Actions. Cambridge, UK, Cambridge University Press.

Terveen, L. G. (1995). An Overivew of Human-Computer Collaboration. Knowledge-Based Systems Journal. Vol. 8, Issue 2-3, 1995

Automatic Documentation Generation: Including Examples

Cécile L. Paris

Information Technology Research Institute
University of Brighton
Lewes Road
Brighton, BN2 4AT
UK
e-mail: Cecile.Paris@itri.bton.ac.uk

Abstract. Good documentation is critical for user acceptance of any system, and empirical studies have shown that examples can greatly increase effectiveness of system documentation. However, studies also show that badly integrated text and examples can be actually detrimental compared to using either text or examples alone. It is thus clear that in order to provide useful documentation automatically, a system must be capable of providing well-integrated examples to illustrate its points.
Previous work on example generation has concentrated on the issue of retrieving or constructing examples. In our work, we looked at the *integration* of text and examples. We identified how text and examples co-constrain each other and showed that a system must consider example generation as an integral part of the generation process. We implemented a system capable of producing documentation that integrated text and examples.

1 Introduction

Good documentation is critical for user acceptance of any system, and, increasingly, it comes in both conventional manuals as well as on-line facilities. These are often based on hypertext or similar retrieval methods. Advances in areas such as knowledge-based systems, Natural Language Generation and multi-media now make it possible to investigate the automatic generation of documentation from the underlying knowledge bases. This has several important benefits: it is easily accessible; it avoids frequent problems of inconsistency (as the information presented is obtained directly from the knowledge bases); and not the least, it can take the user, and the dialogue context into account.

Examples can greatly contribute to the effectiveness of documentation. Empirical studies have found that the inclusion of examples in documentation can greatly increase

---

This work was carried out with Vibhu Mittal, when both Dr. Mittal and the author were at the University of Southern California/Information Sciences Institute. The author gratefully acknowledges support from NASA-Ames grant NCC 2-520 and DARPA contract DABT63-91-C-0025.

user comprehension, e.g., [18, 2]. In order to provide useful documentation automatically, then, a system must not only generate good descriptions, but it must also provide examples. This raises at least two issues: (1) finding appropriate examples and (2), making effective use of them. While the first issue has been investigated previously, e.g., [20, 22], the second one remains largely unstudied. This is the issue we addressed in our effort to build a user-oriented documentation facility for the Explainable Expert System (EES) framework [24].

Building on work in psychology, education, computational generation of examples and natural language generation, we studied how text and examples interact with each other. Our aim was to build a system which can provide appropriate and well-structured examples in the context of the surrounding text. In this paper, we argue that example generation should be considered an integral part of the documentation generation process, i.e., that examples *must* be *integrated* within the surrounding text. Indeed, psychological evidence shows that badly integrated text and examples can be detrimental compared to using either text or examples alone, e.g., [1]. We present a text generation system that achieves this integration by planning a presentation (text and examples) taking into account relevant factors in the generation of these two rhetorical devices. Finally, we present a specific example from our system, in which documentation about a specific programming language is generated.

2   Previous work and Open Issues

There have been considerable efforts in analyzing the type of examples that may be useful to present to the user (e.g., [10]), as well as in deciding whether an example should be retrieved or constructed, and on how to retrieve the appropriate example, e.g., [21, 20, 23]. Other work has focused on *when* to present examples [27]. However, none of these studies looked at generating both text and examples, and thus did not look at the issue of ensuring their integration.

In natural language generation, researchers have used examples as one of the rhetorical strategies used to produce texts, e.g., [9, 17], but did not address the issue of choosing the examples to fit a specific description and integrating them into the text.

Finally, there is a large body of work on the use of examples in education, e.g., [6], cognitive science and psychology, e.g., [19], and documentation, e.g., [2]. Although much of this work is not immediately computationally applicable, it suggests constraints to take into account when generating texts and examples.

Our work builds on the work mentioned above and our own analysis of documentation material to develop a system that generates appropriate examples in the context of a surrounding text to form a coherent, well-structured presentation.

3   Interactions between Text and Examples

In order to identify the relevant factors in the interaction between text and examples, the system must consider at least the following points:

1. what should be presented through text, through examples, or using both text and examples?

2. if examples are to be included, will there be one or multiple examples? If more than one example, how many? what information should each one convey? How should they be ordered?
3. how should the example(s) be positioned with respect to the surrounding text? within, before, or after the text?
4. can the example(s) cause additional text to be generated that may not otherwise have been presented?

To address these issues, the production of the examples and the surrounding text have to be considered together. For example, to decide which aspects of the presentation should be illustrated with examples, a system must know the important features to convey. But, feature importance depends upon the context, and is based on factors such as the type of text (e.g., tutorial *vs* reference) and what the discourse is about [12]. Much of this information is important when constructing a text as well, and will already be available in the discourse planning context. A module for generating examples can thus take advantage of this information.

A LIST contains zero or more pieces of data elements. Examples of
lists are:

```
(aardvark)            ;; a list of one element
(red yellow green)    ;; a list of several elements
(2 3 5 11 19)         ;; a list can contain numbers
(3 french fries)      ;; data elements can be of
                      ;; different types
```

Given the three lists: (1 2), (3 4) and (5 6), the following is also a list:
```
((1 2) (3 4) (5 6))       ;; a list can contain other lists
```

Fig. 1. Using prompts to make explicit the information contained in the ordering of the examples [25].

The interaction actually goes both ways: a decision on which aspects of the information are to be presented through examples affects the textual description as well.[1] Consider for instance, the following definition of the LISP concept list:

A list consists of a left parenthesis, zero or more data elements, followed by a right parenthesis. *The data elements can be either symbols, numbers, or a combination of these two types.*

Compare this definition with that in Fig. 1. In the figure, the information that, above, is expressed in italics was instead communicated through examples. It is thus clear that in this case, the text planning component must know whether and what examples are being presented.

---

[1] Note that these issues are similar to the ones that arise in the planning and presentation of *other* explanatory devices – such as diagrams, pictures and analogies, e.g., [4].

Another source of interaction occurs when an example embodies more than one point, or when a group of examples illustrate a point together. In such a case, the system needs to generate a *prompt*, that is a marker focusing attention on the points being made. (For example, the comments next to the examples in Fig. 1 are prompts.) Since these prompts can be textual, they will also need to be planned by the text-planner. To plan them, the system needs to know not only what the examples illustrate but also what is implied by their ordering. Consider again the definition in Fig. 1. The examples illustrate the fact that the data elements in a list can be of different types and in any number. The order of the examples is important as examples are introduced from simplest to most complex, each building on the previous one. In this case, the author chose to make explicit the information that is implicit in the ordering of the examples and included a comment (a prompt) for each example.

Furthermore, it might be necessary to include yet more text between the examples to ensure the coherence of the presentation, or in order to set up an example properly. This is also done in Fig. 1, where the three lists (1 2), (3 4), and (5 6) are introduced before the last example.

Finally, the examples are given after the features they illustrate have been mentioned in the text. Studies have shown that this results in the most understandable texts [5]. Note, however, that while each group of examples follows the mention in the text of the feature they illustrate, they are interspersed with text.

To generate coherent descriptions which include examples, the generation of examples must thus be tightly integrated within the generation process: text and examples must co-constrain each other. In the next sections, we describe our documentation context, present a system that achieves the desired integration and illustrate it with an actual scenario.

4 Generating integrated explanations

Our system is part of the documentation facility we built for the Explainable Expert Systems (EES) framework [24], a framework for building expert systems capable of explaining their reasoning as well as their domain knowledge. In EES, a user specifies both a domain model (in the high level knowledge representation language Loom [7][2]), and problem solving principles, that is, methods for solving problems in the domain. Given these and a variabilized goal to achieve, EES generates an expert system to solve goals of the same form.

The problem solving methods have to be written in a specific plan language, IN-TEND, which was developed in the project. INTEND is specified in the Backus-Naur Form (BNF),[3] a fragment of which is shown in Fig. 2. The grammar contains productions, and, optionally 'filter-functions' on the productions, that is, tests that have to be satisfied. For instance 'pred-relation-form-test' is a filter on the pred-relation-form production.[4]

---

[2] Loom is a KL-ONE type language.

[3] For use by the generation facility, the grammar is transformed into an equivalent form in Loom.

[4] Transforming the BNF form to a Loom representation was a fairly straightforward task. How-

The grammar of INTEND is quite complex, and thus provides a good test-bed for an on-line documentation facility. With such an on-line facility, users can get information as to what might be wrong when a plan does not parse, as well as descriptions of the various constructs involved, together with examples.

```
if-form := '( 'IF predicate-form 'THEN expression
                           { 'ELSE expression } ') ;
restricted-expression := var-name | concept-desc |
                      function-form | predicate-form ;
predicate-form := pred-relation-form | pred-logical-form |
                pred-action-form ;
pred-relation-form := '( relation-name restricted-expression + ')
                          |> pred-relation-form-test ;
pred-action-form := action-form   |> pred-action-test ;
pred-logical-form :=
          '( 'AND predicate-form + ') |
          '( 'OR  predicate-form + ') |
          '( 'NOT predicate-form ');
function-form := '( relation-name restricted-expression + ')
                    |> function-relation-form-test ;
```

Fig. 2. A fragment of the INTEND grammar.

The documentation for the grammar symbol `predicate-form`, whose BNF definition is shown in Fig. 2, is shown in Fig. 3. (This is taken from our domain of local area networks.) Consider the examples and the textual explanation in this figure. The first three examples are *positive*, while the fourth is a *negative* example (or a *counterexample*). The mutual constraints of the text and the examples can be seen again in many places:

1. The examples illustrate features mentioned in the text, namely the syntax of the `predicate-relation-form`.
2. The first three examples are introduced with 'background' text, to make sure they are understood as positive examples:
   "Examples of predicate-relation-forms are ... "
3. Because the positive examples are introduced with text, they occur together, rather than interspersed with the negative example.
4. The sentence "However, the following is not a ... " is generated to make an explicit contrast between positive and negative examples, as well as mark the negative example.

---

ever, the filter-functions on the productions could not be extracted automatically. These were annotated by hand.

5. The negative example selected causes the generation of additional text both *before* and *after* the presentation of the example. This is because the example is not just *not a* `predicate-relation-form`, but it is also a `function-form`, a different (but similar) construct which can be contrasted with the `predicate-relation-` `-form`. Additional text is generated first to introduce the negative example as a contrast to the positive ones, and then to explain the differences between the two similar constructs.

A predicate-form is a restricted-expression. It returns a boolean value, and the number of arguments in a predicate-form is equal to the arity of the relation. A predicate-form can be of three types: a predicate-relation-form, a predicate-action-form, or a predicate-logical-form.

A predicate-relation-form is a relation-name followed by some arguments. The arguments are restricted-expressions, such as variables, concepts, function-forms and predicate-forms. Examples of predicate-relation-forms are:

```
(INDICATOR-STATE LED-1      ON)
(HARDWARE-STATUS LANBRIDGE-2 FAULTY)
(CONNECTED-TO     DECSERVER-1 VAX-A)
```

However, the following example is not a predicate-relation-form, but a function-form, because the number of arguments is not equal to the arity of the relation:

```
(CONNECTED-TO DECSERVER-1)
```

The difference between a function-form and a predicate-relation-form is that the function-form takes one less argument than the arity of the relation, and returns the range of the relation, while the predicate-logical-form takes as many arguments as the arity and returns a boolean value.

A predicate-action-form is ...

Fig. 3. The documentation for 'predicate-form'.

This scenario also illustrates the other aspects that have to be taken into consideration when generating integrated text and examples:

1. It is not enough to know the important features to convey. The system also has to differentiate between *variable* features and *fixed* features. Fixed features are those that cannot vary. In this scenario, the fact that a `predicate-relation-form` must begin and end with a parenthesis is a fixed feature. On the other hand, variable features are those which can vary within a certain range in a positive example – in this case, the relation-name is a variable feature. It is usually necessary to provide several examples to communicate the variable nature of the feature [3]. In this case, several relation names are used in an attempt to ensure the user realizes their variable nature. On the other hand, it is not always necessary to explicitly state fixed features, as they will become obvious from several examples.

2. The presentation order of the examples is especially important to communicate the *critical features* of a concept. Critical features are features which, if modified, cause the example to change from positive to negative. In this case, the relationship between the arity and the number of arguments is a critical feature. By contrasting the third and fourth example, which are identical except for the number of arguments, the pair highlights the critical feature. In general, examples should be pairwise maximally different if they are positive examples, and minimally different if they are a positive-negative pair [5].

This scenario illustrates again the close relationship between text and examples. Having discussed this close relationship, we now describe how our generation system can generate integrated explanations, and present a trace of the system as it generates the explanation presented in this scenario.

4.1 The Generation Framework

Our framework implements the integration of text and example within a text-generation system. More specifically, we use a text-planning system that constructs text by explicitly reasoning about the communicative goal to be achieved, as well as how goals relate to each other rhetorically to form a coherent text [15, 17, 16]. Given a top level communicative goal (such as (KNOW-ABOUT HEARER (CONCEPT PREDICATE-FORM))),[5] the system finds plans capable of achieving this goal. Plans typically post further subgoals to be satisfied. These are expanded, and planning continues until primitive speech acts are achieved. The result of the planning process is a discourse tree, where the nodes represent goals at various levels of abstraction, with the root being the initial goal, and the leaves representing primitive realization statements, such as (INFORM ...) statements. The discourse tree also includes *coherence relations* [8], which indicate how the various portions of text resulting from the discourse tree will be related rhetorically. This tree is then passed to a grammar interface which converts it into a set of inputs suitable for input to a grammar.

Plan operators can be seen as small schemas which describe how to achieve a goal; they are designed by studying natural language texts and transcripts. They include a goal, substeps, and conditions for their applicability. These can refer to the system knowledge base, the user model, or the context (the current text plan tree and the dialogue history). Two of the plan operators used in our system are shown in Fig. 4. The first one is used to describe objects by describing a concept in terms of its parent and possibly elaborating on this description. The second one can be used to elaborate upon a description by describing the sub-types of a concept.

Using this framework, the generation of examples can be accomplished by explicitly posting the goals of providing examples while constructing the text, i.e., some of the plan operators include the generation of examples as one of their steps. This ensures that the examples embody specific information that either illustrates or complements the information in the accompanying textual description, and that the text to be generated will reflect the presence of examples. The constraints of the plan operators indicate

---

[5] See the references given above for details on the notation used to represent these goals.

how the text and the examples co-constrain each other. Because the same planning mechanism is used to plan the text and the examples, integration is achieved in a straightforward way.

```
( define-text-plan-operator
   :effect (know-about H (concept ?c))
   :constraints (and (isa? ?c object)
                     (isa? ?c ?parent))
   :nucleus (bel H (isa ?c ?parent))
   :satellites (((elaboration ?concept) *optional*)))

( define-text-plan-operator
   :effect (elaboration ?concept)
   :constraints (disjoint-covering ?c ?d-c)
   :nucleus ((setq ?d-j (order-maxim-of-end-weight ?d-c))
             (inform S H (disjoint-cover ?c ?d-j)))
   :satellites (((foreach ?d-j (know-about H (?d-j given ?c))))))
```

Fig. 4. Some sample plans from our application.

4.2 A Trace of the System

We illustrate how our system integrates text and examples by working through the generation of the example shown in Fig. 3, that is, a description of a grammar concept for a non-expert user.

The system initially begins with the top-level goal: (KNOW-ABOUT H (CONCEPT PREDICATE-FORM)), meaning: achieve the state where the hearer knows (or understands) the concept of predicate-form. The text planner searches for applicable plan operators, and, finding the first plan presented in Fig. 4,[6] posts the two subgoals indicated in the plan: one to give a make the hearer believe that (predicate-form) is a restricted-expression (its parent in the Loom hierarchy), and another (optional) to provide more information (elaborate).

At this point, the discourse tree has two un-expanded nodes: (BEL H (ISA PREDICATE-FORM RESTRICTED-FORM)) and (ELABORATION PREDICATE-FORM). The planner expands the first subgoal by first indicating the concept-parent relationship ("a predicate form is a restricted expression") and then informing the user of the attributes differentiating a predicate-form from a restricted-expression ("it returns a boolean value ... ").

The goal to elaborate upon a concept is expanded in turn. The plan chosen here is the one shown in Fig. 4, which presents the different types of predicate-forms

---

[6] When several plans are available, the system chooses one using *selection heuristics* designed by [17].

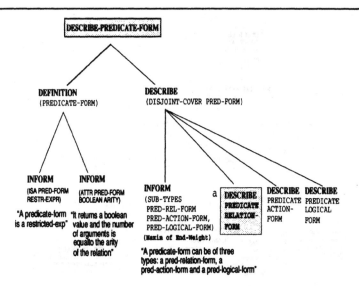

Fig. 5. A skeletal fragment of the text plan generated for the initial text.

that exist, namely `predicate-relation-form`, `predicateaction-form`, and `predicate-logical-form`. Because these sub-types might be of differing complexity, and it is important to present the information from the simplest one to the most complex one (according to the maxim of end-weight in linguistics [26]), one step of the plan operator explicitly orders the sub-types before presenting them to the user. This ordering is done based on some general complexity heuristics: in this case, `predicate-action-form` is considered more complex than `predicate-relation-form` because it is allowed to have an `action-form` (a goal-posting construct) as one of its arguments. The `predicate-logical-form` is considered most complex because it is recursive in definition. After informing the user of the sub-types, goals to elaborate upon each of the sub-types are posted and expanded in turn. Each such elaboration results in posting the goal of describing each sub-type. This portion of the planning process is recorded in the skeletal text-plan shown in Fig. 5.[7]

Let's consider the expansion of the goal: (KNOW-ABOUT H (CONCEPT PREDICATE-RELATION-FORM)). Unlike for the similar initial goal given to the system, the system does not pick the operator that defines the concept in terms of its parent, since the concept-parent relationship between a `predicate-relation-form` and a `predicate-form` has already been mentioned (since `predicate-relation-form` was introduced as a sub-type of `predicate-form`). Instead, a plan operator that describes the concept syntax is chosen. In this case, the syntax is:

---

[7] All the text plans shown in this paper are simplified versions of the actual plans generated: they do not show the coherence relations that hold between the text spans resulting from this planning, and the communicative goals are not written in their formal notation, in terms of the hearer's mental states, for readability's sake.

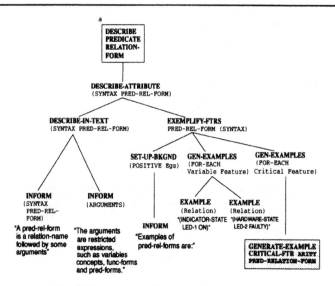

Fig. 6. Plan fragment for the predicate-relation-form.

(relation-name arguments+).

Instantiating the plan, the system realizes that it can describe the syntax by both text and examples (from the syntax definition, the system attempts to construct examples that match this syntax). The steps of the plan operator now compute the parameters that determine what get explained via text, via examples or both. In this case, the system determines that there is one critical feature,[8] i.e., the number of arguments in the predicate-relation-form must be equal to the arity of the relation, and one variable feature, i.e., the relation-name. (Critical, fixed and variable features are determined by modifying the definitions and seeing whether an example of the modified definition becomes a negative example of the concept, using the Loom classifier [14].)

At this point, the system also determines that the parentheses do not need to be mentioned in the text as they will be mentioned in all the examples, are *fixed-features*, and more than one example will be presented. The system now has enough information to continue with the presentation planning process: it constructs the text: "a predicate-relation-form is a relation-name followed by . . . ", and posts a goal to generate examples. The plan chosen to achieve this goal posts the goal to generate text to introduce the examples for the variable features as background, the goal to generate the examples for the variable feature, and the goal to generate examples for the critical features.

The system picks two positive examples to illustrate cd cdthe variable feature. In general, as mentioned before, adjacent positive examples must be as different from one another as possible. In this case, the system picks two different relations, and the first

---

[8] A critical feature is a feature that **must** be present in an example to make it an example. Taking it away would produce a negative example.

two examples are generated. This part of the text plan is shown in Fig. 6.

Now the system must generate an example for the critical feature, i.e., that the number of arguments of a `predicate-relation-form` must be equal to the arity of the relation. Because this is a critical feature, the system decides to generate one pair of positive-negative examples to highlight the feature. The positive example of the pair will be presented first because the discourse tree shows that positive examples were already given and introduced with text. It is thus possible to simply give a new positive example without introducing it. To present the negative example, the system posts the goal of *contrasting* the positive example given.

There are two ways in which a negative example can be constructed in this case: by changing the number of arguments from two to three, or from two to one. The system constructs descriptions of both types, and checks to see whether one of these is a known concept (this can done easily using the classifier in Loom). It finds that a relation with one argument is a construct in the grammar, namely a `function-form`. It thus uses that as a negative example, after posting the appropriate goal to generate text to introduce the example. It also posts a goal to elaborate with text on the differences between a `function-form` and a `predicate-relation-form` to ensure that the user is not further confused by the use of a (possibly) new term. The relevant portions of the text-plan are shown in Fig. 7.

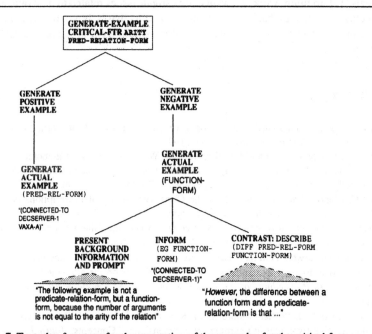

Fig. 7. Text-plan fragment for the generation of the examples for the critical feature.

The planner continues expanding goals in this fashion, until all the goals are primitive speech-acts (such as INFORM). Finally, the completed discourse tree is passed to an interface which converts the INFORM goals into the appropriate input for the sentence generator. The interface chooses the appropriate lexical and syntactic constructs to form the individual sentences and connects them appropriately, using the rhetorical information from the discourse tree. For example, it chooses "However" to reflect the CONTRAST relation.

5 Conclusions and Future Work

In this paper, we have shown how examples and text interact with and co-constrain each other. It is important to recognize this interaction in order to provide an appropriate, well-structured and coherent presentation to the user. We have also argued that a generation system capable of providing examples as part of its presentation must consider example generation as an integral part of the generation process. We have presented our documentation system which illustrates this idea.

While our system is already capable of generating integrated text and examples, some issues remain to be studied. In particular, we limited ourselves for now to a specific discourse context: generating documentation of the EES grammar to a non-expert user. We have also investigated the issue of generating text for tutorial *vs* reference manuals [13]. In future work, we want to investigate issues related to goal (and example) interaction at a more global level than currently done: that is, how can a system "re-use" an example that was given to illustrate a different concept in a previous part of the dialogue.

References

1. Paul Chandler and John Sweller. Cognitive Load Theory and the Format of Instruction. *Cognition and Instruction*, 8(4):292–332, 1991.
2. Davida H. Charney, Lynne M. Reder, and Gail W. Wells. Studies of Elaboration in Instructional Texts. In Stephen Doheny-Farina, editor, *Effective Documentation: What we have learned from Research*, chapter 3, pages 48–72. The MIT Press, Cambridge, MA., 1988.
3. D. C. Clark. Teaching Concepts in the Classroom: A Set of Prescriptions derived from Experimental Research. *Journal of Educational Psychology Monograph*, 62:253–278, 1971.
4. Steven K. Feiner and Kathleen R. McKeown. Automating the generation of coordinated multi-media explanations. *Computer*, 24(10):33–42, October 1991.
5. Katherine Voerwerk Feldman. The effects of the number of positive and negative instances, concept definitions, and emphasis of relevant attributes on the attainment of mathematical concepts. In *Proceedings of the Annual Meeting of the American Educational Research Association*, Chicago, Illinois, 1972.
6. John C. Houtz, J. William Moore, and J. Kent Davis. Effects of Different Types of Positive and Negative Examples in Learning "non-dimensioned" Concepts. *Journal of Educational Psychology*, 64(2):206–211, 1973.
7. Robert MacGregor. A Deductive Pattern Matcher. In *Proceedings of the 1988 Conference on Artificial Intelligence*, St Paul, Mn, August 1988. American Association of Artificial Intelligence.

8. William Mann and Sandra Thompson. Rhetorical structure theory: Toward a functional theory of text organization. *Text: An Interdisciplinary Journal for the Study of Text* 8(2):243–281.

9. Kathleen R. McKeown. *Text Generation: Using Discourse Strategies and Focus Constraints to Generate Natural Language Text.* Cambridge University Press, Cambridge, England, 1985.

10. Edwina Rissland Michener. Understanding Understanding Mathematics. *Cognitive Science Journal*, 2(4):361–383, 1978.

11. Vibhu O. Mittal. *Generating Natural Language Descriptions with Integrated Text and Examples.* PhD thesis, University of Southern California, Los Angeles, California, 1993.

12. Vibhu O. Mittal and Cécile L. Paris. Categorizing Example Types in Instructional Texts: The Need to consider Context. In *Proceedings of AI-ED 93: World Conference on Artificial Intelligence in Education*, Edinburgh, Scotland, 1993. AACE.

13. Vibhu O. Mittal and Cécile L. Paris. Generating Natural Language Descriptions with Examples: Differences between introductory and advanced texts. In *Proceedings of the Eleventh National Conference on Artificial Intelligence – AAAI 93*, pages 271–276. American Association for Artificial Intelligence, 1993.

14. Vibhu O. Mittal and Cécile L. Paris. Generating Examples For Use in Tutorial Explanations: The Use of a Subsumption Based Classifier. In *Proceedings of the Eleventh European Conference on Artificial Intelligence (ECAI-94)*, pages 530–534, Amsterdam, August 1994. John Wiley and Sons.

15. Johanna D. Moore and Cécile L. Paris. Planning text for advisory dialogues. In *Proceedings of the Twenty-Seventh Annual Meeting of the Association for Computational Linguistics*, pages 203 – 211, Vancouver, British Columbia, June 1989.

16. Johanna D. Moore and Cécile L. Paris. Planning Text for Advisory Dialogues: Capturing Intentional, and Rhetorical Information. *Computational Linguistics*, 19(4):651–694, December 1993.

17. Johanna Doris Moore. *A Reactive Approach to Explanation in Expert and Advice-Giving Systems.* PhD thesis, University of California – Los Angeles, 1989.

18. Lynne M. Reder, Davida H. Charney, and Kim I. Morgan. The Role of Elaborations in learning a skill from an Instructional Text. *Memory and Cognition*, 14(1):64–78, 1986.

19. Brian J. Reiser, John R. Anderson, and Robert G. Farrell. Dynamic Student Modelling in an Intelligent Tutor for Lisp Programming. In *Proceedings of the Ninth International Conference on Artificial Intelligence*, pages 8–14. IJCAI-85 (Los Angeles), 1985.

20. Edwina L. Rissland. Example Generation. In *Proceedings of the Third National Conference of the Canadian Society for Computational Studies of Intelligence*, pages 280–288. CIPS, Toronto, Ontario, May 1980.

21. Edwina L. Rissland and Kevin D. Ashley. Hypotheticals as Heuristic Device. In *Proceedings of the National Conference on Artificial Intelligence*, pages 289–297. AAAI, 1986.

22. Edwina L. Rissland, Eduardo M. Valcarce, and Kevin D. Ashley. Explaining and Arguing with Examples. In *Proceedings of the National Conference on Artificial Intelligence*, pages 288–294. AAAI, August 1984.

23. Daniel D. Suthers and Edwina L. Rissland. Constraint Manipulation for Example Generation. COINS Technical Report 88-71, Computer and Information Science, University of Massachusetts, Amherst, MA., 1988.

24. William R. Swartout, Cecile L. Paris, and Johanna D. Moore. Design for explainable expert systems. *IEEE Expert*, 6(3):58–64, 1992.

25. David S. Touretzky. *LISP: A Gentle Introduction to Symbolic Computation.* Harper & Row Publishers, New York, 1984.

26. Paul Werth. *Focus, Coherence and Emphasis.* Croom Helm, London, England, 1984.

27. Beverly Woolf and David D. McDonald. Context-Dependent Transitions in Tutoring Discourse. In *Proceedings of the Third National Conference on Artificial Intelligence*, pages 355–361. AAAI, 1984.

Market-Oriented Programming (Abstract)

Michael P. Wellman

University of Michigan
Ann Arbor, MI USA
wellman@umich.edu
http://ai.eecs.umich.edu/people/wellman/

Market-oriented programming is an approach to distributed computation based on market price mechanisms. The economic perspective on decentralized (computational) decision-making has several advantages. It is well known that-in some circumstances-markets are an effective institution for coordinating activities with minimal communication. Moreover, economic science has developed an extensive analytic framework for studying such multiagent systems.

The idea of market-oriented programming is to exploit the institution of markets and our models of them to build computational economies to solve particular problems of distributed resource allocation. This is inspired in part by economists' metaphors of market systems "computing" the activities of the agents involved, and also by Artificial Intelligence researchers' view of modules in a distributed system as autonomous agents. In market-oriented programming we take these metaphors literally, and directly implement the distributed computation as a market price system. That is, the modules, or agents, interact in a very restricted manner-by offering to buy or sell quantities of commodities at fixed unit prices. When this system reaches equilibrium, the computational market has indeed computed the allocation of resources throughout the system, and dictates the activities and consumptions of the various modules.

In our computational realization of a market price system, we implement consumer and producer agents and direct them to bid so as to maximize utility or profits, subject to their own feasibility constraints. To date, we have tested this approach with applications to simple problems in transportation planning, distributed engineering design, and network information services. Current work is developing more complex models in these domains, as well as investigating new applications in allocation of computational resources, and provision of distributed information services in a digital library.

References

1. SH Clearwater, editor, Market-Based Control: A Paradigm for Distributed Resource Allocation, World Scientific, 1995.
2. MP Wellman. A market-oriented programming environment and its application to distributed multicommodity flow problems. Journal of Artificial Intelligence Research, 1:1-23, 1993. [ftp://ftp.eecs.umich.edu/people/wellman/jair93.ps]
3. MP Wellman. A computational market model for distributed configuration design. AI EDAM, 9:125-133, 1995.
4. MP Wellman. Market-oriented programming: Some early lessons. In Clearwater, 1995.

Belief Increasing in SKL Model Frames

Matías Alvarado[1] and Gustavo Núñez[2]

[1] LSI, Technical University of Catalonia
Pau Gargallo 5, 08028 Barcelona, Spain
e-mail: matias@lsi.upc.es
[2] Integral Tecnology of Information
Diego Rivera 31, 91000 Xalapa, Ver., México
email: GNunez.TSCW@cid.mhs.compuserve.com

Abstract. Three-Valued Strong Kleene Logic [16], provides an adequate framework to deal with belief increasing. In this paper, *undefined* truth-value is used to denote opinionless information. Through an informative refinement, such information could become to be *true* or *false* in a step by step way. Our approach is based upon model frames [9], that are sets of informatively ordered three-valued interpretations. A relation of compatibility among frames, being a partial informative order, is defined. Belief increasing is accomplished by using the compatibility relation that is based on concatenation operation over model frames. A correspondence between model frames and analytic tableaux is outlined. It provides to deal with model frames by using that powerful proof method [11].

1 Introduction

Classical approaches to belief change are the Alchourron-Gärdenfors-Makinson (AGM) [1] and the *Update Theory* of Katsuno and Mendelzhon (KM) [15]. In order to change the logically closed belief base ψ with a sentence μ, AGM proposal provides with *expansion, contraction* and *revision* operations. *Expansion* is applied whenever μ is consistent with ψ, obtaining logical closure from $\psi \cup \{\mu\}$; *contraction* to get out from ψ the sentence μ together with some deductively-related formulas; and *revision* being a $\neg\mu$-contraction followed by a μ expansion. Alchourron *et al.* proposed the so called *rationality postulates* to be satisfied by any *revision operator*. On the other hand, KM approach provides eight postulates to update with μ any arbitrary sets of sentences ψ (not only logically closed ones as AGM does). In case of inconsistency between ψ and μ, semantically, AGM results in the closest model to ψ satisfing μ, while KM release, for each model of ψ, the models of μ closest to it [15].

The main drawback of those fruitful approaches to belief change consists, essentially, in the lack of flexibility to deal with no-considered revision or updating cases, or the contraintuitive results that they provide dealing with ambiguous information. Brewka and Hertzberg [6] as well as Del Val and Shoham [7] propose to use *Action Theory* through axioms of action encoding the *circumstances of especific updating or revision*. We coincide to consider that the point is the cappability to handle particular information based on a general framework.

Thus, the paramount of this paper is twofold:

- Provide a intuitive framework for representation and change of belief using model frames defined by Doherty [9]
- Outline an equivalence between model frames and Analytic Tableaux such that this flexible proof method [11] is used to deal with belief in a computational perspective intuitions preserving.

In section 2, three-valued SKL is introduced together with Belnap's informative partial order over model frames. From SKL and the informative order we outline our epistemic definitions in section 3, developing a (constructive-like) logic of belief. In section 4 correspondence between epistemic model frames and analytic tableaux is mentioned showing that tableaux proof method is well applied in our intend. In the last section a brief comparison between AGM paradigm and *Update Theory* with respect to our approach is developed.

2

2.1 Strong Kleene Logic

For Strong Kleene Logic, propositional language $\mathcal{L}$ is defined from a finite set of sentences Σ and the primitive connectives negation $\neg$ and disjunction $\vee$. From those connectives the conjunction $\wedge$ and implication $\rightarrow$ are defined in the classical way. Let $\mathcal{F}$ be the set of $\mathcal{L}(\Sigma)$-formulas. Semantical definitions for disjunction and negation in the Strong Kleene Logic are given in Table 1. Let *true*, *false* and *undefined* be truth-values denoted with t, f and u.

Table 1

φ	ψ	$\varphi \vee \psi$	φ	$\neg\varphi$
t	t	t		
t	f	t		
t	u	t		
f	t	t	t	f
f	f	f	u	u
f	u	u	f	t
u	t	t		
u	f	u		
u	u	u		

Definition 1. A three-valued interpretation I, is a valuation function from $\mathcal{F}$ to $\{t, f, u\}$ in accordance with logical connectives definition. I is equivalent to $I^t \cup I^f \cup I^u$ in such a way that I^t is the set of *true* formulas, I^f the set of *false* formulas and I^u the set of undefined formulas. When I^u is the empty set we say that I is complete with respect to *true* and *false* truth-values. Let $\mathcal{I}(\mathcal{F})$ be the set of three-valued interpretations of formulas in $\mathcal{F}$.

2.2 Informative Order

In this section we concern with the approach that use an informative order to deal with knowledge and belief (see *e.g* [2, 4, 9]), in order not reduce them to truth-semantic-logical aspect. Herein an informative order over interpretations of sets of beliefs is given. Underline objective is to deal with belief change in a step by step way. The intuitive point is that seems natural to consider the following:

- Having *true, false* and *undefined* statemens, *true* or *false* ones provide more information than *undefined* statements.

We propose that when undefined information turns up defined, as true or false, beliefs could increase.

We observe that increasing of belief can be considered a belief expansion-like operation of Alchourron, Gärdenfors and Makinson Paradigm [1, 14]. It is well known, however, that in the semminal AGM approach, change of belief includes also elimination and revision of current beliefs by using *contraction* and *revision* operations. On the other hand, *Updating Theory* [15] is the classical approach to belief updating. As mentioned in the introduction, this approach has subtle differences with the AGM one and constitutes the other significant view of belief change. In section 5 we outline the way in which our proposal can deal with contraction, revision and updating operations. Now, the informative partial order defined for Doherty over $\{t, f, u\}$ set [9] is introduced.

Definition 2. The **Degree of information** among t, f and u truth-values, is defined as follows: $u \preceq_i t$, $u \preceq_i f$ and t, f are not comparable.

Let Υ be a subset of $\mathcal{I}(\mathcal{F})$. The informative partial order $\preceq_i$ is introduced over Υ in the following way: given an $I, I' \in \Upsilon$, $I \preceq_i I'$ is satisfied if and only if $I^t \subseteq I'^t$, $I^f \subseteq I'^f$ and $I^u \supseteq I'^u$. The order $\preceq_i$ is a partial one on Υ.

Intuition of that order is that given two interpretations of a set $\mathcal{P}$ of formulas, interpretation with more *undefined* formulas is less informed than the one having more *true* or *false* formulas. Then, for $\mathcal{P} \subseteq \mathcal{F}$ such that $I(P) \preceq_i I'(P)$ for every $P \in \mathcal{P}$, I' is more informed than I with respect to $\mathcal{P}$, denoted $I \preceq_i^{\mathcal{P}} I'$. In this case it is said that I' is an **informative refinement** of I with respect to $\mathcal{P}$.

Example : Let $\mathcal{P} = \{P\}$ be the only sentence of language $\mathcal{L}$; $I_0 = (u)$, $I_1 = (t)$, $I_2 = (f)$ be the interpretations of $\mathcal{F}$. Then I_1, I_2 are informative refinements of I_0 and thus more informed than it.

The following formal structure providing a suitable framework for our epistemic approach is an extension of model frame defined by Doherty [10]. The underling objective is to capture the dynamic manner in which beliefs change. We consider that it deppends of *worlds being explored*. Gradual exploration is allowed by using the informative order $\preceq_i$ among model frames.

Definition 3. A **model frame** is an ordered 3-tuple $\mathcal{M} = \langle \Upsilon, I_0, \preceq_i \rangle$, where $\Upsilon \subseteq \mathcal{I}(\mathcal{F})$ is a set of interpretations and $I_0 \in \Upsilon$ is called the current (actual or present) interpretation. For any $I' \in \Upsilon$, we assume that $I_0 \preceq_i I'$. Thus, any interpretation in $\mathcal{M}$ is at least as informed as I_0.

Notice that as interpretation I_0 remains fix, it constitutes an invariant and characterizes the model frame. Following definition will be used in the following comments and in belief definition.

Definition 4. An **interpretation** J is **maximal** in $\mathcal{M}$ if and only if there is no J' in $\mathcal{M}$ such that $J \prec_i J'$.

A model frame can be seen as a set of possible worlds that provides *a description of the state of the things together with its possibles extensions* (see fig 1). Whenever worlds corresponding with the (informatively) maximal interpretation in the model frame contain undefined statements, extension of belief could be performed as it should show below (see 4).

On the other hand, informative order $\preceq_i$ can be considered an accsessibility relation among interpretations in Υ as follows: I' is accessible (compatible) for I whenever I' is an informative refinement of I. Moreover, if for every $I \in \Upsilon$, in a model frame $\mathcal{M}$, $I(\alpha) \in \{t, f\}$, then this last one is a structure of Kripke[3].

3   Belief

In this section a belief definition is proposed. Propositional language $\mathcal{L}$ is extended by adding a modal operator of **belief**, B . The language extended with these modal operators is denoted $\mathcal{BL}$ by belief language. The following satisfaction definition is relative to model frame.

Definition 5. A sentence $\alpha \in \mathcal{F}$ is **satisfied** by the interpretation $I \in \Upsilon$ of the model frame $\mathcal{M}$, denoted $I \models_{\mathcal{M}} \alpha$, if and only if $I(\alpha) = T$. It is said that the frame satisfies α, $\mathcal{M} \models \alpha$, if every $I \in \Upsilon$ satisfies α. For a set Γ such that any sentence of Γ is satisfied by $\mathcal{M}$, is said that the frame $\mathcal{M}$ satisfies Γ, $\mathcal{M} \models \Gamma$.

Notice that this satisfaction definition is for no modal formulas only; for belief modal ones is given below. Relativity of model frame satisfaction is welcome in our aim to encourage the point of view considering belief relative to actual information and context. This semantical flexibility can be syntactically well treated using a method based on Analytic Tableaux. Now we give belief definition.

Definition 6. A formula α is **believed** in the interpretation I of the model frame $\mathcal{M}$, denoted $I \models_{\mathcal{M}} B(\alpha)$, if and only if, for every maximal J of $\mathcal{M}$ with $I \preceq_i J$, $J \models \alpha$ (see fig 2). Whenever for every I of $\mathcal{M}$, $I \models_{\mathcal{M}} B(\alpha)$, it is said that $\models_{\mathcal{M}} B(\alpha)$.

---

[3] A structure of Kripke is a 3-tuple $< W, R, \nu >$ such that W is a nonempty set of worlds, R a possibility relation and ν a valuation function [18].

Then, a statement is belief in $\mathcal{M}$ if it is *true* in the interpretation I_0 or if being undefined in I_0, it becomes *true* in every maximal interpretation of the frame.

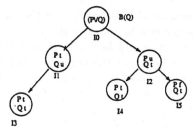

Figure 2: Belief

3.1 Consistency over Belief Increasing

Our formalism provides the possibility to reason from initial, possibly not consistent beliefs set, in a not trivial way. Each one of the contradictory sentences, if any, are considered in different *parts* of the total frame. In fact, increasing (expansion) of beliefs happens in different directions, being consistent each one of them. Now we define compatibility relation among model frames; based upon it, in addition to concatenation and unification operations over frames, change of the initial beliefs, as increasing or modification, is considered. (A comparison with Logic of Explicit and Implicit Belief in [19].)

3.2 Compatible frames

We are interested in model frames that *change* in order to model the dynamic character of a cognitive process. A model frame defined by Doherty in [9] is static; is beforehand given and does not change at all. However, solution to our requirements can be done by introducing an operation, namely of *concatenation*, among Doherty's model frames. The intuitive idea of concatenation is the following:

– To add information to a maximally informed world in the frame, if possible, in such a way that it allows to increase beliefs.

Let $\mathcal{M}_1 = <\Upsilon_1, I_0^1, \preceq_i^1>$, $\mathcal{M}_2 = <\Upsilon_2, I_0^2, \preceq_i^2>$ be two model frames.

Definition 7. Model frame $\mathcal{M} = <\Upsilon, \preceq_i, I_0^1 >$ is the *concatenation* of $\mathcal{M}_2$ with $\mathcal{M}_1$, denoted $\mathcal{M} = \mathcal{M}_1 \odot \mathcal{M}_2$, if and only if
1) I_0^2 is a maximal interpretation of $\mathcal{M}_1$.
2) $\Upsilon = \Upsilon_1 \cup \Upsilon_2$,

By definition, $I_0^1 \preceq I'$ for every $I' \in \Upsilon_1 \cup \Upsilon_2$. Notice that concatenation is defined over maximal interpretations only. Thus, further information is added to maximally informed worlds in the frame. It could be of interest to define concatenation for every interpretation in the model frame but this is behind the scope of this work.

Notice that frame concatenation is based upon the informative orders of model frames. Then, the possibility to concatenate M_2 to M_1 depends on the fact that interpretations in M_2 could be informative refinaments of a maximal interpretation in M_1 (see fig 3 and the next example). Concatenation is applied to increase belief from *undefined* statements by changing them to *true* or *false*, providing a constructive way to obtain beliefs from opinionless information.

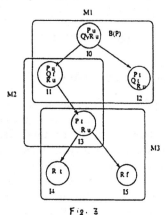

Fig. 3

Now we define an accessibility relation among model frames. Jaako Hintikka's intuitions about use accessibility relation of Kripke' semantics of possible worlds [18] to model knowledge and belief [14], are very suited, being the formalisation weakness that does not capture adequately such intuitions[4] Using concatenation, a relation of possibility, called of compatibility, *is defined*. That relation captures the constructive and dynamic manner in which we think epistemic and doxastic alternatives (worlds) are conceived by a limited rational agent. The intuitive idea of compatibility is the following:

- Given a current frame describing a situation, any frame being coherently more informed than it, is compatible with it. (It is worth to think in the particular case when frames are defined by a single world.)

Definition 8. A model frame M_2 *is compatible with* model frame M_1 if and only if, there is a succession of model frames $N_1, \ldots N_n$ such that $N_1 = M_1$, $N_n = M_2$, and N_{i+1} is concatenated to N_i for $i = 1, \ldots, n-1$.

Then, compatible model frames with M_1 correspond to informative refinements that can be obtained from a maximal world in M_1 (see example 2). Thus, M_2 is compatible for M_1 if it is more informed than M_1 in some of the directions with undefined information that M_1 has. By definition, any concatenated frame to M_1 is compatible with it.

---

[4] In [19] a wide analysis about this point is developed.

Let $\mathcal{N}_1, \ldots \mathcal{N}_l$ model frames with interpretation set $\Upsilon_1, \ldots, \Upsilon_l$, respectively. The following is a remarkable fact.

Proposition 9. *If each set of interpretations Υ_i for $i = 1, \ldots, l$ is a singleton, then each model frame is a world. In that case, accessibility relation is over possible worlds.*

Thus, compatibility relation is a step by step possibility relation among sets of possible worlds in Kleene's three-valued logic.

Proposition 10. *Partial order over Υ set of a model frame $\mathcal{M}$ corresponds to an accessibility relation inside $\mathcal{M}$.*

Example : Let the following set of statements, with initial interpretation I_0 such that $I_0(P) = u$ for every $P \in \mathcal{P}$.

$$
\begin{aligned}
\mathcal{P} = \{ & Misery \rightarrow Rebelion, & (1) \\
& Rebelion \rightarrow Negotiation \vee Repression, & (2) \\
& Rebelion \wedge Negotiation \rightarrow Solution, & (3) \\
& Rebelion \wedge Repression \rightarrow War, & (4) \\
& Solution \rightarrow \neg Misery, & (5) \\
& War \rightarrow MoreMisery & (6) \}
\end{aligned}
$$

Informative order is indicated in the following model frame (fig 4). In the figure we use the initial letter of each predicate to deal with it, except to denote *Rebelion* with *Rb* and *Repression* with *Rp*. Formulas without indicated truthvalue are considered undefined. It is assumed that *true* and *false* formulas in upper interpretations are present in the following ones.

In the example we can draw the possible scenarios that could be allowed from a (unhappy) situation. It depends on the way in which opinionless statements describing the initial situation become *true*. At the final steps of current frame, there are two compatible (possible) evolving frames —not resolved yet in the example— of current frame. One with a good (desired) evolution corresponds with that eventually statement (3) is *true*; the other, with unhappy evolve, corresponds with having as *true* statement (4). (It depends on the beliefs of the active (implicit) agents.) In each case a compatible model frame can be concatenated to the current one.

4 Analytic Tableaux as Frames of Beliefs

We will use as proof system the analytic tableaux method [11] because its flexibility is adequated to introduce doxastic conditions over sets of formulas [2, 9, 17]. There are already characterization of Gentzen type provers for three-valued logics [3]. In fact, Avron distinguishes between the ones that are based upon a logic in which the *undefined* truth-value denotes incomplet or unknown information, from those that use *undefined* denoting inconsistent information. The most known of the first ones corresponds with Kleene's and Lukasiewicz' logics[5]. Moreover, there are multivalued-logic theorem provers [5, 20].

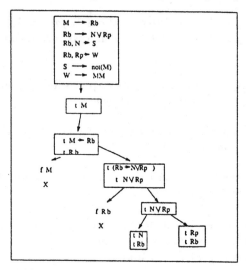

Fig. 4 Analytic Tableaux as Frame of Belief

Our proposed approach uses *undefined* as incomplete or unknown. We can add doxastic conditions through tableaux like rules, or as belief statements in open branches of tableaux containing current interesting information. It is easy to show from the last example the natural manner in which a frame of beliefs can be represented through an analytic tableaux (see fig 4). The correspondence can be established under the following considerations:

- Current model frame is contained in the set of paths of the associated tableaux.
- The informative order over interpretations in the model frame allows the order in which classical tableaux rules are applied over the set of formulas.
- Whenever a formula becomes *true* in the frame, the closure that such change of value conveys is performed by application of classical tableaux rules.
- Classical α, β, π, ν-rules of tableaux [11] when applied over true formulas evolve in tableaux paths such that its model frames counterparts are the virtual concatenations of current model frame.
- Virtual extensions (by concatenation) of the model frame correspond with tableaux extensions through open branchs.

Incorporation of above considerations can be done appending to classical tableaux rules, the following one denoted UD:

- Whenever an *undefined* formula becomes *true* or *false*, then a tableaux is opened and all its logical consequences are deduced.

According to UD rule, whenever an *undefined* formula becomes *true* or *false*, a tableaux is opened and classical rules are applied. In the associated tableaux of the example, β-rule was applied over implication and disjunctive formulas as soon as they turned up *true*, and its logical consequences obtained. It is assumed that every tableaux satisfies all the formulas in upper tableaux. Closed tableaux are marked with X and corresponds with incompatible (impossible) situations for model frame.

5   Related Works and Discussion

In the introduction was mentioned that classical approaches to belief change are those of AGM paradigm [1, 14] and Update Theory (UT) [15]. The first one defines operations of *expansion*, *contraction* and *revision* over logically closed sets (called belief sets,) while the second deals with *belief updating* for arbitrary sets. In the proposed approach, using concatenation operation, it follows increasing (expansion) of belief. Now we can outline the way in which it is possible to deal with contraction, revision and update of beliefs in a nonless natural way.

Intuitive idea of revision of a beliefs set ψ with new information μ is to modify as little as possible ψ in such a way that it entails μ, preserving consistency. In our approach it conveys the modification of the frame $\mathcal{M}$ such that μ becomes *true* in all maximal interpretation of $\mathcal{M}$.

If μ is *true* or *undefined* in every interpretation of $\mathcal{M}$ then is an μ-belief expansion on $\mathcal{M}$, while if μ is false in some interpretation, it arises a contradiction in $\mathcal{M}$. In this case is proceeded in the following manner:

- It should be *erased* interpretations of the frame, by turning *undefined* formulas that being *true* conveys contradictions with formula μ.

As much as needed to preserve consistency in the frame are the erased interpretations. Syntactical operativity is performed using the analytic tableaux associated with the model frame. Contradiction in analytic tableaux appears whenever an open branch of the tableaux becomes close. The erasure of contradictory interpretation in the frame corresponds with the erasure of the closed branches in the tableaux that were generated by making μ *true*. Unconsistency over tableaux branch is backward translated until it disappears. Thereafter contradiction is eliminated, is possible that μ becomes to be *true* in all maximal interpretation of the *revised* frame $\mathcal{M}'$.

We observe that erasure can be done in several ways. It is necessary to consider additional criteria in order to obtain certain erasure(s) among the possible ones. Adopted criteria can be translated over Analytic Tableaux as rules, constraints or strategies over deduction process [19].

Now we make some observations:

1.) In the case of expansion, there are open branches in the associated tableaux to the frame, over which the operation is done.

2.) The erasure of frame interpretations could be considered the contraction operation over the frame.

3.) In AGM approach, revision operation of ψ by μ is equivalent to contraction for $\neg A$ and expansion by μ. This is the manner in which revision of a model frame is performed.

Thus, expansion, contraction and revision operation can be performed over model frames.

With respect with belief updating a similar thing should be done. Intuitive idea of UT is that the world has changed and is necessary to update beliefs. Whenever the updating formula μ do not conveys contradiction with the old beliefs in ψ, revision and updating are equivalent. The case in which contradictions arise, seems that UT generalizes the AGM approach [7]. There are situations in which UT allows different alternatives to belief updating that AGM does not.

However, UT axiomatization, given certain information, results in unintuitive updatings. This is the case when μ is a disjunction that is not in ψ but is entailed by it (remember that UT deals with arbitrary sets.) This situation corresponds with update ψ with so-called *ambiguous* information [6]. Minimal change criterio of UT expressed by axiom U2 (see [15]), conveys unintuitive results in spite of being information describing so simple situations; *e.g.* flipping a coin, the result provided by UT due axiom U2, is the last visible-side-coin, that is a biased one. The same is applicable to deal with the undefinition of a person that having a job, receives a new (might be better) job proposal. *UT* chooses always the old job.

Model frames approach provides to deal with different alternatives for updating with ambiguous information. We have reasons to be optimistics to deal with *problematic* questions of belief change using the proposed approache. Alternative scenarios can be coherently included in a model frame without any kind of implicit bias. While an alternative is not justified enough, it cannot be a belief in the frame, but nor is excluded. In this step it is a local belief satisfied under more especific circumstances. Further information is needed in order to become a global belief. In this case, the other alternative statements, if any, is neither globally rejected. It could remain as local information as well. Further details constitute the material of our current research.

Concluding Remarks

This paper proposes to deal with belief increasing (expansion) using model frames that are sets of informatively ordered possible worlds in three-valued Strong Kleene Logic. The *undefined* truth-value is used to indicate current but opinionless information. *True* and *false* information is considered more informed than the *undefined* one, and it constitutes an informative order. From that order, a compatibility relation over model frames is defined, such that in addition to concatenation frames operation, belief change is allowed. The proposed formalism provides to deal, locally, with contradictory or incoherent beliefs. Using the informative order in a step by step manner ideal reasoning and logical omniscience are avoided. The epistemical framework has a suited syntactical proof method using analytic tableaux.

Part of our forthcoming work is the introduction as far as possible, of strategies for tableaux calculi in modal logic that has been recently developed in [8].

Acknowledgements This work was benefitted with worth comments from Ll. Godó and R. Rodríguez (IIIA-CSIC, Spain), J. Larrosa (LSI-UPC, Spain), S. Demri (LIFIA-IMAG, France) and anonymous referees. First author is supported by a PhD fellowship of Universidad Nacional Autónoma de México. Participation of second author was during a *Visiting Professor Stage* in Technical University of Catalonia.

References

1. C. Alchourron, P. Gärdenfors and D. Makinson: *On the Logic of Theory Change: Partial Meet Contraction and Revision Function.* Journal of Symbolic Logic. Vol. 50 (1985) 510-530.
2. M. Alvarado: *A Posteriori Knowledge: from Ambiguous Knowledge and Undefined Information to Knowledge.* In Procc. of ECSQARU '95 *Lecture Notes in Artificial Intelligence* **946**. Fribourg, Switzerland (1995).
3. A. Avron: *Natural 3-Valud Logics Characterization and Proof Systems.* Journal of Symbolic Logic Vol. 56 No. 1, March 1991.
4. N. Belnap: *A useful four-valued logic* In Dunn and Epstein (Eds.) *Modern Uses of Logic.* Reidel Publishing Co, 1976.
5. Beckert: *3TAP Tableau-Based Theorem Prover.* Karlsruhe University, Germany (1994)
6. G. Brewka and J. Hertzberg: *How to do thing with worlds.* Journal of Logic and Computation Vol No. (1993).
7. A. Del Val and Y. Shoham: *A unified view of Belief Revision and Update.* Journal of Logic and Computation Vol. 4 No. 5 pp 797-810 (1994)
8. S. Demri: *Uniform and Non uniform Strategies for Tableaux Calculi for Modal Logic.* In Procc. of *Workshop on Logics in Artificial Intelligence JELIA'94*, LNAI 738, Springer Verlag (1994)
9. P. Doherty, W. Lukasciewicz: *NML3. A Non-Monotonic Logic with Explicit Defaults.* Journal of Applied Non-Classical Logic Vol. 2 No. 1 (1992)
10. C. Geisler and K. Konolige: *A resolution method for quantified modal logics of knowledfge and belief.* In Procc of *Reasoning About Knowledge Conference*, (1986).
11. M. Fitting: *First-Order Modal Tableaux.* Journal of Automated Reasoning 4 (1988) pp. 191-213.
12. P. Gärdenfors: *Knowledge in Flux.* The MIT Press (1988).
13. M. Ginsberg: *Bilattices and Modal Operators.*
14. J. Hintikka: *Knowledge and Belief* (Cornell University Press 1962).
15. H. Katsuno and A. Mendelzon *Propositional knowledge base revision and minimal change.* Artificial Intelligence 52 (1991) 263 - 294.
16. S. Kleene: *Introduction to Metamathematical.* North Holland Ed. (1952)
17. K. Konolige: *A Deduction Model of Belief and its Logics* (Morgan Kaufmann, 1986).
18. S. Kripke: *A completness theorem in modal logic.* The Journal of Symbolic Logic. **24 - 1** (1959) pp. 1-14.
19. G. Núñez, M. Alvarado: *An Approache to Belief in Strong Kleene Logic.* Report de Recerca LSI-95-27, Technical University of Catalonia (1995)
20. N. Zabel: *Nouvelles Techniques de Deduction Automatique en Logiques Polyvalentes Finies et Infinies du Premier Ordre*, PhD Thesis. Institut National Polytechnique de Grenoble (1993)

Sensitivity of Combination Schemes under Conflicting Conditions and a New Method

A. V. Joshi, S. C. Sahasrabudhe, K. Shankar

Electrical Engineering Department, Indian Institute of Technology,
Powai, Bombay 400 076, India

Abstract. In the theory of evidential reasoning, Dempster's rule is used for combining belief functions based on independent evidences. There has been a lot of debate over the counter-intuitive nature of results obtained by this rule [4, 8, 14, 15]. Dubois and Prade [1, 3] have shown that Dempster's rule is not robust and is sensitive to inaccurate estimates of uncertainty values. Many authors have suggested modifications which overcome this drawback.

In this paper, we first bring out the limitation of the combination rule introduced by Zhang [16]. Subsequently, we focus our study on two other rules. The first one was proposed by Dubois and Prade [2, 3] and is known as Disjunctive rule of combination. Incidentally, this rule also appeared in the Hau and Kashyap's work [5]. The other combination rule was due to Yager [13]. Even though these rules are robust, we show that in some cases these rules treat evidences asymmetrically and give counter-intuitive results. We then propose a combination rule which doesn't have these drawback. An intuitive justification for this rule is also provided.

1 Introduction

The Dempster-Shafer theory has attracted the attention of AI researchers, especially those working in the area of development of knowledge based systems primarily because of its ability to represent ignorance and the Dempster's rule of combination. It is well-known that Dempster's rule gives counter-intuitive results in a highly conflicting situation and is not robust. This problem is attributed to the normalization that is carried out in the combination rule. A detail discussion on this problem can be found in [3]. Dubois and Prade have shown that the result of the combination in such cases depends on how one represents an unlikely proposition. There are quite a few combination rules which overcome this sensitivity problem. Dubois and Prade [2, 3] and Yager [13] suggested alterations to Dempster's rule which avoid normalization. These rules are robust but are non-associative. In this paper, we show that in certain situations these rules give counter-intuitive results. We also take up the recent proposal by Zhang [16] and show that although it is commutative and associative, it is not robust. On the backdrop of this discussion, we propose a combination rule which is robust and quite general in nature. We also provide an intuitive justification for this rule.

The paper is organized in the following manner: Section 2 gives an outline of Dempster-Shafer theory. Section 3 describes the sensitivity of Dempster's rule and the modifications proposed by various authors in detail. Limitations of Dubois and Prade's proposal and Yager's modification are discussed in section 4. A new combination rule is proposed in Section 5. Section 6 concludes the paper.

2   The Dempster-Shafer Theory

The Dempster-Shafer theory [7] assumes that the answer to a particular question lies in a finite set X called *frame*. The elements of this set X are mutually exclusive and exhaustive. An element of a frame represents an *elementary* proposition and there is a one-to-one correspondence between subsets of frame and propositions. A mapping $m : 2^X \longrightarrow [0, 1]$ satisfying

$$m(\emptyset) = 0; \tag{1}$$

$$\sum_{C \subseteq X} m(C) = 1 . \tag{2}$$

is called a *basic probability assignment* (bpa). A *focal element* is a subset of frame which has non-zero bpa. The union of all focal elements is termed as *core*. *Total belief* in a proposition is defined as:

$$Bel(C) = \sum_{B \subseteq C} m(B) . \tag{3}$$

Plausibility of a proposition C is defined as:

$$Pl(C) = 1 - Bel(\bar{C}) . \tag{4}$$

It is a measure of extent to which C is believed to be true. The degree of uncertainty or ignorance about C is represented by $[Bel, Pl]$ interval.

Two belief functions Bel_1 and Bel_2 based on independent evidences can be combined using Dempster's rule combination. The result of combination is a new belief function $Bel_1 \oplus Bel_2$ reflecting the pooling of evidences. The combination rule is defined as:

$$m(C) = \frac{\displaystyle\sum_{\substack{i,j \\ A_i \cap B_j = C}} m_1(A_i) \cdot m_2(B_j)}{1 - \displaystyle\sum_{\substack{i,j \\ A_i \cap B_j = \emptyset}} m_1(A_i) \cdot m_2(B_j)} . \tag{5}$$

provided, $\displaystyle\sum_{\substack{i,j \\ A_i \cap B_j = \emptyset}} m_1(A_i) \cdot m_2(B_j) < 1$; otherwise the combination is not defined.

Note that m_1 and m_2 are bpa's corresponding to Bel_1 and Bel_2 respectively.

3   Sensitivity of Dempster's Rule and Other Combination Schemes

Zadeh [15] criticized normalization in the Dempster's rule on the grounds that it can lead to misleading results. He has also shown that it gives counter-intuitive result in case of a highly conflicting condition [14].

It has been demonstrated by Dubois & Prade that Dempster's rule is sensitive to inaccurate estimates of uncertainty values [3]. Consider the following example: Let $X = \{a, b, c\}$ and

$$m_1(a) = \delta, \qquad m_1(b) = 0.1, \qquad m_1(c) = 0.9 - \delta \qquad (6)$$
$$m_2(a) = 0.9 - \delta, \qquad m_2(b) = 0.1, \qquad m_2(c) = \delta \qquad (7)$$

Application of Dempster's rule results in,

$$m(b) = m_1 \oplus m_2(b) = \frac{0.01}{2\delta \cdot (0.9 - \delta) + 0.01} \cdot \qquad (8)$$

The plot of $m(b)$ against δ is shown in Fig.1.

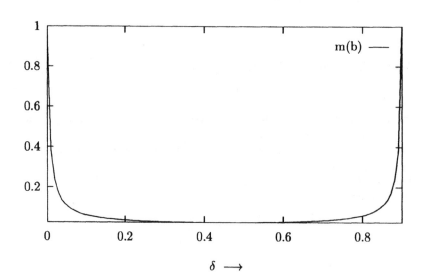

Fig. 1. Plot of m(b) against δ in Dubois and Prade's example

If we vary the value of δ from 0.01 to 0.001 the conclusion swings from 'b' unlikely to 'b' most likely proposition. Thus, the rule is sensitive to representation of unlikeliness of a proposition.

The above example was a modification of Zadeh's example in abstract form:

$$m_1(a) = 0.99, \qquad m_1(b) = 0.01 \qquad\qquad (9)$$
$$m_2(c) = 0.99, \qquad m_2(b) = 0.01 \qquad\qquad (10)$$

Combining these two belief functions by Dempster's combination rule, we obtain $m(b) = 1$. As we can see there is a strong conflict between the two evidences. The first evidence rules out 'c' while the second evidence rejects 'a' and both these evidences weakly support 'b'. Zadeh feels that the combination should not assign certainty to 'b' and expects a large uncertainty in this case.

However, Shafer [8] doesn't agree with Zadeh and argues that this result is perfectly logical and acceptable. He defends this result by quoting Sherlock Holmes motto:*if we eliminate impossible; then whatever remains, however improbable, is the truth.* Shafer also points out that in practice, evidence seldom rules out anything conclusively. Further, he feels that perhaps there is a common uncertainty underlying two belief functions which need to be sorted out before combining them.

Shafer [7, 8] introduced the concept of "discount factors" to take into account the unreliability of sources. However, it doesn't mitigate the lack of robustness of the rule.

Dubois and Prade [2] introduced a *Disjunctive combination rule* where-in the mass associated with the null hypothesis in the combination is assigned to the disjunction of the conflicting hypothesis. By doing so, the decision is deferred until further evidence is obtained. If we assume that one of the sources is unreliable and we are not in a position to tell which one amongst them is; then Disjunctive rule of combination can be used. This rule also appeared in the work of Hau & Kashyap [5]. Mathematically, it can be expressed as:

$$m(C) = \sum_{A \cap B = C} m_1(A) \cdot m_2(B) + \sum_{\substack{A \cap B = \emptyset \\ A \cup B = C}} m_1(A) \cdot m_2(B) \ . \qquad (11)$$

In cases, where the result due to conflict is unreliable, Yager [13] suggested the following rule:

$$m(C) = \sum_{A \cap B = C} m_1(A) \cdot m_2(B) \qquad \forall C \subset X \ . \qquad (12)$$

$$m(X) = m_1(X) \cdot m_2(X) + \sum_{A \cap B = \emptyset} m_1(A) \cdot m_2(B) \ . \qquad (13)$$

The Disjunctive rule and Yager's rule are robust but are non-associative.
There was another proposal of hybrid combination rule from Dubois and Prade [3](p.256). It is a combination of Dempster's rule and the Disjunctive rule.

There is also a possibility that the frame we are considering is non-exhaustive. Dubois and Prade [3] analyzed the problem in this context. Similar approach can be found in Smets [11, 12]. Smets accounted for this possibility by considering the open world assumption in his widely known *transferable belief model.*

Zhang [16] put forth the following *Center Combination Rule*:

$$m(C) = k \cdot \sum_{A \cap B = C} \frac{|C|}{|A| \cdot |B|} m_1(A) \cdot m_2(B) \ . \tag{14}$$

He showed that the results of this rule are consistent with those obtained by probabilistic approach in the famous three prisoners problem. The interesting property of this combination rule is that it is commutative as well as associative. However, it is easy to verify using Zadeh's example that it is not robust.

McLeish [6] studied the conditions under which the result obtained by probabilistic method and belief function approach give same results and proposed a new scheme for combining belief functions.

Halpern and Fagin [4] didn't approve the arguments concerned with counter-intuitive results obtained using Dempster's rule. They argued that the source of these problems lies in confusing between two views of belief viz. belief as a generalized probability and belief as evidence. They contemplated that if we view beliefs as a generalized probability, then it makes sense to update them while if we view them as representing evidence, then combining them is sensible. They have substantiated their arguments by many examples. However there is no consensus over this issue and Zadeh's example doesn't fit well in their argument.[1]

Shi et.al [10] introduced a new rule for updating evidence called *proportional sum*. Out of the two views espoused by Fagin and Halpern [4], this rule corresponds to the view of belief as a generalized probability as compared to Dempster's rule which treat belief as evidence. Thus, according to them, there are two rules in the evidence theory framework; one for combining belief and the other for updating them.

Shafer [9] cautions that in certain cases, it is illegitimate to use Dempster's combination rule as we can get misleading results.

4 Limitation of Disjunctive Rule and Yager's Rule

Let us consider a simple example where frame X consists of just two elements. Let $X = \{ a, b \}$ and the two belief functions be:

$$m_1(a) = s_1, \quad m_1(b) = 1 - s_1 \tag{15}$$
$$m_2(a) = s_2, \quad m_2(ab) = 1 - s_2 \tag{16}$$

Combining these two belief function by Yager's rule and Disjunctive rule, we obtain,

$$m_1 \oplus m_2(a) = s_1 \tag{17}$$
$$m_1 \oplus m_2(b) = (1 - s_1) \cdot (1 - s_2) \tag{18}$$
$$m_1 \oplus m_2(ab) = s_2 \cdot (1 - s_1) \tag{19}$$

---

[1] Personal communication with Joe Halpern.

From (17) we find that the second evidence has no effect whatsoever on $Bel(a)$. It affects 'a' only to the extent of changing it's plausibility. This is counter-intuitive for two reasons. First of all, we expect our belief in 'a' to go up as support for 'a' in Bel_2 viz.s_2 increases. Secondly, increase in plausibility together with a fixed value of belief implies increase in ignorance about 'a'.

On the other hand if we vary s_1 we notice that $Bel(a)$ also changes and it is directly proportional to s_1. Thus, these rules treat the two evidences asymmetrically. This kind of behavior of the combination rules is certainly not desirable.

Application of Dempster's rule for the above example yields,

$$m_1 \oplus m_2(a) = s_1/k \tag{20}$$

$$m_1 \oplus m_2(b) = (1 - s_1) \cdot (1 - s_2)/k \tag{21}$$

where $k = (1 - s_2 \cdot (1 - s_1))$
Equations (20) and (21) indicate that Dempster's rule doesn't have these drawbacks.

Hence, there are situations when outcome of Dempster's combination rule is acceptable while that of other rules is not.
Similar results can be obtained if we change the belief function Bel_2 as below:

$$m_2(b) = s_2, \quad m_2(ab) = (1 - s_2)$$

The above example can be generalized as follows:
Let the frame be $X = \{x_1, x_2, \ldots, x_n\}$

$$m_1(x_1, x_2, \ldots, x_k) = s_1, \quad m_1(x_{k+1}, x_{k+2}, \ldots, x_n) = (1 - s_1) \tag{22}$$

$$m_2(x_1, x_2, \ldots, x_k) = s_2, \quad m_2(X) = (1 - s_2) \tag{23}$$

$$\text{or} \quad m_2(x_{k+1}, x_{k+2}, \ldots, x_n) = s_2, \quad m_2(X) = (1 - s_2) \tag{24}$$

It can be easily verified that the same conclusion holds.

Remark. The counter-intuitive behavior of Disjunctive rule and Yager's rule may be due to violation of assumptions one makes when using these rules. Perhaps it is not appropriate to make these assumptions in cases like these. However, it is very difficult to know before hand all the situations where it is legitimate to make certain assumptions and where it is not.

5 A New Combination Rule

We have observed in the previous sections that there are cases when Dempster's rule gives counter-intuitive results. We have also seen that few modifications schemes which were proposed to overcome some drawbacks of Dempster's rule, also have limitations. As mentioned earlier, these rules depart from Dempster's rule only when there is a conflict between the evidences. So far there aren't any objections to Dempster's rule when both the evidences are concurring. Thus, the assignment $m(\emptyset)$ in the combination plays a crucial role in any combination rule because its distribution decides its properties. In the Dempster's combination rule the conflicting information is totally lost and the non-empty sets are correspondingly scaled up. Yager's proposal puts the conflicting mass into the frame indicating ignorance and hence there is no inflation of proper subsets of the frame. These are the two extremes and we have seen in the previous sections that blind use of either of these rule leads to problems. This motivated us to propose the following combination rule:

$$m(C) = \left(\sum_{A_i \cap B_j = C} m_1(A_i) \cdot m_2(B_j) \right) \cdot (1 + m(\emptyset)) \qquad \forall C \subset X \ .$$

$$m(X) = 1 - \sum_{C \subset X} m(C) \ .$$

where

$$m(\emptyset) = \sum_{A_i \cap B_j = \emptyset} m_1(A_i) \cdot m_2(B_j) \ .$$

The underlying assumption of this rule is that our level of ignorance is directly proportional to the degree of conflict. If there is no conflict between the evidences, the combination rule becomes Dempster's rule. As the conflict increases, we become more and more uncertain leading to a state where decision making becomes very difficult based solely on belief values. The results in this situation deviate from those obtained using Dempster's rule depending on the degree of conflict and tend to approach Yager's rule. In the extreme case when the two evidences are totally contradicting, we obtain Yager's rule. This is a condition where we are in a state of dilemma. We really can't say anything and it is as if we know nothing. Hence, Yager's rule aptly represents this state of mind.

Thus, the assumption of level of ignorance being directly proportional to the amount of conflict is reasonable and intuitively satisfying.

Now we show that the above rule is a convex combination of Dempster's rule and Yager's rule for proper subsets of the frame.

For each proper non-empty subset, the convex combination of Dempster's rule and Yager's rule can be written as:

$$\alpha \overbrace{\left[k \sum_{A_i \cap B_j = C} m_1(A_i) \cdot m_2(B_j) \right]}^{Dempster's\ rule} + (1-\alpha) \overbrace{\left[\sum_{A_i \cap B_j = C} m_1(A_i) \cdot m_2(B_j) \right]}^{Yager's\ rule}$$

where $k = \frac{1}{1-m(\emptyset)}$ and $0 \leq \alpha \leq 1$.

With the condition $\alpha \cdot k = 1$, we obtain the above proposed rule.

It can be seen that each non-empty proper subsets get additional mass from $m(\emptyset)$ depending upon its own support in the combination. The rest of the mass remains uncommitted. It is easy to check that this combination rule is commutative and non-associative but is robust. The non-associative nature of rule

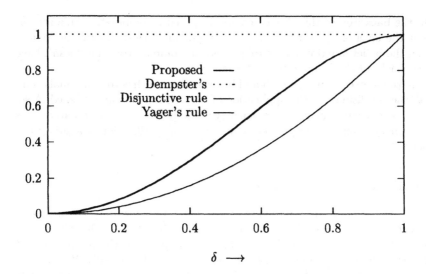

Fig. 2. Plot for Zadeh's example

can be attributed to the method of redistribution of $m(\emptyset)$. In this sense, these properties are similar to those of Disjunctive rule and Yager's rule. Fig.2 shows the plot of $m(b)$ obtained by the three combination rules for Zadeh's example.

Although the above rule is quite general, its utility needs to be established in practical applications.

Incidentally, elicitation of precise numbers from an expert, satisfying certain conditions, is not an easy task. Say, an expert puts a belief in a particular hypothesis to be 73%. What happens if, say, we represent or change it to 75%? How meaningful are the numbers obtained by combining belief functions? These are some of the intriguing questions which are beyond the realm of Dempster-Shafer theory. We have seen in earlier section that some of the modifications to Dempster rule are made so that the results agree with those obtained by probabilistic approach; while others try to resolve the uncertainty. All these things make the comparison of different combination rules difficult.

6   Conclusion

In this paper we remarked using Zadeh's example that Zhang's center rule of combination lacks robustness. Further we have shown that Disjunctive rule and Yager's rule give counter-intuitive results in some cases. In addition, these rules exhibit a tendency of treating evidences asymmetrically. Hence, care must be taken when applying these rules.

On the backdrop of this discussion we proposed a combination rule assuming that the level of ignorance is directly proportional to the degree of conflict between the belief functions. This rule is robust, commutative and doesn't have the drawbacks of the Disjunctive and Yager's rule.

From the above discussion it should be clear that one has to really make sure that all the conditions for the application of a particular rule are satisfied. Also, there can be pathological cases and one may possibly have many alternative rules to choose from. Hence, the right choice and need for justification of assumptions is crucial.

Acknowledgments

This work was supported by Indian Space Research Organization. We are grateful to Prof.P.G.Poonacha, Electrical Engineering Department for helpful suggestions. We acknowledge the help of Joeseph Halpern for the interesting net discussion on Zadeh's example and the combination rules. Finally, We are also thankful to anonymous referees for their comments which helped in improving this draft.

References

1. D. Dubois and H. Prade. Combination and Propagation of Uncertainty with Belief Functions: A Reexamination. Proc. 9th IJCAI, pages 111–113, Los Angeles, 1985.
2. D. Dubois and H. Prade. A Set-theoretic View of Belief Functions. *International Journal of General Systems*, 12:193–226, 1986.
3. D. Dubois and H. Prade. Representation and Combination of Uncertainty with Belief Functions and Possibility Measures. *Computational Intelligence*, 4:244–264, 1988.
4. J. Halpern and R. Fagin. Two Views of Belief: Belief as Generalized Probability and Belief as Evidence. *Artificial Intelligence*, 54:275–317, 1992.
5. H. Hau and R. Kashyap. Belief Combination and Propagation in a Lattice Structured Inference Network. *IEEE Transactions on Systems, Man and Cybernetics*, 20(1):45–57, 1990.
6. M. McLeish. A Study of Probabilities and Belief Functions under Conflicting Evidence. In B. Bouchon, R. Yager, and L. Zadeh, editors, *Uncertainty in Knowledge Bases*, Lecture Notes in Computer Science, pages 41–49, France, 1990. Springer-Verlag.
7. G. Shafer. *A Mathematical Theory of Evidence*. Princeton University Press, New Jersy, 1976.
8. G. Shafer. *Analysis of Fuzzy Information*, volume 1, chapter Belief Functions and Possibility Measures, pages 51–83. CRC Press, 1987. J. Bezdek Editor.
9. G. Shafer. *Readings in Uncertain Reasoning*, chapter Belief Functions, pages 473–481. Morgan Kauffman, 1990. G. Shafer and J. Pearl Eds.
10. Shi ShengLi, M.E.C Hull, and D.A. Bell. A New Rule for Updating Evidence. In Z. Ras and M. Zemankova, editors, *Methodology for Intelligent Systems*, number 869 in Lecture Notes in Artificial Intelligence, pages 95–104, Berlin, 1994. Springer-Verlag.

11. P. Smets. *Non-standard Logics for Automated Reasoning*, chapter Belief Functions, pages 253–286. Academic Press, 1988. D. Dubois and H. Prade Eds.

12. P. Smets. The Combination of Evidence in Transferable Belief Model. *IEEE Transactions on Pattern Analysis and Machine Intelligence*, 12(5):447–458, 1990.

13. R. Yager. On the Dempster-Shafer Framework and New Combination Rules. *International Journal of Man-Machine Studies*, 41:93–137, 1987.

14. L. Zadeh. Review of Shafer's A Mathematical Theory of Evidence. *AI Magazine*, 5(3):81–83, 1984.

15. L. Zadeh. A Simple View of the Dempster-Shafer Theory of Evidence and Its Implication for the Rule of Combination. *AI Magazine*, 7:85–90, 1986.

16. L. Zhang. *Advances in the Dempster-Shafer Theory of Evidence*, chapter Representation, Independence and Combination of Evidence in the Dempster-Shafer Theory, pages 51–69. Wiley Professional Computing. John Wiley & Sons, New York, 1994. R. Yager and M. Fedrizzi and J. Kacprzyk Eds.

Two Conditional Logics for Defeasible Inference: A Comparison Preliminary Version

Verónica Becher

postmaster@becher.uba.ar
Univesidad de Buenos Aires, ARGENTINA

Abstract. We compare two conditional logics for defeasible inference: Alchourrón's defeasible logic DFT and Boutilier's CO logic. The two logics share the distinguishable characteristics common to most logics for defeasible inference. Namely, their conditional connective defeat the rules of Modus Ponens, Strengthening the Antecedent, Transitivity, and Contraposition. Although both logics have possible worlds semantics, Boutilier's is relational while Alchourrón's is non-relational. In this note we reveal the connection between the two, concluding that the conditional sentences validated by both logics are precisely the *same*.

1 Introduction

In this note we compare two modal conditional logics for defeasible inference: Alchourrón's DFT [2] and Boutilier's CO [3]. Both are conditional logics with possible worlds semantics. Boutilier gives a relational semantics, requiring a reflexive transitive and totally connected binary relation between worlds. He regards the accessibility relation as a plausibility ordering of possible worlds. In contrast, Alchourrón gives non-relational semantics, based on a selection function Ch that picks all presuppositions for a given proposition. Both logics have an axiomatic presentation, and are sound and complete. In this note we investigate their connection. Both conditional constructions share the distinguishable characteristics with respect to the conditional connective common to most logics for defeasible inference. Namely, they defeat the rules of Modus Ponens, Strengthening the antecedent, Transitivity, and Contraposition.

2 Alchourrón's DFT Logic

Alchourrón's modal conditional logic is based on a propositional language $\mathbf{L}_{CPL}$ (over variables $\mathbf{P}$, the set of atomic variables in the language) augmented with an S5-necessity operator $\Box$ and a revision operator f. The resulting modal language is denoted by $\mathbf{L}_M$. The possibility operator $\Diamond$ defined in terms of $\Box$ as usual: $\Diamond A \equiv_{df} \neg\Box\neg A$. Alchourrón bases his construction on the very idea that in a *defeasible conditional* the antecedent is a *contributory* condition of its consequent (as opposed to be a sufficient condition for the consequent). Hence, he defines a defeasible conditional $A >_{DFT} B$ meaning that the antecedent A jointly with the set of assumptions that comes with it is a sufficient condition for the consequent B. In order to represent in the object language the joint assertion of the proposition expressed by a sentence A and the set of assumptions (or presuppositions) that comes with it he uses a *revision operator* f. Let $A_1, \ldots A_n$ the set of assumptions associated with A, then fA stands for the joint assertion (conjunction) of A with all the A_i (for all $1 \leq i \leq n$), where A is always one of the conjuncts of fA. Four constraints are imposed to the revision operator f:

f.1 $(fA \supset A)$ (Expansion)
f.2 $(A \leftrightarrow B) \supset fA \leftrightarrow fB)$ (Extensionality)
f.3 $\Diamond A \supset \Diamond fA$ (Limit Expansion)
f.4 $[f(A \vee B) \leftrightarrow fA] \vee [f(A \vee B) \leftrightarrow fB] \vee [f(A \vee B) \leftrightarrow (fA \vee fB)]$
(Hierarchical Ordering)

Condition **f.1** is quite natural since fA stands for conjunction of A and its presuppositions. The second asserts that equivalent sentences have equivalent presuppositions. **f.3** insures the existence of consistent presuppositions for any sentence that is not a contradiction. We will see below that the formulation of condition **f.3** carries some consequences that we analyze in semantic terms. Finally, **f.4** asserts that the presuppositions of a disjunction are either the presuppositions of one of the disjuncts, or else the disjunction of the presuppositions of each of the disjuncts. Alchourrón defines a defeasible conditional $A >_{DFT} B$ meaning that the antecedent A jointly with the set of assumptions that comes with it is a sufficient condition for the consequent B. To reflect his intuition, Alchourrón adopts the following definition due to Lennart Åquist :

$$A >_{DFT} B \equiv_{df} \Box(fA \supset B)$$

Alchourrón gives a formal semantic interpretation of the object language $\mathbf{L}_M$ based on standard non-relational S5-models. He defines a model for $\mathbf{L}_M$ as $M_{DFT} = \langle W, Ch, \| \ \| \rangle$ where W is a non-empty set of possible worlds, $\| \ \|$ is the valuation function ($\| \ \|$ maps $\mathbf{P}$ into 2^W), and Ch is a *selection function* such that for each sentence A of $\mathbf{L}_M$ $Ch(A) \subseteq W^1$. That is, $Ch(A)$ is the proposition of the joint assertion of A and its assumptions, i.e., the worlds in which fA are true. Hence, Alchourrón defines:

$$\|fA\| = Ch(A)$$

The function Ch satisfies the following four constraints, in exact correspondence to the four properties of the revision operator f.

Ch.1 $Ch(A) \subseteq \|A\|$
Ch.2 If $\|A\| = \|B\|$ then $Ch(A) = Ch(B)$

---

[1] Alchourrón defines the selection function Ch as Ch^α meaning that the selection is indexed by the particular preferences of an individual α (as opposed to be a universal selection function for every individual). For the purposes of this note, the distinction is not relevant; moreover, wherever we write Ch it could be read as Ch^α.

Ch.3 If $\|A\| \neq \emptyset$ then $Ch(A) \neq \emptyset$

Ch.4 $Ch(A \vee B) = \{ Ch(A) \text{ or } Ch(B) \text{ or } (Ch(A) \cup Ch(B)) \}$

Condition **Ch.3** embodies a requirement in which Alchourrón's and Boutilier's logic differ. **Ch.3** reflects that every consistent proposition must contain some minimum, preferred or chosen elements. This condition is known as the *Limit Assumption* [1]. Although it is a very sensible property when using selection function semantics, it becomes inapplicable in models where the minimum can not be defined, where there is an infinite chain of minimal elements, as in the real numbers. Truth conditions in model M_{DFT} are defined as follows:

$w \in \|\Box A\|$ iff $\|A\| = W$,

$w \in \|A \Rightarrow B\|$ iff $\|A\| \subseteq \|B\|$

Truth in a Model $M_{DFT} \models A$ iff $\|A\| = W$

Logical Truth $\models A$ iff $M_{DFT} \models A$ for all M_{DFT}

Truth of a defeasible conditional in a model is defined as:

$$M_{DFT} \models (A >_{DFT} B) \text{ iff } Ch^{\alpha}(A) \subseteq \|B\|$$

Alchourrón also gives an axiomatic presentation of his logic, having the conditional connective $>_{DFT}$ as primitive. The following definitions are used in his axiomatization. $NA \equiv_{df} (\neg A >_{DFT} \bot)$, and $(A \succeq B) \equiv_{df} [N(\neg A \wedge \neg B) \vee \neg((A \vee B) >_{DFT} \neg A)]$.

DFT1 $\vdash_{DFT} (A >_{DFT} A)$

DFT2 $\vdash_{DFT} [A >_{DFT} (B \wedge C)] \equiv [A >_{DFT} B) \wedge (A >_{DFT} C)]$

DFT3.1 $\vdash_{DFT} [(A >_{DFT} C) \wedge (B >_{DFT} C)] \supset [(A \vee B) >_{DFT} C]$

DFT3.2 $\vdash_{DFT} (A \succeq B) \supset [((A \vee B) >_{DFT} C) \supset (A >_{DFT} C)]$

DFT4 $\vdash_{DFT} (A >_{DFT} B) \supset N(A >_{DFT} B)$

DFT5 $\vdash_{DFT} \neg(A >_{DFT} B) \supset N\neg(A >_{DFT} B)$

DFT6 $\vdash_{DFT} (\neg A >_{DFT} \bot) \supset A$

Rule of Extensionality If $\vdash_{DFT} (A \equiv B)$ then $\vdash (A >_{DFT} C) \equiv (B >_{DFT} C)$ and $\vdash_{DFT} (C >_{DFT} A) \equiv (C >_{DFT} B)$.

¿From the fact that Alchourrón bases his logic DFT over S5, DFT.4 and DFT.5 are axioms of his system. He observes that they have a paradoxical flavor since they can be interpreted as asserting that a defeasible conditional is never contingent: it is always impossible or necessary. DFT.4 and DFT.5 reveal the global nature of a defeasible conditional with respect to the contextual model M_{DFT}. So, conditionals are contingent in the set of all models. In the next section we will see that Boutilier's conditionals have precisely the same behaviour. We end up this section with the following observation about Alchourrón's conditional connective, reflecting a limiting case of the definition.

Observation In the particular case where the Choice function $Ch(A) = \|A\|$ for every $A \in L_M$ Alchourrón's defeasible conditional connective $>_{DFT}$ collapses into the S5-strict conditional $\Rightarrow$[2].

---

[2] $A \Rightarrow B \equiv_{df} \Box(A \supset B)$.

In this limiting case the Choice function induces an ignorant revision function f, where every sentence is becomes its own presupposition. Then, the conditional $>_{DFT}$ looses all its defeating properties.

3 Boutilier's Conditional Logic CO

Boutilier presents a family of conditional logics for belief revision and default reasoning. In this section we concentrate in one of them that he called CO. This modal logic is based on a bimodal language $\mathbf{L}_B$, which is defined as a propositional language $\mathbf{L}_{CPL}$ (over variables $\mathbf{P}$, the set of atomic variables in the language) augmented with two modal operators. $\Box$ is the modality for accessibility and $\overline{\Box}$ is its complement denoting inaccessibility. The sentence $\Box\alpha$ is read as usual as "α is true at all *accessible* worlds." In contrast, $\overline{\Box}\alpha$ is read "α is true at all *inaccessible* worlds." A CO-model is a triple $M_{CO} = \langle W, R, \| \ \| \rangle$, where W is a set of worlds with valuation function $\| \ \|$ (the function $\| \ \|$ maps $\mathbf{P}$ into 2^W), and R is an accessibility relation over W. Boutilier requires that R to be reflexive, transitive and totally connected (that is, either wRv or vRw for all w, v)[3]. Semantically, R is interpreted as a *plausibility ordering* over possible worlds; wRv is read as: v is at least as plausible as w. Satisfaction of a modal formula at world w in a model M_{CO} is given by:

$M_{CO} \models_w \Box\alpha$ iff for each v such that wRv, $M_{CO} \models_v \alpha$.
$M_{CO} \models_w \overline{\Box}\alpha$ iff for each v such that not wRv, $M_{CO} \models_v \alpha$.

Boutilier defines several new connectives as follows: $\Diamond\alpha \equiv_{df} \neg\Box\neg\alpha$; $\overline{\Diamond}\alpha \equiv_{df} \neg\overline{\Box}\neg\alpha$; $\ddot{\Box}\alpha \equiv_{df} \Box\alpha \wedge \overline{\Box}\alpha$; and $\ddot{\Diamond}\alpha \equiv_{df} \neg\ddot{\Box}\neg\alpha$. These connectives have the following truth conditions: $\Diamond\alpha$ ($\overline{\Diamond}\alpha$) is true at a world if α holds at some accessible (inaccessible) world; $\ddot{\Box}\alpha$ ($\ddot{\Diamond}\alpha$) holds iff α holds at all (some) worlds.

For any CO-model $M_{CO} = \langle W, R, \| \ \| \rangle$, α is valid on M_{CO} (written $M_{CO} \models \alpha$) iff $M_{CO} \models_w \alpha$ for each $w \in W$. Let's notice that validity in a model is expressible in logic CO as $M_{CO} \models \ddot{\Box}\alpha$. Therefore, the $\ddot{\Box}$ modality behaves as an S5 accessibility modality, denoting truth at every possible world. A sentence α is CO-valid, written $\models_{CO} \alpha$ just when $M_{CO} \models \alpha$ for every CO-model M_{CO}.

The conditional logic CO is the smallest $S \subseteq \mathbf{L}_B$ such that S contains classical propositional logic and the following axiom schemata, and is closed under the following rules of inference:

K $\Box(A \supset B) \supset (\Box A \supset \Box B)$
K' $\overline{\Box}(A \supset B) \supset (\overline{\Box}A \supset \overline{\Box}B)$
T $\Box A \supset A$
4 $\Box A \supset \Box\Box A$
S $A \supset \overline{\Box}\Diamond A$

---

[3] Reflexivity follows from total connectedness; so, to specify a CO-model transitivity and total connectedness suffice.

H $\diamondsuit(\Box A \wedge \overline{\Box} B) \supset \overline{\Box}(A \vee B)$

Nes From A infer $\overline{\Box} A$

MP From $A \supset B$ and A infer B.

Axiom **4** ensures transitivity of the accessibility relation R and **S** ensures total (or strong) connectedness[4]. Axiom **T** ensures reflexivity. The system CO is characterized by the class of CO-models; that is, $\vdash_{CO} \alpha$ iff $\models_{CO} \alpha$. Let's remark that the class of CO models are S4.3 models with a unique chain of clusters (this is ensured by total connectedness).

Boutilier defines the comparative *plausibility* of two propositions in a model. A is at least as plausible as B, written $A \succeq_{CO} B$ just when, for every B-world w, there is some A-world that is at least as plausible as w. This is expressed in $\mathbf{L}_B$ as $\overline{\Box}(B \supset \diamondsuit A)$.

The conditional connective is defined in the bimodal language as follows:

$$(A \succ_o B) \equiv_{df} \overline{\Box}(A \supset \diamondsuit(A \wedge \Box(A \supset B)))$$

The conditional $A \succ_o B$ holds in a model when either there are no A worlds at all, or, when every A-world has access to some point where every accessible world satisfying A also satisfies B. Under the interpretation of the accessibility relation R as a plausibility ordering, the conditional $A \succ_o B$ states that the (possibly infinite) chain of most plausible A-worlds must satisfy B. Contrasting with Alchourrón DFT-logic, Boutilier does not assume the existence of *the most plausible* A-worlds. In the case where such worlds do exist, obviously $A \succ_o B$ holds just when B holds at all such worlds. In contrast, suppose there is some unending chain of more and more plausible A-worlds. If some B-world lies in this chain having the property that B-holds whenever A does, at all (still) more plausible worlds in the chain, then $A \succ_o B$ ought to be considered true. Even though no *most* plausible A-world exists, B would hold at the *hypothetical limit* of A-worlds in this chain. The requirement that there exists a set of most plausible A-worlds in the ordering is the *Limit Assumption* (L.A.). Since CO makes no commitment to the L.A. this is a point in which the Boutilier's and Alchourrón's formalsms differ. A particular kind of CO-models are those that satisfy the L.A.

The set of most plausible A-worlds in a model M_{CO} that satisfies the L.A. is defined as:

$$Pl(M_{CO}, A) = \{w \in W : M_{CO} \models_w A \text{ and } M_{CO} \models_v \diamondsuit A \text{ implies } vRw \text{ for all} \\ v \in W\}$$

When dealing with CO-models that cumply the L.A. the definition of a conditional can be expressed semantically as follows:

$$M_{CO} \models A \succ_o B \text{ iff } Pl(M_{CO}, A) \subseteq \|B\|$$

$A \succ_o B$ is true in a model M_{CO} just when B is true at each of the most plausible A-worlds.

---

[4] Notice that axiom **S** of total connectedness is only expressible in a bimodal language.

4   The Connection between DFT and CO

In this section we compare the two logics and reveal their connection. We presume that the unnested conditional fragments of DFT and CO coincide for corresponding models in the two logics. In order to see semantically whether this equivalence holds we should first define the notion of correspondence between models of the two logics. We are forced to make the following assumptions. Let logical language L defined over a set of propositional variables P. We will assume that language L either deals with infinite conjunctions, or else the set of propositional variables is finite. The reason for this assumption is that Alchourrón's Choice function is intrinsically linguistic, that is, it is defined from $L \rightarrow W$. Hence, in order to show correspondence with Boutilier's semantics we ought to denote the elements of W with sentences of L. We take W as the set of possible worlds that can be described by L, that is, the set of all maximal consistent extensions of L. We assume W is non-empty. Let's see first how a CO-model $M_{CO} = \langle W, R, \| \ \| \rangle$ that satisfies the Limit Assumption induces a Choice function Ch_R, and gives rise to a corresponding DFT-model M_{DFT}.

Definition 1. Let a CO-model $M_{CO} = \langle W, R, \| \ \| \rangle$ that satisfies the Limit Assumption, and let $A \in L$. The Choice function Ch_R induced by the accessibility relation R is defined as:

$$Ch_R(A) = \{w \in \|A\| : w' Rw, \ \forall w' \in \|A\|\}$$

We shall prove that Ch_R satisfies the expected four properties of a Choice function.

Proposition 2. *Ch_R satisfies the following properties:*

C.1 $Ch_R(A) \subseteq \|A\|$
C.2 *If* $\|A\| = \|B\|$ *then* $Ch_R(A) = Ch_R(B)$
C.3 *If* $\|A\| \neq \emptyset$ *then* $Ch_R(A) \neq \emptyset$
C.4 $Ch_R(A \vee B) = \{ \ Ch_R(A) \ or \ Ch_R(B) \ or \ Ch_R(A) \cup Ch_R(B) \ \}$

Proof. That Ch_R satisfies **C.1** and **C.2** is obvious by definition 1.
To see **C.3** suppose $Ch_R(A) = \emptyset$. Then, there is no $w \in \|A\|$ such that $w' Rw$ for all $w' \in \|A\|$. Since R is a well-founded total preorder, $\|A\| = \emptyset$.
Let's see **C.4**. By Definition 1, $Ch_R(A \vee B) = \{w \in \|A \vee B\| : w' Rw, \ \forall w' \in \|A \vee B\|\}$ Since $\|A \vee B\| = \|A\| \cup \|B\|$, we have: $Ch_R(A \vee B) = \{w \in (\|A\| \cup \|B\|) : w' Rw \ \forall w' \in (\|A\| \cup \|B\|)\}$, which can be written as:

$$Ch_R(A \vee B) = \{w \in \|A\| : w' Rw, \forall w' \in \|A\| \cup \|B\|\} \bigcup \{w \in \|B\| : w' Rw, \forall w' \in \|A\| \cup \|B\|\} \tag{1}$$

Since R is a total preorder, encoding the comparative plausibility of two propositions in a model, one of the following three cases holds. Either, (a) the proposition of A is stricltly more plausible than proposition of B, written $A \succ_{CO} B$, which says that for every B-world w, there is some A-world v such that wRv but not

vRw. Or, (b) the proposition of B is striclty more plausible than the proposition of A, $B \succ_{CO} A$; or else (c) propositions for A and B are equally plausible, $A \succeq_{CO} B$ and $B \succeq_{CO} A$.

Suppose case (a) holds. It becomes clear that the set of of A-worlds accessible by every world in $\|A \cup B\|$ is presicely the same as the set of A-worlds from every A-world, since there is always an A-world strictly more plausible than a B-world. Thus the first set in expression 1 becomes:

$$\{w \in \|A\| : w'Rw \; \forall w' \in (\|A\|\cup\|B\|)\} = \{w \in \|A\| : w'Rw \; \forall w' \in \|A\|\} = Ch_R(A)$$

Let's inspect the second set in 1. Since A-worlds are striclty more plausible than B-worlds there can be no B-worlds accessible from every A-world, so, $\{w \in \|B\| : w'Rw \; \forall w' \in (\|A\| \cup \|B\|)\} = \emptyset$. We conclude that whenever $A \succ_{CO} B$, $Ch_R(A \vee B) = Ch_R(A)$

Case (b) is analogous to case (a), for which we obtain $Ch_R(A \vee B) = Ch_R(B)$, whenever $B \succ_C OA$

It remains to analyze expression 1 for case (c). We have that proposition of A is at least as plausible as proposition of B ($A \succeq_{CO} B$), and B is at least as plausible as A ($B \succeq_{CO} B$). So, for every B-world w, there is some A-world v such that wRv, and for every A-world v', there is some B-world w' such that $v'Rw'$. As R is a total preorder, the set of A-worlds accessible from every A-world is *the same* as the set of A-worlds accessible form every $(A \vee B)$-world. And the set of B-worlds accessible from every B-world is *the same* as the set of B-worlds accessible from every $(A \vee B)$-world. Hence,

$$\{w \in \|A\| : w'Rw \; \forall w' \in (\|A\|\cup\|B\|)\} = \{w \in \|A\| : w'Rw \; \forall w' \in \|A\|\} = Ch_R(A)$$

and

$$\{w \in \|B\| : w'Rw \; \forall w' \in (\|A\|\cup\|B\|)\} = \{w \in \|B\| : w'Rw \; \forall w' \in \|B\|\} = Ch_R(B)$$

So, $Ch_R(A \vee B) = Ch_R(A) \bigcup Ch_R(B)$ whenever $A \succeq_{CO} B$ and $B \succeq_C OA$

Therefore, from cases (a) (b) and (c) we obtain $Ch_R(A \vee B) = \{ Ch_R(A)$ or $Ch_R(B)$ or $Ch_R(A) \cup Ch_R(B) \}$

Now let's see how a DFT-model $M_{DFT} = \langle W, Ch, \| \;\| \rangle$ induces a reflexive transitive and totally connected accessibility relation R_{Ch} among the worlds of W and gives rise to a CO-model $M_{CO} = \langle W, R_{Ch}, \| \;\| \rangle$.

Definition 3. Let M_{DFT} a DFT model with choice function $Ch : \mathbf{L} \rightarrow 2^W$. The *accessibility relation* R_{Ch} induced by Ch is defined as follows.

$wR_{Ch}v$ iff there is $A \in \mathbf{L}$ such that $w, v \in \|A\|$, and $v \in Ch(A)$.

We shall see that R_{Ch} is a reflexive transitive and totally connected accessibility relation in W. We make use of the following two lemmas.

Lemma 4. *Let* $A, B \in \mathbf{L}$ *such that* $\|A\| \subseteq \|B\|$ *and let* $v \in W$. *If* $v \in \|A\|$ *and* $v \in Ch(B)$ *then* $v \in Ch(A)$.

Lemma 5. *Let* $A, B \in \mathbf{L}$, *such that* $\|A\| subseteq \|B\|$. *If* $Ch(A) = \|A\|$ *and* $(Ch(A) \cap Ch(B)) \neq \emptyset$ *then* $Ch(A) \subseteq Ch(B)$.

Proposition 6. R_{Ch} *is reflexive transitive and totally connected accessibility relation in* W.

Proof. To see that R_{Ch} is reflexive, we have to show that for every $w \in W$, $w R_{Ch} w$. By definition 3, $w R_{Ch} w$ iff there is some $A \in \mathbf{L}$ such that $w \in Ch(A)$. Let the sentence A denote the unitary proposition $\{w\}$. By condition C.1, $Ch(A) \subseteq \|A\|$. Hence, $Ch(A) = \{w\}$.

Let's see that R_{Ch} is transitive. Let any three worlds $w, v, u \in W$, such that $w R_{Ch} v$ and $v R_{Ch} u$, Let's denote with $A \in \mathbf{L}$ the proposition $\{w, v, u\}$. By property C.1 $Ch(A) \subseteq \{w, v, u\}$ and by C.3 if $\|A\| \neq \emptyset$ then $Ch(A) \neq \emptyset$ Then at least one of w, v, u is in $Ch(A)$.

1. Suppose $u \in Ch(A)$. Straightforwardly by Definition 3, $w R_{Ch} u$.
2. Suppose $v \in Ch(A)$. Since $v R_{Ch} u$, by Definition 3 there is $B \in \mathbf{L}$ such that $\{v, u\} \subseteq \|B\|$ and $u \in Ch(B)$. Let $\|B\| = \{v, u\}$. By Lemma 4 $v \in Ch(B)$. Then $Ch(B) = \|B\|$ By lemma 5 $Ch(B) \subseteq Ch(A)$ Then $u \in Ch(A)$. Hence $w R_{Ch} u$.
3. Finally suppose $w \in Ch(A)$. By Lemma 4 $w \in Ch(B1), w \in Ch(B2)$, for $B1 = \{w, v\}, B2 = \{w, u\}$. Since $w R_{Ch} v$, by Definition 3 $w, v \in \|B1\|, v \in Ch(B1)$. By lemma 5 $Ch(B1) \subseteq Ch(A)$ Then $v \in Ch(A)$. It follows as case 2.

To prove that R_{Ch} is totally connected we should see that for any pair of worlds $u, v \in W$ either $u R_{Ch} v$ or $v R_{Ch} u$. We have to show that it is impossible that not $u R_{Ch} v$ and not $v R_{Ch} u$.

Let's suppose not $u R_{Ch} v$ and not $v R_{Ch} u$. Then, for every sentence $A \in \mathbf{L}$ such that $u, v \in \|A\|$ it ought to be that $u \notin Ch(A)$ and $v \notin Ch(A)$. But this is impossible, as the following example illustrates. Consider the unitary propositions $\|B\| = \{u\}$ and $\|C\| = \{v\}$, so $\|B \vee C\| = \{u, v\}$. By properties C.1 and C.3, $Ch(B \vee C) \subseteq \|B \vee C\|$ and $Ch(B \vee C) \neq \emptyset$ if $\|B \vee C\| \neq \emptyset$ Then, either u, v or both should belong to $Ch(B \vee C)$.

We can now assert that for each DFT-model there is a corresponding CO-model satisfying L.A. and vice-versa.

Proposition 7. *For each CO-model* $M_{CO} = \langle W, R, \| \| \rangle$ *satisfying the Limit Assumption there is a corresponding DFT-model* $M_{DFT} = \langle W, Ch_R, \| \| \rangle$.
For each DFT-model $M_{DFT} = \langle W, Ch, \| \| \rangle$ *there is a corresponding CO model* $M_{CO} = \langle W, R_{Ch}, \| \| \rangle$.

We are now able to prove the important result of this note, which reveals the connection between the two logics, DFT and CO: the two logics validate the *same* unnested conditional sentences. In order to show this result we should state a common language for the two logics where to express the flat conditional assertions they validate. Let $\mathbf{L}_>$ the language of unnested conditional sentences, formed from a denumerable set **P** of propositional variables together with the connectives $\neg, \supset, and >$ (the connectives $\wedge, \vee \equiv$ are defined in terms of $\neg, \supset$ as usual). So we shall prove that the conditional sentences validated by DFT and CO are the same. To show this correspondence, let's consider the conditional sentences of DFT with their connective $>_{DFT}$ replaced by $>$, and the conditional sentences of CO with their conditional connective $>_{CO}$ also replaced by $>$.

Theorem 8. *Let M_{CO} and M_{DFT} be corresponding models, and let any sentence $A > B \in \mathbf{L}_>$, then $M_{CO} \models A > B$ iff $M_{DFT} \models A > B$.*

Proof. $M_{CO} \models A > B$ iff $Pl(M_{CO}, A) \subseteq \|B\|$ iff $\{w \in \|A\| : w'Rw$ for all $w' \in \|A\|\} \subseteq \|B\|$ iff $Ch(A) \subseteq \|B\|$ iff $M_{DFT} \models A > B$.

The next theorem states that the conditionals derivable by both logics coincide. This result is not surprising given the previous result and the fact that both CO and DFT are sound and complete.

Theorem 9. *Let M_{CO} and M_{DFT} be corresponding models, and let any sentence $A > B \in \mathbf{L}_>$, then $M_{CO} \vdash_{CO} A > B$ iff $M_{DFT} \vdash_{DFT} A > B$.*

In DFT one can define a restricted necessity operator Bel_{DFT} that stands for belief as follows: $\mathsf{Bel}_{DFT}(A) \equiv_{df} \top >_{DFT} A$ Reciprocally, Boutilier defines in CO the belief modality Bel_{CO} in $\mathbf{L}_B$. The sentence $\mathsf{Bel}_{CO}(A)$ holds in a revision model when A is true at each most plausible worlds: $M_{CO} \models \mathsf{Bel}_{CO}(A)$ iff $Pl(M_{CO}, A) \subseteq \|A\|$ iff $M_{CO} \models \top >_{CO} A$. Syntactically Boutilier's belief operator can also be defined as: $\mathsf{Bel}_{CO}(A) \equiv_{df} \ddot{\Box}\Diamond\Box A$. So, as a corollary of Theorem 8 we have that the two notions of belief coincide.

5 Concluding Remarks

We have shown by semantic means that the unnested conditional fragments of Alchourrón's DFT logic and Boutilier's CO logic are equivalent. The two logics are modal conditional logics with roughly the same motivation: both are intended for a *defeasible* inference. The equivalence may be suggesting that the field of study is becoming mature, so that different logics with the same motivation turn out to be equivalent in a relevant portion.

An important aspect is that of the nested occurrences of the conditional connective. It seems that different intuitions correspond to whether the nesting of the conditional connective appears in the antecedent or in the consequent of a conditional construction. Alchourrón shows that certain nested conditionals collapse into the flat portion of DFT; in particular, he proves that $(A \wedge (A > B)) > B$ has the same truth value as $A > B$. The same behaviour occurs for these kind of nested conditionals in Boutilier's CO logic. Since the two logics have corresponding models, we conjecture they induce the same nested conditionals. However, this presumption deserves proper study, that we consider as future research.

Acknowledgements

I'm grateful to Carlos Alchourrón for his valuable comments on an earlier draft of this paper. This research has been supported by a fellowship in the Informatics Programs at the University of Buenos Aires.

References

1. D. Lewis. 1973. *Counterfactuals.* Blackwell, Oxford.
2. C. Alchourrón. 1993. Defeasible, Strict and Counterfactual Conditionals. Non-monotonic Inference Relations. In *Conditionals and Artificial Intelligence* Edited by Crocco, Fariñas del Cerro, Herzig. Toulouse, France.
3. C. Boutilier. 1992. Conditional Logics for belief revision and Default Reasoning. PhD. Thesis. Technical Report KRR-TR-92-1. University of Toronto, Toronto, Ontario.
4. C. Boutilier. 1994. Conditional Logics of Normality: A Modal Approach. *Artificial Intelligence*, 68:87-154.
5. C. Boutilier. 1994. Unifying Default Reasoning and Belief Revision in a Modal Framework. *Artificial intelligence*, 68: 33-85.

Underlying Semantics for the Assessment of Reiter's Solution to the Frame Problem

Tania Bedrax-Weiss[1] and Leopoldo E. Bertossi[2]

[1] CIRL and University of Oregon, 1269 University of Oregon, Eugene OR 97403-1269
[2] Departamento de Ciencia de la Computacion, Escuela de Ingenieria, Pontificia
Unviersidad Catolica de Chile, Casilla 306, Correo 22, Santiago, Chile

Abstract. This paper presents an application of Sandewall's methodology [16] for assessing nonmonotonic entailment criteria for reasoning about actions and change. We establish the correctness of Reiter's general solution to the frame problem [14] for a broad and well characterized class of problems. This is done by: (1) identifying a nonmonotonic entailment criterion corresponding to Reiter's solution; (2) discovering ontological and epistemological assumptions that we believe underly the domains of possible applicability of Reiter's approach; (3) defining an underlying semantics corresponding to these assumptions; and (4) providing a semantic correspondence between the models selected by the entailment criterion and the models obtained from the underlying semantics.
We also compare our methodology to Kartha's evaluation [6] of Reiter's general solution with respect to action logic semantics [4].

1 Introduction

This paper presents an application of Sandewall's methodology [16] for assessing nonmonotonic entailment criteria for reasoning about actions and change. We establish the correctness of Reiter's general solution to the frame problem based on the situation calculus [14] for a broad and well characterized class of problems. Given a preliminary axiomatization describing the effects of actions. Reiter's solution is a syntactic completion of this axiomatization. A summary of this process is presented in Section 2. Sandewall's methodology is briefly presented in Section 3. In Section 4 we assess Reiter's solution according to Sandewall's methodology. In Section 5, we compare our methodology to Kartha's evaluation [6] of Reiter's general solution with respect to action logic semantics [4]. Finally, we present the conclusions and future work.

2 Reiter's General Solution

Reiter [14] proposes a formalism to reason about action in first-order logic. Building on work by Haas [5], Pednault [9], and Schubert [17], he syntactically transforms a preliminary axiomatization into a specification that completely describes each fluent at states that result from action executions. The preliminary specification is given in the situation calculus [8] with predicates, fluents, actions, and a function symbol. do. The function symbol do takes as argument an action and a situation and denotes the situation that results from executing the action in that situation. A distinguished predicate. $Poss$. is introduced to this language to specify the conditions under which actions may be possible to execute. If these conditions are satisfied in the state the action is to be executed. it will be referred to as a legal action. It will be referred to as an illegal action. otherwise.

2.1 Axiomatization

The preliminary axiomatization consists of knowledge about S_0. the initial state of the world. which need not be complete. state independent knowledge which defines the initial database. plus the following axioms:

Action Precondition Axioms: For each action name A we will have a precondition axiom of the form

$$Poss(A(\bar{x}). s) \equiv \pi_A(\bar{x}. s).$$

Positive Effects Axioms: For all pairs formed by a fluent R and an action name A. where the action causes fluent R to become true, an axiom of the form:

$$Poss(A(\bar{x}). s) \wedge \gamma(\bar{x}. \bar{y}. s) \supset R(\bar{y}. do(A(\bar{x}). s)). \tag{1}$$

That is. if action A is possible. and the preconditions for fluent R represented by the metaformula $\gamma(\bar{x}. \bar{y}. s)$ are true at state s. then fluent R becomes true in the successor state $do(A(\bar{x}). s)$ obtained after executing action A in state s. Here. $\bar{x}$ and $\bar{y}$ are parameters of the action and the fluent. respectively.

Negative Effects Axioms: For all pairs formed by a fluent R and an action name A. where the action causes fluent R to become false. an axiom of the form:

$$Poss(A(\bar{x}). s) \wedge \psi(\bar{x}. \bar{y}. s) \supset \neg R(\bar{y}. do(A(\bar{x}). s)). \tag{2}$$

The syntactic completion process is the following. For each fluent we combine the positive effect axioms that contain that fluent into a general single positive effect axiom.

$$Poss(a. s) \wedge \lambda(a. s) \supset R(do(a. s)). \tag{3}$$

In this axiom. a is a variable for actions that is considered (tacitly) universally quantified. Similarly, we obtain a general negative effect axiom for each fluent of the form:

$$Poss(a. s) \wedge o(a. s) \supset \neg R(do(a. s)). \tag{4}$$

The general effect axioms do not solve the frame problem. Reiter relies on a "Generalized Completeness Assumption" to do so. He makes the common sense assumption that relatively few actions change the value of any particular fluent and that the actions that do so are completely known. This assumption. though. is made at a metalevel so the transformation remains first-order. After this assumption is made, we can construct the:

Successor State Axiom:

$$Poss(a. s) \supset [R(do(a. s)) \equiv [\lambda(a. s) \vee (R(s) \wedge \neg o(a. s))]]. \tag{5}$$

This axiom is tacitly universally quantified over actions. Intuitively, if action a is possible, then fluent R is true at the successor state that results from the execution of action a if and only if a is one of the actions causing R to be true (for which the fluent preconditions are true), or R was already true when a was executed and a is not one of the actions causing R to be false. There is one successor state axiom for each fluent. In order for things to work properly, unique names axioms [11] are required for actions and states.

It is important to point out that Reiter's solution to the frame problem [14], works only for deterministic actions, that is, actions whose effects are completely known and where the preconditions of the actions are valid in the state they are executed in. Nonetheless, there is nothing in the logic to prevent the execution of illegal actions (actions whose preconditions are not satisfied in the state they are executed), so we must consider them but we choose to ignore its effects.[3]

2.2 Reiter's Nonmonotonic Entailment Criterion

Reiter's approach is monotonic only after the described syntactic transformation has been performed. This method is reminiscent of Clark's completion of logic programs [3]. From this point of view, Reiter's solution represents a syntactic method of selection of the intended models.

Assume that we have a set of formulas Σ corresponding to a preliminary axiomatization of a domain as described at the beginning of Section 2.1. Let $\mathcal{R}(\Sigma)$ denote Reiter's syntactic completion of Σ, as described above. A particular entailment criterion, $\approx_R$, is associated with this completion process with a natural definition: for a formula φ in the language of Σ.

$$\Sigma \approx_R \varphi \quad \Leftrightarrow \quad \mathcal{R}(\Sigma) \models \varphi. \tag{6}$$

On the right-hand side of the equivalence we have the classical entailment criterion, i.e. defined in terms of a "surface semantics" for a first-order predicate calculus. This surface semantics is essentially given in terms of models for first-order languages that represent worlds that evolve in time. Thus, they consider all the possible histories of the world. The criterion $\approx_R$ on the left-hand side is nonmonotonic and can be interpreted as a model preference criterion that selects some of the models of Σ in the class determined by the surface semantics in order to check the validity of φ.

The preferred models of Σ can be inductively defined on actions as follows. In the base case (no actions are executed), select all first-order models which satisfy the initial domain description. In the inductive step we make use of the successor state axiom. There can be two cases: an action may be legal or illegal in that state. If a legal action is executed, select all first-order models such that for each pair (fluent, action), if the successor state axiom for the fluent mentions the action, the value of the fluent in the selected model is true if and only if in equation (5) a is in $\setminus$ or if it was true and a does not belong to o, and it

---

[3] In a real application one actually restricts to the case of accessible states, that is, . states that can be reached after a finite sequence of legal actions.

is negative otherwise. It can be checked that a fluent will be assigned only one value [14]. so at least one model is always selected.

If the action is illegal (its preconditions are not satisfied in the state the action is executed), nothing can be derived. We interpret this as a selection of all possible models of the "successor situation". As we have said before, there is no way to exclude this case from consideration since there is nothing in the logic that restricts the execution to legal actions only.[4] If we introduce a predicate of executability that restricts actions to this case, the definition of the selected models restricted to this predicate remains the same, but without illegal actions.

Remark. The models of Σ we have constructed are exactly those of $\mathcal{R}(\Sigma)$.

The class of models selected by Reiter's entailment criterion will be compared to those defined according to Sandewall's methodology in the following sections.

3   Sandewall's Methodology

Sandewall's methodology [16] consists of first, identifying a class of problems (or domains) one wishes to work with characterized by different epistemological and ontological assumptions about the domains. Epistemological assumptions are assumptions about what kind of information about the description of the domain is available such as, whether there is complete or incomplete information about the initial state, whether there is information about states other than the initial one, etc. There are also ontological assumptions, assumptions about the kinds of worlds that are allowed to exist in the domain, such as, whether there are concurrent actions or not, whether there are delayed effects, etc.

Secondly, Sandewall defines an underlying semantics for the identified class of problems. The underlying semantics takes into account the assumptions underlying the class. The semantics is basically, a simulation semantics where the starting point is a scenario description or a *chronicle* (a description of a representative of the class of problems to be simulated consistent with the identified epistemological assumptions) and where the simulation is generated by an interaction between an ego and a world. This interaction intuitively represents an interaction between a single agent (the ego) who perceives the reality of the problem simulation and invokes actions, and the world, who changes (or not) in response to the ego's actions. Thus, the world "knows" of the action descriptions and the ontological assumptions. We describe the relevant assumptions and the simulation in the following sections. This simulation yields the intended models for the given scenario description.

4   Analysis of Reiter's Solution

In order to compare the intended models to those selected by Reiter's formalism, we must first obtain a translation of Reiter's preliminary axiomatization

---

[4] Notice that *do* is a total function.

into a scenario description in Sandewall's logic. This translation will define a structure called a chronicle which contains several kinds of axioms: observations (corresponding to the description of the initial domain description), action laws (corresponding to a translation of the effect axioms), and a schedule (corresponding to a sequence of actions that will define the state about which we want to query). We give a brief description of this translation later on.

Secondly, the intended models are obtained from this chronicle according to the underlying semantics. Finally, we state the semantic correspondence between the models selected by Reiter's formalism and Sandewall's underlying semantics.

4.1 Ontological and Epistemological Assumptions

By taking a philosophical approach to the situation calculus, to Reiter's solution, and to the problems with inertia (worlds resisting change), we discover the ontological and epistemological assumptions which characterize the class of problems for which Reiter's solution is intended to be applicable. Epistemological assumptions are those that refer to the description of the domain and ontological assumptions are those that refer to the properties of the domain, as in [16].

Ontological Assumptions From the situation calculus we can recognize two assumptions: *single step actions* executed from one situation to the next and *sequential actions* since no concurrent actions are allowed. More assumptions are identified in Reiter's framework: *inertia* restricted to legal actions only since the successor state is undetermined for illegal actions, *deterministic actions, alternative results of actions*, i.e., state-dependent actions, *structural dependency*, i.e., definitions of fluents in terms of properties of a different object, and *local dependency*, i.e., restrictions on fluents imposed by features of the same object.

Epistemological Assumptions We identified the following assumptions: *incomplete knowledge about the initial state, each change is completely characterized* in the sense that all actions that produce a change are known, *the axiomatization is consistent*, and *actions are defined in terms of preconditions*, so the effects of an action are completely known only if it is a legal action.

4.2 Translation into Sandewall's Logic

Sandewall defines an Elementary Feature Logic which is basically a first-order temporal logic [16]. This logic is a language to describe a chronicle or a particular scenario of a domain. The entailment criteria are defined separately by giving its intended set of models. In order to assess Reiter's solution must translate the preliminary axiomatization into a chronicle in Sandewall's logic and define the set of intended models for his entailment criterion.

The translation is straightforward so we will only briefly sketch how this is done. We will interpret each situation as corresponding to a timepoint[5], and such that the initial situation corresponds to timepoint 0, and situation s_i corresponds

---

[5] We follow Sandewall's logic, but the analysis could have been done with situations.

to timepoint i. For each statement of the form $R(x, S_0)$ we introduce an observation statement of the form $[0]R(x) \overset{\wedge}{=} T$. The symbol $\overset{\wedge}{=}$ assigns an observed value (the symbol at the right) to the symbol at the left. For each statement that does not mention any state φ, we introduce an observation statement of the form $[]\varphi$. To translate the effect and precondition axioms into action laws we need to compile for each action, the effect axioms and precondition axioms that mention that action to obtain a first-order equivalent "action law":

Take action $A(\bar{x})$ and all the axioms of the form 1 and 2 that mention the action and write an axiom of the following form, where we have already substituted $Poss(A(\bar{x}), s)$ by its definition.

$$[t, t + 1]A(\bar{x}) \Rrightarrow \quad [t]\pi_A(\bar{x}) - [t]\backslash - [t + 1]R := T \wedge$$
$$[t]\pi_A(\bar{x}) - [t]o - [t + 1]R := F \wedge$$
$$[t]\pi_A(\bar{x}) - [t]\epsilon - [t + 1]Q := T \wedge \ldots$$

The symbol $:=$ has an implicit meaning of possible change, that is, it means that the fluent will have the value at the right of the symbol regardless of what its value was at time t.

A sequence of actions $do(a_{n-1}, \ldots, do(a_1, do(a_0, S_0)) \ldots)$ will be translated:

$$[0]a_0, [1]a_1, \ldots, [n - 1]a_{n-1}.$$

The models of this chronicle are recovered from the class of structures determined by the underlying semantics. We will compare these models to those selected by Reiter's nonmonotonic entailment criterion as defined in Section 2.2. This will be done in the following section.

4.3   Assessment

According to Sandewall's methodology described in Section 3, we identified the class of problems we intend to solve with Reiter's solution. This class was defined according to the ontological and epistemological assumptions. We need to characterize the intended models that correspond to this class by means of the underlying semantics. This underlying semantics is defined as a simulation (interaction) between an ego and a world.

Underlying Semantics The interaction between the ego and the world determines all the possible histories of the particular instance of the domain for a sequence of actions. More precisely, given: (a) an arbitrary axiomatization, (b) a sequence of transactions, (c) an ego, and (d) a world (all of these satisfying the ontological and epistemological assumptions), the interaction will determine the possible histories of that chronicle. The intended models will be obtained from these histories, called *developments*.

Formally, a *development* is a tuple $\langle B, M, O_s, R, \mathcal{F}, \mathcal{C} \rangle$, where:

B: is the set of interpretations of the form $\{0, \ldots, k\}$ for breakpoints (which in the case of single-step actions coincide with the timepoints), where k corresponds to the current state.

M: is the valuation for timepoints (assigns members of B to timepoints) and objects in the universal object domain.

O: is the object domain

R: is the history of the fluent changes from timepoint 0 to timepoint k, actually, we consider this to be an indexed set of assignments of values to fluents,

$\mathcal{F}$: is the set of actions that have been executed.

$\mathcal{C}$: is the set of actions that currently are being executed; since only one action can be executed at a time, it will always contain a single action.

In $\mathcal{F}$ actions are time stamped indicating the starting and termination times, while in $\mathcal{C}$ actions are only time stamped with the starting times.

The moves of the ego and the world are recorded in the developments as follows: If the ego chooses an action, a specified in the chronicle, the world updates $\mathcal{C}$ with the tuple $\langle t, a \rangle$ and reacts to the action in two possible ways: (1) If the preconditions of a are satisfied in R, it updates that history by overriding any previous fluent values with new ones as determined by the action laws in the chronicle. It also updates B by adding a new timepoint $t + 1$ and removes $\langle t, \tau \rangle$ from $\mathcal{C}$ and adds $\langle t, \tau, t + 1 \rangle$ to $\mathcal{F}$. (2) If the preconditions are not satisfied in R, it branches out (one change each time it branches) generating all possible updates for R, and it updates B, $\mathcal{C}$, and $\mathcal{F}$ as before.

The interaction goes on repeatedly for all actions defined in the chronicle and for all histories that arise up to a time t. This interaction is defined for every initial state of the particular domain and every valuation of the timepoints that satisfies the time restrictions imposed by the chronicle (sequential single-step transactions). This generates all the possible histories of the world, given all the possible executions of actions in all possible initial states.

The developments are tree structures. Since the initial state of the domain description is not completely specified, we will have several tree structures corresponding to the evolution of the world, namely, the trees whose history component of the initial development is consistent with the given initial state. The models that define the underlying semantics are obtained from the developments. They are first-order logic models of the history slices of the developments at all timepoints.

The underlying semantics defined in this way is independent of Reiter's entailment criterion, since it depends only on the assumptions made about the domain in question. It is also true that the underlying semantics completely captures these assumptions [2].

Semantic Correspondence In this section we state the correspondence between the first-order models of the values assigned to fluents in both frameworks: Reiter's and Sandewall's. This result applies in the legal as well as in the illegal case.

Let us consider a chronicle Γ, arising from a preliminary axiomatization Σ, of a particular domain description in Reiter's formalism. This chronicle contains a sequence of actions A. The underlying semantics provides the set of models for Γ according to the execution of A.

Theorem 1. *The class of first-order models of Γ arising from the underlying semantics at each time slice coincides with the set of first-order models of $\mathcal{R}(\Sigma)$.*[6]

The proof of the theorem is done by induction on the executed actions. The complete proof can be found on [2].

Note that the models of the chronicle according to both frameworks are formally different since Reiter's models contain information about the fluents at each situation, while Sandewall's models contain the history of the fluents at each point in time. This is why we are forced to compare only the first-order models of the values of the fluents at corresponding timepoints.[7]

This theorem can be thought of as stating that Reiter's solution is applicable to all domains that belong to the class defined according to the ontological and epistemological assumptions of Section 4.1.

From the theorem and remark 2.2 we can obtain a soundness and completeness result:

Corollary 2. *For any sentence φ, $\Sigma \models_R \varphi$ iff φ is true in all models of Σ arising from the underlying semantics.*

5 Comparison to Kartha's Evaluation

Kartha [6] has already presented an analysis of Reiter's solution with respect to Gelfond and Lifschitz's action logic $\mathcal{A}$ [4]. He proves that Reiter's solution captures the semantics of $\mathcal{A}$ starting from a description (chronicle) in $\mathcal{A}$ and then translating it into Reiter's formalism. This translation is sound and complete.

Although our work is similar to Kartha's in the sense that we both characterize and compare the models for a given scenario description, there are several differences. In $\mathcal{A}$ the semantics of a description is fixed, i.e., the entailment criterion is the same for all descriptions, forcing the translation to be from $\mathcal{A}$ into Reiter's formalism. Sandewall's logic, on the other hand, is only a base logic, that is, the entailment criterion is independent of the language used to describe the chronicle. Because of this, we can assess different nonmonotonic entailment criteria by defining equivalent selection criteria in Sandewall's framework. Sandewall's methodology provides a certain degree of flexibility that is not present in Kartha's approach.

There is another difference with respect to both methodologies. Sandewall gives a general language and a general list of assumptions which he restricts when he identifies exactly the class of problems to be addressed. Any assessment

---

[6] See Remark 2.2.
[7] We are indebted to Matt Ginsberg for pointing this out to us.

based on $\mathcal{A}$. on the other hand. must extend the language and semantics (if necessary). So the difference is one of narrowing or extending the language.

Another difference is that Sandewall analyses a criterion with respect to the ontological and epistemological assumptions that underlie a particular domain while Kartha's evaluation considers the models given by two different entailment criteria. In this sense. Sandewall's methodology may be said to check the models selected by the entailment criterion against "reality". whereas Kartha is forced to compare models. that is. abstractions of reality.

Our work is a little bit less restrictive than Kartha's work since we restrict the domains that can be considered to those that can be expressed in Reiter's framework. while Kartha restricts to those expressible in the language $\mathcal{A}$. The difference appears to be that the language $\mathcal{A}$ considers named actions and fluents with no quantification over any of these. so it can be seen as a propositional case. Reiter's framework is full first-order logic.

6   Conclusions

We have made several contributions: (1) we identified a nonmonotonic entailment criterion corresponding to Reiter's syntactic compilation and we inductively defined the preferred models: (2) we identified the ontological and epistemological assumptions that underlie the situation calculus and Reiter's solution in general: (3) we defined an underlying semantics that corresponds to the class of assumptions. thereby extending Sandewall's work: (4) we stated a semantic correspondence between Reiter's models and the models of the underlying semantics: and (5) as a consequence. we obtained that Reiter's solution is correct and complete for a broad class of problems.

7   Future Work

There are still several issues that need to be addressed. We have only considered Reiter's original solution. not its extension to some kinds of ramifications [7]. In [15. 10]. Reiter formalizes the evolution of a database according to his solution to the frame problem [14]. In [1]. this formalization was positively assessed with Sandewall's methodology. In that paper. there was a restriction to ground databases. i.e.. without null values. It seems interesting to extend their results to null values by making a logical reconstruction of the database as described by Reiter [12. 13]. Other extensions to databases may also be considered. such as, concurrent actions and active databases.

8   Acknowledgments

We are grateful to Ray Reiter. Erik Sandewall. and Javier Pinto for stimulating conversations and advice. This research has been supported partly by DIUC. SAREC/CONICYT. Fundacion DICTUC. and FONDECYT (#1930554) grants.

partly by the Air Force Office of Scientific Research under contract 92-0693 and by ARPA/Rome Labs under contracts F30602-91-C-0036 and F30602-93-C-00031. Tania Bedrax-Weiss is specially thankful to CIRL and to David Etherington. Leopoldo Bertossi visited Linköping University in Sweden and is grateful to Erik Sandewall for his hospitality.

References

1. Bedrax-Weiss, T., Bertossi, L.: An assessment of Reiter's general monotonic solution to the frame problem and its applicability to database updates. ECAI-LAC (1994)
2. Bedrax-Weiss, T., Bertossi, L.: An assessment of Reiter's general monotonic solution to the frame problem and its applicability to database updates. Tech. Rept. P. Universidad Catolica de Chile. Dept. de Ciencia de la Computacion. Santiago. Chile. RP-PUC-DCC-94-1 (1994) 1-25
3. Clark. K.L.: Negation as failure. Logic and Databases. Plenum Press. New York (1978) 292-392
4. Gelfond. M. and Lifschitz. V.: Describing action and change by logic programs. Joint International Conference and Symposium on Logic Programming (1992)
5. Haas. A.: The case for domain-specific frame axioms. Workshop: The frame problem in artificial intelligence. (1987) 343-348
6. Kartha. G.N.: Soundness and completeness theorems for three formalizations of action. IJCAI-93. Chambery. France (1993) 724-729
7. Lin. F., Reiter. R.: State constraints revisited. Journal of Logic and Computation. Special issue on actions and processes 4 (1994) 655-678
8. McCarthy. J., Hayes. P.: Some philosophical problems from the standpoint of artificial intelligence. Machine Intelligence 4 (1969) 463-502
9. Pednault. E.: ADL: Exploring the middle ground between STRIPS and the situation calculus. KR-89. (1989) 324-332
10. Reiter. R.: Formalizing database evolution in the situation calculus. Fifth Generation Computer Systems. Tokyo. Japan (1992)
11. Reiter. R.: Equality and domain closure in first-order databases. JACM 27 (1980) 235-249
12. Reiter. R.: Towards a logical reconstruction of relational databases theory. On Conceptual Modelling: Perspectives from Artificial Intelligence. Databases and Programming Languages. Springer-Verlag (1984) 191-233
13. Reiter. R.: A sound and sometimes complete query evaluation algorithm for relational databases with null values. JACM 2 (1986) 349-370
14. Reiter. R.: The frame problem in the situation calculus: a simple solution (sometimes) and a completeness result for goal regression. AI and Math. Theory of Computation: Papers in Honor of John McCarthy. Academic Press. (1991) 359-380
15. Reiter. R.: On specifying database updates. Tech. Rept. University of Toronto. Dept. of Computer Science. Toronto. Canada. KRR-TR-92-3 (1992)
16. Sandewall. E.: Features and Fluents. The Representation of Knowledge about Dynamical Systems 1. Oxford University Press (1994)
17. Schubert. L.: Monotonic solution of the frame problem in the situation calculus: an efficient method for worlds with fully specified actions. Knowledge Representation and Defeasible Reasoning. Kluwer Academic Press. (1990) 23-67

Modeling Intentions with Extended Logic Programming

Michael da Costa Móra[1]* and José Gabriel Lopes[2]** and Helder Coelho[3]

[1] CRIA UNINOVA/Portugal - CPGCC UFRGS/Brazil
2825 Monte da Caparica, Portugal
mdm@fct.unl.pt
[2] CRIA UNINOVA/Portugal
2825 Monte da Caparica, Portugal
gpl@fct.unl.pt
[3] INESC/Portugal
R. Alves Redol, 7, 1000 - Lisbon
hcoelho@eniac.inesc.pt

Abstract. As far as we are concerned, the existing theories of intentions adopt a designer's perspective, i.e., intentions and related mental states are approached from a designer's point-of-view. Such theories are logic-based and enable one to reason about the agents. However, they are not adequate to be used by the agent, to reason about itself. We argue that adopting an agent perspective may simplify some aspects of such theories, and enable the definition of a logic that agents may use to reason. Also, this change of perspective raises some questions that are, in general, ignored by traditional theories, namely the relations among other attitudes and intentions and between intentions and actions. We present preliminary definitions of a theory of intentions that adopt this different perspective. We also discuss some of the traditionally ignored questions, unveiling potential extensions to the definitions presented here.

Keywords: theories of intentions; mental states modeling; event calculus; distributed artificial intelligence.

1 Introduction

Intentions, among all the mental states that characterize an intelligent agent, are considered fundamental building blocks, as they cannot be reduced to other more basic mental states. Since agents are resource bounded, it is not possible for them to continuously weigh their competing motives and beliefs. Intentions play their role as a compromise with a specific possible future which, once chosen, is abandoned only in certain circumstances, thus avoiding such continuous weighing of other attitudes. According to Bratman [2], intentions play three functional roles in a rational agent: (1) intentions pose problems for the agent, who needs to determine ways to overcome them;

---

* Supported by CNPq/Brazil, contract number 200636/93-6(NV).
** Work supported by project IDILIO, contract number STRDA-C-TIT-139/92, funded by JNICT.

(2) intentions constitute a *screen of admissibility* for adopting other intentions, i.e., an agent cannot adopt an intention which conflicts with previously adopted ones; and (3) the agent must track the success of its intentions and persist on its execution, in case of failure. Following Bratman's analysis, many formal theories of rational agency[4] have appeared [4] [11] [7] [14]. Such theories are meant to be formal specifications of a rational agent in terms of its mental states and the relations among them. However, none of these theories are suitable to be used by the agent as a formal basis for it to reason. According to our view, while allowing agent designers to reason about properties of agents, such theories of intentions ought to be expressed in a logic the agent may use to reason, in order to decrease the gap between specifications and real agents. In this paper, we make the preliminary definitions of a theory of intentions that adopts an *agent perspective*, instead of a designer's one. As the underlying logic, we use Logic Programming extended with explicit negation (or ELP – Extended Logic Programming) with its semantics being given by the paraconsistent version of the Well-Founded Semantics augmented with Explicit Negation (WFSX) [1].

Intentions are temporal attitudes, as they guide future planning activities and track present actions. Therefore, we need some formalism to deal with time. Most of the existing theories use a variation of dynamic logic [Eme 80], defined in their modal logic environment by the standard modal operators. However, in order to allow the previously mentioned change of perspective, we need a formalism with which the agent may reason, as discussed before. So, on top of the logical basis provided by ELP, we define a variation of the Event Calculus (EC) [8], inspired on previous extensions by Messiaen [9] and Shanaham [12]. The ELP, together with the EC, constitute the logical framework which will be used for building our theory of intentions.

This paper is organized as follows: in section 2, we present ELP and its paraconsistent WFSX semantics; in section 3, we define the EC and justify our choice; in section 4, we present the preliminary definitions of our theory of intentions; finally, in sections 5 and 6, we discuss some related questions and draw some conclusions.

2 Extended Logic Programs

An extended logic program is a set of rules of the form $L \leftarrow L_1, \ldots, L_n,$ *not* $L_{n+1}, \ldots,$ *not* L_m $(0 \leq n \leq m)$ where L and L_i are objective literals. An objective literal is either an atom A or its explicit negation $\neg A$. *not* L is a default literal, where *not* stands for negation as failure. Literals are either objective or default literals. By *not* $\{a_1, \ldots, a_n, \ldots\}$ we mean $\{not\ a_1, \ldots, not\ a_n, \ldots\}$. $\mathcal{H}(\mathcal{P})$ denotes the set of all ground objective literals of a program P and is called extended Herbrand base of P. We present here the definition of the paraconsistent version of WFSX, that allows for contradictory programs.

Definition 1 (Interpretation). An interpretation I of an extended logic program P is any set $T \cup not\ F$, where T and F are subsets of $\mathcal{H}(\mathcal{P})$ which verify

---

[4] Also, many non-formal models of intentions, related some way to Bratman's ideas, have appeared. See, for instance, [5] [15].

the coherence principle: if $\neg L \in T$ then $L \in F$. Set T contains all *true* ground objective literals in I, set F contains all *false* ground objective literals in I. The truth value of the remaining objective literals is *undefined* (the truth value of a default literal *not L* is the 3-valued complement of L).

Through some program transformations, which produce (possibly more than one) non-negative programs, it is possible to get all the consequences of the original program, even those leading to contradictions, as well as those arising from contradictions. It can be shown that the operator that is used to obtain such a set of consequences (name Φ_P) is monotonic under set inclusion of interpretations, for any program P[5]. Hence, it has a least fixpoint, which can be obtained by iterating Φ_P starting from the empty set.

Definition 2 (Paraconsistent WFSX). The paraconsistent WFSX of an extended logic program P, denoted by $WFSX(P)$, is the least fixpoint of Φ applied to P. If some literal L belongs to the paraconsistent WFSX of P we write $P \models_p L$. A program P is said to be *contradictory* iff, for some positive literal L, both $P \models_p L$ and $P \models_p \neg L$ hold. P is said to be consistent iff it is not contradictory.

ELP with the WFSX semantics presents some characteristics that are very useful when we are to model intentions and related mental states, namely its ability to deal with contradictory programs and to allow the detection of such contradiction, through the notion of contradictory program. Also, this concept is based on the definition of $\models_p$, which is computable and may be used not only by the designer, when (s)he is proving properties, but also by the agent, when it is reasoning.

3 The Event Calculus

In order to represent and reason about action and time, we use the Event Calculus. Initially proposed by Kowalski and Sergot [8] to overcome some drawbacks of the Situation Calculus, this formalism has inspired many variations. Here, We present a definition of the Event Calculus derived from the ones proposed by [9] and [12]. Although we do not make extensive use of the EC in this paper, it is necessary when we deal with topics related to action planning (see section 5). It is presented here because our purpose is to settle the logical framework used to develop our theory of intentions.

As in [8], the ontological primitives are *events*, which initiate and terminate periods during which *properties* hold. We use the ELP language to define them. Later on, we will extend this basic ontology to deal with concurrent actions. The core clauses of our EC are:

$$holds\_at(Prop, T) \leftarrow initially(Prop), persists(0, Prop, T). \tag{1}$$

[5] Due to lack of space, the formal definitions of such operators are not presented here. For details, refer to [1].

$$holds\_at(Prop, T) \leftarrow happens(Evt, Act, TEvt), initiates(Evt, Prop),$$
$$TEvt < T, persists(TEvt, Prop, T).$$

$$persists(TEvt, Prop, T) \leftarrow not\ clipped(TEvt, Prop, T). \tag{2}$$

$$clipped(TEvt, Prop, T) \leftarrow happens(IntEvt, Act, TIntEvt), \tag{3}$$
$$terminates(IntEvt, Prop), not\ out(TIntEvt, TEvt, T).$$

$$out(TIntEvt, TEvt, T) \leftarrow (T \leq TIntEvt); (TIntEvt < TEvt). \tag{4}$$

The predicate $holds\_at(P, T)$ represents that property P holds at time T. The predicate $happens(E, A, T)$ represents that an uniquely identified event E has occured or will occur, at time T. This event denotes a specific instance of action A. By now, time points are to be interpreted as natural numbers, being 0 the initial time point. We assume the usual definition for the relations $\neq$, $<$ and $\leq$. Predicates $initiates(E, P)$ and $terminates(E, P)$ indicate, respectively, that an event E initiates or terminates the interval during which property P holds. Predicate $persists(TE, P, T)$ represents that a property P holds in an interval between TE and T if that interval is not interrupted (i.e., clipped) by an event which terminates the holding property. Predicate $initially(P)$ states that property P holds from "the beginning of times" (there is no event that initiates it). Predicates $initiates/2$ and $terminates/2$ capture a problem domain. Predicate $happens/3$ will describe courses of events, meaning that action A is performed when event E occurs.

3.1 Extending the EC to Deal with Concurrent Actions

We need concurrent actions because we are setting the logical foundations for a theory of intentions, and at some moment it will be necessary to model an agent that interacts with some other agent. So there may be situations where their joint action will be required. In this formulation of the EC it is easy to represent concurrent occurrences of actions, as suggested in [12]: it is enough to state that they happen at the same time point, such as $\{happens(e1, A1, x)., happens(e2, A2, x).\}$. Problems arise when the concurrent execution of such actions produce results different from those expected if the actions were performed independently. In order to overcome this problem, we need to modify the EC formulation in two aspects: (1) it is necessary to state the properties that the concurrent execution of two or more actions initiates/terminates, and how to represent such a concurrent occurrence, as well; (2) we need some way to express that an event can cancel the effects of another one occurring at the same time. For instance, consider the supermarket trolley problem [12]. If one *pushes* a supermarket trolley, the effect of such an action is to move the trolley forward; if one *pulls* such a trolley, the effect is to move it backward. But, if one *pushes* and *pulls* it at the same time, the trolley will spin around, or stay still. Thus, in this kind of situation, we should be able to state that the concurrent occurrence of *push* and *pull* on the same object produces a different effect, and does not necessarily initiate/terminate their usual properties.

In order to solve problem (1), we introduce a new term $conc/2$, which relates 2 types of events that, together, form a new one, along with a new axiom for the predicate $happens$, which we will call, from now on, $occurs$, to avoid some looping problems[6]. The *compound event* $conc(E1, E2)$ happens whenever $E1$ and $E2$ happen concurrently.

$$occurs(conc(Evt1, Evt2), TConc) \leftarrow happens(Evt1, A1, TConc), \tag{5}$$

---

[6] The predicate $occurs/2$ will be true if a simple event or a compound event happens.

$$happens(Evt2, A2, TConc), Evt1 \neq Evt2.$$
$$occurs(Evt, TEvt) \leftarrow happens(Evt, A, TEvt).$$

It is also necessary to represent, through *initiates/2* and *terminates/2*, the properties that are affected by compound events. To overcome problem (2), we introduce a new predicate *cancels/2*. A formula *cancels(Act1, Act2)* states that if an action of type *Act1* occurs, it cancels the effects of an action of type *Act2* occurring at the same time. It is also necessary to modify some of the EC axioms, namely axiom 3.

$$clipped(TE, P, T) \leftarrow occurs(C, TC), terminates(C, P), \qquad (6)$$
$$not\ cancelled(C, TC), not\ out(TC, TE, T).$$
$$cancelled(Evt, T) \leftarrow happens(Evt2, Act2, T), \qquad (7)$$
$$happens(Evt, Act, T), cancels(Act2, Act).$$

Note that, if we do not introduce the *cancels* predicate and the above modifications, we may get incorrect conclusions, since the effects brought about by the events that form the compound event would still be caused.

Example 1. Consider the following representation of the trolley car problem [12]

$$initiates(conc(E1, E2), spinning) \leftarrow happens(E1, push, \_), happens(E2, pull, \_).$$
$$terminates(conc(E1, E2), forward) \leftarrow happens(E1, push, \_), happens(E2, pull, \_).$$
$$terminates(conc(E1, E2), backward) \leftarrow happens(E1, push, \_), happens(E2, pull, \_).$$
$$initiates(E, forward) \leftarrow happens(E, push, T).$$
$$terminates(E, backward) \leftarrow happens(E, push, T).$$
$$terminates(E, spinning) \leftarrow happens(E, push, T).$$
$$initiates(E, backward) \leftarrow happens(E, pull, T).$$
$$terminates(E, forward) \leftarrow happens(E, pull, T).$$
$$terminates(E, spinning) \leftarrow happens(E, pull, T).$$

and the following possible course of events

$$happens(e1, push, 2). \quad happens(e2, pull, 5).$$
$$happens(e3, pull, 15). \quad happens(e4, push, 15).$$

No predicate *holds_at(P, T)*, when $T = 20$, belong to the model. Informally, this happens because the effects of *push* and *pull* are still individually considered, and since *clipped/2* tests for events that terminate properties, each one is terminated by the other. If we add

$$cancels(push, pull). \quad cancels(pull, push).$$

then we will have $\{holds\_at(spinning, 20)\}$, as desired, since the effects of *pull* and *push* are not individually accounted. After these modifications, the final EC axioms are the basic ones, (1) – (4) extended with axioms (5) – (7)[7].

---

[7] It would also be necessary to introduce a standard event *start*, which happens at the initial time 0; and the definition of $\neg hold\_at(P, T)$. Notice that we are not (yet) benefiting from the ELP to define the EC. Its properties are used only when the mental states are defined.

4 Towards a Theory of Intentions

A theory of intentions is meant to formalize the properties of intentions and its relation to other mental states. Following Bratman's analysis [2] of what intentions and their roles are, we may point some of the desired properties of intentions. Intentions must be mutually consistent, i.e., an agent is not supposed to adopt intentions that preclude each other. Exactly what to do when an agent is faced with a new intention that is contradictory with a previously existing one is yet to be decided. Cohen and Levesque [4] suggest that the newly arriving intention should be discarded if it introduces a contradiction, although they do characterize such a behavior as fanatical[8]. Intentions are believed to be satisfiable or, at least, they are not believed to be impossible. It is not rational that an agent intends something it believes to be impossible, since it must try to overcome the problems posed by its own intentions. It is, indeed, rational to intend something that we do not know if it is possible or not. Agents do not need to intend all the consequences of their intentions, even those that they are able to foresee – the so-called *side-effect* problem[9][11]. For example, an agent who owns an out-of-order car will formulate (suppose) an intention to repair it, and will decide to take the car to a mechanic. As a consequence, it will have to spend some money to pay the service. Although spending money is a consequence of his intention to repair the car, he probably does not intend to spend money. Suppose that, when it arrives at the garage, it is told that they are not able to fix the car. Since the agent's intention is not satisfied, it would take the it to another garage (remember that an agent must track the success of the accomplishment of his intentions, and persist acting in order to achieve them). But now, suppose that our agent is told that, since he is the $1,000,000^{th}$ client, the repair will be for free. Although spending money was a foreseen consequence of his intentions, it was not an intention by itself. So, the agent may (and certainly will) accept the free repair. In summary, the side-effect (spending money for repairing the car) was not intended, although it was *intentionally chosen*[10]. An agent must commit to its intentions, i.e., an agent who has an intention must persist in trying to achieve it through out changing circumstances. This is a delicate question: the notion of commitment is at the core of the idea of intentions, and it is certainly necessary, since agents are resource bounded and cannot continuously weigh their competing motives and beliefs[10]. Also, it is very useful to allow agents to infer other agent's intentions, to coordinate their actions more easily. However, the degree of such commitment varies according to many factors, namely changes in beliefs, changes in motives, action's priorities and so. For instance, an agent cannot persist forever on an intention, since this intention could no longer be compatible with its motives and beliefs, what would lead to quite irrational behaviors. As we will see further, in section 5, commitment may be achieved through adequate policies with respect to adoption and abandonment of intentions.

Some work has been devoted to theories of intentions (or theories of rational agency). Cohen and Levesque [4] were the first ones to develop a formal theory of intentions, based on Bratman's analysis. Although it has been used as a starting point

---

[8] Later, in the same work [4], they consider relativizing intentions to its cause, an arbitrary condition. But, it has been argued that this approach contradicts Bratman's analysis [13].

[9] Side-effects are the non-intended consequences of one's intentions.

[10] As Bratman states, intentions are a subset of the agent's choices. See [2] for a more detailed discussion.

for a very fruitful work ([6][3], among others), it does not meet some of the desired properties we have presented, namely it suffers from the side-effect problem. Also, its notion of commitment is deeply connected to the semantics of intentions, preventing its adequate treatment [13]. Konolige and Pollack [7] solve some of these problems presenting a formalism also based in modal logics but with a different semantics (not based in the accessibility relation among possible worlds). However, as the authors state, it is limited to static aspects of intentions, not encompassing questions such as adoption and abandonment of intentions. In common, those theories share a *designer's perspective*[11], i.e., they are conceived to be used by agent designers to prove properties about them. We argue that adopting an *agent's perspective*, where the theory is to be used by the agent when reasoning about the world (i.e, the agent builds the world model while reasoning) is more adequate: it simplifies some traditional problems, namely the side-effect problem, and induces us to deal with some questions that are, in general, ignored by traditional theories. We present here the preliminary definitions of such a theory, up to the point where these "ignored question" emerge[12].

Definition 3 (Agent Structure). An agent structure is a tuple $< B, I, A, T >$ such that (i) B is a set of extended logic programming sentences[13] – it is the set of agent's beliefs; (ii) I is a not deductively closed set of extended logic programming sentences – it is the set of agent's intentions; (iii) A is a set of *initiates*/2 and *terminates*/2 clauses – it is the description of the actions the agent is capable of performing; (iv) T is the set of EC axioms -- the time axioms.

This agent structure is the core definition of an agent, in our theory. It is not an architecture, in the sense of [5], since it defines only some of the agent's mental states and the relation among them, and not the whole agent. But, unlike most of the existing theoretical approaches, this theory supplies, additionally to those specifications, a logical framework that enables the agent to reason and behave. By the above definition, an agent G, with an agent structure $G_E = < B, I, A, T >$ *believes* in a sentence b iff $b \in B$ and *intends* a sentence i iff $i \in I$. The side-effect problem is avoided, since the only intentions an agent has are those belonging to I (remember that it is not closed under deduction). Its logical consequences, both with respect to other intentions and with respect to its beliefs, are excluded.

According to the language definition presented so far (ELP + EC), an intention will be one of the three different kinds of sentences: (i) *happens(Evt, Act, Time)* which states that an agent intends an action *Act* to be performed at time *Time*; (ii) *holds_at(Prop, Time)* which states that an agent intends to be in a world state where property *Prop* holds, at time *Time*; (iii) *time independent sentences* properties, that are meant to be maintained, as long as they are valid intentions. These are called *maintenance intentions* [4]. New intentions cannot contradict them and modifications in the agent's beliefs, stating that such property does not hold anymore, should make the agent act on that intention[14].

Example 2. Suppose the car repair problem described in section 4. The agents beliefs, action description and intentions would be, respectively $B = \{holds\_at(bad\_$

---

[11] This term, as long as the term *agent's perspective*, is borrowed from [14].

[12] We shall discuss them in section 5.

[13] Whether this set is closed under deduction or not depends on the approach we use to deal with beliefs. In general, it is not necessarily closed under deduction.

[14] This kind of intention is out of our scope, in this work.

$car, t1)\}$, $\mathcal{A} = \{initiates(spend\_money, E) \leftarrow act(E, take\_car\_mec)\}$, $\mathcal{I} = \{holds\_at(car\_is\_repaired, t2), happens(e1, take\_car\_mec, t3)\}$.

According to the definitions, logical consequences of the intentions are not intentions by themselves. So, although we are able to derive $holds\_at(spend\_money, t4)$, in any $t4 > t3$, from $\mathcal{B} \cup \mathcal{I} \cup \mathcal{A} \cup \mathcal{T}$, it does not belong to $\mathcal{I}$, so it is not an intention, and the agent does not need (in fact, he will not) to persist on it.

The definition of agent structure is still too generic, and does not assure that intentions will have the desired properties, as stated in section 4. Some restrictions must apply. Thus, we extended our definition to *rational agent structure*.

Definition 4 (Rational Agent Structure). Let *now* be a function of type $now :\rightarrow \mathcal{N}$ that returns the current time point. A rational agent structure is a tuple $< \mathcal{B}, \mathcal{I}, \mathcal{A}, \mathcal{T} >$ such that (i) $\mathcal{B}$ is a set of extended logic programming; (ii) $\mathcal{I}$ is a not deductively closed set of extended logic programming sentences, such that

1. its elements are not mutually contradictory, nor contradictory with the agent's beliefs, i.e., $\not\exists i \in \mathcal{I} . [(\mathcal{B} \cup \mathcal{I} \cup \mathcal{A} \cup \mathcal{T} \models_p i) \land (\mathcal{B} \cup \mathcal{I} \cup \mathcal{A} \cup \mathcal{T} \models_p \neg i)]$
2. $\forall(holds\_at(P, T)) \in \mathcal{I} . (now < T)$; and
3. $\forall(happens(E, P, T)) \in \mathcal{I} . (now < T)$;

$\mathcal{A}$ is a set of $initiates/2$ and $terminates/2$ clauses; $\mathcal{T}$ is the set of EC axioms.

Notice that, in constraint number 1, in the above definition, it is not enough to state just $\not\exists i \in \mathcal{I} . (\mathcal{B} \cup \mathcal{I} \cup \mathcal{A} \cup \mathcal{T} \models_p \perp)$, because we would be considering logical consequences of intentions as reasons to invalidate them. Also, constraint number 1 guarantees the satisfaction of the last basic requirement of intentions with respect to beliefs, namely that they are not believed to be impossible (if we include in $\mathcal{I}$ some sentence i which is believed to be impossible, i.e., $\neg i \in \mathcal{B}$, a contradiction would raise, offending restriction number 1).

The different perspective adopted — an agent-based one, instead of a designer-based one — may be noticed in many aspects, namely the definitions presented so far take into account not what is possible to derive with this framework - as it would be in a design tool - but what the agent in fact generates, while reasoning. Also, the definitions and restrictions are based on the notion of $\models_p$, which is clearly computable[15] and may be used by the agent while reasoning.

5 Further Work

As stated in section 4, this change of perspective also introduces some problems that are usually ignored in traditional theories. Mainly, these problems are connected with the dynamic aspects of intentions: how do they appear? how do they vanish? Remember that intentions guide the agents behavior. Consequently, it is not enough to define intentions and relating mental states just as sets of logical sentences with some constraints, because we are only able to determine valid states of the mental attitudes. Those dynamic aspects are ignored[16].

We may classify such aspects in two types: *motive-to-intentions process* and *intention-to-action process*. Motive-to-intention process relates to the origin of intentions. During

---
[15] See [1] for more details.
[16] And, in fact, the same happens with the existing theories that adopt a designer's perspective.

decision making, agents adopt intentions that will guide their behavior. Such intentions are restricted by its beliefs and are formed from other pro-attitudes, such as obligations, necessities, desires and so. Most of the existing theories do not focus this aspect[17]. Intention-to-action process relates to the production of actions. When the time comes, the agent has to transform his intentions into actions in order to fulfill those intentions. This has long been studied in the planning field, but no connection has been established with theories of agency[18]. These questions will influence two major aspects of intentions, namely intention revision (adopting and abandoning intentions) and commitment.

Suppose that an agent tries to adopt a new intention that is contradictory with existing ones. Must he ignore the newly arriving intention in favor of the older one? This would be quite reasonable, since intentions are aimed to avoid the continuous balancing of other mental states, and the agent had already committed to the older intentions. But, in some situations, this might not be the case. For example, suppose (also) that the agent in question is a robot performing some task and that he starts to run out of energy. Presumably, he should form a new intention, namely to stop and get recharged. However, according to the above description, such an intention would be ignored, since it would conflict with the existing one. In order to decide whether to continue the ongoing task or to recharge, it would be necessary to establish revision criteria that take into account the origin of intentions. We could define, for example, that intentions that come from obligations are stronger than the ones originating from desires; and that the ones coming from necessities are even stronger. In fact, it is necessary to define the other pro-attitudes that must be part of the rational agent structure, and how they must relate to intentions, introducing concepts like priorities among motives. Also changes in these pro-attitudes may cause the abandonment of intentions. If an intention i is adopted because of an obligation o (suppose, for instance, an order given by someone) and, afterwards, such obligation is retracted (for instance, the order is canceled), the agent should also abandon the respective intention. This notion of motives of intentions is also interesting to correctly define the notion of commitment. An agent must commit to an intention as long as (as in section 4) he does not believe it to be impossible, or to have not yet been achieved, and (differently from the existing theories) as long as the motives to that intention are still valid. Also, the tracking of the success of actions performed to achieve intentions may be used to decide whether to continue trying to achieve them or not.

6 Conclusion

In this paper, we sketched the basic definitions of a theory of intentions that adopt an agents' perspective, instead of a designers' one. We have presented the logical basis, namely ELP with a paraconsistent version of WFSX and a variation of the Event Calculus, on which we based the preliminary definitions of such a theory of intentions. Preliminary definitions, because we have only showed how to treat the static aspects of intentions, namely its semantics and its relation to beliefs. As discussed in section 5, a complete theory must encompass also those dynamic aspects of intentions. We will

---

[17] An exception would be [5], but it is an architecture definition, indeed.

[18] Exceptions would be [5] and [14], where intentions are connected to preconceived strategies for achieving them.

focus, in further work, on what we have called the *motive-to-intention process*, since it deeply affects the intention revision process. We are convinced that the change of perspective we have suggested here is more adequate for a theory of agency, since it provides tools for the agents, focus on aspects so far left apart and still provides tools with which we may reason about the agent. Also, we believe that this approach reduces the gap between agent specification and agent implementation.

References

1. J.J. Alferes. *Semantics of logic programs with explicit negation.* PhD thesis, Universidade Nova de Lisboa, Lisbon, Portugal, october 1993.
2. M.E. Bratman. What is intention? In P.R. Cohen, J.L. Morgan, and M. Pollack, editors, *Intentions in Communication*, chapter 1. The MIT Press, Cambridge, MA, 1990.
3. C. Castelfranchi. Social power. In Y. Demazeau and J.P. Muller, editors, *Descentralized AI - Proceedings of the First European Workshop on Modelling Autonomous Agents and Multi-Agents Worlds (MAAMAW'89)*, Amsterdam, The Netherlands, 1990. Elsevier Science Publishers.
4. P.R. Cohen and H.J. Levesque. Intention is choice with commitment. *Artificial Intelligence*, 42:213–261, 1990.
5. M. Corrêa and H. Coelho. Around the architectural approach to model conversations. In *Proceedings of the Fifth European Workshop on Modelling Autonomous Agents and Multi-Agents Worlds (MAAMAW'93)*, 1993.
6. N. Jennings. On being responsible. In E. Werner and Y. Demazeau, editors, *Descentralized AI 3 - Proceedings of the Third European Workshop on Modelling Autonomous Agents and Multi-Agents Worlds (MAAMAW'91)*, Amsterdam, The Netherlands, 1992. Elsevier Science Publishers.
7. K. Konolige and M. Pollack. A representationalist theory of intentions. In *Proceedings of the XII International Joint Conference on Artificial Intelligence (IJCAI'93)*, Chambéry, France, 1993. IJCAI inc.
8. R.A. Kowalski and M.J. Sergot. A logic-based calculus of events. *New Generation Computing*, 4:67–95, 1986.
9. L. Messiaen. *Localized abductive planning with the event calculus.* PhD thesis, Katholieke Universiteit Leuven, Leuven (Heverlee), 1992.
10. P. Quaresma and G.P. Lopes. Unified logical programming approach to the abduction of plans and intentions in information-seeking dialogues. *Journal of Logic Programming*, 24(1&2), 1995. Special Issue on Computational Linguistics and Logic Programming.
11. A.S. Rao and M.P. Georgeff. Modelling rational agents within a bdi-architecture. In R. Fikes and E. Sandewall, editors, *Proceedings of the Knowledge Representation and Reasoning'91 (KR&R'91)*, San Mateo, CA., 1991. Morgan Kauffman Publishers.
12. M. Shanaham. A circumscriptive calculus of events. *Artificial Intelligence*, 2, 1995. To appear.
13. M. Singh. A critical examination of the cohen-levesque theory of intentions. In *Proceedings of the Tenth European Conference of Artificial Intelligence (ECAI'92)*, Vienna, Austria, 1992. ECAI inc.
14. M. Singh. *Multiagent systems: a theoretical framework for intentions, know-how, and communications.* Springer-Verlag, Heidelberg, Germany, 1994. Lecture Notes in Artificial Intelligence (LNAI 799).
15. E. Werner. A unified view of information, intentions and ability. In Y. Demazeau and J.P. Muller, editors, *Descentralized AI 2 - Proceedings of the Second European Workshop on Modelling Autonomous Agents and Multi-Agents Worlds (MAAMAW'90)*, Amsterdam, The Netherlands, 1991. Elsevier Science Publishers.

Labelled Theorem Proving for Substructural Logics

Claudia M. G. M. Oliveira[1]

Departamento de Engenharia de Sistemas
Instituto Militar de Engenharia - RJ
e-mail: cmgo@ime.eb.br

Keywords: *Theorem Proving, Automated Reasoning, Substructural Logics*

Abstract. In this paper we will present an implementation of a theorem prover for substructural logics, as they are presented in the framework of Labelled Deductive Systems [3]. This implementation is an instance of a general theorem proving environment described in [4].

1 General Considerations

The starting point of this work is the abstract specification of an environment for theorem proving. Here we give a brief overview of this system, which is fully described in [4]. It is formed by two levels of representation. Firstly, the logical level is a database and a first order inference procedure. The second level is a program interpreter whereby programs interact with the logical level in order to introduce new information, query the database and implement changes in the inference procedure. We highlight the novelties of the architecture with the help of the following diagram.

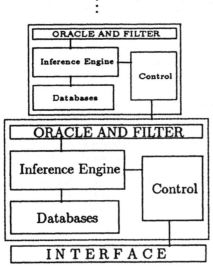

For our purpose here the **Control** is simply an interpreter of a Prolog-like language, with the main primitives: *prove* which activates the **Inference Engine** to perform a derivation; *assert* which introduces a new sentence into the databases. The **Database** system is a collection of databases defined as pairs $< s, \Gamma >$, where s is a label and Γ is a multiset of clauses. We refer to each clause $C \in \Gamma$ as $s : C$. The inference engine is such that, if used as a classical prover it is equivalent to resolution.

With the addition of mechanisms of **Filter** and **Oracle** it can become the implementation of a scope of non-classical logics. Basically, a **Filter** is a program in the language interpreted by the control which restricts the derivations, by evaluating the labels of the formulas in one resolution step and validating/invalidating the step according to some theory of labels. If a filter $f_3(s_1, s_2, s_3)$ is applied after a successful resolution step then s_1 is the label of the near parent clause, s_2 is the label of the far parent clause and s_3 is the resulting label. If f_3 succeeds then the resolvents label is s_3 and the derivation proceeds; otherwise the derivation backtracks. For example, consider the following database: $\{a_1 : \neg A \lor B, a_2 : A\}$, if we consider labels as multisets and a filter $f(s_1, s_2, s_1 - s_2)$, then the first resolvent of the derivation of $a_1 \cup a_2 : \neg B$ is $a_2 : \neg A$ since $f(a_1 \cup a_2, a_1, a_2)$. Likewise, an **Oracle** is a program which extends resolution such that an alternative direction will be given to the proof-search whenever an unsuccessful path is reached. An oracle will seek to solve the problem outside the current setting, it will use extra data. If an oracle $o_3(L, s_1, s_2)$ is applied after a failed resolution step then L is the literal which failed to be resolved and s_1 is the current resolvent's label and s_2 is the resulting label. If o_3 succeeds then the resolvent's label is s_3 and the derivation proceeds; otherwise the derivation backtracks. For example, consider the following database: $\{a_1 : \neg A \lor B\}$, and oracle o_3 then the first resolvent of the refutation of $a_1 \cup a_2 : \neg B$ is $a_2 : \neg A$ (with filter f) and since there is no way forward the oracle will compute in some other way the unresolved literal (question the user, for instance). A similar concept is used to improve theorem proving (see [5] and [1]) for certain classes of theories, which by an appropriate knowledge representation can have their search space drastically reduced.

We present the implementation of substructural logics in the above architecture. We we will limit our case studies to the propositional implicational fragments of substructural logics. By the implementation of a logic we mean the specification in our system of the following: 1) the normalization policy; 2) the database labelling policy; 3) the querying mechanism; 4) the filtering policy; 5) the oracle.

Our strategy for demonstrating the correctness of our implementation is as follows: we present a setting of our system whereby it represents a certain logic L; we present the semantics of its LDS counterpart; then we make the correspondence between derivability in our system and satisfyability and consequence in the LDS-semantical presentation.

2 Substructural Logics

The denomination *Resource Logic* has been applied to a number of logical systems where part of the deductive process is to keep track of and restrict the use of assumptions (data) and the order of the application of rules.

One particular subclass of resource logics are *Substructural Logics* [3]. These are logics in which the history of the proof must be carefully kept because the use of every item of data must be validated. The labels are used to *name* assumptions and propagation of the labels is done throughout the deductive process (*naming* the conclusions) according to a labelling discipline.

In order to analyse a group of such logical systems according to the properties of each of their respective consequence relations, a list of Hilbert type axioms schemas is laid out in the table below. Axioms 1, 2, 3 and 6 gives us Linear logic; 1, 2, 3, 5 and 6, BR1; 1, 2, 3, 4 and 6 Relevance Logic; 1, 2, 3, 4, 5 and 6, Intuitionistic Logic. We will give the above systems' LDS presentation an algorithmic formulation.

Axiom	Property
1.$A \rightarrow A$	identity
2.$(A \rightarrow B) \rightarrow ((B \rightarrow C) \rightarrow (A \rightarrow C))$	right transitivity
3.$(A \rightarrow B) \rightarrow ((C \rightarrow A) \rightarrow (C \rightarrow B))$	left transitivity
4.a.$(A \rightarrow B) \rightarrow ((A \rightarrow (B \rightarrow C)) \rightarrow (A \rightarrow C))$ b.$(A \rightarrow (B \rightarrow C)) \rightarrow ((A \rightarrow B) \rightarrow (A \rightarrow C))$	distribution
5.$(A \rightarrow (B \rightarrow A))$	weakening
6.$(A \rightarrow (B \rightarrow C)) \rightarrow (B \rightarrow (A \rightarrow C))$	permutation

2.1 Normal Form Translation

The normal form translation we propose was devised to transform implicational propositional sentences into clauses preserving the various possible substructural interpretations of the implication. Classical normal form translation rules are not all valid, in particular the ones that change the structure of the sentence, for instance in (1) $(A \wedge B) \vee C \equiv (A \vee C) \wedge (B \vee C)$ the left of the equivalence is basicly the same as (2) $(A \rightarrow B) \rightarrow C$. The idea is to maintain the structure of the formula using a special predicate SUB. Sentence (2) becomes $SUB(A, B) \vee C$. This predicate always occurs with the same sign if we take that $SUB(A, B)$ replaces $\neg(A \rightarrow B)$ in some contexts. Therefore it is never resolved during the resolution process: it must be evaluated as a sub-proof of the current proof, and the elimination of the literal SUB depends on the success of this sub-proof. For instance, for the clauses

$$0.1. \neg A \vee B \,, \, 0.2. \, SUB(A, B) \vee C \,, \, 0.3. \neg C$$

we have the following refutation

0.4. $SUB(A, B)$	res. 0.3. and 0.2.	1.3. $\neg A$	res. 1.2. and 0.1.
1.1. A	new assumption	1.4. $\square$	res. 1.3. and 1.1
1.2. $\neg B$	new goal	0.5. $\square$	sub − proof elimination

We propose a unified normalization policy for resource logics. The translation of an implicative sentence into a clause is done by the function τ.

Definition 1 *The propositional implicational wffs are defined as follows:*
1) if A is a proposition then A is an atomic wff (atom);
2) if F_1 and F_2 are wffs then so is $(F_1 \to F_2)$

Corolary 1 *Every wff F is either an atom or for some n there exists wffs $F_1, \cdots, F_n$ such that F is $(F_1 \to (F_2 \to (\cdots \to (F_{n-1} \to F_n)\cdots)))$ and F_n is atomic. Proof: Trivial, by induction on the structure of F.*

Definition 2 (translation function) *The function τ is defined from the set of implicative sentences to the set of clauses as follows:*

$$\tau(F) = \begin{cases} F & \text{if } F \text{ is a literal} \\ \neg F_1 & \text{if } F = N(F_1) \text{ and } F_1 \text{ is a literal} \\ \tau_O(F_1, F_2) & \text{if } F = (F_1 \to F_2) \\ \tau_A(F_1, F_2) & \text{if } F = N(F_1 \to F_2) \end{cases}$$

$$\tau_O(F_1, F_2) = \tau_S(F_1) \vee \tau(F_2)$$
$$\tau_A(F_1, F_2) = \tau(F_1) \wedge \tau(N(F_2))$$

$$\tau_S(F) = \begin{cases} \neg F \\ \quad \text{if } F \text{ is a literal} \\ SUB(\tau(F_1) \wedge \cdots \wedge \tau(F_{n-1}), F_n) \\ \quad \text{if } F = (F_1 \to (F_2 \to (\cdots \to (F_{n-1} \to F_n)\cdots))) \\ \quad \text{and } F_n \text{ is a literal} \end{cases}$$

where SUB is a new unique predicate symbol.

Function τ_O deals with disjunctions; τ_A deals with conjunctions; τ_S deals with nestings of implications and avoids distribution by using a new predicate symbol SUB (according to corolary 1). Negation is only applied to literals. The following properties of the language generated by function τ will be useful later on when we discuss the correctness of the implementation.

Corolary 2 *If F is an implicative sentence then $\tau(F)$ is a disjunction of literals. Proof: We proceed by induction on the structure of F.*

1. *if F is atomic then $\tau(F) = F$;*
2. *if $F = (F_1 \to F_2)$ then $\tau((F_1 \to F_2)) = \tau_O(F_1, F_2) = \tau_S(F_1) \vee \tau(F_2)$ and by the induction hypothesis $\tau(F_2)$ is a disjunction, then: (a) if F_1 is a literal then $\tau_S(F_1) \vee \tau(F_2) = \neg F_1 \vee \tau(F_2)$ is a disjunction; (b) if $F_1 = (F'_1 \to (F'_2 \to (\cdots \to (F'_{n-1} \to F'_n)\cdots)))$ then: $\tau_S(F_1) \vee \tau(F_2) = SUB(\tau(F'_1) \wedge \cdots \wedge \tau(F'_{n-1}), F'_n) \vee \tau(F_2)$ is a disjunction.*

The results below follow from corollary 2 and the definition of τ.

Corolary 3

1. *A SUB-literal is never generated as an atom by function τ.*
2. *If F is an implicative sentence then $\tau(N(F))$ is a conjunction of disjunctions.*
3. *If F is an implicative sentence then the last clause in the conjunction generated by $\tau(N(F))$ is a negated literal.*
4. *The first term of a SUB literal is a conjunction of disjunctions.*
5. *The second term of a SUB literal is an atom.*

Example 1 *Function τ applied to $(A \to B) \to C$ is computed as follows:*
$$\tau((A \to B) \to C) = \tau_O((A \to B), C) \qquad = \tau_S((A \to B)) \vee \tau(C)$$
$$= SUB(\tau(A), \tau(B)) \vee C = SUB(A, B) \vee C$$

We will use function τ before introducing data to the database. If on the other hand we want to query the system with Q we will input τ with $N(Q)$. Each instance of predicate $SUB(x, y)$ will be computed by the oracle procedure based on a program which assumes x (asserts it to the system) and tries to prove y.

2.2 Linear Logic

We assume the reader is familiar with the definition of the metabox discipline in an LDS. In sumary, a metabox is an environment of labelled formulas where:

1. the rule **Modus Ponens** can be applied; the metabox discipline will determine the conditions on the premisses and the propagation of labels;

2. the **Box Goal Rule** can be applied, whereby another metabox may be created (opened); the new metabox inherits the discipline of the original which includes conditions for importing assumptions from previous boxes, and exiting-from-box conditions.

The conditions on the Modus Ponens and Box Goal rules are changeable with the logical system being used.

Consider the LDS proof system for implicational Linear Logic in the following definition.

Definition 3 *The metabox discipline of Linear Logic of* $\rightarrow$ *is an LDS system with the following rules:*

1. *Labels are multisets of atomic labels;*

2. *Modus Ponens is applied to labelled formulas:* $\dfrac{\alpha : A, \ \beta : A \rightarrow B}{\alpha \cup \beta : B}$

3. *The Box Goal Rule is as follows: assume that in line k of box b we want to show $A \rightarrow B$. Open a box named "a" assume A with new atomic label $\{a\}$ (hence $\{a\} : A$ is the assumption). If $\beta : B$ is derived then the box is successful if $a \in \beta$. Exit the box with $\gamma : A \rightarrow B$ where $\gamma = \beta - \{a\}$.*

The above definition summarizes the basic meta-feature of linear implication which is that all items of data in a derivation must be used exactly once. The number of times all labelled assumptions are used will be registered in the label at any point of the deduction. The figure shows a Linear Logic LDS deduction of the logical theorem

$$(A \rightarrow B) \rightarrow ((B \rightarrow C) \rightarrow (A \rightarrow C))$$

which follows in the calculus from an empty set of axioms.

In order to obtain other substructural implications, in rule 1 of definition 3 labels can be sets of atomic labels. in which case the operator $\cup$ in rule 2 would be set union. In rule 3, the exit from box conditions can be relaxed or others imposed, and the operator $-$ would be set difference. The reader may refer to [3] and [2] for an extensive presentation of this class of logics. The main point is that all these conditions and label operations are recursive.

$$\boxed{\begin{array}{l} \{a_1\} : A \to B \\[4pt] \boxed{\begin{array}{l} \{a_2\} : B \to C \\[4pt] \boxed{\begin{array}{llll} \{a_3\} : A \\ \{a_1\} : A \to B & reit. \\ \{a_1, a_3\} : B & M.P. \\ \{a_2\} : B \to C & reit. \\ \{a_1, a_3, a_2\} : C & M.P. \end{array}} \\[4pt] \text{exit:}\{a_1, a_2\} : A \to C \end{array}} \\[4pt] \text{exit:}\{a_1\} : (B \to C) \to (A \to C) \end{array}}$$

$$exit : \emptyset : (A \to B) \to (B \to C) \to (A \to C)$$

2.3   Implementation

Although there is an implemention of the prover for substructural logics in a Prolog-like language we give it here a much shorter presentation. The reader will be satisfied that the programs we will describe are recursive and therefore any such language is capable of implementing them.

We will use a meta-language composed of the predicates $assert(l, \alpha)$ which stores a sentence α into database l; and $prove(\alpha, s_1, s_2)$ which derives the sentence α from the installed databases with initial label s_1 and final label s_2.

The database labelling: In order to introduce a sentence α into the database system, we have program $assert(l, \tau(\alpha))$ which generates a new atomic label l and adds $< l, \tau(\alpha) >$ to the database system.

Queries: In the case of a query F, $\tau(N(F))$ will, in general, produce more then one clause. So $prove((F_1 \to (\cdots \to (F_n \to A)\cdots)), l_0, l_f)$ produces $< l_1, \tau(F_1) >, \cdots, < l_n, \tau(F_n) >$ and $l_1 \cup \cdots \cup l_n : \neg A$ starts the derivation[1].

The inference rule: The inference rule is resolution with filter and oracle. For an application of a resolution step we write

$$\frac{l_1 : L_1 \vee C_1, \ l_2 : L_2 \vee C_2}{l_1 - l_2 : C_1 \vee C_2}$$

where L_1 is a literal, L_2 is $\neg L_1$, C_1 and C_2 are clauses. The filter is $f(l_1, l_2, l_1 - l_2)$ or in short $l_1 - l_2$, whatever the operation $-$ is set to be. **The oracle:** The normalization policy we have described is to be used in conjuntion with a special oracular program. When introducing predicate

---

[1] It is simple to conceive a program $\cup(l_1, l_2, l_1 \cup l_2)$ generating such label.

SUB in the translation function we intended that a SUB-literal should never be resolved but should be evaluated by the oracle. Therefore we have a program:

$op(SUB(A_1 \wedge \cdots \wedge A_n, A), l_0, l_f) : -$
  $assert(l_1, A_1) \& \cdots \& assert(l_n, A_n)$
  $\& prove(A, l_1 \cup \cdots \cup l_n \cup l_0, l_f).$

Example 2   *We run:* $assert(\{l_1\}, \tau((((A \rightarrow B) \rightarrow C) \rightarrow D) \rightarrow (E \rightarrow F)))$ *which creates* $< \{l_1\}, SUB(SUB(A, B) \vee C, D) \vee \neg E \vee F >$. *We query the system with* $\tau(N(E \rightarrow ((((A \rightarrow B) \rightarrow C) \rightarrow D) \rightarrow F))$ *which generates* $< \{l_2\}, E >, < \{l_3\}, SUB(\neg A \vee B, C) \vee D >$ *and starts a derivation with* $\{l_1\} \cup \{l_2\} \cup \{l_3\} : \neg F$ *with oracle* op_3 *and filter* f_3 *as above. The derivation process is computed as follows:*

level 1

1.1. $\{l_1\}$	$: SUB(SUB(A, B) \vee C, D) \neg E\, F$	input
1.2. $\{l_2\}$	$: E$	input
1.3. $\{l_3\}$	$: SUB(\neg A \vee B, C)\, D$	input
1.4. $\{l_1, l_2, l_3\}$	$: \neg F$	query
1.5. $\{l_2, l_3\}$	$:SUB(SUB(A, B) \vee C, D) \neg E$	(res. 1.4,1.1) + filter
1.6. $\{l_3\}$	$:SUB(SUB(A, B) \vee C, D)$	(res. 1.5,1.2) + filter
1.7. $\emptyset$	$:\square$	oracle for 1.6

level 2:

2.1. $\{l_4\}$	$: SUB(A, B)\, C$	input
2.2. $\{l_3, l_4\}$	$: \neg D$	query
2.3. $\{l_4\}$	$:SUB(\neg A \vee B, C)$	(res. 2.2,1.3) + filter
2.4. $\emptyset$	$:\square$	oracle for 2.3

level 3:

3.1. $\{l_5\}$	$: \neg A\, B$	input
3.2. $\{l_4, l_5\}$	$: \neg C$	query
3.3. $\{l_5\}$	$: SUB(A, B)$	(res. 3.2,2.1) + filter
3.4. $\emptyset$	$:\square$	oracle for 3.3

level 4:

4.1. $\{l_6\}$	$: A$	input
4.2. $\{l_5, l_6\}$	$: \neg B$	query
4.3. $\{l_6\}$	$: \neg A$	(res. 4.2,3.1) + filter
4.4. $\emptyset$	$:\square$	(res. 4.3,4.1) + filter

3 Semantical Aspects

In this section we will present the semantical interpretation for the implementation of substructural logics given previously. First we will present a model-theoretic semantics extracted from [3]. In that work the LDS presentation is proved to be sound and complete with respect to this semantics. Likewise we will demonstrate soundness and completeness thus establishing the equivalence of both presentations.

Definition 4 *1. If X is a non-empty set, h is an assignment giving a truth value $h(Y, q) \in \{0, 1\}$ to each atomic q in a propositional language and each Y built out of elements of X then a pair (X, h) is:*

*(a) a **LL** (linear) structure if we assume that Y is a multiset;*

*(b) a **BR1** (basic resource) structure if we assume that Y is a multiset and h is monotonic in Y, i.e. $Y_1 \subseteq Y_2 \Rightarrow h(Y_1, q) \leq h(Y_2, q)$.*

*(c) a **R** (relevance) structure if we assume that Y is a set;*

(d) an intuitionistic structure if we assume that Y is a set and h is monotonic in Y

2. In each of the above cases, the function h can be extended to a function h^* on implicational formulas by letting:

$$h^*(Y, A \rightarrow B) = 1 \; iff \; \forall Y'(h^*(Y', A) = 1 \Rightarrow (h^*(Y \cup Y', B) = 1)$$

The assignment function in the case of a database system like ours is defined with respect to the data stored as in the next definition.

Definition 5 *Let Γ be a set of databases $< l_i, \{\tau(\alpha_i)\} >$. Then we define $h(\{l_1, \cdots, l_n\}, A) = 1$ iff*

$$\frac{\{l_1\} : \tau(\alpha_1), \cdots, \{l_n\} : \tau(\alpha_n), \{l_1, \cdots, l_n\} : \tau(\neg A)}{\emptyset : \square}$$

In order to prove soundness and completeness of our implementation we will need the following lemma regarding the language generated by function τ and the assertion programs.

Lemma 1 *If F is an implicational formula then* $\dfrac{l_1 : \tau_S(F), l_2 : \tau(F) \vee C}{l_1 - l_2 : C}$

Proof: We proceed by induction.

1. *F is an atom, then from the definition of τ, $\tau_S(F) = \neg F$ and $\tau(F) = F$, hence* $\dfrac{l_1 : \neg F, l_2 : F \vee C}{l_1 - l_2 : C}$

2. *F is $(F_1 \rightarrow F_2)$; by corollary 1 F_2 is $(F_1^2 \rightarrow (\cdots \rightarrow (F_n^2 \rightarrow A) \cdots))$ where A is an atom, for some $n \geq 0$. Then $l_2 : \tau(F_1 \rightarrow F_2) \vee C$ is translated as: (i) $l_2 : \tau_S(F_1) \vee \tau_S(F_1^2) \vee \cdots \vee \tau_S(F_n^2) \vee A \vee C$ and $l_1 : \tau_S(F_1 \rightarrow F_2)$ is translated as $SUB(\tau(F_1) \wedge \tau(F_1^2) \wedge \cdots \wedge \tau(F_n^2), A)$. By the execution of:*

$op(SUB(\tau(F_1) \wedge \tau(F_1^2) \wedge \cdots \wedge \tau(F_n^2), A), l_1, l_f) : -$
  $assert(l_1^1, \tau(F_1)) \& assert(l_1^2, \tau(F_1^2)) \& \cdots \& assert(l_1^{n+1}, \tau(F_n^2))$
  $\& prove(A, \; l^1{}_1 \cup \cdots \cup l^{n+1}{}_1 \cup l_1, l_f).$

and the derivation starting with (ii) $l^1{}_1 \cup \cdots \cup l^{n+1}{}_1 \cup l_1 : \neg A$ has the first resolution step (between (i) and (ii)) results in

$$(l^1{}_1 \cup \cdots \cup l^{n+1}{}_1 \cup l_1) - l_2 : \tau_S(F_1) \vee \tau_S(F^2{}_1) \vee \cdots \vee \tau_S(F^2{}_n) \vee C$$

By the induction hypothesis

$$l^1{}_1 : \tau(F_1)$$
$$\dfrac{(l^1{}_1 \cup \cdots \cup l^{n+1}{}_1 \cup l_1) - l_2 : \tau_S(F_1) \vee \tau_S(F^2{}_1) \vee \cdots \vee \tau_S(F^2{}_n) \vee C}{(l^2{}_1 \cup \cdots \cup l^{n+1}{}_1 \cup l_1) - l_2 : \tau_S(F^2{}_1) \vee \cdots \vee \tau_S(F^2{}_n) \vee C}$$

$\vdots$

$$l^{n+1}{}_1 : \tau(F^2{}_n)$$
$$\dfrac{(l^{n+1}{}_1 \cup l_1) - l_2 : \tau_S(F^2{}_n) \vee C}{l_1 - l_2 : C}$$

Corolary 4 *If F is an implicational formula then*

$$\dfrac{l_1 : \tau(N(F)), l_2 : \tau(F) \vee C}{l_1 - l_2 : C}$$

To further simplify the notation of the derivability relation we introduce the following definition.

Definition 6 *If $\alpha_1, \cdots \alpha_n$ and β are implication formulas then we define:*

$$l_1 : \alpha_1, \cdots, l_n : \alpha_n \vdash_{res} l : \beta \; iff \; \dfrac{l_1 : \tau(\alpha_1), \cdots, l_n : \tau(\alpha_n), l : \tau(N(\beta))}{l - l_1 - \cdots - l_n : \square}$$

Lemma 2 (Cut) *If $F_1, \cdots, F_n$, $E_1, \cdots, E_n$, α and β are implicational formulas then if:*

$l_1 : F_1, \cdots, l_n : F_n \vdash_{res} \{l_1, \cdots, l_n\} : \alpha$, *and*

$k_1 : E_1, \cdots, k_n : E_m \vdash_{res} \{k_1, \cdots, k_m\} : (\alpha \to \beta)$ *then*

$l_1 : F_1, \cdots, l_n : F_n, k_1 : E_1, \cdots, k_n : E_m \vdash_{res} \{l_1, \cdots, l_n, k_1, \cdots, k_m\} : \beta$

Proof: It follows from definitions 4 and 6 and corollary 4.

Theorem 1 (Completeness) *Let Γ be $< l_i, \{\tau(\alpha_i)\} >$, $1 \leq i \leq n$ then $h(\{l_1, \cdots, l_n\}, \alpha) = 1$ iff $l_1 : \alpha_1, \cdots, l_n : \alpha_n \vdash_{res} \{l_1, \cdots, l_n\} : \alpha$. Proof: We proceed by induction in both directions.*

1. If α is atomic then it follows directly from the definition 5 of h ;

2. In order to prove that

$$h(\{l_1, \cdots, l_n\}, \alpha) = 1 \ implies \ l_1 : \alpha_1, \cdots, l_n : \alpha_n \vdash_{res} \{l_1, \cdots, l_n\} : \alpha$$

we suppose that α is $(F_1 \to F_2)$ then $h(\{l_1, \cdots, l_n\}, (F_1 \to F_2)) = 1$ iff by definition $\forall K(h(K, F_1) = 1 \Rightarrow h(\{l_1, \cdots, l_n\} \cup K, F_2) = 1)$ and by the induction hypothesis we have that, for $< K, \tau(F_1) >$, in particular,

$$\frac{l_1 : \tau(\alpha_1), \cdots, l_n : \tau(\alpha_n), K : \tau(F_1), \{l_1, \cdots, l_n\} \cup K : \tau(N(F_2))}{\emptyset : \square} \ which \ is$$

generated when $\dfrac{l_1 : \tau(\alpha_1), \cdots, l_n : \tau(\alpha_n), \{l_1, \cdots, l_n\} : \tau(N(F_1 \to F_2))}{\emptyset : \square}$.

Thus by definition $l_1 : \alpha_1, \cdots, l_n : \alpha_n \vdash_{res} \{l_1, \cdots, l_n\} : (F_1 \to F_2)$.

3. In order to prove that

$$l_1 : \alpha_1, \cdots, l_n : \alpha_n \vdash_{res} \{l_1, \cdots, l_n\} : \alpha \ implies \ h(\{l_1, \cdots, l_n\}, \alpha) = 1$$

we suppose that α is $(F_1 \to F_2)$, we assume that

(1) $\dfrac{l_1 : \tau(\alpha_1), \cdots, l_n : \tau(\alpha_n), \{l_1, \cdots, l_n\} : \tau(N(F_1 \to F_2))}{\emptyset : \square}$ *and also that*

(2) $\dfrac{k_1 : \tau(\gamma_1), \cdots, k_m : \tau(\gamma_m), \{k_1, \cdots, k_m\} : \tau(N(F_1))}{\emptyset : \square}$ *From (1) we get*

(3) $\dfrac{l_1 : \tau(\alpha_1), \cdots, l_n : \tau(\alpha_n),}{\dfrac{K : \tau(F_1), \{l_1, \cdots, l_n\} \cup K : \tau(N(F_2))}{\emptyset : \square}}$ *then by lemma 2*

(4) $\dfrac{l_1 : \tau(\alpha_1), \cdots, l_n : \tau(\alpha_n), k_1 : \tau(\gamma_1), \cdots, k_m : \tau(\gamma_m),}{\dfrac{\{l_1, \cdots, l_n, k_1, \cdots, k_m\} \cup K : \tau(N(F_2))}{\emptyset : \square}}$

From (3) and (4) and by the induction hypothesis we get that

$$h(\{k_1, \cdots, k_m\}, F_1) = 1 \text{ implies } h(\{l_1, \cdots, l_n, k_1, \cdots, k_m\}, F_2) = 1$$

Hence, since no condition was imposed on $\{k_1, \cdots, k_m\}$ we have that

$$h(\{l_1, \cdots, l_n\}, (F_1 \rightarrow F_2)) = 1$$

4 Conclusions

We presented as case study the implementation of the implication fragment of substructural logics. The normalization function, labelling policy, filtering and oracle procedures were defined. We have shown that the implementation is sound and complete with respect to possible world semantics. The study of the implementation of other connectives in these logics is under way.

5 Acknowledgements

This work is been part of a yet unsponsored software development project Witty, under the supervision of Prof. Roberto Lins de Carvalho at LNCC - CNPq. I appreciate his contribution.

References

1. Leo Bachmair, H. Gazinger, and U. Waldmann. Refutational theorem proving for hierarchic first-order theories. *Applicable Algebra in Engineering, Communication and Computing*, 5:193–212, 1994.
2. Marcello D'Agostino and Dov M. Gabbay. A generalization of analytic deduction via labelled deductive systems. part I: basic substructural logics. *Journal of Automated Reasoning*, 13, 1994. To appear.
3. Dov Gabbay. Labelled deductive systems - part i. 5th Draft, Dec 1990. To be published by Oxford University Press.
4. Claudia Oliveira. *An Architecture for Labelled Theorem Proving*. PhD thesis, University of London - Imperial College, 1995.
5. Mark E. Stickel. Automated deduction by theory resolution. *Journal of Automated Reasoning*, 1:333–355, 1985.

Labelled Abduction

Nicia Cristina Rocha Riccio[1] and Ruy J. G. B. de Queiroz[2]

[1] Departamento de Sistemas e Computação, Universidade Federal da Paraíba
Campina Grande, PB 58109-970, Brazil
[2] Departamento de Informática, Universidade Federal de Pernambuco
C.P. 7851, Recife, PE 50732-970, Brazil

Abstract. The intention here is to develop a theory of machine learning (in particular, abductive reasoning) using the framework of D. Gabbay's *Labelled Deductive Systems (LDS)*, in the light of Gillies' perspective on the dichotomy 'deductive versus inductive logic' where controlled inference serves as the bridging notion. From this point of view, abductive reasoning, a topic that attracts much interest in AI and automated reasoning research, can be seen as a kind of controlled deduction where the control component will be represented by the labels of the *LDS* framework; this work investigates the possibility of treating the meta-level considerations of the abductive reasoning in terms of the informations handled by the labels on the labelled formulae of such framework.

1 Introduction

D. Gillies' 'logic = inference + control' formula [4], a recent perspective on the dichotomy 'deductive vs. inductive logic', points to a key concept pervading much of recent work on logic and computation: 'controlled inference'. The main observation is that whilst control is creeping into deductive logic, controlled inference is becoming the norm in inductive logic, representing the so-called rapprochement between deductive and inductive logic. In terms of logic and computation, controlled inference can be seen as a kind of generalized concept of object level deduction where elements of the so-called meta-level have a decisive role to play in the formulation of deduction rules. In the light of this perspective, abductive reasoning can be seen as a kind of *controlled* deduction, where the meta-level considerations of the abductive problem will be the deductive system control component.

Abduction is a natural form of reasoning in any scientific field when new knowledge may be gained by observation of real world facts. It is also a common form of everyday reasoning and its formalization has recently attracted much attention in the AI community. Abduction and induction are always together and were wrongly considered as a single argument (frequently also together with deduction). C. S. Peirce himself (considered the father of abduction) [9] assumes this confusion and attributes it to the narrow formalist character of the inference conception adopted by the logicians.

The initial informal view of abduction relates it to the notion of explanation, and its logical schema is the inference of α from the premisses $\alpha \rightarrow \varphi$ and φ. This inference rule is clearly unsound from the deductive point of view. The material implication, however, is necessary but not sufficient in determining an abductive problem solution. The characterization of abduction must impose additional external (meta-logical) conditions on explanations, with the aim of selecting 'good reasons' for an event φ among all the formulae that logically imply φ in the background theory.

Certain approaches to Logic Programming propose to formalize abduction by transforming it into a kind of deduction. For instance, in [1] the concept of predicate completion is used to transform an abduction problem into a normal (deductive) query problem. A more recent work [10], on the other hand, describes the extension of logic programming to perform abduction. In [11] abduction is recognized as a separate reasoning activity; a formalism to write rules of abduction is described and a variety of abduction rules are discussed. In [5] analytical proof systems are proposed as suitable tools to face the meta-level and proof theoretical questions involved in abduction. A logical characterization of abduction is proposed in [7], and some interesting properties to abductive methods are discussed. A method of propositional abduction using modal logic is proposed in [6].

We shall here attempt to sketch the a theory of machine learning (in particular, abductive reasoning) using the framework of D. Gabbay's *Labelled Deductive Systems (LDS)*. The idea is to use meta-level information handled by the labels on the labelled formulae to represent the preference criterion (meta-level characteristics) of an abductive problem.

2   Abductive reasoning in logical form

An abduction problem in a logic L consists of a background theory Θ and a formula φ to be explained, such that $\Theta \not\vdash_L \varphi$. A solution of the problem given by the pair $\langle \Theta, \varphi \rangle$ is to be chosen among formulae α such that $\Theta \cup \{\alpha\} \vdash_L \varphi$.

However, material implication alone is inadequate to capture causality. Actually, most characteristics that make the explanation interesting are meta-level considerations that cannot be expressed in the object level [1].

Other conditions, whose meaning is more interesting from a logical point of view, are generically stated in terms of logical consequence: for example, an abductive explanation α must be consistent with the theory Θ, i.e. $\Theta \not\vdash_L \neg\alpha$ and it must be minimal, in the sense that for any other α' that logically implies φ in the context of Θ, if $\vdash \alpha \rightarrow \alpha'$, then $\vdash \alpha' \rightarrow \alpha$ [5].

In [7] is given an interesting definition of the abductive relation that we will consider in our own work. The general characterization of abductive reasoning proposed in the referred work supposes 3 (three) parameters as necessary to define an abductive problem: (i) the logic underlying the theory Θ; (ii) the preference criterion among the hypothesis; (iii) a set of alternative hypothesis that a good explanation has to stand comparison with.

In practical reasoning, in fact, a hypothesis is accepted as a good reason for the truth of a given fact as long as a better one is not found. That is, being 'good' is judged in relation to a set of alternative hypothesis that does not necessarily contains all the γ's such that $\Theta \vdash_L \gamma \rightarrow \varphi$: the absolute 'best' explanation is actually never used nor looked for.

The three place relation $\Theta \vdash_L \alpha \rightsquigarrow \varphi$ is used in [7] to express the abductive relation 'in the background theory Θ, α is a good reason for φ, in the logic L'; the preference relation is denoted by the symbol $\sqsubseteq$ and the function $Cand$, applied to a theory Θ and a formula φ to be explained, is assumed to return the set of alternative candidates that constitute the test stand for any acceptable explanation of φ in Θ.

The abductive relation is defined in [7] as follows:

Definition 1. $\Theta \vdash_L \alpha \rightsquigarrow \varphi$ if $\Theta \vdash_L \alpha \rightarrow \varphi$ and for every $\gamma \in Cand(\Theta, \varphi)$, if $\gamma \sqsubseteq \alpha$, then $\alpha \sqsubseteq \gamma$. Where, $\alpha \sqsubseteq \gamma \equiv_{def} \vdash_L \gamma \rightarrow \alpha$ and $Cand(\Theta, \varphi) \equiv_{def} \{\gamma : \Theta \vdash_L \gamma \rightarrow \varphi\}$.

This definition will be used in our own work, with some little differences.

In [5], the underlying idea is to solve the abduction problem $\langle \Theta, \varphi \rangle$ by building a formula α that closes the open branches of a tableau for $\Theta \cup \{\neg\varphi\}$. Here our intention is to propose a similar method, but using a labelled deductive system in which, besides the logical and syntactical restrictions imposed in the referred method, we shall consider some kind of meta-level restriction which will be handled by the labelled formulae of the LDS.

3   The LDS framework

The approach to proof theory called *Labelled Deductive Systems (LDS)* is based on a generalization of the functional interpretation of logical connectives, the so-called 'Curry-Howard interpretation' [2]. It is an enriched system of natural deduction, in the sense that terms representing proof-constructions (the labels) are carried alongside formulae. The declarative unit of a logical system is a *labelled* formula '$t : A$'. The label t represents information which is needed to modify A or to supplement (the declarative information) in A which is not of the same type or nature as A itself. Whilst formulae are part of the logical calculus, terms are expressions of the functional calculus. Moreover, there is a certain harmony between the functional calculus on the labels and the logical calculus on the formulae.

According to Gabbay [3], logic has recently been widely applied in computer science and artificial intelligence, and strong interest and intensive research was directed in the area of non-monotonic and non-classical logics. The meta-level features of logical systems have not received too much attention in pure logic community, nevertheless it seems to be of crucial importance to the needs of computer science.

Gabbay argues [3] that, since the difference between one logic and another are meta-level considerations, it is possible (and highly desirable) to put forward a general framework where meta-level features can live side by side with object level features. And, according to him, the best framework to provide this is that of *LDS*.

An *LDS* system is a triple $\langle L, \Gamma, M \rangle$, where L is a logical language, Γ is a set of labels and M is a discipline of labelling formulae of the logic, together with deduction rules and with agreed ways of propagating the labels via the application of the deduction rules. The way the rules are used is more or less uniform to all systems.

Depending on the logical system involved, the intuitive meaning of the labels varies. Whereas in the traditional logical systems the consequence is defined using proof rules on the formulae, in the *LDS* methodology the consequence is defined by using rules on both formulae and their labels. The meta features can be reflected in the algebra or logic of the labels and the object features can be reflected in the rules of the formulae.

4 *LDS* as a framework for abduction

An abductive problem will be defined here similarly as it was in [1]. However, in order to manipulate the meta-level characteristics the theory must be completely labelled following a meta-level criterion given by the user and according to the problem domain. Moreover, there must be defined an ordering, possibly partial, among the labels that will reflect the preference criterion (meta-logical). For instance, this meta-logical criterion can be interpreted as probability measures, possibility distributions, cost, etc.

4.1 Characterizing abduction via logic

An abductive problem, then, is a triple $\langle \Theta, \varphi, \sqsubseteq \rangle$, where:

- Θ is a background theory consisting of formulae labelled following any preference criterion;
- φ is a formula to be explained such that, $\Theta \not\vdash_L \varphi$ and $\Theta \not\vdash_L \neg\varphi$;
- $\sqsubseteq$ is an ordering relation among the labels denoting the preference criterion among the formulae.

In fact, the fundamental conditions in order to an explanation be accepted as 'interesting' may be separated in two groups. In the former we have the consistence and minimality conditions, and possibly some syntactical restriction, all of them defined in the object level. In the second group we have the conditions or preference criterion from the meta-level (domain dependent) that will be treated by the labels.

The role set of minimal and Θ-consistent explanations will be generated deductively using labelled natural deduction [2], and after that the most plausible explanations will be selected following the meta-logical criteria.

In the object level, solutions to the problem $\langle \Theta, \varphi, \sqsubseteq \rangle$ can be found among the formulae that complete the proof of φ on the basis of the theory Θ.

Definition 2. Let R be a deduction tree. R is said to be **acceptable** if to each formula from all its leaves no elimination or introduction rule of logical connectives can be applied, considering the theory Θ, or if the formula is a member of Θ.

Definition 3. Let R be an acceptable deduction tree associated to an abductive problem $\langle \Theta, \varphi, \sqsubseteq \rangle$. $F(R)$ is the set composed of the formulae present in the leaves of R. $Exp(R)$ is defined as: (i) $Exp(R) = \emptyset$, when $\forall \alpha \in F(R)$, $\alpha \in \Theta$; (ii) $Exp(R) = \bot$, or undefined, when φ is not Θ-consistent; (iii) $Exp(R) = \{\alpha_1 \wedge \alpha_2 \wedge ... \wedge \alpha_n$, such that $\alpha_i \in F(R)$ and $\alpha_i \notin \Theta\}$, when (i) and (ii) do not occur.

Definition 4. The set of all candidates to be an explanation for the abductive problem $\langle \Theta, \varphi, \sqsubseteq \rangle$ will be represented by $Cand(\Theta, \varphi)$ and is composed by all $Exp(R_i)$ where each R_i is an acceptable tree associated to the abductive problem $\langle \Theta, \varphi, \sqsubseteq \rangle$.

Using these definitions, the following theorem establishes completeness and a form of soundness in the process of candidates generation.

Theorem 5. Let $\langle \Theta, \varphi, \sqsubseteq \rangle$ be an abductive problem. Then, every element of $Cand(\Theta, \varphi)$ is a non-contradictory explanation for $\langle \Theta, \varphi, \sqsubseteq \rangle$ (soundness) and any minimal and non-contradictory explanation for $\langle \Theta, \varphi, \sqsubseteq \rangle$ is an element of $Cand(\Theta, \varphi)$ (completeness).

4.2 The logical and the functional calculus

As stated before, the logical calculus that will be used to the object level solution will be the natural deduction system in the style of Prawitz [8]. For the meta-level solution we will need a functional calculus. We considered the rules of labelled natural deduction [2], and formulated similar rules of introduction and elimination for logical connectives. The rules to the propositional logic are as follows:

Conjunction

$$\frac{x : A \qquad y : B}{I_\wedge(x,y) : A \wedge B}(\wedge - I)$$

$$\frac{x : A \wedge B}{E_{1\wedge}(x) : A}(\wedge - E_1) \qquad \frac{x : A \wedge B}{E_{2\wedge}(x) : B}(\wedge - E_2)$$

Disjunction

$$\frac{x : A}{I_{1\vee}(x) : A \vee B}(\vee - I_1) \qquad \frac{y : B}{I_{2\vee}(y) : A \vee B}(\vee - I_2)$$

$$[y : A] \qquad\qquad [z : B]$$
$$\vdots \qquad\qquad\qquad \vdots$$
$$\frac{x : A \vee B \qquad f(y) : C \qquad\qquad g(z) : C}{E_\vee(x, \lambda y.f(y), \lambda z.g(z)) : C}(\vee - E)$$

Implication

$$[x : A]$$
$$\vdots$$
$$\frac{f(x) : B}{I_\rightarrow(\lambda x.f(x)) : A \rightarrow B}(\rightarrow - I) \qquad \frac{x : A \qquad y : A \rightarrow B}{E_\rightarrow(x,y) : B}(\rightarrow - E)$$

Negation

$$[x : A]$$
$$\vdots$$

$$\frac{f(x) : \perp}{I_\neg(\lambda x. f(x)) : \neg A}(\neg - I) \qquad \frac{x : A \qquad y : \neg A}{E_\neg(x, y) : \perp}(\neg - E)$$

Reductio ad Absurdum

$$[x : \neg A]$$
$$\vdots$$

$$\frac{f(x) : \perp}{R(\lambda x. f(x)) : A}$$

The search for a solution to an abductive problem is summarised as follows:

1. The attempt to construct a proof of φ from Θ (the solution at the object level).
2. The generation of the set of all minimal candidates ($Cand(\Theta, \varphi)$) to complete the proof of φ.
3. The labels propagation from the possible generated candidates until the formula φ (top-down).
4. The candidates comparison in order to select the most plausible one.

4.3 The proof construction and the generation of candidates

The first and second steps will be executed deductively from the conclusion (the fact φ) to the premisses, using the rules of natural deduction, considering our theory Θ.

In fact, in abductive reasoning the proof φ cannot be completed only with the background theory. At some point in the proof construction there will be no more elements in Θ which let us continue. At this moment we stop with an acceptable deduction tree. In most cases, we get a set of acceptable trees and each of them gives us a possible candidate that will compose the set $Cand(\Theta, \varphi)$.

Logically speaking, each $\alpha_i \in Cand(\Theta, \varphi)$ is a possible explanation for φ, but it may be that only one of them (or perhaps none of them) was really the cause for φ. That is the biggest question on abductive reasoning: as stated before, we cannot assure that the found solution is the correct solution. What we want to assure in this work is that, given the logical criterion (from the object level) and the meta-logical criterion provided by the user (the labels and their ordering), the solution (or solutions) we get, is(are) the best one(s).

4.4 The propagation of the labels

The propagation of the labels is the simplest step. It is the intermediate step between the object level solution and the meta-level solution.

To each formula $\alpha \in Cand(\Theta, \varphi)$ generated by the attempt to construct the proof of φ we must attribute a hypothetic label that will be propagated besides the labels of other sentences of Θ used in the deduction, following the functional calculus rules described above. So, for each candidate we will have a deduction tree that will culminate in φ. As each of these trees must be using different deduction rules to prove φ, the final labels found to the formula φ in the bottom of the deduction tree will be different (see the example in section 5). This difference means exatly the degree of plausibility of each candidate to be the cause of φ.

4.5   The candidates comparison

To choose between the various candidates is the crucial point of abduction. The characteristic of being the 'best' is very subjective, it is exactly what we mean as meta-level preference criterion, and probably it depends on the kind of problem we are dealing with. That is why the labels ordering must be given by the user. We believe this specific question is also dependent on the problem and the application area, and so, we propose that there must not be a fixed way to compare the labels. We must provide a variety of options and the user will choose that one he/she considers more adequate to the kind of problem he/she is dealing with.

The first point to consider are the logical criteria, as stated by definition 1, and some syntactical restriction can also be stated as in [5]. Integrity constraints can also be treated in the object level.

After the object level criterion, we can state some intuitive ways in which to compare the labels.

The first criterion that must be applied is the **unification criterion** following which we can eliminate similar functions and atomic labels[3] in order to reduce the most we can the number of elements we have to compare.

After that we can directly apply the **atomic labels preference criterion**, that is, we have only to verify which label is preferable following the order $\sqsubseteq$ given by the user.

An other important criterion is the **number of elements** (atomic labels and functions) present in the final label. If the label with a smallest number of elements have no atomic label with a smaller preference than all the atomic labels of the biggest final label, the first one (the smallest) is preferable than the last one (the biggest). The same occur with the number of facts and the number of rules used in the deduction: a final label which was constructed by the utilization of more facts than rules of the theory is preferable than other one which used more rules.

The last criterion we can apply is the one considering the **label type**. In this case we have the following preferences:

1. $l \sqsubseteq x$, if l labels a formula from the theory and x is a hypothetic label.
2. $f(l) \sqsubseteq x$, if l labels a formula from the theory, f is any function and x is a hypothetic label.
3. $f(a) \sqsubseteq f(b)$, if both a and b label formulae from the theory and $a \sqsubseteq b$ in the user ordering.
4. $f(a, b) \sqsubseteq f(c, d)$, if a, b, c and d label formulae from the theory and if $a \sqsubseteq c$, $a \sqsubseteq d$, $b \sqsubseteq c$ and $b \sqsubseteq d$ in the user ordering.

All these criteria are rather generic and can be used in any application domain of abductive reasoning. However, when dealing with specific cases it is possible to state other criteria of candidates comparison according to the labels meaning.

---

[3] We are calling atomic labels that ones which label a formula from the theory or a hyphotetic label.

In the next section we will show an example in propositional logic in order to make clearer the method discussed above.

5   An example

Suppose a theory Θ compposed of the following labelled sentences:
$$\Theta = \{\, l_1 : A \to D,$$
$$l_2 : E \to C \wedge D,$$
$$l_3 : B \vee F \to D\}$$

And the observed fact φ to be explaned is D .

The attempt to construct a proof of D from Θ and, after that, the labels propagation, gives us the following 5 (five) deduction trees:

To $\alpha = A$, and supposing A labelled by a hypothetic label x, we have:

$$\frac{x : A \quad l_1 : A \to D}{E_\to(x, l_1) : D}$$

To $\alpha = E$, suppose E labelled by y:

$$\frac{\dfrac{y : E \quad l_2 : E \to C \wedge D}{E_\to(y, l_2) : C \wedge D}}{E_{2\wedge}(E_\to(y, l_2)) : D}$$

To $\alpha = B \vee F$, suppose $B \vee F$ labelled by z:

$$\frac{z : B \vee F \quad l_3 : B \vee F \to D}{E_\to(z, l_3) : D}$$

To $\alpha = B$, suppose B labelled by t:

$$\frac{\dfrac{t : B}{I_{1\vee}(t) : B \vee F} \quad l_3 : B \vee F \to D}{E_\to(I_{1\vee}(t), l_3) : D}$$

To $\alpha = F$, suppose F labelled by w:

$$\frac{\dfrac{w : F}{I_{2\vee}(w) : B \vee F} \quad l_3 : B \vee F \to D}{E_\to(I_{2\vee}(w), l_3) : D}$$

Considering the 5 (five) possibilities, our candidate set is:
$$Cand(\Theta, D) = \{A, E, B \vee F, B, F\}$$

and at this point we have 5 (five) possible labels to the formula D (our φ). The next step is to compare the 5 (five) options and to choose the most plausible.

First of all, we must consider the logical criterion of minimality: if $\gamma \to \alpha$ then $\alpha \sqsubseteq \gamma$. The candidates B, F and $B \vee F$ can be treated conform this criterion (i.e. $B \to B \vee F$ and $F \to B \vee F$). So, $B \vee F \sqsubseteq B$ and $B \vee F \sqsubseteq F$ and then we can eliminate both B and F as candidates.

Continuing, we have now only 3 (three) labels to compare; they are:

$$E_\to(x, l_1) \, , \, E_{2\wedge}(E_\to(y, l_2)) \, , \, E_\to(z, l_3)$$

Suppose we have the following ordering among the labels:

$$l_1 \sqsubseteq l_3, l_2 \sqsubseteq l_3, l_1 \sqsubseteq l_2, l_2 \sqsubseteq l_1$$

Considering the unification criterion, we can compare the first and the last labels. By doing that we eliminate the function $E_\to$ and all we have to compare is (x, l_1) and (z, l_3). Since x and z are hypothetic labels we have no way to compare them. Then we finish with l_1 and l_3 and we verify that $l_1 \sqsubseteq l_3$ in the preference ordering. So we can conclude that $A \sqsubseteq B \vee F$.

Now we must compare the first two labels: $E_\to(x, l_1)$, propagated from the candidate A, and $E_{2\wedge}(E_\to(y, l_2))$, propagated from the candidate E.

Considering the number of elements criterion, the single atomic label we can compare in the first final label is l_1, since x is a hypothetic label. In the other final label (the one which has more elements) the single atomic label we can compare is l_2, since y is a hypothetic label. As $l_1 \sqsubseteq l_2, l_2 \sqsubseteq l_1$, that is, they have the same preference order, we select the smallest final label as the preferable one. So, we conclude that:

$$\Theta \vdash_L A \rightsquigarrow D$$

meaning that 'A is a good reason for D'.

6 Final remarks

Following Gillies' perspective, the rapprochement between deductive and inductive logic is actual and necessary and brings us to the concept of *controlled inference* which can be perfectly associated with the *LDS* framework, where the elements of the so-called meta-level (the labels) have a decisive role to play. Here we have presented the first elements of a theory of abductive reasoning (seen as a form of controlled deduction) using the *LDS* framework. Most works on abductive reasoning deal with the object level only. In this work we treat both object and meta-level aspects of an abductive problem: the set of possible explanations to an observed fact φ is generated deductively (the object level) and, after that, the most interesting explanation is chosen considering the preference criterion stated by the user (the meta-level). This way it is possible to give an abductive problem a more plausible solution (even though it could be a wrong solution since abduction is generally unsound). Moreover, since the preference criterion, which depends on the meaning of the labels, may vary, this characterization of abduction can easily be adapted to different problem domains.

In the next step of our project of characterizing abduction via *LDS*, we shall consider the following points:

- The extension to first order logic.

- Case studies will help evaluating the method proposed, for example cases where the meaning of the labels are numerical measures such as: probability measures, possibility distributions, reliability degrees, etc. In all these cases it is possible to define a calculus with the numeric labels.
- An investigation of the use of various non-classical logics (such as intuitionistic, linear, relevant), since the *LDS* framework considers the logic underlying the theory as a parameter, and a precise definition of explanation in an abductive problem will be dependent on the logic.

References

1. Luca Console, Daniele Theseider Dupre, and Pietro Torasso. On the relationship between abduction and deduction. *Journal of Logic and Computation*, 1(5):661–690, 1991.
2. Ruy J. G. B. de Queiroz and Dov M. Gabbay. An introduction to labelled natural deduction. *Proc 3dr Adv. Summer Sch. in AI, Sept 21-25'92*, 1992. Paper available via anonymous ftp from theory.doc.ic.ac.uk, file intro-lnd.{dvi,ps}.gz in /papers/deQueiroz.
3. Dov M. Gabbay. *LDS - Labelled Deductive Systems, Volume I - Foundations.* Oxford University Press, 1994. First Draft 1989. Current Draft, 465pp.,May 1994. Published as MPI-I-94-223, Max-Planck-Institut für Informatik, Saarbrücken, Germany.
4. Donald Gillies. A rapprochement between deductive and inductive logic. *Bulletin of the Interest Group in Pure and Apllied Logics*, 2(2):149–166, 1994.
5. Marta Cialdea Mayer and Fiora Pirri. First order abduction via tableau and sequent calculi. *Bulletin of the Interest Group in Pure and Applied Logics*, 1(1):99–117, 1993.
6. Marta Cialdea Mayer and Fiora Pirri. Propositional abduction in modal logic. *Bulletin of the Interest Group in Pure and Applied Logics*, 1995. Special Issue on *Proc. Tableaux Workshop 1994*, (to appear).
7. Marta Cialdea Mayer and Fiora Pirri. Towards a logical characterization of abductive reasoning. *Bulletin of the Interest Group in Pure and Applied Logics*, 1995. Special Issue on *Mechanised Deduction on the Logics of Practical Reasoning*, (to appear).
8. Prawitz, D. *Natural Deduction. A Proof-Theoretical Study*, volume 3 of *Acta Universitatis Stockholmiensis. Stockholm Studies in Philosophy.* Almqvist & Wiksell, Stockholm, 113pp, 1965.
9. Thomas A. Sebeok and Jean Umiker Sebeok. "Você conhece o meu método": Uma justaposição de Charles S. Peirce e Sherlock Holmes. In *O signo de três*. Editora Perspectiva, 1991. From the original : *The sign of three.* Indiana University Press, 1983.
10. Francesca Toni. *Abductive Logic Programming.* PhD thesis, University of London, February 1995. Department of Computing, Imperial College of Science, Technology and Medicine.
11. Wlodek Zadrozny. Is there a prototypical rule of abduction? (yes, e.g. in proximity based explanation). *J. Expt. Theor. Artif. Intell.*, 6:147–162, 1994.

PROMAL: Programming in Modal Action Logic*

Odinaldo Rodrigues[1] and Mario Benevides[2]

[1] Imperial College, Dept. of Computing
London - SW7 2BZ - UK
e-mail: O.Rodrigues@doc.ic.ac.uk
[2] COPPE/UFRJ, Prog. de Eng. de Sistemas
Rio de Janeiro-RJ, Brazil, Cx. Postal 68511 CEP 21945-970
e-mail: mario@cos.ufrj.br

Abstract. In this work we present PROMAL: Programming in Modal Action Logic, a formalism to deal with the planning problem. This formalism is based on the concepts of Modal Action Logic (MAL) and may be regarded as an extension of SLD-Resolution to allow the clauses of a Definite Set to have literals with modalities.

The modalities are intended to capture the notion of state change caused by the execution of actions. As in previous works in MAL, we call the information about a system's state **scenario**. Besides accomplishing proofs of properties of specific scenarios it is possible to search scenarios where desired properties hold.

1 Introduction

Modal Action Logic - MAL ([5],[4],[8]) is a neat and suitable way to represent information about system's states and the way these states change by the execution of actions. Thus being well suited to express the dynamics of a planning system too.

Logic Programming has had increased popularity since the idea of using logic as a programming language was first introduced by Kowalski ([6]) and Colmerauer ([1]). In part this happens because it is intuitive to use and yet it is well formalised.

In this work, we join some concepts from these two areas in a formalism to deal with the planning problem. We present PROMAL – Programming in Modal Action Logic – an extension of SLD-resolution so that it can handle with literals with modalities. The modalities are intended to capture the notion of change caused by the execution of actions.

It is unavoidable to relate this work with previous ones about the planning problem. Among these is STRIPS ([3]). STRIPS could be seen as a system divided into four main modules: a theorem prover; a search strategy; a set of operators (used to describe actions) and world models (to represent the information about states). This division

---

* An earlier version of this paper was published in the IX Brazilian Conference on Artificial Intelligence (SBIA'92) - In Portuguese. This is an extension and formalisation of that work.

makes it difficult to have a clear understanding of how a search for a solution to a problem is performed.

Another system is Warren's WARPLAN ([10]). WARPLAN is written in PROLOG and uses its built-in theorem prover to accomplish proofs of properties of scenarios. One of the most interesting features of WARPLAN is its ability to correct plans. Whenever a property required in the goal does not hold in the state reached by the execution of actions in the plan being built, WARPLAN tries to correct it by inserting actions where they do not compromise the properties already achieved.

A related approach to PROMAL can be found in [2]. That work introduces MOLOG, a system that allows modalities in the clauses and has inference rules according to the particular modal system it is intended to work under.

Our system differs from the ones above because we incorporated in its own language, elements of the underlying formalism and yet maintained a procedural semantics easy to understand and program. In particular, a plan is built by the refutation process itself and is obtained as part of the answer for the goal.

2   Language

We now present the language of PROMAL:

Definition 1 Alphabet.
- A set of n-place predicative symbols
- A set of n-place function symbols
- A set of variables
- A set of constants
- A finite set of action names $(\boldsymbol{Ac})$
- Logical symbols: $\leftarrow$,[,] and ,.

Definition 2 Language symbols.   A *term* is either a variable, a constant or an expression of the form $f(t_1, t_2, \ldots, t_n)$, where f is a n-place function symbol and t_1, t_2, ... and t_n are terms.

A *positive literal* is an expression of the form $p(t_1, t_2, \ldots, t_n)$, where p is a n-place predicate symbol and t_1, t_2, ... and t_n are terms.

An *action* is an expression of the form $[\alpha(t_1, t_2, \ldots, t_n)]$, where α is a n-place action name and t_1, t_2, ... and t_n are terms.

Remark.   The expression $[\![\alpha]\!]^k$ will denote the sequence of actions $[\alpha_1][\alpha_2] \ldots [\alpha_k]$, where $[\alpha_1]$, $[\alpha_2]$, ... and $[\alpha_k]$ are (possibly) distinct actions.

Definition 3 Atoms.   A *pure atom* is a positive literal. A *modal atom* is an expression of the form $[\![\alpha]\!]^k q$ where q is a positive literal and $k > 0$.

We will use the term *atom* to refer to either a modal atom or a pure atom indistinctively .

We are now in a position to define the clauses of our system:

Definition 4 Clauses.   A *non-modal definite clause* is an expression of the form $q \leftarrow a_1, a_2, \ldots, a_m (m \geq 0)$, where each a_i $(0 \leq i \leq m)$ is an atom and q is a pure atom.

A *modal definite clause* is an expression of the form $[\![\alpha]\!]^k q \leftarrow a_1, a_2, \ldots, a_m$ $(m \geq 1)$, where each a_i $(1 \leq i \leq m)$ is an atom and $[\![\alpha]\!]^k q$ is a modal atom. We will often refer to a modal definite clause as a *modal rule* and to the sequence $[\![\alpha]\!]^k$ as its *modal part* or *prefix*.

A *goal clause* is an expression of the form $\leftarrow a_1, a_2, \ldots, a_m \quad (m \geq 1)$, where each $a_i \ (1 \leq i \leq m)$ is an atom.

The *empty clause* ($\square$) is a clause with empty antecedent and consequent and it is to be understood as a contradiction.

We will often refer to a non-modal definite clause whose antecedent is non-null as a *non-modal rule*, and to a non-modal definite clause with a null antecedent as a *fact*.

Definition 5 Modal Sets. A *modal definite set* is a set of modal and non-modal definite clauses.

A *modal quasi-definite set* is a set constituted by modal and non-modal definite clauses and exactly one goal clause.

Definition 6 Selection function for Goal clauses. A *selection function for goal clauses* is a function from a set of goal clauses to a set of atoms.

The selection function which always selects the leftmost atom in a goal clause is called the *standard selection function*.

Before stating the rules of the system it is interesting to introduce some concepts. In PROMAL we have information specific to the initial state of the system and information about its general behaviour. A pure atom states a property of the initial state of the system, here called Initial Scenario. A modal atom states a property of some scenario, namely the scenario reached by the execution of the sequence of actions of its prefix in the Initial Scenario. The modal atom $[\alpha]q$, e.g., states the information that the property q holds in the state reached from the Initial Scenario by the execution of $[\alpha]$.

The conditional clauses, i.e. the modal and non-modal rules, are intended to verify in all scenarios, because they state information about the behaviour of the system. It follows that the information about the Initial Scenario is what can be deduced by ordinary SLD-Resolution.

The structure of the representation of a problem may be seen in Figure 1. The Modal Rules are intended to represent the notion of change. As we mentioned earlier, a modal atom like $[\alpha]q$ represents the information that q is a property of the scenario reached from the Initial Scenario by the execution of $[\alpha]$. In other words, an action ($[\alpha]$) was executed to reach a scenario in which q holds. Now consider a proof of such an atom ($[\alpha]q$):

The Non-Modal Rules work exactly as ordinary rules of SLD-Resolution, except that they apply to all scenarios (and here we have an implicit Necessitation Rule applied to them).

Consider the rule:

$$q \leftarrow a_1, a_2, \ldots, a_m$$

This rule states that if the properties a_1, a_2 and a_m hold in the Initial Scenario, then the property q also holds in the Initial Scenario. However, in our system this rule states more information. If the properties a_1, a_2 and a_m hold in the scenario reached from the Initial Scenario by the execution of $[\alpha]$, then the property q also holds in that scenario, i.e., if $[\alpha]a_1$, $[\alpha]a_2, \ldots, [\alpha]a_m$ hold then so does $[\alpha]q$. These clauses are not enough to express the notion of change. It is necessary to state the way in which the scenarios relate to each other, i.e., how they change.

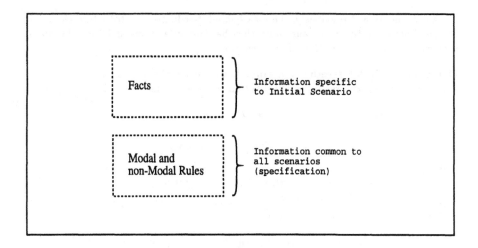

Fig. 1. Structure of the representation of a problem in PROMÁL

A modal rule such as

$$[\alpha]q \leftarrow a_1, a_2, \ldots, a_m \tag{1}$$

states that whenever all the properties a_1, a_2 and a_m hold in a scenario, for instance S, then property q also holds in the scenario reached from S by the execution of $[\alpha]$. For example, suppose the atom $[\alpha]q$ was to be proved. By using rule (1), this could be achieved by proving that properties a_1, a_2, ... and a_m all hold in the Initial Scenario. Now, suppose we wanted to prove $[\beta][\alpha]q$. Since the clauses in the specification apply to all scenarios, then in particular they also apply to a scenario reached by the execution of $[\beta]$. Thus, the rule

$$[\beta][\alpha]q \leftarrow [\beta]a_1, [\beta]a_2, \ldots, [\beta]a_m \tag{2}$$

is also in the system, even though implicitly. A proof of $[\beta]a_1$, $[\beta]a_2$, ... and $[\beta]a_m$ would therefore yield a proof of $[\beta][\alpha]q$ by using (2). Each application of rules by this process reduces the length of the prefix of the literal chosen by the selection function, so that they eventually become pure atoms to be proved in the Initial Scenario.

3 Rules of PROMAL

The mechanism of PROMAL will be explained by first introducing the modal f-reduction rule described informally above. Later on, the modal f-extension rule, which allows it to be used as a planning system, will be presented.

3.1 Modal f-reduction rule

All the properties of the Initial Scenario are represented by the facts and what can be deduced from them by using non-modal clauses, i.e., via pure SLD-Resolution. They represent the basic case of the rule.

As we mentioned previously, the idea behind f-reductions is to reduce the prefix of modal atoms in the goal clause until they become pure atoms and hence becoming properties to be proved in the Initial Scenario.

Definition 7 Modal f-reduction rule. Let G be a goal clause, D a modal (or non-modal) clause and ψ a renaming substitution to D in presence of G. If G is

$$\leftarrow g_1, g_2, \ldots, g_n$$

and

$$f(G) = g_i = [\![\beta]\!]^j [\![\gamma]\!]^k q \quad (j \geq 0, k \geq 0) \tag{3}$$

and $D\psi$ is

$$[\![\alpha]\!]^k q' \leftarrow a_1, a_2, \ldots, a_m \quad (k \geq 0, m \geq j) \tag{4}$$

and there exists a mgu θ of $\{[\![\gamma]\!]^k q, [\![\alpha]\!]^k q'\}$, then the application of a modal f-reduction of G by D results in a new goal clause

$$G' = \leftarrow (g_1, g_2, \ldots, g_{i-1}, [\![\beta]\!]^j a_1, [\![\beta]\!]^j a_2, \ldots, [\![\beta]\!]^j a_m, g_{i+1}, \ldots, g_n)\theta.$$

It is required that $m \geq j$ (in (4)) in order to ensure that only properties of the Initial Scenario are proven from its facts. Otherwise, it would be possible to find a refutation from $\leftarrow [\alpha]q$ and $q \leftarrow$ (by letting $k = 0$, $m = 0$ and $[\![\beta]\!]^j = [\alpha]$, in (3) and (4)). From the rule above we can now define the concepts of modal $\mathrm{SLD}(f)$-deduction and modal $\mathrm{SLD}(f)$-refutation:

Definition 8 Modal $\mathrm{SLD}(f)$-deduction. Let f be a selection function, S a modal quasi-definite set and G the goal clause in S. A *modal $\mathrm{SLD}(f)$-deduction of G from S* is a sequence $d = (C_1, C_2, \ldots, C_n)$ of clauses ending in G, i.e., $C_n = G$ and $\exists r \leq n$ such that:

a) for all $i < r$, C_i is a modal or non-modal definite clause of S;
b) C_r is the goal clause of S; and
c) for all $i > r$, C_i is derived from C_{i-1} and C_j (for some $j < r$) via the modal f-reduction rule.

Definition 9 Modal $\mathrm{SLD}(f)$-refutation. A *modal $\mathrm{SLD}(f)$-refutation* from a quasi-definite set S is a modal $\mathrm{SLD}(f)$-deduction of the empty clause from S.

Though we have presented a first-order version of a modal $\mathrm{SLD}(f)$-refutation, we think that a propositional example is better to illustrate the rule stated above. A more detailed first-order example will be presented in a future section. In all examples shown, f is the standard selection function.

Example 1 A modal $SLD(f)$-refutation.

Modal Definite Set S:

Facts of the Initial Scenario	Specification
1. p	4. $[\alpha]q \leftarrow p, s$
2. r	5. $[\beta]s \leftarrow r$
3. t	6. $[\beta]p \leftarrow t$

A modal SLD(f)-refutation from $S \cup \{\leftarrow [\beta][\alpha]q\}$:

1.	r	
2.	t	
3.	$[\alpha]q \leftarrow p, s$	
4.	$[\beta]s \leftarrow r$	
5.	$[\beta]p \leftarrow t$	
6.	$\leftarrow [\beta][\alpha]q$	
7.	$\leftarrow [\beta]p, [\beta]s$	RED(3)
8.	$\leftarrow t, [\beta]s$	RED(5)
9.	$\leftarrow [\beta]s$	RED(2)
10.	$\leftarrow r$	RED(4)
11.	$\square$	RED(1)

3.2 Modal f-extension rule

With the modal f-reduction rule just defined it is possible to prove properties of specific scenarios, i.e., given a scenario and a property we could say if that property holds in that scenario. But as far as it is concerned to the planning problem it would be more interesting if we could state a property and then find out a scenario in which it holds. In order to make this possible it is necessary to include a new rule in the formalism, to be called the f-extension rule.

Definition 10 Modal f-extension rule. Let G be a goal clause, D a modal (or non-modal) clause and ψ a renaming substitution to D in presence of G. If G is

$$\leftarrow g_1, g_2, \ldots, g_n$$

and

$$f(G) = g_i = [\![\alpha]\!]^k q \quad (k \geq 0)$$

and $D\psi$ is

$$[\![\beta]\!]^j [\![\gamma]\!]^k q' \leftarrow a_1, a_2, \ldots, a_m \quad (j > 0, k \geq 0)$$

and there exists a mgu θ of $\{[\![\alpha]\!]^k q, [\![\gamma]\!]^k q'\}$ then the application of a modal f-extension of G by D results in a new goal clause

$$G' = \leftarrow \ [\![\beta]\!]^j g_1, [\![\beta]\!]^j g_2, \ldots, [\![\beta]\!]^j g_{i-1}, a_1, a_2, \ldots, a_m, [\![\beta]\!]^j g_{i+1}, \ldots, [\![\beta]\!]^j g_n.$$

The sequence $[\![\beta]\!]^j$ is called the *sequence of extensions* up to G'.

The definitions of modal deduction and modal refutation are now changed to accommodate the new rule.

Definition 11 Generic modal SLD(f)-deduction. Let f be a selection function, S a modal quasi-definite set and G the goal clause of S. A *generic modal SLD(f)-deduction of G from S* is a sequence $d = (C_1, C_2, \ldots, C_n)$ of clauses ending in G, i.e., $C_n = G$, a sequence $A = ([\![\alpha]\!]_0, [\![\alpha]\!]_1, \ldots, [\![\alpha]\!]_{n-r})$ of action sequences, a sequence of mgu's $\theta_0, \theta_1, \ldots, \theta_{n-r}$ and $\exists r \leq n$ such that:
a) $[\![\alpha]\!]_0 = \epsilon$ and $\theta_0 = \epsilon$;
b) for all $i < r$, C_i is a modal or non-modal definite clause of S;
c) C_r is the goal clause of S; and

d) for all $i > r$, C_i is derived from C_{i-1} and C_j (for some $j < r$) via the modal f-reduction or the modal f-extension rule and

    1. If C_i is derived via modal f-reduction, then $[\![\alpha]\!]_{i-r} = ([\![\alpha]\!]_{i-r-1})\theta_{i-r}$.

    2. If C_i is derived via modal f-extension, then $[\![\alpha]\!]_{i-r} = ([\![\beta]\!]^j [\![\alpha]\!]_{i-r-1})\theta_{i-r}$, where $[\![\beta]\!]^j$ is the sequence of extension of C_i.

    3. If there exists e ($r < e < n$) such that C_e is derived from C_{e-1} and C_j, for some $j < r$ and C_j is a fact, then there doesn't exist i ($i > e$) such that C_i was derived via the modal f-extension rule.

Every time a modal f-extension is applied, the system jumps from the current state to the next one reached by the execution of the actions in the sequence of extensions.

Condition $d.3$ is imposed in order to ensure that once a literal is proven in the Initial Scenario further applications of the modal f-extension rule are not allowed. A subsequent application of a extension rule would affect soundness of PROMAL. The reason is that f-reductions with rules always keep the antecedent part of the rule used in the new goal clause. Since the rules hold in all scenarios, whenever a further f-extension is necessary it can be performed without affecting the result, because the new sequence of extensions will be applied to the whole of the previous goal clause, which includes that antecedent. On the other hand, an application of a f-reduction to a fact effectively retracts one literal of the goal clause.

Definition 12 Generic modal SLD(f)-refutation. A *generic modal SLD(f)-refutation from a quasi-definite set S* is a generic modal SLD(f)-deduction of the empty clause from S.

Finding a generic modal refutation corresponds to finding a solution to the planning problem. The sequence of actions found in the deduction of the empty clause corresponds to the reverse sequence of actions to be executed from the Initial Scenario to reach a scenario where the properties stated in the goal clause hold, i.e., a plan to the given goal.

3.3 A Modal Intuitive Notion to PROMAL

In PROMAL, the Necessitation Rule is implicitly applied over the clauses in the Specification. This is how the information about the system behaviour is extended to all of its states. The Necessitation Rule must not be applicable to the facts though, as they state information specific to the Initial Scenario.

The modal f-reduction rule is also based in Axiom K (of the modal systems):

$K:$ $\Box (p \rightarrow q) \rightarrow (\Box p \rightarrow \Box q)$

which distributes the necessity operator over implication.

Let's consider a modal f-reduction of $\leftarrow [\![\beta]\!]^j [\![\alpha]\!]^k q$ by $[\![\alpha]\!]^k q \leftarrow a_1$:

(1) By Necessitation, we have

$$[\![\beta]\!]^j ([\![\alpha]\!]^k q \leftarrow a_1)$$

(2) By Axiom K, we have

$$[\![\beta]\!]^j [\![\alpha]\!]^k q \leftarrow [\![\beta]\!]^j a_1$$

and now we can perform an *extension*[3] resulting in a new goal clause $\leftarrow [\![\beta]\!]^j a_1$.

---

[3] similar to that of SLD-Resolution

A query of the form $\leftarrow q$ in respect to the generic modal f-reduction rule, should be considered as the implicit query $\leftarrow [\![\beta]\!]^k q$, for some action sequence $[\![\beta]\!]^k$.

This rule does not contradicts our previous assumptions about clauses, since a goal clause can be considered as applicable to all scenarios.

To illustrate the above definition and the representation of a problem in our formalism we will take an example from the blocks world. In this example, the world consists of a table on which some wood blocks lay. A block may be either on the table or on top of exactly another block. Given an initial configuration of the blocks on the table, the objective is to find a sequence of actions which, when executed, changes the disposition of the blocks to a desired configuration.

The possible positions of the blocks are stated via the following predicates:

- $table(X)$ - block X is on the table
- $clear(X)$ - there is no block on top of block X
- $on(X, Y)$ - block X in on top of block Y
- $free(X)$ - block X is on the table and clear
- $dif(X, Y)$ - block X is not equal to block Y

There are two actions to change the configuration of the blocks: $[sta(X, Y)]$ - to stack block X on top of block Y, and $[uns(X, Y)]$ - to unstack the block X from top of block Y. Their pre-conditions (or enabling context) is shown below in the item *Representation of the Problem* as the antecedents of the corresponding rules. In the initial configuration, block a is on top of block b, block b is on top of block c, which is on the table. The goal is to find a sequence of actions whose execution leads the system to a state in which block b is free. The Initial and Goal configurations may be seen in Figure 2.

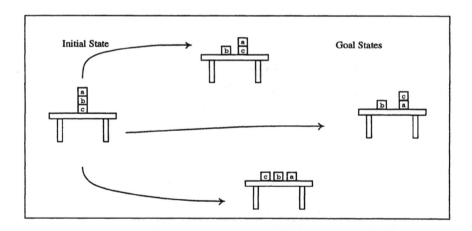

Fig. 2. Configurations for the given problem

Representation of the Problem

Initial Scenario	**Specification**

Initial Scenario

1. $dif(a, b)$
2. $dif(a, c)$
3. $dif(b, a)$
4. $dif(b, c)$
5. $dif(c, a)$
6. $dif(c, b)$
7. $clear(a)$
8. $table(c)$
9. $on(a, b)$
10. $on(b, c)$

Specification

11. $free(X) \leftarrow table(X), clear(X)$
12. $[uns(X, Y)]dif(W, Z) \leftarrow dif(W, Z)$
13. $[uns(X, Y)]table(X) \leftarrow clear(X), on(X, Y)$
14. $[uns(X, Y)]clear(Y) \leftarrow clear(X), on(X, Y)$
15. $[uns(X, Y)]clear(Z) \leftarrow clear(Z)$
16. $[uns(X, Y)]table(Z) \leftarrow table(Z)$
17. $[uns(X, Y)]on(W, Z) \leftarrow dif(W, X), on(W, Z)$
18. $[sta(X, Y)]dif(W, Z) \leftarrow dif(W, Z)$
19. $[sta(X, Y)]on(X, Y) \leftarrow dif(X, Y),$
    $\qquad table(X), clear(X), clear(Y)$
20. $[sta(X, Y)]clear(Z) \leftarrow dif(Z, Y), clear(Z)$
21. $[sta(X, Y)]table(Z) \leftarrow dif(Z, X), table(Z)$
22. $[sta(X, Y)]on(W, Z) \leftarrow on(W, Z)$

In the example below, clauses [1-9] are the clauses from the representation of the problem used in the refutation; the clause (10) is the initial goal clause; and the second line of goal clauses (11-22) represents:

1) the rule used in the derivation (modal f-reduction − RED; or modal f-extension − EXT) and which previous clause it was applied to;
2) the renaming substitution for the clause used in the derivation;
3) the mgu used in the derivation; and
4) the sequence of extension of the new goal clause.

Example 2. A generic modal SLD(f)-refutation
1. $dif(b, a)$
2. $clear(a)$
3. $on(a, b)$
4. $on(b, c)$
5. $free(X) \leftarrow table(X), clear(X)$
6. $[uns(X, Y)]table(X) \leftarrow clear(X), on(X, Y)$
7. $[uns(X, Y)]clear(Y) \leftarrow clear(X), on(X, Y)$
8. $[uns(X, Y)]clear(Z) \leftarrow clear(Z)$
9. $[uns(X, Y)]on(W, Z) \leftarrow dif(W, X), on(W, Z)$
10. $\leftarrow free(b)$
11. $\leftarrow table(b), clear(b)$

RED 5 $\quad \psi = \epsilon \qquad\qquad \theta = \{X/b\} \qquad\qquad\qquad [\![\alpha]\!]_1 = \epsilon$

12. $\leftarrow clear(b), on(b, Y), [uns(b, Y)]clear(b)$

EXT 6 $\quad \psi = \epsilon \qquad\qquad \theta = \{X/b\} \qquad\qquad\qquad [\![\alpha]\!]_2 = [uns(b, Y)]$

13. $\leftarrow clear(X), on(X, b), [uns(X, b)]on(b, Y), [uns(X, b)][uns(b, Y)]clear(b)$

EXT 6 $\quad \psi = \{Y/y_1\} \quad \theta = \{y_1/b\} \qquad\qquad [\![\alpha]\!]_3 = [uns(X, b)][uns(b, Y)]$

14. $\leftarrow on(a, b), [uns(a, b)]on(b, Y), [uns(a, b)][uns(b, Y)]clear(b)$

RED 2 $\quad \psi = \epsilon \qquad\qquad \theta = \{X/a\} \qquad\qquad\qquad [\![\alpha]\!]_4 = [uns(a, b)][uns(b, Y)]$

15. $\leftarrow [uns(a, b)]on(b, Y), [uns(a, b)][uns(b, Y)]clear(b)$

RED 3 $\quad \psi = \epsilon \qquad\qquad \theta = \epsilon \qquad\qquad\qquad\quad [\![\alpha]\!]_5 = [uns(a, b)][uns(b, Y)]$

16. $\leftarrow dif(b, a)on(b, Y), [uns(a, b)][uns(b, Y)]clear(b)$

RED 9 $\quad \psi = \{Y/y_1\} \quad \theta = \{X/a, y_1/b, W/b, Z/Y\} \quad [\![\alpha]\!]_6 = [uns(a, b)][uns(b, Y)]$

17. $\leftarrow on(b, Y), [uns(a, b)][uns(b, Y)]clear(b)$
RED 1 $\psi = \epsilon$ $\theta = \epsilon$ $[\![\alpha]\!]_7 = [uns(a, b)][uns(b, Y)]$
18. $\leftarrow [uns(a, b)][uns(b, c)]clear(b)$
RED 4 $\psi = \epsilon$ $\theta = \{Y/c\}$ $[\![\alpha]\!]_7 = [uns(a, b)][uns(b, c)]$
19. $\leftarrow [uns(a, b)]clear(b)$
RED 8 $\psi = \epsilon$ $\theta = \{X/b, Y/c, Z/b\}$ $[\![\alpha]\!]_9 = [uns(a, b)][uns(b, c)]$
20. $\leftarrow clear(a), on(a, b)$
RED 7 $\psi = \epsilon$ $\theta = \{X/a, Y/b\}$ $[\![\alpha]\!]^{10} = [uns(a, b)][uns(b, c)]$
21. $\leftarrow on(a, b)$
RED 2 $\psi = \epsilon$ $\theta = \epsilon$ $[\![\alpha]\!]_{11} = [uns(a, b)][uns(b, c)]$
22. $\square$
RED 3 $\psi = \epsilon$ $\theta = \epsilon$ $[\![\alpha]\!]_{12} = [uns(a, b)][uns(b, c)]$

The last action sequence of the refutation ($[\![\alpha]\!]_{12} = [uns(a, b)][uns(b, c)]$) corresponds to the plan found to solve the initial problem. In this case, in order to get block b free, we would have to unstack block a from top of block b and then unstack block b from top of block c. An illustration of the solution to the problem can be seen in Figure 3.

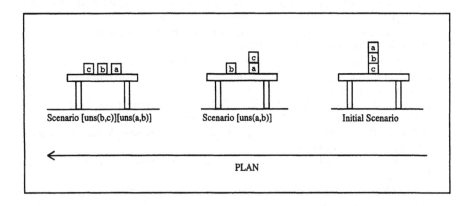

Fig. 3. A solution to the given problem

4 Conclusions

In this work we presented PROMAL, a formalism that can be used in the Planning Problem. PROMAL uses modalities to express the notion of action and can accomplish proofs of specific scenario properties as well as search scenarios where desired properties hold.

PROMAL could be regarded as an extension of SLD-Resolution. The extended language allow literals with modalities and provides an elegant and intuitive way to express the notions of change and state change.

A plan that leads the system from the Initial State to a state where the properties in the goal hold is built during the process of refutation. It is also possible to prove properties of specific scenarios, i.e., verify whether a desired property hold in a particular scenario.

We think that an analysis of ways to obtain negation in this context, in order to get more expressive power in the language and make it easier to specify problems should be very useful as well as extend the formalism so it can deal with multiple agent reasoning.

Acknowledgements

Odinaldo Rodrigues is supported by CNPq (Conselho Nacional de Desenvolvimento Científico e Tecnológico) - Grant 200347/93-4. Mario Benevides is partially supported by CNPq.

References

1. A. Colmerauer, H. Kanoui, P. Roussel, and R. Pasero. Un système de communication homme-machine en français. Technical report, Université d'Aix-Marseille, 1973. Groupe de Recherche en Intelligence Artificielle.

2. L. Fariñas del Cerro. Molog: A system that extends prolog with modal logic. *New Generation Computing*, 4:35–50, 1986.

3. R. E. Fikes and N. J. Nilsson. STRIPS: A new approach to the application of theorem proving to problem solving. In *Proceedings of 2nd IJCAI*, Imperial College, London, England, 1971.

4. R. Goldblatt. *Axiomatizing the Logic of Computer Programming*. Lecture Notes in Computer Science. Springer-Verlag, New York, Heidelberg, Berlin, 1982.

5. D. Harel. *First Order Dynamic Logic*, volume 68 of *Lectures Notes in Computer Science*. Springer-Verlag, 1979.

6. R. A. Kowalski. Predicate logic as a programming language. In *IFIP-74*, pages 569–574, 1974.

7. J. W. Lloyd. *Foundations of Logic Programming*. Symbolic Computation. Springer-Verlag, 1984.

8. T.S.E. Maibaum. A logic for the formal requirements specification of real-time / embedded systems. Technical report, Dept. of Computing, Imperial College, London, 1987.

9. Odinaldo Teixeira Rodrigues. Prolog modal de ação e revisão de crenças em conjuntos definidos. Master's thesis, COPPE - Universidade Federal do Rio de Janeiro - Brazil, 1993. In Portuguese.

10. David H. D. Warren. A system for generating plans. Technical report, Department of Artificial Intelligence, Edinburgh University, June 1974. Memo 76.

A Goal Directed Reasoning
for Semi-Normal Default Theories

Gerson Zaverucha[1]   Sheila R. M. Veloso[1,2]

[1]Programa de Engenharia de Sistemas e Computação / COPPE
[2]Departamento da Ciencia da Computação / IM
Universidade Federal do Rio de Janeiro
Caixa Postal 68511
211945-970 Rio de Janeiro, Brazil
E-mail: {gerson, sheila}@cos.ufrj.br

Abstract Determining whether a given formula holds in any extension of a Default Logic (DL) theory is called in [8] *goal directed reasoning*. Reiter [14] presented a goal-directed proof theory for normal default theories. But Reiter and Criscuolo [15] showed that semi-normal defaults were needed in DL to give priorities between defaults to eliminate anomalous extensions. Moreover, Marek and Truszczynski [11] showed that any DL theory can be represented as a semi-normal default theory. Etherington [4, 5] developed a forward procedure for constructing default extensions of a subclass of semi-normal default theories. Since a theory may have many extensions, it seems wasteful to compute an entire extension when one is only concerned with goal directed reasoning. Moreover, the given formula may not be contained in the currently computed extension.This paper presents a goal-directed proof theory for semi-normal default theories. A proof of soundness is presented for plain ordered network semi-normal default theories. We show that if there is a proof of a given formula, then an extension containing this formula can be constructed by Etherington's procedure. We also present a goal-directed proof procedure to compute a default proof.

1 Introduction

Reiter's [14] Default Logic (DL) is one of the most used and investigated approaches for the formalization of nonmonotonic reasoning. However its proof theory has been developed only for some special theories. As defined by Kautz and Selman [8], determining whether a given formula holds in any extension of a default theory is called *goal directed reasoning*. Originally, Reiter [14] presented a goal-directed proof theory for normal default theories. But Reiter and Criscuolo [15] showed that semi-normal defaults were needed in DL to give priorities between defaults to eliminate anomalous extensions. Moreover, Marek and Truszczynski [11] showed that any DL theory can be represented as a semi-normal default theory. Then, Etherington [4, 5] developed a forward procedure for constructing default extensions of finite, ordered network default theories.

As pointed out by Besnard [3] and by Antoniou et al [1], the existence of extensions for semi-normal default theories can only be guaranteed if they are plain with a modified order definition on them. Other procedures for constructing default extensions were also developed by Zhang and Marek [20], Marek and Truszczynski [11], Junker and Konolige [7], Schwind and Risch [17] and Antoniou et al [2]. Goal-directed proof theories have been developed only for semi-monotonic default theories (see Reiter [15], Poole [13-14], Lukasziewicz [9, 10], Guerreiro et al [6] and Rothschild and Schaub [16]).

This paper presents a goal-directed proof theory for semi-normal default theories. A proof of soundness is presented for plain ordered network semi-normal default theories. We show that if there is a proof of a given formula, then an extension containing this formula can be constructed by Etherington's procedure. As Etherington, we also conjecture that the proof theory presented is sound for plain arbitrary ordered semi-normal default theories.

The motivation for the proof theory presented here was taken from the one originally given for normal default theories by Reiter. However, most of the difficulty in the present case comes from the lack of semi-monotonicity so one has to ensure that once a default is applied, the conditions required for doing so remain satisfied when other defaults are also applied. Since a theory may have many extensions, it seems wasteful to compute an entire extension when one is only concerned with goal directed reasoning. Moreover, the given formula may not be contained in the currently computed extension.

We also present a goal-directed proof procedure to compute a default proof. Being goal directed, this proof procedure does not require the construction of extensions. Although Kautz and Selman [8] have shown that backwards procedures are not necessarily more efficient than forward ones, we believe that they are, at least, more intuitive and elegant.

In the next section we first give some background definitions, present Etherington's procedure for constructing extensions and also Reiter's proof theory. In section 3, we present our goal-directed proof theory, its soundness proof, some examples and a goal-directed proof procedure to compute a default proof. Finally, in section 4 we give some conclusions.

2 Background

In this section we present some background definitions, Etherington's procedure for constructing extensions and also Reiter's proof theory.

Definition 2.1. A default rule is *semi-normal* if it is of the form $\alpha : \beta \wedge \gamma \,/\, \gamma$. A default theory (W, D) is *semi-normal* iff all defaults in D are semi-normal. ◆

Definition 2.2. A *clausal* default theory (W, D) is a default theory in which all formulas occurring in W and D are clausal formulas (i.e. quantifier-free formulas in conjunctive normal form). ◆

Definition 2.3 (Etherington's order $\leq$ and $<$) Let $\Delta = (W,D)$ be a closed, semi-normal default theory. Without loss of generality, assume all formulae are in clausal form. The partial relations $\leq$ and $<$ on literals are defined as follows:

(1) If $\alpha \in W$ then $\alpha = (\alpha_1 \vee ... \vee \alpha_n)$, for some $n \geq 1$.

For all $\alpha_i, \alpha_j \in \{\alpha_1,...,\alpha_n\}$, if $\alpha_i \neq \alpha_j$, let $\neg \alpha_i \leq \alpha_j$.

(2) If $\delta \in D$, then $\delta = (\alpha: \beta \wedge \gamma) \,/\, \beta$. Let $\alpha_1,...,\alpha_r,\ \beta_1,..,\beta_s$, and $\gamma_1, ...,\gamma_l$ be the literals of the clausal forms of α, β and γ, respectively. Then:

 (i) If $\alpha_i \in \{\alpha_1,...,\alpha_r\}$ and $\beta_j \in \{\beta_1, ..,\beta_s\}$, let $\alpha_i \leq \beta_j$.

 (ii) If $\gamma_i \in \{\gamma_1 \cdots \gamma_l\}$, $\beta_j \in \{\beta_1, ..,\beta_s\}$ and $\gamma_i \notin \{\beta_1, ..,\beta_s\}$, let $\neg \gamma_i < \beta_j$.

 (iii) Also, $\beta = \beta_1 \wedge ... \wedge \beta_m$, for some $m \geq 1$.

 For each $i \leq m$, $\beta i = (\beta_{i,1} \vee .. \vee \beta_{i,mi})$ where $mi \geq 1$.

 Thus if $\beta_{i,j}, \beta_{i,k} \in \{\beta_{i,1}, ..., \beta_{m,mm}\}$ and $\beta_{i,j} \neq \beta_{i,k}$, let $\neg \beta_{i,j} \leq \beta_{i,k}$.

(3) the relations $\leq$ and $<$ are transitive and if $\alpha < \beta$ and $\beta \leq \gamma$ or $\alpha \leq \beta$ and $\beta < \gamma$ then $\alpha < \gamma$. ◆

Definition 2.4 (Etherington's order). A semi-normal default theory is *ordered* iff there is no literal α such that $\alpha < \alpha$. ◆

As shown first by Besnard [3] and later by Antoniou et al [1], the existence of extensions cannot be guaranteed for finite ordered semi-normal default theories.

Definition 2.5 (Antoniou et al [1] order). Given a clausal, semi-normal default theory T, define relations $<<$ and $\underline{<<}$ on the literal of T just like $<$ and $\leq$ as in definition 2.3, with the only difference that condition 2ii) is deleted. ◆

Definition 2.6 (Besnard[3] plain theories). A semi-normal default theory (W,D) is *plain* if it is clausal, propositional and D is finite. ♦

Theorem 2.1 (Etherington-Besnard-Antoniou et al's existence of extensions). A semi-normal plain ordered default theory has at least one extension. ♦

Definition 2.7 Let $\delta = (\alpha: \beta / \gamma)$ then Prereq(δ) is α, Justif(δ) is β and Conseq(δ) is γ. Similarly, if T is a set of defaults then Prereq(T) = $\wedge$\{Prereq(d) / d $\in$ T\}, Justif(T) = $\wedge$\{Justif(d) / d $\in$ T\} and Conseq(T) = $\cup$\{ Conseq(d) / d $\in$ T\}. If X is a set of sentences, Consist(X) means that X is consistent.

Definition 2.8 (Etherington's procedure of constructing default extensions)
$H_0 := W$;   j:=1;
repeat

        j := j+1; $h_0 := W$; $GD_0 := \emptyset$;   i:=0;
      repeat

          $D_i := \{(\alpha: \beta / \gamma) \in D \mid h_i \vdash \alpha, h_i \not\vdash \neg \beta, H_{j-1} \not\vdash \neg\beta\}$;
          if $\neg$null (D_i - GD_i) **then**
               choose δ from (D_i - GD_i);
               $GD_{i+1} := GD_i \cup \{\delta\}$;
               $h_{i+1} := h_i \cup$ Conseq(δ) ;
          end if;
          i:= i+1;
        until null (D_{i-1} - GD_{i-1});
        $H_j := h_{i-1}$;
until $H_j = H_{j-1}$ ♦

Definition 2.9 (Etherington's network default theory). A default theory Δ = (W,D) is a *network* theory iff it satisfies the following conditions:
(i) W contains only
    a) literal and
    b) disjuncts of the form $(\alpha \vee \beta)$ where α and β are literals
(ii) D contains only normal or semi-normal defaults of the form $(\alpha: \beta / \beta)$ or $(\alpha: \beta \wedge \gamma_1 \wedge ... \wedge \gamma_n / \beta)$ where α, β and γ_i are literals. ♦

Theorem 2.2 (Convergence). For plain, ordered, network default theories, Etherington's procedure always converges on an extension. ♦

A conjecture that this theorem can also be generalized for arbitrary ordered semi-normal theories is founded in Etherington [4, 5] where a more restrictive definition of D_i's are given.

We now present Reiter's [14] proof theory for closed normal default theories.

Definition 2.10 (Reiter's default proof theory). Given a closed normal default theory Δ = (W, D) and a sentence G, a finite sequence T_0, ...,T_n (n $\geq$ 0) of finite subsets of D, is *a default proof of G from Δ* iff

(i) W $\cup$ Conseq(T_0) $\vdash$ G
(ii) for $0 \leq i \leq n$

    W $\cup$ Conseq(T_i) $\vdash \bigwedge$(Prereq(T_{i-1}))

(iii) $T_n = \emptyset$.
(iv) Consist (W $\cup$ \{Conseq(T_i)| $0 \leq i \leq n$\}). ♦

3 A Goal-Directed Reasoning For Semi-normal Default Theories

The proof theory presented here is similar to the one proposed by Reiter in definition 2.10. It generates a sequence of default sets, the prerequisite of each being proved by the consequents of the previously generated ones. The difference here is that, due to the lack of semi-monotonicity, the consistency check is done globally, for each generated set, having to take into account the whole set of defaults D, instead of locally, as in the case of normal defaults, with just the set of defaults used in the proof.

Definition 3.1 Let $\Delta = (W,D)$ be a closed semi-normal default theory, X be a finite set of sentences, T and Γ be finite sets of closed defaults and α be a sentence. Define:

a) Prove(X, α,T, Γ) $\leftrightarrow$ Consist (X $\cup$ Conseq(T $\cup$ Γ)) $\wedge$

$$(X \cup Conseq(T) \vdash \alpha) \wedge Applic(X, T, T \cup \Gamma)$$

b) Applic(X, T, Γ) $\leftrightarrow$ $\exists$ T' $\subseteq$ D (Prove(X, Prereq(T), T', Γ) $\wedge$

$$\neg Block(X, T, T \cup \Gamma)), \text{ if } T \neq \emptyset$$

True, if $T = \emptyset$

c) $\neg$Block(X, T, Γ) $\leftrightarrow$ $\forall$S $\subseteq$ D ((Consist(X $\cup$ Conseq(T $\cup$ Γ $\cup$ S) $\wedge$

$$X \cup Conseq(T \cup \Gamma \cup S) \vdash \neg Justif(T))$$

$$\rightarrow \neg Applic(X \cup Conseq(\Gamma), S, \Gamma)) \qquad \blacklozenge$$

The intended meaning of each of these meta-predicates is the following:

• Prove(X, α, T, Γ) means that α is a logical consequence of X $\cup$ Conseq(T), where T is a set of defaults which can be applied from X in the presence of T $\cup$ Γ, such that X $\cup$ Conseq(T $\cup$ Γ) is consistent.

• Applic(X, T, Γ) means that the defaults in the set T are applicable in the context where the sentences in X are taken as true and the defaults in Γ had already been applied. (T is applicable from X in the presence of Γ)

• $\neg$Block(X, T, Γ) means that the defaults in T can not be blocked in the context of X in the presence of Γ, i.e. any set of defaults S that would block defaults in T by having $\neg$Justif(T) as a logical consequence of X and the consequents of S $\cup$ T $\cup$ Γ can not be applied in the context of X $\cup$ Conseq(Γ) in the presence of Γ.

Definition 3.2 Given a closed semi-normal default theory $\Delta = (W, D)$ and a sentence G, a finite sequence T_0, ...,T_n ($n \geq 0$) of finite subsets of D, is *a goal directed default proof of G from Δ* iff

(i) Prove(W, G, T_0, $\emptyset$);

(ii) $T_1...T_{n-1}$, are obtained from the definition of Prove(W, G, T_0, $\emptyset$) such that for $0 \leq i \leq n$:

Applic(W, T_i, $\cup$ {T_j | $0 \leq j \leq i$}) and $\neg$Block(W, T_i, $\cup$ {T_j | $0 \leq j \leq n$});

(iii) $T_n = \emptyset$.

We will write $\Delta \vdash_{DL} G$ iff there is a goal directed default proof of G from Δ. Let $P_G = T_0,...,T_n$ be the goal directed default proof of G from Δ. Then DS(P_G) = $\cup$ {T_j/ $0 \leq j \leq n$}, is called the *default support* of P_G. $\blacklozenge$

Example 3.1 Consider $\Delta = (\emptyset, D)$, with D={d_1,d_2,d_3,d_4,d_5} where:

$d_1 = : x / x$

$d_2 = : y \wedge \neg z / y$

$d_3 = u : \neg t / \neg t$

$d_4 = x: z \wedge t / z$

$d_5 = y : u / u$

We show that $\Delta \vdash_{DL} z$, with $T_0 = \{d_4\}$, $T_1 = \{d_1\}$ and $T_2 = \emptyset$.

We have to show

1) Prove($\emptyset$, z, {d4}, $\emptyset$) (definition 3.2 (i))

From definition 3.1 a), we must have:

2a) Consist ($\emptyset$ $\cup$ Conseq({d4} $\cup$ $\emptyset$))

2b) ($\emptyset$ $\cup$ Conseq({d4}) $\vdash$ z)

2c) Applic($\emptyset$, {d$_4$}, {d4} $\cup$ $\emptyset$)

Since 2a) and 2b) are satisfied one must show 2c), which reduces to

3) Prove($\emptyset$, Prereq({d$_4$}), {d$_1$}, {d$_4$})

4) $\neg$Block($\emptyset$, {d$_4$}, {d$_4$,d$_1$})

Since 3) is easily verified, one must show 4). Applying definition 3.1c) the only possible choice for S to satisfy the antecedent of 4) is S={d$_3$}. So the condition

5)$\neg$Applic(Conseq({d$_1$, d$_4$}), {d$_3$}, {d$_1$, d$_4$}) has to be tested.

From definition 3.1b) and 3.1c) this reduces to verify one of the following, with X, T and Γ properly instantiated:

6) for each T'$\subseteq$ D, $\neg$Prove(X, Prereq(T), T, Γ)

7) Block(X, T, T $\cup$ Γ)

So let T'={d$_5$}. To check 6), applying definition 3.1a) one of the following conditions must be satisfied with X, T and Γ properly instantiated::

8a) $\neg$Consist(X $\cup$ Conseq(T $\cup$ Γ)

8b) W $\cup$ Conseq(T) $\not\vdash$ Prereq(T)

8c) $\neg$Applic(X, T, T $\cup$ Γ)

Since conditions 8a) and 8b) fail, one must verify 8c) instantiated:

9)$\neg$Applic(Conseq({d$_1$, d$_4$}), {d$_5$ }, {d$_1$, d$_4$, d$_5$})

which reduces to showing 6) or 7) again.

So, let T' = {d$_2$}. Again, conditions 8a) and 8b) fail, so one must verify 8c) instantiated:

10) $\neg$Applic(Conseq({d$_1$, d$_4$, d$_5$}), {d$_2$} {d$_1$, d$_4$, d$_5$})

Since 6) does not hold, as

Prove(Conseq({d$_1$, d$_4$, d$_5$, d$_2$}), Prereq ({d$_2$}), $\emptyset$, {d$_1$, d$_4$, d$_5$, d$_2$})

is verified, one must test 7) instantiated:

11) Block(Conseq({d$_1$, d$_4$, d$_5$}),{d$_2$}, {d$_1$, d$_4$, d$_5$, d$_2$})

In definition 3.1c) let S' = $\emptyset$, which satifies the following conditions:

Consist(Conseq{d$_1$, d$_4$, d$_5$, d$_2$}

Conseq({d$_1$, d$_4$, d$_5$, d$_2$}) $\vdash$ $\neg$Justif({d$_2$}) and

Applic(Conseq({d$_1$, d$_4$, d$_5$, d$_2$}), $\emptyset$, {d$_1$, d$_4$, d$_5$, d$_2$})

So, 11) is satisfied, which implies that 10) holds. Since there are no more choices for T' condition 9) holds. Hence condition 5) is verified. Since there are no more choices for S, 4) is verified. So conditions 2c) and 1) are also satisfied.

It remains to be shown condition ii) from definition 3.2. That is:

Applic($\emptyset$, {d$_4$},{d$_4$})

Applic($\emptyset$, {d$_1$},{d$_4$, d$_1$}) and

$\neg$Block($\emptyset$, {d$_1$}, {d$_4$,d$_1$}).

They are all easily verified. Also note that T$_0$ ={d$_2$}, T$_1$= $\emptyset$ is not a default proof for y for. when verifying $\neg$Block($\emptyset$, {d$_2$}, {d$_2$}), letting S = {d$_4$} = { x:(z $\wedge$ t) / z}, one gets :

Consist(Conseq({d$_2$, d$_4$}),

Conseq({d$_2$, d$_4$} $\vdash$ $\neg$Justif(d$_2$) and

Applic(Conseq({d$_2$}),d$_4$, {d$_2$}),.

which makes $\neg$Block($\emptyset$, {d$_2$}, {d$_2$}) false. $\blacklozenge$

Example 3.2 Consider Δ = ($\emptyset$, D), where D={d$_1$,d$_2$,d$_3$} with:

d$_1$ = : p $\wedge$ $\neg$r /$\neg$r

d$_2$ = : q $\wedge$ $\neg$p /$\neg$p

d$_3$ = : r $\wedge$ $\neg$q /$\neg$q

The theory Δ has no extension and one can show that Δ $\not\vdash$ Conseq(d$_i$), for i=1, 2, 3. To illustrate this, take i=2.

Since all defaults in D have no pre-requisite, the only part of the predicate Applic which has to be verified is the one that concerns to ¬Block. One possible candidate to $T_0, ..., T_n$ would start with $T_0 = \{d_2\}$ and check whether

a)Prove($\emptyset$, ¬p, T_0, $\emptyset$) holds, which reduces to verifying whether

a')¬Block($\emptyset$, T_0, T_0) holds.

The only possible choice for S that satisfies the antecedent of a') is S={d_3}. For S={d_3} one has to check:

b)¬Applic(Conseq (T_0), S, T_0)

To verify b) one has to verify

c)Block(Conseq (T_0), S, $T_0 \cup$ S),

i. e. that there exists S' such that

i) Consist(Conseq($T_0 \cup$ S $\cup$ S'),

ii) Conseq(S $\cup$ $T_0 \cup$ S') $\vdash$ ¬Justif(S) and

iii) Applic(Conseq ($T_0 \cup$ S), S', $T_0 \cup$ S)

Take S'={d_1}, which is the only possible candidate to satisfy i) and ii). To verify iii) one has to check:

d)¬Block (Conseq ($T_0 \cup$ S), S', $T_0 \cup$ S $\cup$S').

The only choice for S that satisfies the antecedent of d) is S" = {d_2}. It is easy to verify that Applic(Conseq($T_0 \cup$ S $\cup$ S'), S",$T_0 \cup$ S $\cup$ S') holds. Take $S_1=\emptyset$ when checking ¬Block (Conseq ($T_0 \cup$ S $\cup$S'), S", $T_0 \cup$ S $\cup$S' $\cup$ S").

This leads one to conclude that d) does not hold, which implies that iii) is false, hence c) also does not hold. Therefore b) and a) are both false. ♦

Example 3.3 Consider $\Delta = (W, D)$, where W = {a, b} and D = {d_1, d_2, d_3} as in example 2.

The theory Δ has no extension but $T_0 = \emptyset$ is a goal directed default proof for any $\alpha \in$ Th(W). That is why we require the guarantee of existence of extensions. ♦

Remark 3.1 If we apply our proof theory to theories satisfying the strong existence property, as defined by Guerreiro et al.[6] (i.e. Th(W) is a subset of every default extension, which always exists), then we could assert its soundness.♦

Theorem 3.1 (Soundness). Let $\Delta = (W,D)$ a plain ordered network closed semi-normal default theory and G a sentence. If $\Delta \vdash_{DL} G$, then there exists a default extension E of Δ so that $G \in E$.

Proof From $\Delta \vdash_{DL} G$, let $P_G = T_0,...,T_n$ be the goal directed default proof of G from Δ. In Etherington's algorithm, definition 2.8, for j=1, all defaults in P_G can always be in some D_i and can be chosen to define a h_i, choosing first, all defaults in T_{n-1}, then the defaults in T_{n-2}, until all defaults in T_0 are chosen, in this order. Some other defaults S which does not occur in DS(P_G), can be chosen to construct H_1.

Suppose there is $S \in D_i$ such that W $\cup$ Conseq(DS(P_G) $\cup$ S) $\vdash \neg$ Justif(T_k) for some k, $0 \le k \le n$, i.e., for some, $d \in T_k$, W $\cup$ Conseq(DS(P_G) $\cup$ S) $\vdash$ ¬Justif(d). Thus, for j= 2, T_k would not be contained in H_2. However, since ¬Block(W, T_i, DS(P_G)) holds, one has Applic(W $\cup$ Conseq(DS(P_G)), S, DS(P_G)), i.e. we have one of the following:

a) for all $\theta \subseteq D$, we have one of the following:

(i) ¬ Consist(W $\cup$ Conseq(DS(P_G) $\cup$ θ);

(ii) W $\cup$ Conseq(DS(P_G) $\cup$ θ) $\not\vdash$ Prereq(S);

(iii) ¬ Applic(W $\cup$ Conseq(DS(P_G)), θ, DS(P_G) $\cup$ θ).

b) Block(W $\cup$ Conseq(T), S, DS(P_G)).

Case (a) is impossible since with $\theta = \emptyset$, we have:

i') Consist(W $\cup$ Conseq(DS(P_G)) and

ii') W $\cup$ Conseq(DS(P_G)) $\vdash$ Prereq(S) and

iii') Applic(W ∪ Conseq(DS(P_G)), ∅ , DS(P_G)).

Thus case b) holds, i.e., there exists S' such that

Applic(W ∪ Conseq(DS(P_G)), S', T) holds.

So, a proof π for Prereq(S') will be generated.

Thus, in lieu of choosing S in "**choose δ from** $(D_i - GD_i)$", pick those defaults which occur in π and then choose S'. In this way when defining D_i after these choices $S \not\subseteq D_i$ (since Block(W ∪ Conseq(DS(P_G)), S, DS(P_G)) holds), which guarantees that Conseq(T_k) $\subseteq H_2$.

The same argument can be used when obtaining all other H_j's.

By the convergence theorem 2.2, Etherington's procedure converges to an extension E of Δ, and by the reasons given above Conseq(DS(P_G)) $\subseteq$ E.

Hence, $G \in E$, as W ∪ Conseq(T_0) $\vdash$ G. ♦

We now present a goal directed proof procedure.

Definition 3.3 Given a closed semi-normal default theory $\Delta = (W, D)$ and a sentence G, a goal directed default proof of G from Δ is obtained from the instantiation of the output parameter UD (used defaults) in the following procedure:

GDP(W, D, G, UD) ← Pr(W, D, G, ∅, UD);

Pr(X, D, α, UD', UD) ← ∃ T ⊆ D (Consist (X ∪ Conseq(T ∪ UD')) ∧
        X ∪ Conseq(T) ⊢ α) ∧ Appl(X, D, T, T ∪ UD', UD))

¬Pr(X, D, α, UD', UD) ← ∀ T ⊆ D (¬Consist (X ∪ Conseq(T ∪ UD')) ∨
        (X ∪ Conseq(T) ⊬ α) ∨
        ¬Appl(X, D, T, T ∪ UD', UD))

Appl(X, D, ∅, UD, UD) ← True
Appl(X, D, T, UD', UD) ← Pr(X, D, Prereq(T), UD', UD) ∧
        ¬Blk(X ∪ Conseq(UD), D, T, UD,UD)
¬Appl(X, D, T, UD', UD) ← ¬Pr(X, D, Prereq(T), UD', UD) ∨
        Blk(X ∪ Conseq(UD), D, T, UD,UD)

¬Blk(X, D, T, UD', UD) ← ∀S ⊆ D ((Consist(X ∪ Conseq(T ∪ UD' ∪ S) ∧
        X ∪ Conseq(T ∪ UD' ∪ S) ⊢ ¬Justif(T))
        → ¬ Appl(X ∪ Conseq(UD'), D, S, UD, UD))

Blk(X, D, T, UD', UD) ← ∃S ⊆ D ((Consist(X ∪ Conseq(T ∪ UD' ∪ S) ∧
        X ∪ Conseq(T ∪ UD' ∪ S) ⊢ ¬Justif(T)) ∧
        Appl(X ∪ Conseq(UD'), D, S, UD, UD)) ♦

The intended meaning of each of these meta-predicates is the following:

• GDP(W, D, G, UD) asks whether G has a goal-directed default proof UD from (W, D).

• Pr(X, D, α, UD', UD) means that there exists a set of defaults T such that α is a logical consequence of X ∪ Conseq(T), which can be applied from X in the presence of T ∪ UD', such that X ∪ Conseq(T ∪ UD') is consistent.

• Appl(X, D, T, UD', UD) means that the defaults in the set T are applicable in the context where the sentences in X are taken as true and the defaults in UD had already been applied. (T is applicable from X in the presence of UD)

• ¬Block(X, D, T, UD', UD) means that the defaults in T can not be blocked in the context of X in the presence of UD, i.e. any set of defaults S that would block defaults in T by having ¬Justif(T) as a logical consequence of X and the consequents of S ∪ T ∪ UD' can not be applied in the context of X ∪ Conseq(UD') in the presence of UD.

The proof procedure was described to be implemented with a depth-first search strategy.

4 Conclusions

We have presented a goal-directed proof theory for semi-normal default theories. Its motivation was taken from the one originally given by Reiter for normal default theories. However, most of the difficulty in the present case comes from the lack of semi-monotonicity. So one has to ensure that once a default is applied, the conditions required for doing so remain satisfied when other defaults are also applied.

The argument of the proof theory's soundness uses Etherington's procedure to construct an extension containing all consequents of the defaults given by the proof theory. Similarly to Etherington, we also conjecture that the proof theory presented is sound for plain arbitrary ordered semi-normal default theories. Moreover, if we apply our proof theory to default theories satisfying the strong existence property then we could assert its soundness.

We have also presented a goal-directed proof procedure to compute a default proof. Since a theory may have many extensions, it seems wasteful to compute an entire extension when one is only concerned with goal-directed reasoning. Moreover, the given formula may not be contained in the currently computed extension.[1]

As future works, we would like to adapt this work to provide a proof-theory for the family of Prioritized Default Logics developed in [18, 19], to implement our proof procedure and to show its correctness.

Acknowledgements

The authors are partially financially supported by the Brazilian National Research Council (CNPq) grant numbers 30.0282/90-7 and. 35.0160/93-7, respectively.

References

[1] Antoniou, G. , Langetepe, E. and Sperschneider, V. 1993. New proofs in default logic theory. Unpublished draft.

[2] Antoniou, G. , Langetepe, E. and Sperschneider, V. 1993. Computing extensions of default logic- preliminary report. LPAR-93.

[3] Barback, M. D., Lobo, J. 1994. A Resolution-based Procedure for Default Theories with Extensions. Proceedings of the Workshop W5 (with ICLP-94) on Nonmonotonic Extensions of Logic Programming: Theory, Implementation and Applications, S. Margherita Ligure, Italy.

[3] Besnard, P. 1989. An introduction to default logic. Springer Verlag.

[4] Etherington, D. W. 1988. Reasoning with Incomplete Information, Pitman, London.

[5] Etherington, D.W. 1987. Formalizing Nonmonotonic Reasoning Systems. Artificial Intelligence 31:41-85.

[6] Guerreiro, R. A. T., Casanova, M. A. and Hemerly, A. S. 1990. Contributions to a Proof Theory for Generic Defaults, Proc. 9th European Conference on Artificial Intelligence, Stockholm, Sweden.

[7] Junker, U. and Konolige, K. 1990. Computing the extensions of autoepistemic and default logic with a TMS. In Proc. of AAAI-90.

[8] Kautz, H. A., Selman, B. 1989. Hard Problems for Simple Default Logics. Proc 1st International Conference on Principles of Knowledge Representation and reasoning,

---

[1]The authors became aware after finishing this paper that a resolution-based procedure was presented in [3]. It can be viewed as an implementation of our proof theory, although its soundness and completeness is defined for a larger class of semi-normal theories.

Toronto, Ontario, Canada.

[9] Lukasziewicz, W. 1990. Nonmonotonic Reasoning: formalization of commonsense reasoning. Ellis Horwood.

[10] Lukasziewicz, W. 1988. Considerations on Default Logic. Computational Intelligence, 4, pp 1-16.

[11] Marek, W., Truszczynski, M.: Nonmonotonic logic: context dependent reasoning. Springer Verlag 1993.

[12] Poole, D. L. 1987. A Logical Framework for Default Reasoning. Artificial Intelligence, 36, pp 27-47.

[13] Poole, D. L. Goebel, R. and Aleluinas, R. 1987. Theorist: a logic reasoning system for defaults and diagnosis. N. Cercone and G. McCalla (eds). The Knowledge Frontier: Essays in the representation of Knowledge, Springer Verlag, New York, pp 331-352.

[14] Reiter, R. 1980. A Logic for Default Reasoning. Artificial Intelligence, 13, pp. 81-132.

[15] R. Reiter, G. Criscuolo: Some representational issues in default reasoning. J. Computers and Maths. with Appls. 9 (1983) 1-13.

[16] Rothschild, A. and Schaub, T. 1993. A computational approach to default logics. Proc. of Dutch / German Workshop on Nonmonotonic Reasoning Techniques and Their Applications, eds. Brewka, G and Witteveen, C.

[17] Schwind, C. B. and Risch, V. 1991. A tableaux-based characterization for default logic. In R. Kruse, editor, Proc. of European Conference on Symbolic and Quantitative Approaches to Uncertainty, pp. 310-317, Springer Verlag.

[18].G. Zaverucha: A Prioritized Contextual Default Logic: Curing Anomalous Extensions with a Simple Abnormality Default Theory. In:Bernhard Nebel and Leonie Dreschler-Fischer, eds. Proc. KI-94, Saarbrucken, Germany, LNAI 861 (Springer 1994) 260-271.

[19].G. Zaverucha: On Cumulative Default Logic With Filters. Submitted (also Technical Report ES-321/94, COPPE/ UFRJ).

[20] Zhang, A. and Marek, W. 1990. On the classification and existence of structures in default logic. Fundamenta Informaticae 8(4), pp. 485-499.

Towards New Learning Strategies
in Intelligent Tutoring Systems

Esma Aïmeur   Claude Frasson   Carmen Alexe

Université de Montréal
Département d'informatique et de recherche opérationnelle
2920 Chemin de la Tour
Montréal, H3C 3J7, Québec, Canada
E-mail : {aimeur, frasson, alexe} @iro.umontreal.ca
Tel : 1-514-343 7019
Fax : 1-514-343 5834

Abstract. Co-operative tutoring systems replace the prescriptive approach developed by traditional intelligent tutoring systems with a constructive one based on the use of the computer as a way to exchange, control and build knowledge. This paper proposes two new learning strategies, learning by disturbing and learning by co-teaching, that extend the spectrum of possibilities in terms of co-operation and place the learner into a higher degree of abstraction. Learning by disturbing method allows to check the ability of the learner to distinguish between wrong and correct solutions. Learning by co-teaching provides an example of discussions between the teacher and the co-teacher that is useful for inducing correct solutions presented in a pedagogical form. Co-operation can be improved using elicitation techniques that can serve to extract learner's knowledge which can be further compared with the expert solution in order to identify his knowledge level. These techniques strengthen the efficiency of the learning strategies and serve as a basis for developing tutoring systems or learning environments including their co-operative aspects. We show how these strategies can be dynamically selected in an architecture of an intelligent tutoring system in which the knowledge level of the learner is frequently evaluated. We give an example of eliciting dialogues in a medical environment.

keywords : Intelligent tutoring systems, Elicitation, Troublemaker, Co-teacher, Learning strategy, Co-operative system.

1 INTRODUCTION

Traditional Intelligent Tutoring Systems (ITS) have been designed for adapting learning of a particular domain to individual student. Most ITS are composed by a tutor which uses four components: domain expertise, pedagogical expertise, student model and interface. The domain expertise (often called curriculum) is a knowledge base of information about the domain to be taught. The pedagogical expertise provides teaching techniques to be utilized by the tutor. The student model provides an image of the state of the student (knowledge, reasoning and possibly misconceptions), which is dynamically updated as the student progresses through tutoring sessions. The interface enables communication between the student and the tutor. Since their appearance at the beginning of the eighties, ITS have evolved in the same vein as AI approaches, aiming to reproduce the behavior of a competent human tutor who adapts his teaching techniques according to the student's learning profile. Thus the resulting simulated tutor intends to provide the learner with individual treatment taking into account both his/her previous knowledge and how new knowledge is acquired. In such a prescriptive approach the training control is entirely assumed by the tutor.

Various teaching techniques have been explored in order to facilitate knowledge acquisition by the learner: learning by example, by doing, by playing, by deduction, by induction, by abduction, etc. The resulting systems were generally heavy to control and not efficient from a pedagogical point of view. They were also complex to build, taking into account on one hand the multiplicity of expertise to incorporate, and on the other the difficult handling of the student model with its large amount of data and relationships (Self, 1988). A drawback of most of the ITS lies in their prescriptive approach based on centralized decision and coaching.

Since the mid of the eighties, the tutor-tutee model has been challenged. J. Self and his colleagues first argued that the role played by the computer as an authorized teacher for transmitting certified knowledge should be de-emphasized. They suggested (Gilmore & Self, 1988) that the computer can cooperate with the student in the learning process and so facilitate knowledge acquisition through interactions under learner's control. An extension of this approach was presented by Chan (Chan & Baskin, 1990) with the learning companion who simulates the behavior of a second learner (the companion) who would learn together with the human learner. Various alternatives to this co-operative approach were then conceived leading more recently (Palthepu et al, 1991, Van Lehn et al, 1994) to an inverted model of ITS called "learning by teaching" in which the learner could teach the learning companion by giving explanations. This method is important in the sense that it strengthens the knowledge acquisition process forcing the learner to structure the knowledge. An explanation of this principle derived from the self-explanation effect (Chi et al, 1989) was given in (Frasson & Kaltenbach, 1993).

In the meantime, the domain of expert systems was also evolving towards more efficient techniques of knowledge acquisition from the expert. Various methods were defined and particularly elicitation techniques (Firlej & Hellens, 1991) which consist of obtaining explanations from the expert through an interaction designed to detect knowledge to acquire and which is normally difficult to explain. This approach gains in efficiency by taking into account the context in which the interaction is realized, particularly in co-operative systems (Aïmeur & Frasson, 1995b).

This article aims at determining how co-operative tutoring systems can be improved using two approaches. First by using elicitation techniques that improve the quality and accuracy of the dialogue between the learner and the system, clarifying the context in which the learner is placed. Secondly, by introducing new learning strategies that strengthen knowledge acquisition through dialogue between real and virtual learners. After reviewing the existing learning forms we present two new approaches called *learning by disturbing* and *learning by co-teaching*. We show how these strategies can be dynamically selected in an architecture of an intelligent tutoring system in which the knowledge level of the learner is frequently evaluated. We give an example of eliciting dialogues in a medical environment.

2 DIFFERENT FORMS OF LEARNING STRATEGIES

The principle of co-operative tutoring systems (also called social learning systems) is based on the use of the computer not as a directive training means but instead as a way to exchange, control and build knowledge. Several experiences have shown that two persons working together could learn more than in individual training. In that sense, several models have been developed which generally are called social learning systems, co-operative systems, or collaborative systems.

2.1 One-on-one learning

This approach preceded the co-operative systems and consisted in simulating the computer as an intelligent tutor who can understand the learner and provide adaptive tutoring. The learner receives knowledge directly from the tutor who communicates and acts according to a prescriptive behavior. Most of traditional ITS adopt this approach with adaptive features more or less marked, according to the complexity of the student model used to provide feedback. The teacher's knowledge is without doubt higher then that of the learner.

As alternatives to one-on-one strategy, co-operative strategies comprise an additional element, namely peer interaction. Co-operative learning systems, called also social learning systems, adopt a constructive approach based on the use of the computer more as a partner then as a teacher in the process of knowledge transfer. Multiple agents that are either computer simulated or real human beings can work on the same computer or share a computer network.

2.2 Learning with a companion

The idea of introducing a *co-learner* in the learning process arose with the perception that knowledge should result more in a building process than in a transmission process (Gilmore & Self, 1988). In this scope, the learner could co-operate with a co-learner having quite similar objectives and level of knowledge. A learner is inclined to more easily understand explanations given by a co-learner, who has understood, knows what to do and to answer, than the teacher. The co-learner is supposed to have recently passed through the same understanding problem and so is more aware of the level of explanation and detail to give to solve the problem. The knowledge level of the co-learner is slightly higher than the learner. Chan and Baskin proposed a three-agent learning situation (Chan & Baskin 1990) which consists in a co-operation between a human learner and a simulated learning companion who learn together under the guidance of the teacher. The *companion* and the learner perform the same task and exchange ideas on the problem. The learner and the co-learner (the companion) work together and ask the teacher for help only if they cannot find a solution. The role of the teacher is then to alternatively present problems and critiques of the learner's solution. The process is gradual in the sense that each learner produces a solution then checks the other's solution. Finally the teacher checks the solutions which are submitted to him in order to correct any remaining error. The companion and the learner have quite similar knowledge levels, while the tutor has a higher knowledge level.

2.3 Learning by teaching

An additional form derived from the learning companion was also proposed by Chan & Baskin (1990). The idea was to encourage the human learner to teach the companion, by providing examples, explaining why the solution given by the companion is not adequate. The approach is called learning by teaching and has been further elaborated by other studies (Palthepu et al, 1991, Van Lehn et al, 1994). Explanation of this approach can be found in the learning theory of Gagné (Gagné, 1984) who shows that a strong knowledge acquisition is achieved when a learner is able to fully explain the solution of a task using his own inference mechanism and this last exercise is in itself a knowledge acquisition method.

As we can see, each method requires a dialogue between the learner and the system, and explanations are fundamental. The learner can ask for an explanation to justify his opinion, propose an alternate solution, help another learner to formulate his questions, recognize the wrong interpretations and understand the motivation of another learner. Elicitation techniques are generally used to obtain knowledge from an expert in order to build a knowledge based system. They also can serve to extract learner's knowledge which can be compared with the expert solution in order to identify his knowledge level. In the next section we will briefly review the elicitation methods.

3 METHODS OF KNOWLEDGE ELICITATION

Knowledge acquisition consists of extracting and organizing knowledge using manual, semi-automatic (interactive) and automatic (machine learning) techniques. Knowledge acquisition draws on methods of knowledge elicitation and modelling. *Knowledge elicitation* consists of acquiring knowledge semi-automatically. This requires constructing conjointly the description language (extracted from domain concepts and relations) and the domain knowledge model. The modelling activity consists of constructing an expert model which includes a model of the problem solving process and a model of the domain knowledge. Two types of knowledge elicitation methods can be distinguished : direct and indirect.

The direct methods (Firlej & Hellens, 1991) are referred to non contrived methods. They permit the expert to state their knowledge "naturally" without being constrained by a structure predefined by the knowledge engineer. We will refer to the use of these methods as direct knowledge transfer. These methods include interview techniques (Gallouïn, 1988), protocol analysis techniques, direct observation (Boy et al, 1988) etc.

Indirect methods correspond to contrived methods. They constrain the experts to state their knowledge with the help of predefined structures such as tables, repertory grid decision trees, networks, etc. These structures can help to extract knowledge which is difficult to formulate. Indirect methods are capable of complementing direct methods. Types of indirect methods include repertory-grid (Gaines & Shaw, 1992, Boose & Bradshaw, 1993), card sorting (Major, 1991), laddering techniques (Rugg et al, 1990), etc.

The difference between direct and indirect methods is that with direct methods the knowledge engineer depends entirely on the information provided by the expert (i.e. "tell me what you know") whereas with indirect methods the knowledge engineer interacts with the expert (i.e. "let me see if I understand you correctly"). Direct methods are more natural and provide more flexibility for the expert. This makes them easier to use but increases the risk of substantial omissions in the knowledge. Indirect methods need a structure capable of representing the experts knowledge, this structure must be defined before these methods may be used. However indirect methods are more reliable than direct ones, because the expert becomes more precise, thus reducing the time factor which is crucial for the knowledge engineer : they allow rapid testing of the knowledge once it has been made explicit.

Introducing elicitation methods in a co-operative approach present multiple advantages, they reduce the quantity of information exchanged in the dialogue, they reduce the cognitive complexity of human memory, they remove ambiguities, they facilitate the focus of the dialogue between co-operative agents. An important aspect of a co-operative approach is the dialogue which is used to negotiate and find a solution to address the differences between interpretations. The dialogue can take various forms such as consultation and critique, elicitation and communication.

4 NEW LEARNING STRATEGIES

We have seen above the main four forms of co-operative systems. We consider now a general context in which a learner has to build a model of a given task. The elicitation methods chosen in our approach are indirect methods. They are constrained by the expert solution that is used as a guideline for the elicitation process. In this way, the learner has to model the task in a hierarchical form. To understand and acquire the knowledge related to this task we use elicitation techniques that force the learner to describe the characteristics of the task and then decompose the task into sub tasks. The process continues for each level of decomposition of the tasks. We present two new learning forms and explain how they take advantage of elicitation techniques.

4.1 Learning by disturbing

This learning form suggests (Figure 1) that the computer can be simulated as two agents: a teacher and a troublemaker. The elicitation is performed between the teacher, the troublemaker and the human learner. It is a disturbing approach, because when the teacher elicits the characteristics of tasks and their decomposition from the learner, the troublemaker sometimes tries to lead the learner astray by giving him false indications and other times good indications. The troublemaker and the learner have the same knowledge level and criticize each other.

Fig. 1. Learning by disturbing

The learner explains the troublemaker under the guidance of the teacher. In case of an incorrect solution the teacher gives the solution of the expert to the learner.

Advantage of the method: this approach forces the learner to solve the problems or questions proposed by the troublemaker. The teacher asks questions to the learner and the troublemaker interrupts the dialogue to give his own solution. This solution is sometimes right and sometimes wrong. The same process applies when the learner gives a solution to the teacher (after a question from the teacher). This method forces the learner to take confidence in his/her actions or conclusions and distinguish between wrong and correct solutions. In addition, it strengthens the knowledge acquisition process.

4.2 Learning by co-teaching

This learning form suggests (Figure 2) that the computer can be simulated as two agents: a teacher and a co-teacher. The elicitation is performed between the teacher, the co-teacher and the human learner. This approach is referred to as learning by co-teaching, because the teacher and the co-teacher have the same knowledge level and talk each other. In specific cases the co-teacher can be composed by two experts: an expert in pedagogy and the domain expert (Aïmeur & Frasson, 1995a) when they elicit the characteristics of tasks and their decomposition from the learner.

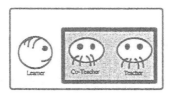

Fig. 2. Learning by co-teaching

Advantage of the method: the learner is watching the two teachers and can particularly benefit from the given advice. This is a fully co-operative approach. When the learner gives a solution to a problem or answers a question the teacher and the co-teacher discuss the solution. In case of conflict the teacher and the co-teacher take the expert solution which is embedded in the knowledge base. After justifications from the learner the solution of the expert is presented to him. An indirect advantage of the method is to provide the user with various expert point of views which is a good way for integrating (chunking) the knowledge.

To strengthen these new learning strategies we include both direct and indirect elicitation methods in each learning strategy. For eliciting a task to perform, we need direct methods in order to obtain information on the learner's profile (Aïmeur & Frasson, 1995b). Indirect methods will be used to understand and acquire the knowledge related to the task, forcing the learner to describe the characteristics of the task and then decompose the task into sub tasks. The process continues for each level of decomposition of the tasks. These methods are constrained by the expert's solution that is used as a guideline for the elicitation process. In this way, the learner has to model the task in a hierarchical form.

5 ARCHITECTURE OF A TUTORING SYSTEM BASED ON MULTIPLE LEARNING STRATEGIES

In order to benefit from the flexibility provided by different learning strategies, we propose an architecture (Figure 3) which incorporates a *metatutor* module into the traditional ITS scheme comprising student model, user interface, tasks database and knowledge domain. The role of this metatutor is to choose a suitable strategy according to various parameters related to the characteristics of the learner. An important aspect of this architecture is that *each tutoring strategy is associated with elicitation methods* which foster the communication between the learner and other actors (teacher, companion, troublemaker, etc.) and strengthen knowledge acquisition. The adaptive feature of this architecture is assured by choosing the proper learning strategy according to the student's evolution.

• The first stage is achieved by the identification module which is part of the student model. For that purpose, the learner has to answer a set of questions elaborated by psychologists. The analysis of the answers is done by an analyzer which is able to determine the profile and the history of the learner. The profile concerns the learning style, the intentions and the characteristics of the learner and the history deals with a database of errors previously made by the learner.

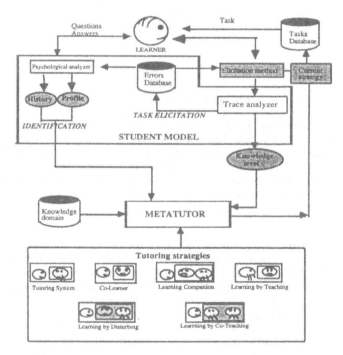

Fig. 3. Architecture of a multi-strategies tutoring system

•   The basic principle of a tutoring cycle is to propose a task to the learner together with a learning strategy. Based upon a first approximation assessment of the learner knowledge level, the identification module is able to select in the tasks database a first task, called target task, to be proposed to the learner. The default (initial) strategy is the one-on-one learning, able to coach the user in a directive way.

•   During the execution of the task the trace analyzer determines the level of knowledge at which the learner is placed. A *metatutor* module, containing selection rules, receives the knowledge level, the history and the profile of the learner as input and recommends the choice of a new learning strategy that will become the new current strategy.

The knowledge level is determined according to Gagné's theory (Gagné, 1984), in which instruction is a set of events external to the learner. We consider that these events can place the student in different learning levels corresponding to the main steps of the cognitive process (Frasson & Kaltenbach, 1993).

The different levels (seven levels) are successively *indetermination* (the learner has no prerequisites), *acceptance* (no information given about the knowledge to acquire), *motivation* (learner motivated and aware of objectives), *attention* (recall of previously learned capabilities done), *presentation* (introduction of learning tools and stimuli (text, video, demonstration, etc.), *initiation* (learner mastery of knowledge in particular simple situations), *integration* (learner aware of some solutions for more complex situations than those associated with the previous level), generalization. (learner can transfer the knowledge in various situations). Levels 1 to 4 represent the conditioning steps (the student is prepared to learn), while levels 5 to 7 correspond to the steps of effective knowledge acquisition. Notice that during the first steps (levels 1 to 4) the student is not really active in the learning process (he is guided). His active participation increases from levels 5 to 7 where he is finally capable of generalizing the solution.

Part of this architecture is already implemented in Smalltalk, in the SAFARI project intended to develop multiple types of tutoring systems. The different learning strategies are experimented in a complex learning environment dealing with intensive care medicine. In the Surgical Intensive Care Unit (SICU) a specialized nurse assists a patient and manipulates different medical devices. Figure 4 shows an example of the main characteristics of dialogues for knowledge elicitation during a patient assessment task, used in learning by co-teaching strategy integrated into the SICU environment. The learner executes the task (tries to realize the different steps of the task) and the resulting trace of the learner actions is produced by a trace analyzer.

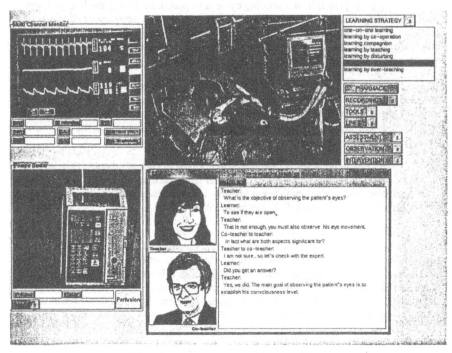

Fig. 4. Learning in intensive care unit

6 CONCLUSION

Co-operative tutoring systems replace the prescriptive approach developed by traditional ITS with a constructive one based on the use of the computer as a way to exchange, control and build knowledge. Various forms of co-operative systems were recently introduced in which the learner can work by talking either to the tutor or the companion, to exchange ideas or hypothesis on possible solutions or to obtain explanations or additional examples. We have presented two new learning forms that extend the spectrum of possibilities in terms of co-operation. They place the learner into a higher degree of abstraction. Learning by disturbing method allows to check the ability of the learner to distinguish between wrong and correct solutions. Learning by co-teaching provides an example of discussions between the teacher and the co-teacher that is useful for inducing correct solutions presented in a pedagogical form. This architecture is currently in evaluation particularly for tuning the selection rules which switch from the different strategies.

REFERENCES

Aïmeur, E. & Frasson, C. (1995a). Application d'une méthode d'explicitation dans un environnement de système tutoriel coopératif. *Environnements interactifs d'apprentissage avec ordinateur, tome 2, Editions Eyrolles,* (pp. 197-208).

Aïmeur, E. et Frasson C. (1995b) Eliciting The Learning Context In Co-Operative Tutoring Systems, IJCAI-95 Workshop on Modelling Context in Knowledge Representation and Reasoning , Montréal.

Boose, J. & Bradshaw, J.M. (1993). Expertise Transfer and Complex Problems: using AQUINAS as a Knowledge-Acquisition Workbench for Knowledge-Based Systems. In *Readings in Knowledge Acquisition and Learning*, (pp. 240-252), Edited by B.G. Buchanan & D.C. Wilkins, Morgan Kaufmann Publishers.

Boy, G., Faller, B. & Sallantin, J. (1988). Acquisition et ratification des connaissances. In *Actes des journées nationales du PRC-GRECO, Intelligence Artificielle*, (pp. 321-356), Toulouse.

Chan, T.W. & Baskin, A.B. (1990). Learning Companion Systems. In C. Frasson & G. Gauthier (Eds.) *Intelligent Tutoring Systems: At the Crossroads of Artificial Intelligence and Education*, Chapter 1, New Jersey: Ablex Publishing Corporation.

Chi, M.T.H., Bassok, M., Lewis, M.W., Reimann, P. & Glaser, R. (1989). Self Explanations: How students study and use examples in learning to solve problems.*Cognitive Science,5*, (pp. 121-152).

Firlej, M. & Hellens, D. (1991). Knowledge Elicitation : a Practical Book Prentice Hall International (UK) Ltd.

Frasson, C., Kaltenbach, M. (1993). Strengthening the Novice-Expert shift using the self-explanation effect. *Journal of Artificial Intelligence in Education*, special issue on student modelling, vol 3(4), (pp. 477-494).

Gagné R.M.,(1984). The conditions of learning, 4 ed, *Les éditions HRW Ltée*, Montréal.

Gaines, B. R. & Shaw, M. L. (1992). Knowledge acquisition tools based on personal construct psychology. *Knowledge Engineering Review*, 8, (pp. 49-85).

Gallouïn, J.F. (1988).Transfert de Connaissances, Systèmes Experts : Techniques et Méthodes, Editions Eyrolles.

Gilmore, D. & Self, J. (1988). The application of machine learning to intelligent tutoring systems. In J. Self, (Ed.) *Artificial Intelligence and Human Learning, Intelligent computer-assisted instruction*, New York: Chapman and Hall, (pp. 179-196).

Major, N.P. (1991). CATO An Automated Card Sort Tool. In *Proceedings of the Fifth European Knowledge Acquisition for Knowledge-Based Systems Workshop*, University of Strathclyde.

Palthepu, S., Greer, J., & McCalla, G. (1991). Learning by Teaching. *The Proceedings of the International Conference on the Learning Sciences*, AACE.

Rugg, G., Mcgeorge, P. & Shadbolt, N. (1990) On the use of laddered grids in knowledge elicitation. *Artificial Intelligence Group*, Technical Report , Feb, 1, University of Nottingham.

Self, J. (1988). Bypassing the untractable problem of student modelling. *International Conference of Intelligent Tutoring Systems*, Montreal, Canada, (pp. 18-24).

Van Lehn, K, Ohlsson, S. & Nason, R. (1994). Application of simulated students: an exploration. *Journal of artificial intelligence in education*, vol 5, no 2, (pp.135-175).

Modeling the Influence of Non-Changing Quantities

Bert Bredeweg   Kees de Koning   Cis Schut

Department of Social Science Informatics (S.W.I.)
University of Amsterdam, Roetersstraat 15
1018 WB Amsterdam (The Netherlands)
Telephone: +31-20-525 6788, Telefax: +31-20-525 6896
E-mail: bert@swi.psy.uva.nl

Abstract. In qualitative modelling, information is lost by abstracting from quantitative formulae. We show that when the behaviour of two similar systems is compared, non-changing quantities from these formulae can have a significant influence on the qualitative prediction. We propose the addition of a new ontological primitive for representing these influences in qualitative models, and provide a calculus for exploiting this primitive in the reasoning process. Augmentation with the new primitive enhances the power of the qualitative simulator, resulting in a more appropriate prediction of behaviour, and also improves the explanation capacities of the model. The latter feature is of major importance for tutoring systems using qualitative reasoning.

1   Introduction

A description of behaviour, generated by a qualitative simulator, consists of a set of states modelling qualitatively distinct behaviours of the simulated device. The notion of change is the key concept for generating such a description. In the qualitative simulator we use [1], changes are initiated by active processes that influence certain quantities, as introduced in QPT [8]. These direct changes may propagate through proportionalities, leading to indirect changes in other quantities. Following this approach, the causal knowledge about changes in the device behaviour is represented (explicitly) in the qualitative model by influences and proportionalities.

It turns out that the use of these dependencies produces incorrect behaviour analyses for certain devices, the problem being that either the simulator does not generate the required set of distinct states or that it fails to produce the appropriate causal account of why the behaviour evolves in a certain direction. These shortcomings result from lacking reasoning capabilities in current qualitative reasoning techniques. In particular, they originate from the abstractions introduced by influences and proportionalities. Considering the latter, different monotonic functions such as $f(y_1) = c_1 x_1$ and $f(y_2) = c_2 x_2$ are represented by the same qualitative dependency (increasing monotonic), namely $y_1 \propto_{Q+} x_1$ and $y_2 \propto_{Q+} x_2$. This representation abstracts from the effects resulting from differences between the constants c_1 and c_2. Usually this abstraction introduces no problem. However, when the model includes two similar causal structures this abstraction may lead to faulty predictions. Consider for example two liquids, with equal boiling temperatures ($t_{b1} = t_{b2}$), being heated by two heat sources that produce an equal amount of energy ($H_1 = H_2$). In this situation, the correct behaviour can only be predicted by using the knowledge about the heat capacities of the liquids (c_{h1} and c_{h2}). The heat capacities of the liquids determine the ratio of the heat flow rates and hence which liquid will reach its boiling-point first. Namely:

if $c_{h1} > c_{h2}$ **then** t_{b2} will be reached in the next state
if $c_{h1} = c_{h2}$ **then** both t_{b1} and t_{b2} will be reached in the next state
if $c_{h1} < c_{h2}$ **then** t_{b1} will be reached in the next state

This *causal* knowledge cannot be represented adequately in current approaches to qualitative reasoning. In this paper we present a new dependency that can be used for modelling the influence of these non-changing quantities as *modifiers* on the underlying causal model (consisting of influences and proportionalities). Given this primitive the simulator can support (the communication of) inference steps such as:

The energies produced by heat source1 and heat source2 are equal. The boiling points of Liquid1 and Liquid2 are also equal. Liquid1 will reach its boiling point first because the heat capacity of Liquid1 is lower than the heat capacity of Liquid2, and thus the total amount of heat needed for reaching the boiling point is smaller for Liquid1.

2 Qualitative Reasoning and Teaching Systems

It is widely recognised that for solving physics problems a careful qualitative analysis of the problem situation is essential [10, 2, 9, 6]. A typical difference in the problem solving behaviour of experts and novices is the large amount of time an expert spends on the qualitative analysis. The novice is more likely to skip this phase and start computing formulae right away. One of the problems for physics tutors is to make sure that novices start with a qualitative analysis before they select mathematical formulae. In other words, teaching qualitative reasoning in terms of envisioning the behaviour of a device in a qualitative way is an essential step in teaching physics.

A second reason for using qualitative models as part of an intelligent tutoring system is the notion of explanation. It is well-known that quantitative models can be used for efficient simulation of device behaviour. However, they do not provide many means for generating explanations. In particular, they lack the explicit causal knowledge that is required for the generation of explanations. Qualitative models to a certain extent originated from efforts in trying to cope with this problem [11].

Following the discussion above, two requirements can be pointed out that should be fulfilled by a qualitative simulator in a teaching situation. (1) Precise envisionment: The simulator must predict the behaviours that are manifested by the real system. This means that the simulator may not neglect any states of behaviour, but also that it may not predict any spurious (non-existing) behaviours. A precise envisionment provides the required qualitative facts about the device behaviour that a tutor needs for teaching the qualitative analysis that precedes the selection of formulae. (2) Predictive causal account: The knowledge used by the simulator for predicting the states of behaviour should facilitate an explanation of why certain behaviours occur whereas others do not. This implies that the simulator must be able to provide a predictive causal account of why the behaviour evolves in a certain direction. While using the *Balance Tutor*, a tutoring environment that coaches students in analysing the behaviour of a physical device using qualitative knowledge [4], we have encountered a number of situations in which the underlying qualitative simulator did not satisfy the two requirements mentioned above.

3 Qualitative Formalism

As mentioned before, in the qualitative simulator we use, called GARP [1], the notion of processes represents the prime cause of changes (cf. [8]). The (direct) changes imposed upon a system by *influences* are further propagated by *proportionalities* (indirect changes). In addition to these two causal relations, *corresponding* values can be defined between the magnitudes of specific quantities. Finally, *inequalities* ($<, \leq, =, \geq, >$) can be used for representing non-causal dependencies between quantities. Inequalities are not the same as correspondences: two quantities can be unequal but still have corresponding qualitative values, or vice versa.

Similar to compositional modelling [7], GARP uses the notion of *model fragments* for modelling the behaviour of partial real-world systems. All model fragments have associated with them a set of *conditions* under which they are applicable, and a set of *consequences* that are given once their conditions hold. Typically, conditions specify required objects, inequalities between quantities and/or specific values that quantities must have. Consequences, on the other hand, usually introduce influences and proportionalities between quantities, although inequalities can also be specified in the consequences.

Finally, we use a set of rules for determining how one state of behaviour changes into the next. Typically, *termination rules*, such as the limit rule, specify possible transitions, whereas *ordering rules*, such as the epsilon ordering rule, provide further knowledge on conflict resolution between competing transitions (cf. [3]).

4 Problems with Non-Changing Quantities

In this section we will further elaborate on the specific problem dealt with in this paper. For this purpose we use the balance system (see Figure 1). The problem is to predict the behaviour of balances with containers on each balance arm. Both containers are assumed to be equal in weight. Depending on the difference in mass of the liquids in the containers, one balance arm may be heavier than the other. Therefore, after releasing it from the starting position, the balance may change its position. Through outlets near the bottom of the containers the liquid gradually flows out of the containers. Depending on the pressure at the bottom, the flow rates may be different. As a result, the balance may move to a different position, because the difference in weight between the two balance arms changes. Eventually, when both containers are empty, the balance will reach an equilibrium.

In order to reason about the behaviour of the balance-system, model fragments are needed for the containers containing liquid, the liquid flow out of the containers, the position of the balance (depending on the mass difference between left and right), and the movement of the balance (depending on the flow difference between left and right) (for details see [5]). In the *scenario*, or input system, the balance system is, apart from its physical structure, defined by the quantities *Height* (H_L, H_R), *Volume* (V_L, V_R) and *Width* (W_L, W_R). The *Flow rate* quantities (F_L, F_R) will be introduced by the liquid flow process.

For purposes of clarity, in the example we do not mention the 'fully corresponding' quantities *Amount* and *Mass* (corresponding with *Volume*), *Pressure* (corresponding with *Height*), *Position* (corresponding with $V_L - V_R$), and *Movement* (corresponding with $F_L - F_R$). Furthermore, we assume that the containers are rectangular, and for the moment ignore the depths of the containers by assuming them to be equal.

In the example shown in Figure 1, the following inequalities initially hold: $H_L > H_R$, $V_L = V_R$ and $W_L < W_R$. All these quantities have the initial qualitative value +. When

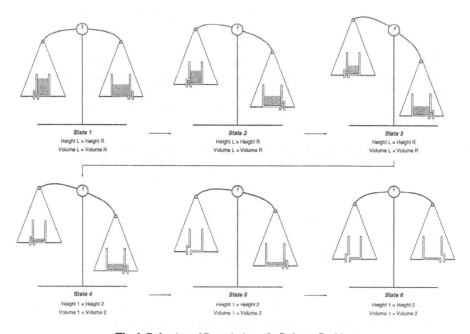

Fig. 1. Behavioural Description of a Balance Problem

presenting this system to the qualitative simulator, a causal structure is produced for the different states of behaviour, as shown in Figure 2. In this model the height of the column determines the flow rate. The flow rate influences the volume of the liquid. Changes in this volume propagate into changes of the height. Changes in the width of the column also propagate into changes in height, that is, if the container would get wider, the liquid column would become lower. This causal structure is applicable for the liquid columns on both sides of the balance.

Notice that in order to predict the behaviour of the balance system the behaviour features of the two balance arms have to be compared. This means analysis of behaviour represented by two *similar* causal structures. It turns out that with the current techniques (in particular, using a causal model consisting of influences and proportionalities), it

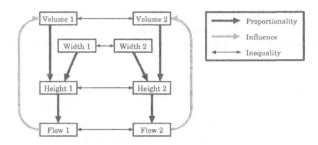

Fig. 2. Causal Dependencies and Inequalities for the Balance Problem

is not possible to derive all the required states as shown in Figure 1. Let us discuss the analysis step by step. From State 1 four transitions must be considered (see also Table 1). First, the "limit" rule states that both containers may become empty (Tr_1 and Tr_2). Next, because the liquid column in the left container is higher, the liquid flow out of that container is faster (pressure at the bottom is higher). Consequently the volume on the left side may become smaller (Tr_3). Finally, because the left column loses liquid faster, the heights may become equal (Tr_4). In this situation, the resulting change is

Termination	Derivative	Value	Value in next state
Tr_1	$\delta V_L = -$	$V_L = +$	$V_L = 0$
Tr_2	$\delta V_R = -$	$V_R = +$	$V_R = 0$
Tr_3	$\delta V_L > \delta V_R$	$V_L = V_R$	$V_L < V_R$
Tr_4	$\delta H_L > \delta H_R$	$H_L > H_R$	$H_L = H_R$

Table 1. Transitions from State 1 to State 2

determined by the "epsilon ordering" rule, favouring Tr_3. However, it is also easy to see that the three other terminations, including their combinations, lead to logically inconsistent, and therefore impossible, successor states of behaviour.

In State 2 the left column is still higher and therefore $F_L > F_R$ is still true. As a result the same transitions as for State 1, except for Tr_3, hold. There is no further knowledge available that allows discrimination between the alternatives. This means that each of the transitions may happen alone or in combination with the others, resulting in seven possibilities. Most of these produce inconsistent results, such as Tr_2 being inconsistent with $V_L < V_R$. Tr_1 is consistent with $V_L < V_R$ but ignores the fact that $H_L > H_R$. Transition Tr_4 produces the only valid state transition from State 2 to State 3.

Things get more complicated when we consider the transitions from State 3. The liquid columns are now equally high and therefore $F_L = F_R$ holds. Only the transitions as shown in Table 2 can therefore be derived. Notice that from the causal chain as shown in Figure 2 we cannot derive that there will be a change in the heights while going from State 3 to State 4. In State 3, the heights are equal and therefore the flows are equal. As a result, the changes in the volumes are equal ($\delta V_L = \delta V_R$), so therefore there will be no change in the relative heights. Namely, $\delta H_L = \delta H_R$ and therefore $H_L = H_R$ does not

Termination	Derivative	Value	Value in next state
Tr_1	$\delta V_L = -$	$V_L = +$	$V_L = 0$
Tr_2	$\delta V_R = -$	$V_R = +$	$V_R = 0$

Table 2. Transitions from State 3 to State 4

change, which is incorrect . Notice that it is possible to derive that, because $V_L < V_R$ and $\delta V_L = \delta V_R$, the left container will be empty before the right container (this follows from Tr_1). But this is inconsistent with $H_L = H_R$. And we already saw that there is no termination that proposes a change for $H_L = H_R$ into $H_L < H_R$ (because the derivatives for the heights are equal).

At this point in the behaviour analysis we lack the causal knowledge to predict and explain that in the next state of behaviour (State 4) the height of the left liquid column will be lower, $H_L < H_R$. The influence of the non-changing quantity *Width* cannot be taken into account, the problem being that the effect of a changing V on H is mediated by the width W of the column, namely $H = f(V)W$. Because $W_L < W_R$, the smaller column will decrease more in height with equal loss of volume ($\delta V_L = \delta V_R$), resulting in $H_L = H_R$ changing into $H_L < H_R$. This piece of causal knowledge cannot be modelled by current approaches to qualitative reasoning, in particular, by simulators reasoning with a QPT-like knowledge representation.

In the next section we will show how this problem can be solved by introducing a new type of dependency: the *I-P modifier* (influence/proportionality modifier).

5 Representing Non-Changing Quantities

One option is to define a qualitative version of the formula $V = W \times H$, for example as: `mult(V,W,H)` or `equal(V,mult(W,H))`. In order to support larger multiplications (for instance, when the *Depth* (D) is taken into account and this formula expands to $V = W \times H \times D$) this representation could be enhanced to allow embedded multiplication relations. Alternatively, intermediate variables could be added. Incorporating the depth would then result in respectively `mult(V,mult(W,H),D)` or `mult(V,X,D)`, `mult(X,W,H)`.

Although using such multiplications may yield a correct simulation of the behaviour, the approach does not allow us to explicitly model the notion of: "the *Width* modifying the causal effect of the *Volume* on the *Height*". In a tutoring situation this hampers the explanation capabilities of the system, because the tutor does not have access to a *causal account* of the predicted behaviour. We therefore adopt another option which is to enrich the ontology for qualitative reasoning with a new primitive, the *I-P modifier*. This enables us to express explicitly that the value of a non-changing quantity affects another relation. Considering the balance example again, we can now express that the width affects the influence of the volume on the height. This may be represented as shown in Figure 3. The positive proportionality relation `Prop1` between *Volume* and *Height* states that an increase (decrease) in the volume causes an increase (decrease) in the height, whereas *Width* acts as a negative modifier of `Prop1`: the larger *Width*, the smaller the influence of *Volume* on *Height*. In Prolog, this could be represented as:

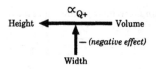

Fig. 3. A negative I-P Modifier

```
prop_pos(Prop1, Height, Volume)
mod_neg(Width, Prop1)
```
Representing more than one modifier for a proportionality is now easy by defining more than one mod_pos or mod_neg relation for the same proportionality.

6 Reasoning with I-P modifiers

In designing a calculus for dealing with modifiers, it is important to keep in mind that these modifiers are only relevant in situations where (1) two similar causal structures are compared, and, (2) inequality constraints exist between those structures, that relate quantities of the same type. We start with the simplest case, in which there is a single proportionality with a single modifier in each of the systems. Let $A_1, B_1, \ldots$ be the quantities of one system, and $A_2, B_2, \ldots$ the corresponding quantities in the other system. Let the following relations hold:

```
prop_pos(Prop1, C1, A1)        prop_pos(Prop2, B2, A2)
mod_neg(B1, Prop1)             mod_neg(B2, Prop2)
```

Then the calculus presented in Table 3 is used to compute the effect of the modified proportionalities on the relation between δC_1 and δC_2[1]. For reasons of clarity, some

Combining prop_pos and mod_neg			
	$B_1 < B_2$	$B_1 = B_2$	$B_1 > B_2$	$B_1 ? B_2$
$\delta A_1 < \delta A_2$	$\delta C_1 ? \delta C_2$	$\delta C_1 < \delta C_2$	$\delta C_1 < \delta C_2$	$\delta C_1 ? \delta C_2$
$\delta A_1 = \delta A_2$	$\delta C_1 > \delta C_2$	$\delta C_1 = \delta C_2$	$\delta C_1 < \delta C_2$	$\delta C_1 ? \delta C_2$
$\delta A_1 > \delta A_2$	$\delta C_1 > \delta C_2$	$\delta C_1 > \delta C_2$	$\delta C_1 ? \delta C_2$	$\delta C_1 ? \delta C_2$

Table 3. A Calculus for Processing Modified Proportionalities

boundary cases are omitted (for instance, if one allows modifiers to be *zero*). These can be defined in a similar way.[2] The table should be read as follows. Take for example the problem described in Section 1:

> **if** heat source 1 and 2 produce an equal amount of energy ($\delta A_1 = \delta A_2$)
> **and** the heat capacity of the liquid 1 is higher ($B_1 > B_2$)
> **then** the temperature of liquid 2 will increase faster ($\delta C_1 < \delta C_2$)

[1] The column for $B_1 ? B_2$ is added because combined modifiers can be ambiguous, as will become clear below. In subsequent tables, similar columns are omitted.
[2] By the same token, analogous calculi are defined for prop_neg's and mod_pos's.

It is now also easy to see how the required transition from State 3 to State 4 (change from $H_L = H_R$ into $H_L < H_R$) can be derived:

if the left container is smaller ($B_1 < B_2$)
and the columns are equal ($\delta A_1 = \delta A_2$)
then the height of the left column will decrease faster ($\delta C_1 > \delta C_2$)

This calculus is sufficient only for computing the influence of a single modifier on a single proportionality for C. Consequently, we have to expand our calculus to incorporate multiple modifiers and multiple proportionalities. We do this by first combining multiple modifiers for each proportionality, then computing the proportionalities one by one, and finally combining the different proportionalities. This is best explained by means of

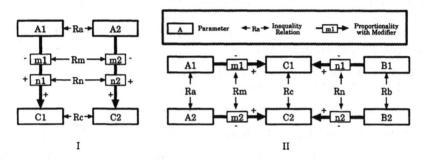

I   II

Fig. 4. Multiple Proportionalities and Modifiers

examples. In Figure 4-I, a schematic representation is given of the following relations:

```
prop_pos(Prop₁, C₁, A₁)      prop_pos(Prop₂, C₂, A₂)
mod_neg(m₁, Prop₁)           mod_neg(m₂, Prop₂)
mod_pos(n₁, Prop₁)           mod_pos(n₂, Prop₂)
```

In addition, there are inequality dependencies between the quantities (R_a, R_m, R_n, and R_c). We now want to calculate the *combined effect* of the inequality relations R_m and R_n on R_c. This is done by using a simple combination calculus, as depicted in Table 4. The right-side table applies to our example, because we want to combine a mod_neg with a mod_pos. Modifier pairs that have opposite inequality relations can be combined (*e.g.*, ">" and "<" yields ">", where the resulting relation is a mod_neg), and equal modifier pairs can be omitted (*e.g.*, ">" and "=" yields ">"). As an example, consider State 2 of the balance problem, were we have $H_L > H_R$, $V_L < V_R$, and $W_L < W_R$. Given $H_L > H_R$, and thus $\delta V_L > \delta V_R$, we use $W_L < W_R$ to derive $\delta H_L > \delta H_R$ (see Table 3). $\delta H_L > \delta H_R$ together with $H_L > H_R$ yields the desired transition to $H_L = H_R$. Now suppose the problem is extended by taking into account the depths (D_L, D_R) of the containers as well. We can now derive that if (for example) $D_L > D_R$, the resulting combined modification, and hence the state transition, is ambiguous:

if $W_L < W_R$ **and** $D_L > D_R$ **then** M_L ? M_R

	<	=	>
<	<	<	?
=	<	=	>
>	?	>	>

Similar relations (*e.g.*, `mod_pos` with `mod_pos`)

Opposite relations (*e.g.*, `mod_pos` with `mod_neg`); resulting relation is of type defined in the top row)

Table 4. Calculi for Combination

Here M_L, M_R are the resulting combined modifiers for both sides. Applying these modifiers to the proportionality relations between volumes and heights yields H_L ? H_R (see Table 3).

If, on the other hand, $D_L = D_R$ or $D_L < D_R$, the same transition to $H_L = H_R$ is found (see the left table in Table 4):

if $W_L < W_R$ and $D_L = D_R$ then $M_L < M_R$
if $W_L < W_R$ and $D_L < D_R$ then $M_L < M_R$

Applying these combined modifiers yields

if $\delta V_L > \delta V_R$ and $M_L < M_R$ then $\delta H_L > \delta H_R$

For proportionality relations with more than two modifiers, the calculus can be applied incrementally. The result of this addition is that all proportionalities can be represented as having exactly one modifier, because non-modified proportionalities can be seen as having one modifier which is equal in both systems. Similarly, the different proportionalities for one quantity can now be combined by adding the inequality relations between modifiers and quantities. Consider the relations in Figure 4-II, illustrating the relations

```
prop_pos(Prop_A1, C_1, A_1)        prop_pos(Prop_A2, C_2, A_2)
mod_neg(m_1, Prop_A1)              mod_neg(m_2, Prop_A2)
prop_pos(Prop_B1, C_1, B_1)        prop_pos(Prop_B2, C_2, B_2)
mod_neg(n_1, Prop_B1)              mod_neg(n_2, Prop_B2)
```

The two proportionality relations influencing C are calculated separately using the calculus from Table 3. This time, we do not calculate the actual inequality between δC_1 and δC_2, but we calculate the *relative influence* of each proportionality. For example, if the left side proportionality relations in Figure 4-II would have caused R_c to change from "=" to ">" provided it was the only proportionality affecting C, then we can say that the relative influence on R_c is ">". When we have done this for all proportionalities affecting C, then we can add them conform the calculus in Table 4.

Summarising, modified proportionalities are dealt with by computing the effect of the modifier on the proportionality using the calculus in Table 3. In the case that multiple modifiers exist for one proportionality, the inequality relations between corresponding modifiers are combined by using the calculus in Table 4. If more than one proportionality affects the same quantity, the relative influences of the inequalities involved are combined by the latter calculus.

7 Discussion and Concluding Remarks

We showed that non-changing quantities may have a significant influence on the prediction of behaviour of physical systems. When comparing similar processes, which regularly occurs in teaching situations as well as in real-life applications, current QR techniques are not capable of modelling the desired behaviour. We presented a new ontological primitive that enlarges the scope of qualitative reasoning by modelling the changes in behaviour that result from influences of non-changing quantities.

Two representations have been discussed. They differ with respect to the explicit representation of the multiplication and the addition of modifiers. The latter is explicit with respect to its role in the prediction of causal behaviour, whereas the multiplication relation can also be used for other (teaching) purposes, for instance providing general background knowledge about the relations between the different quantities. That is, it may be useful to teach a student the multiplication relation explicitly, and not only its causal (more implicit) consequences. On the other hand, knowing which quantity is the modifier (thus by explicit representation) simplifies the realisation of causal explanations for a teaching system.

The extension proposed here is a small, but nevertheless important step. In the development of QR research, the power of qualitative reasoning has increased by gradually lowering the level of abstraction. First, only (qualitative) quantity values were used. An important improvement was the introduction of inequality reasoning, which employs the quantitative values of quantities. We follow this line one step further by introducing the modified proportionality, facilitating the exploitation of constants in the comparison of similar behaving systems. When predicting the behaviour of solitary systems these constants can be omitted, but when comparing similar systems they can influence the behaviour significantly.

References

1. Bredeweg, B.: Expertise in qualitative prediction of behaviour. PhD thesis, University of Amsterdam, The Netherlands (1992)
2. Chi, M.T.H., Feltovich, P.J., Glaser, R.: Categorization and representation of physics problems by experts and novices. Cognitive Science 5 (1981) 121–152
3. de Kleer, J.H., Brown, J.S.: A qualitative physics based on confluences. Artificial Intelligence 24 (1984) 7–83
4. de Koning, K., Bredeweg, B.: The balance tutor. Tech. rep., University of Amsterdam (1993)
5. de Koning, K., Bredeweg, B.: Norm behaviour models. Tech. rep., University of Amsterdam (1994)
6. Elio, R., Sharf, P.B.: Modeling novice-to-expert shifts in problem-solving strategy and knowledge organization. Cognitive Science 14 (1990) 579–639
7. Falkenhainer, B., Forbus, K.D.: Compositional modeling: Finding the right model for the job. Artificial Intelligence 51 (1991) 95–143
8. Forbus, K.D.: Qualitative process theory. Artificial Intelligence 24 (1984) 85–168
9. Gentner, D., Stevens, A.L. (eds): Mental Models. Lawrence Erlbaum, Hillsdale (1983)
10. Larkin, J.H., McDermott, J., Simon, D.P., Simon, H.A.: Expert and novice performance in solving physics problems. Science 208 (1980) 1335–1342
11. Wenger, E.: Artificial Intelligence and Tutoring Systems. Morgan Kaufmann (1987)

Mathema: A Learning Environment
Based on a Multi-Agent Architecture

Evandro de Barros Costa[1], Manoel A. Lopes[2] and Edilson Ferneda[2]

[1] UFAL-CCEN-MAP, PhD student at Electrical Engineering - UFPB
[2] UFPB-CCT-DSC

Universidade Federal da Paraíba
Caixa Postal 10.090, 58.109-970 Campina Grande - PB, Brazil
{evandro,mal,edilson}@dsc.ufpb.br

Abstract. This paper introduces a computer-based learning environment called Mathema. Mathema uses the methaphor of cooperating intelligent agents. The idea is to integrate human learners in a society of artificial tutoring agents, aiming to involve them in a learning situation through a cooperative and interactive process. In Mathema, a multi-agent architecture is adopted. This architecture is a suitable design to support the development of tutoring systems in the sense of the approach above. The architecture is introduced, its components, as well as its functionality.

1 Introduction

In the last few years, the marriage between the notion of cooperative learning [16, 7] and Distributed Artificial Intelligence (mainly through Multi-Agent Systems) [4] has become a very atractive alternative in the search of intelligent computational systems. The idea of cooperative learning seems to be an approach with good acceptance by the education community, in regard to its effectiveness in the teaching/learning process. On the other hand, multi-agent systems are a suitable paradigm for the computational feasibility of cooperative learning. Indeed, this marriage has been present in the various fields of artificial intelligence, where, either humans cooperate with machines aiming *machine learning* [2], or artificial agents cooperate with a human learner.

From this point of view, we are introducing the design of a Cooperative Intelligent Tutoring System supporting the process of teaching/learning, based on a multi-agent architecture. In this kind of system, the learner is a human and the teacher is artificial, although the possibility of machine learning (knowledge acquisition) is also considered. Our proposal follows this approach, focusing on the human learner.

Emphasis on Mathema is on operationality, instead of generality. Therefore, some restrictions, contributing to the efectiviness and feasibility of this type of environment, are defined. In doing so, we intend to substantially minimize some of the main problems present in Multi-agent Systems [15], which are mainly related to generality. For instance, consider the problems related to task description, decomposition and allocation, as well as communication overload among agents in heterogeneous knowledge based systems. Considering these difficulties, we adopt a homogeneous environment, in the sense that the agents have the same representation. Therefore, a common discourse language over a specific, formal and sufficiently rich domain should be adopted. Examples of homogeneous environments are algebra and classical logic. Another issue to be considered is the control mechanism, which may be centralized as will be discussed later.

We adopt in Mathema a teaching/learning cooperative model combining aspects of *learning by being told* and aspects of *learning by doing* [3]. The first one focuses on instructional aspects of traditional intelligent tutoring systems, where the initiative and control of the interaction are prerogatives of the system [8]. The second one focuses on an explorative approach in problem solving situations which are present in the notion of microworld, as proposed by Seymour Papert [10, 11], and based on Piagetian constructivism, where the learner has the possibility to explore freely the environment.

Mathema's model suggests a more collaborative learning approach involving a combination of the interaction and the equilibration piagetian notions [9]. In this case the initiative of interaction can be dynamically changed in function of a negotiation dialogue. Equilibration is a piagetian concept meaning adaptive interaction, which is the combination of two processes, named by Piaget as assimilation and accommodation, occuring simultaneously [1, 12].

In order to accomplish this idea, we propose a multi-agent system based approach. In such way each tutor agent supports, among others elements, features of three fundamental knowledge modules in a classical ITS, designed to know what it teaches (domain module), who it teaches (student model) and how it teaches (pedagogical module) [13]. Thus, we intend to have a more flexible and richer environment, improving the adaptativity of the system with respect to the student.

The functional architecture of Mathema consists essentially of the following agents: a learner (human), a client (representing an external motivator for the learner), a society of artificial tutoring agents (with the role of tutoring system), a society of human agents (bahaving as sources of knowledge to the artificial tutoring agents), an interface agent between the learner and the tutoring system, and a communication agent between the two societies.

In this work, we present some details of Mathema, focusing mainly on its multi-agent architecture. We begin, in Section 2, introducing the structural model of Mathema, including a minimal model which will be used as a reference to Mathema and its general description. In Section 3, we introduce details of the society of artificial tutoring agents. In Section 4, we focus on the functional description of Mathema. Conclusions are presented in Section 5.

2 Structural modeling

In this section, we introduce a general and structural description of Mathema. Before this, we will describe what we have been called minimal reference model, adopted as a basis to suggest the multi-agent architecture defined to Mathema.

2.1 Minimal Model of Reference

In this model we will consider an alternative combining the classical structure of an ITS and the notion of microworld, with a formal protocol of automatic learning named MOSCA, proposed by Reitz [14]. Based on this combination we obtain a Cooperative ITS in the sense that the tutoring system and the learner are involved in a learning process and cooperate with each other, aiming to build a common knowledge related to the domain of discourse. The idea is to establish a compromise between ITS and Microworld, allowing ITS to incorporate some features of Microworlds. To do so, we defined our minimal model according to a perspective of agents, where we essentially have two agents: artificial tutor and human learner. Thus, we intend to provide some degree of flexibility in the system, in order to keep the learner with a more active role while interacting with the system.

With respect to MOSCA, it is opportune to emphasize that its design [14] was initially proposed with the objective to provide the means to control the knowlegde of an artificial agent in a situation of learning by examples. In what follows, we give a brief description of the learning protocol of MOSCA.

2.1.1 MOSCA

MOSCA is a model of interaction composed of five roles: the *Master*, the *Oracle*, the *Probe* (*"Sonda"*, in portuguese), the *Client*, and the *Apprentice*. Each one of these roles represent specific behaviors which can be defined according to the intended objectives. For instance, in Ferneda [5] we find a definition of such roles where the machine is the learner and the others are performed by human agents, intending to have an environment to help in the discovery of concepts in euclidean geometry. These roles can be described informally as:

- the *Apprentice*, yielding a learned hypothesis which fits well the sample of examples and counter-examples previously made available to him;
- the *Oracle*, yielding unrefutable ¡problem,solution¿ pairs;
- the *Client*, which submits problems to the apprentice and expects to receive solutions from him;
- the *Probe*, yielding refutable ¡problem,solution¿ pairs, making him to present the due argumentations; and
- the *Master*, who analyses the apprentice's argumentations and then offers useful criticisms to him.

The learning environment is shown in Figure 1. Additional explanations can be found in Ferneda [5].

2.1.2 Minimal Model

We adopt differents visions of the roles described above considering mainly the change to other point of view where the learner becomes human and the teacher turns to be the machine. Considering now a Tutoring Systems approach, as mentioned earlier, an addition of a redefinition of roles is needed. Besides

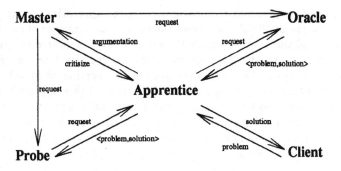

Fig. 1. The MOSCA learning protocol

this, we propose a short modification in the structure of MOSCA. Therefore, the basic structure of our minimal model is shown in Figure 2. In this way, we have a learner (human), an artificial tutor, and a client representing the external environment, working as a kind of motivator of learner (it can be, for example, a teacher).

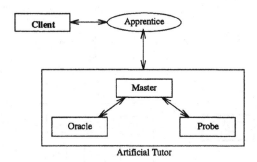

Fig. 2. Minimal Model of reference to Mathema

The artificial tutor includes the roles of Oracle, Probe and Master. Application domain knowledge is distributed between the Oracle and the Probe. The Oracle represents the knowledge base considered as correct. The Probe is a noisy knowledge base aiming the cognitive disequilibrium, in the piagetian sense, of the apprentice (traps) plus a bug catalogue linked with these traps.

The Master is responsible by tutoring properly related to the apprentice, working as a facilitator in a teaching/learning cooperative and interactive process. For this, it has a cognitive apparatus including a knowledge module about the knowledges (meta-knowledge) into the Oracle and into the Probe. Also, it has a dynamic knowledge module about the student (student model) and another about pedagical strategies (pedagogical module), increased with a control module. With this apparatus, the Master dialogues with the apprentice through an interaction and cooperation mechanism aiming the apprentice learning.

Conceptually, the artificial tutor agent can be seen as composed of two levels: an external one and the internal one. In the external level, is located the Master, interacting directly with the Apprentice. In the internal level are the Oracle and the Probe which can be seen as passive entities, serving as knowledge to the Master, executing its tutoring role. An advantage of this approach is that while in MOSCA the direct interations between apprentice and probe, between apprentice and oracle and between apprentice and master generate the necessity of a control protocol of these interations, in the minimal model of Mathema such protocol is dispensable, implying in a considerable simplification.

2.2 General Description of Mathema

According to the intentions declared in the last section, let us present the functional archtecture of Mathema, describing their components. Mathema is an extention of the minimal model introduced above. Its archtecture is shown in the Figure 3.

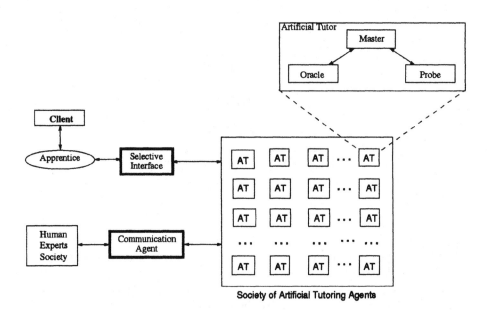

Fig. 3. The architecture of Mathema

The Apprentice and the Client remain with their respective roles as defined in the minimal model in Section 2.1.2. The artifical tutor presented in that section is transformed in a Society of Artificial Tutoring Agents Tutores (SATA), which eventually collaborates among themselves in order to realize the teaching/learning process. We have assotiated with this society another one formed by human experts working as sources of knowledge to that society. Between the Apprentice and the society of tutor agents there is an agent which is responsible by the role of communication and a mechanism of selection to the choose a tutor agent which is more suitable to student profile and which is responsable to realize the tutoring. A communication agent provides the interaction between the two societies, offering the necessary means for the communication and maintenance of SATA, including a language for agents descriptions. In the next section we give a special emphasis on SATA.

3   Society of artificial tutoring agents

A metaphor associated with Mathema is one of a model of social organization, in the sense of a human society. More specifically, the idea is to integrate human learners in a society of artificial tutoring agents (a kind of microsociety), aiming to involve them in a learning situation through a cooperative and interactive process. These agents work in a specific domain, as for instace the algebra domain. Moreover, these agents cooperate among themselves to promote the learning of a certain student. Their specialities are distributed through three dimensions, such as: one is the deep, the other is the laterality, and the last one is composed by different contexts (situated knowledge) in the subject domain. Our objective with these dimensions is to have an environment larger than a specific knowledge. Therefore, having an environment more adaptable to a student, considering his peculiarities and personality.

To each agent are associated the capabilities of: *(i)* solve and propose problems to the learner; *(ii)* learning; *(iii)* solve conflicts; *(iv)* communication; *(v)* cooperation with the others agents.

Related to *(i)*, the system should not only propose the problem to the learner with respect to the inherent interactive process, but also should solve and help to solve the possible problems either proposed to the learner or by the learner. In order to answer the learner requests, the system must have a mean to understand and solve the problem, in addition of explanations about the solution process used. But, this is not a trivial task and in certain cases an open problem. Thus, it becomes necessary to describe the problems in a sistematic way, through of a formal and exact language. It is also necessary that the concept of the problem should be presented in a rigorous form according to Lopes [6].

In the case of capability *(ii)* it is required from the system three forms of learning. The first one, which is fundamental, is originated from the interation with humans experts (human society). The second one is related to the possibility of the system to learn with the learner and about him. Finally, the third one treats the possibility of an agent learns about the other ones. In the first one, the system learns something with the society of humans experts, at the moment in which the system requests it. The possibility of the system to learn about the learner occurs during the process of learning of itself, which is a task of the student model. While that the learning through learner can be verified in a situation where the system detects that the solution offered by the learner is correct, but this doesn't agree with any of their solutions. This imply the trigger of a negociation process between the system and the apprentice, so that the system may assimilate such solution. Finally, the possibility of an agent learns about other one is related to a situation of cooperation where an agent specializes more his knowledge about the capability of the other one.

In *(iii)* we refer to the possibility of cognitive conflicts resolution, that is, disagreements which can emerge between the system knowledge and the learner. These conflicts can be identified in four situations related to a problem resolution process, such as: *a)* tutor is right and the learner is wrong; *b)* the learner is right and the tutor is wrong; *c)* both are right, and; *d)* both are wrong. The situation *a)*, occurs at the moment in which the learner presents his argumentation in the resolution of a problem and the tutor detects some mistake in the same resolution; the case *c)*, happens in a situation in which the tutor recognizes which learner solution is right, but it is not a known solution; finally, even considering that situations *b)* and *d)* occurs in the real world, they will be not considered here.

In *(iv)* and *(v)* we refer the necessity of a communication protocol which allows the cooperation of agents, to exchange messages, when they are involved in the solution of a certain problem.

An artificial tutor agent mantains the structure defined in the minimal model. To be feasible, the view of the society discussed in this paper, has to be enhanced with a module representing its believes on its own capabilities and on the capabilities of another agents. These believes are defined considering how an agent knows which are its capabilities, the capabilities of the members of the society. Therefore, an agent should have an external representation of each agent an its own. This representatiom is needed to help an agent in a situation-problem involving the decision process, and to do so the agent tutor has three levels of knowledge: *a)* knows; *b)* partially unconfident, that is, knows what it doesn't know, but it knows someone in the society that knows and, *c)* totally unconfident, in the sense that it doesn't know, and also doesn't know any other agent that knows.

Related to *a)*, we refer to the situation in which an agent acts about a problem, with the belief that it can solve it, without interacting with other agents. Case *b)*, occurs when an agent cannot solve a problem, but it is the case that it knows other agents that have the capabilities to solve the problem. Finally, in case *c)*, the agent doesn't know how to solve a problem, neither knows an agent that knows. In this case the agent communicates to the other agents and waits for any cooperation. If such cooperation could not be established, the agent communicates the impossibility to solve the problem to the learner and also asks for cooperation with the human experts society. This society, then interacts with a maintenance schema in the SATA, through the communication agent.

4 Functional description

In this section we present a brief description of a tutorial session between the apprentice and the system.

Let us consider the scenario when an apprentice interacts with the tutoring system for the first time. In order to explain the functionality of the system, we describe the following relationships $< Aprenttice, InterfaceAgent >$, $< InterfaceAgent, SATA >$, $< SATA, HumanExpertsSocyety >$.

In this case, a dialog is first established between the Apprentice and the Interface Agent, that besides the communication, triggers a module that is responsible to statically model the Apprentice. The idea is to obtain an identification of the Apprentice, and also to have an initial profile of the Apprentice. This profile has information about the objectives and intentions, which will be obtained as answers of the apprenttice based on fuzzy queries.

Having this fuzzy queries answered, the Interface Agent triggers a module responsible to execute a fuzzy matching between the information obtained from the Apprentice and the objectives and intentions from the Tutoring Agents. The result of this process is the election of an agent, which will then be responsible for the tutoring of the Apprentice. From now on, an interaction process between the Apprentice and the selected agent starts.

Therefore, a dialog to search the subject to be worked is started. From now on a process of teaching/learning is started. In this process the Apprentice and the Tutor are active participants. At this moment situations with different complexities may occur.

The more elementary situation is that one in which a Apprentice is involved with only one Tutor (apprentice/selected agent). This means that the demand of the apprentice was sufficient to be treated by the selected agent.

The complexity starts when the demand of the Appentice involves more than one tutor agent. The upper bound of the complexity is reached when all the society has to be involved to solve the problem. So, when this case takes place, the problem of multi-agents emerge, some of which were already mentioned. The selected agent is responsible for the cooperation control. Therefore, each involved agent cooperates with the selected agent, which in turn interacts with the Apprentice.

The complexity becomes excessive when all the agents working in cooperation cannot attend to the request. In this case, the selected agent (control agent) informs to the Apprentice the impossibility to solve the problem stated in the request. Also, this agent informs the problem, through communication agent, to the human experts society. Then, as soon as this society solves the problem, upgrades the SATA, so that either a new agent may be included, or the knowledge of the existing agents may be improved.

5 Conclusion

In this paper we have introduced the design of the computer-based learning environment called Mathema. We emphasize its multi-agent architecture as an alternative framework to support the development of cooperative ITS (Intelligent Tutoring Systems). The main objective is to have a more flexible and richer environment, improving the adaptativity of the system with respect to the student.

We have presented in details the concept of a society of artificial tutoring agents. This society integrates human apprentice in a learning situation through a cooperative and interactive process, working in a specific and wide domain.

Also, the functionatilities of Mathema were discussed with emphasis on tutoring session involving a novice apprentice and the systems.

At the moment we are investigating suitable tools to describe the communication among agents and a logic formalism to support believes agents.

6 Acknowledgements

We would like to thank Dr. Angelo Perkusich (DEE/UFPb) for fruitful revision of this paper. Also, the first author thanks Dr. Flávio Moreira (PUC-RS) for fruitful discussion about seminal ideas in Mathema.

References

1. Boden, M. A.: Artificial Intelligence in Psychology: Interdisciplinary Essays. Bradford Books (1989)
2. Carbonell, J. G.: Paradigms for Machine Learning. Artificial Intelligence. **40**(1-3) (1989) 1–10
3. Costa, E.: Artificial Intelligence and Education: the role of knowledge in teaching. In: Machine and Human Learning (1991) 249–258
4. Demazeau, Y., Muller, J.-P.: Decentralized AI. In: Demazeau, Y., Muller, J.-P. (Eds): Decentralized Artificial Intelligence. Elsevier Science Publisher, Amsterdam, Holland (1990) 3–13
5. Ferneda, E., Py, M., Reitz, Ph., Sallantin, J.: L'agent rationnel SAID: une application en géométrie. Proceedings of the First European Colloquium on Cognitive Science. Orsay, France (1992) 175–192
6. Lopes, M. A., Rosa, W.: Alguns Aspesctos dos Problemas Solúveis por Decomposição. Proceedings of the Second Symposium on Artificial Intelligence. INPE, São José dos Campos, Brazil (1985)
7. Oliveira, F. M., Viccari, R. M.: Belief Logics and Student Modeling in Intelligent Tutoring Systems. Proceedings of the Iberoamerican Symposium on Informatics and Education. Santo Domingo, Dominican Republic (1992)
8. Oliveira, F. M., Viccari, R. M., Coelho, H.: A topological approach to equilibration of concepts. Proceedings of the XI Brazilian Symposium on Artificial Intelligence. Fortaleza, Brazil (1994)
9. Oliveira, F. M.: Crit rios de Equilibra o para Sistemas Tutores Inteligentes. PhD Thesis. CPGCC, UFRGS, Porto Alegre, Brazil (1994)
10. Papert, S.: Mindstorms: Children, Computers, and Powerful Ideas. Basic Books. New York (1994)

11. Papert S.: Microworlds: Transforming education, in Artificial Intelligence and Education. In: Lawer, R. W., Yazdani, M. (Eds.): Learning Environments and Tutoring Systems 1 (1987)
12. Piaget, J.: La Psychologie de l'Intelligence. Colin. Paris, France (1947)
13. Pontes, E. V., Costa, E. de B. at all: HIPERPLAN: Um ambiente de aprendizagem baseado em hipertextos e planos. Proceedings of the Iberoamerican Symposium on Informatics and Education. Santo Domingo, Dominican Republic (1992)
14. Reitz Ph.: Contribution à l'étude des environnements d'aprentissage. Conceptualisation, Spécification et Prototypage. PhD Thesis. LIRMM, Université de Montpellier II, France (1992)
15. Sichman, J. S., Demazeau, Y., Boissier, O.: When can knowledge-based systems be called agents?. Proceedings of the IX Brazilian Symposium on Artificial Intelligence. Rio de Janeiro, Brasil (1992)
16. Slavin, R. et al.: Learning to cooperate, cooperating to learn. Plenum. New York (1985)

A General Model of Dialogue Interpretation for Concept Tutoring Systems

Alexandre I. Direne

Departamento de Informática – UFPR,
Centro Politécnico, Jardim das Américas,
81.531-990 Curitiba–PR Brazil

Abstract. The paper describes how high-level knowledge about *visual* images can be communicated to students through *system-active* and *system-passive* tutorial interactions. Past work in visual concept tutoring has concentrated on the theoretical principles of how humans acquire expertise in visual recognition. The few implementations there have been are domain-specific. However, a key point that has been neglected is the question of how general knowledge can be used to regulate tutorial dialogues about abnormal image features, while enforcing consistency of such dialogues. We introduce a new *model of interpretation*, which combines meta-level knowledge with domain-specific teaching effects in a computer-based environment which allows the student to *explore* example images or, alternatively, to interact with an *Intelligent Tutoring System* (ITS). We argue that principled knowledge can be acquired by free exploration of the image database browser and that experiential knowledge can be acquired through consistent dialogues guided by the ITS interface.

1   Introduction

This paper describes how high-level knowledge about visual images are interpreted through system-active and system-passive tutorial interactions in the computer-based environment RUI (Representations for Understanding Images). The ideas lend themselves to the design and implementation of a category of Intelligent Tutoring Systems (ITSs) aimed at the teaching of abnormalities in highly visual domains, like medical diagnostic imaging (see Figure 1).

We shall argue that a learner's knowledge and expertise can be best developed through a computer tutor if he or she has access to the same knowledge structures created by experts who directly used computer-based tools to design courseware. However, new computational concepts are needed to cope with the complex phenomenon of knowledge communication (from expert to machine and from machine to student). Related work in the field of ITS gives a comprehensive view of *domain-independent* computer tutors [6, 12, 1, 8].

First, I shall discuss a *domain-specific* approach developed for the Radiology Tutor [11] because it addresses, in computational and pre-computational forms, some aspects of the approach developed here. Sharples and du Boulay view the

```
-  TUTOR: Give a diagnosis for this image.
-  STUDENT: The size of the left ventricle is en-
-  larged. The aorta shows signs of calcification.
-  TUTOR: The size of the left ventricle appears
5  to be markedly enlarged. The aorta as a whole
-  is not calcified. Can you be more specific about
-  which subpart(s) of the aorta is calcified?
-  STUDENT: The aortic arch is calcified.
-  TUTOR: The aortic arch appears to be slightly
10 calcified. What can you say about the size of the
-  heart?
-  STUDENT: The heart size is normal.
-  TUTOR: We have identified that the left ven-
-  tricle is markedly enlarged so the heart is not
15 expected to be normal either. Actually the car-
-  diothoracic ratio is 0.82 giving the heart size
-  markedly enlarged. Which heart chambers are
-  enlarged?
-  STUDENT: ⋯ the right atrium is enlarged ⋯
20 TUTOR: ⋯ The right atrium is not visible in
-  this image. What justification do you have for
-  saying it is enlarged?
-  STUDENT: The superior vena cava is enlarged.
-  TUTOR: That's satisfactory ⋯
```

Fig. 1. Dialogue carried out by RUI about cardiac X-rays

learning of medical visual concepts (such as pathologies), through a computer-based tutor, as the acquisition of competence in a space of feature dimensions where boundaries of pathologies are defined, and that such competence can be developed by interacting with ordered sets of images via the ITS. They point out that, in normal practice, much of a student's knowledge about pathologies tends to be acquired inductively, giving rise to over-generalisation. The immediate consequence is that these over-general beliefs cover not only example images but also non-examples (see Figure 2), requiring the ITS to take further action in order to bring the student's beliefs to a *consistent* and more complete state. Explicit "emendation" teaching, they argue, is needed to diminish the fragility of knowledge which is acquired inductively.

2 Visual Concept Tutoring

Visual concept tutoring is not a new idea but past work has tended to concentrate on the theoretical principles of how humans acquire expertise in visual recognition [4, 5, 10]. The few implementations there have been are domain-specific [3, 11, 9, 13]. However, the problem of building domain-independent

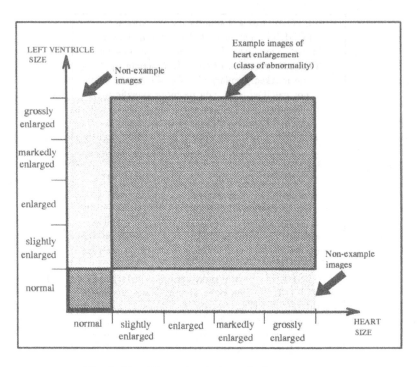

Fig. 2. Two-Dimensional view of a feature space

ITSs that teach visual concepts has been neglected. Also neglected is the question of how meta-level knowledge can be encoded in order to regulate tutorial dialogues about abnormal image features while enforcing consistency of such dialogues.

In trying to understand what constitutes radiological expertise, Lesgold [4] suggests that it involves substantial amounts of both *principled* knowledge and *experiential* knowledge. Principled knowledge refers to the distinct bodies of medical knowledge which are already formalised (e.g. anatomy and theories of medical disease) whereas experiential knowledge involves the integration of these bodies of knowledge in clinical practice to produce accurate diagnoses.

Despite the fact that visual interpretation tasks in different domains have much in common [10], no domain-independent method for ITS design has focused specifically on visual concept recognition. Computer tutors for visual concepts differ from more traditional tutoring systems in that the skills to be communicated to students are closely linked to the interpretation of image patterns as a primary task. Therefore, these systems must include facilities for students to manipulate and display large stocks of visual images. Likewise, design methods and tools for producing these tutors must provide experts with mechanisms for creating and assigning high-level, symbolic descriptions to such images.

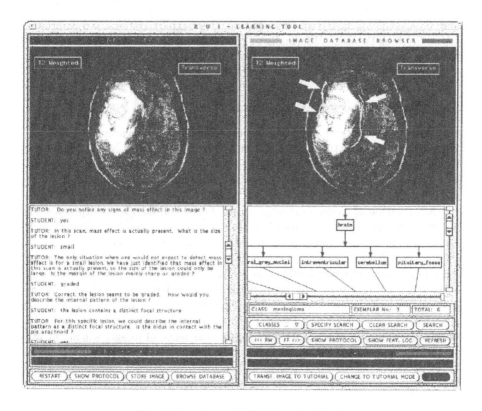

Fig. 3. Snapshot of RUI's Learning Tool

3 The Instructional Level

At the instructional level, RUI's Learning Tool [2] allows a student to acquire expertise by means of two distinct interfaces: the Image Database Browser (IDB) and the Guided Tutorial Mode (GTM). Figure 3 shows a snapshot of the Learning tool where the IDB is displayed on the right side and the GTM on the left side. The IDB aims at the communication of principled knowledge while the GTM aims at the communication of experiential knowledge. In using the IDB, the system-passive interface, students search and select example images based on anatomical information, observe individual feature values as well as feature locations, make interactive measurements of ratios and compare complete diagnoses to acquire the underlying principled knowledge necessary for classifying abnormalities. In using the GTM, the system-active interface, students stretch their experiential knowledge by engaging in Socratic-like dialogues (see Figures 1 and 4) where, constantly challenged by the system, they make use of their conceptual principles to form more accurate and complete diagnoses.

Existing diagnostic expert systems and computer tutors for visual concept recognition, such as the Radiology Tutor [11], CLORIS [9] and ICON [13], are domain-specific teaching tools. In addition, these expert systems and computer tutors overlook the issue of formalising knowledge under the same language used both for experts to author courseware and for students to acquire expertise, *i.e.* a rich, unified, expert-student framework of knowledge communication.

3.1 The IDB and Free Exploration

The IDB interface is conceived as a learning-by-discovery environment. Free exploration encourages students to become autonomous learners by allowing them to compose their own questions, hypothesise about the concepts of a domain and draw conclusions from hypotheses. In visual domains, this includes understanding the nature of visual concepts translated into features such as shape, size and location of anatomical components. Principled knowledge expresses the ability to recognise abnormalities based on deformations and variations of such anatomical structures, projected onto 2-Dimensional image regions [4].

Because of the exploratory nature of the IDB, it only permits students to learn most diagnostic relationships inductively, rather than explicitly discussing these relationships during the interaction. However, knowledge acquired by induction is fragile [11] and, as a result, students could be expected to show misconceptions even after using the IDB. One source of diagnostic error is based upon the possibility of students inferring the existence of images which "fit in" the feature space, but in practice do not occur. That is, as instruction proceeds, students' beliefs are expected to become "over-general," needing explicit (guided) interventions to avoid the problem.

3.2 The GTM and the Model of Dialogue Interpretation

To provide explicit advice and thus help the development of experiential knowledge, the GTM engages students in Socratic-like dialogues similar to those of the earlier Radiology Tutor, a domain-specific ITS for developing the skills of interpreting cardiac X-rays. For example, Figure 1 shows a dialogue with the GTM while teaching about knowledge designed (with RUI) for the domain of cardiac radiology. In fact, a similar dialogue to that in Figure 1 can also be carried out by the Radiology Tutor.

The GTM comments on students' partial diagnoses of images, critiques inconsistencies in such diagnoses, indicates important areas of the image with graphic elements, and gives continuity to the dialogue by asking about other abnormal image features. The GTM guides the interaction by monitoring students' actions as they progress with their hypotheses and by offering intelligent feedback whenever they deviate from accurate diagnoses. To achieve these goals, the GTM is supported by a domain-independent model of dialogue interpretation based on four mechanisms: (1) feature visibility, (2) anatomy granularity, (3) the propagation of domain-specific teaching/protection rules, and (4) default teaching actions.

The *feature visibility* mechanism makes use of visibility information, available from a symbolic image descriptions, matching it against the student's diagnosis and, if necessary, providing feedback. Basically, it helps the student in understanding what knowledge is not directly visible in an image but can still be inferred by a relationship among different features. For an example of this mechanism's effect on the tutorial dialogue see lines 20–24 of Figure 1.

```
-   TUTOR: Give a diagnosis for this image.
-   STUDENT: The brain is affected by the lesion.
-   The lesion size is medium.
-   TUTOR: Quite right, the brain is affected by the
5   lesion. The lesion is of type meningioma. The le-
-   sion appears to be large. Which parts of the brain
-   are affected by the lesion?
-   STUDENT: The cortical grey is affected ...
-   TUTOR: Indeed, the cortical grey appears to be
10  affected by the lesion. ... Do you notice any other
-   indication of meningioma?
-   STUDENT: The lesion is necrotic.
-   TUTOR: That is not a specific sign of menin-
-   gioma. It can be associated with glioma, for
15  example. The image opposite shows a case of
-   glioma where the lesion is necrotic. What do you
-   think the arrows above indicate?
-   STUDENT: The lesion is in contact with the pia
-   arachnoid.
20  TUTOR: Correct, the lesion appears to be in
-   contact with the pia arachnoid. What do you no-
-   tice about the margin of the lesion?
-   STUDENT: The margin of the lesion is mainly
-   sharp. ...
```

Fig. 4. Dialogue carried out by RUI about scans of the head

Sometimes a student's diagnosis, although not incorrect, may require more detailed information to be considered accurate. The *anatomy granularity* mechanism aims at tuning the student's perception on where exactly, in the anatomical structure, the abnormal feature is situated. Lines 5–7 of Figure 1 show a fragment of dialogue where this mechanism is activated, challenging the student to provide a more accurate interpretation about the feature calcification which is not found to be generalised in the aorta. In fact, the aorta is described in the knowledge base by a finer level of granularity consisting of three subcomponents (see Figure 5), in one of which (the aortic arch) the calcification is located.

The third mechanism refers to the *propagation of domain-specific teaching and protection rules*. RUI's dialogue interpreter traverses the anatomical structure (see Figure 5) defined for a class of abnormality, in a depth-first fashion,

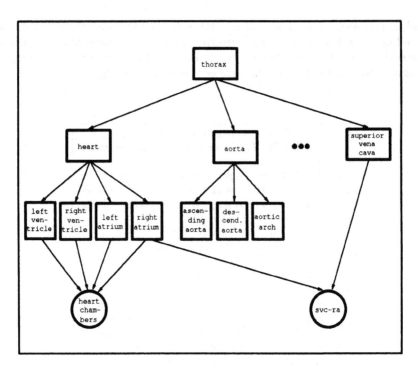

Fig. 5. Anatomical structure of the human chest

searching for such domain-specific rules and gives them control precedence over the other three domain-independent mechanisms (1, 2 and 4). Depending on the conditional clause of a rule, the dialogue interpreter may fire the body of actions of this rule, propagating the effect on the student model which may result in the selection of another rule by this mechanism thus repeating the cycle. Through this mechanism, the GTM avoids the problem of over general student beliefs by eventually firing actions of domain-specific rules which are specially designed by the domain expert to enhance the power of explicit advice. See lines 10, 11 and 13–18 of Figure 1 and lines 4, 5, 10, 11, 16 and 17 of Figure 4 as examples.

Finally, like the above mechanism, the *default teaching actions* mechanism can also be activated by the model of dialogue interpretation to discuss the value V of a feature F in an anatomical component C. However, default teaching actions are generated automatically by meta-level procedures that simply combine V, F and C to construct discourse structures in a slot filling way. It is only executed whenever the dialogue interpreter does not find a domain-specific rule referring to F and C in focus. In other words, even if the expert does not design any domain-specific rules, the dialogue interpreter, combining this mechanism with the first two mechanisms (feature visibility and anatomy granularity), is still capable of guiding tutorial interactions with students. Examples of this mechanism's effect are found in lines 1, 4–7 and 9 of Figure 1 and lines 1, 9, 13–16 and 20–22 of Figure 4.

3.3 The Acquisition of Experiential Knowledge

To provide explicit advice on building diagnoses and thus help the development of experiential knowledge, the GTM engages students in Socratic-like dialogues. Socratic dialogues are meant to be rich dialogues, often based on natural language, where the computer poses a problem and the computer and student together "discuss" it. Students may ask back another question for clarifying some information they believe to be relevant. The computer can acknowledge correct assertions, send warnings about inconsistent points or even, if necessary, alter the course of the student's work. The three most relevant characteristics of Socratic dialogues for the current research are:

C1 - There is only one source of belief, *i.e.* the knowledge communication process is unidirectional and flows from the tutor to the student. This is in accordance with the idea of the more experienced element (tutor) in the conversation guiding the less experienced one (student).

C2 - The hypothetico-deductive approach of the conversation which consists of the student extracting general principles from available evidence, found in image features, about the case in discussion. The student is driven towards forming an initial hypothesis as to the case-problem, examine the validity of the hypothesis and search for further evidence that can support or contradict the hypothesis. The tutor can address a student's incorrect response by treating it as a hypothesis and showing the consequences of the hypothesis. This approach becomes important to help students, when learning classes of abnormalities, in a data-driven (forward) fashion where the system is capable of proposing hypotheses when solving diagnostic problems in a given domain of expertise.

C3 - There is fluidity of the dialogue. The tutor examines the steps in the student's reasoning to make sure that the following question is an appropriate one to be asked, providing for continuity and consistency of the dialogue. This is particularly appropriate when students have to develop their ability in gathering evidence for producing more complete diagnoses.

Despite the difficulties of implementation, these three characteristics make Socratic dialogues a suitable means for helping students extend their knowledge, from principled to experiential, in an explicit and consistent way. Many such computer tutors that adopt Socratic dialogues for teaching in a variety of subject domains (e.g the Radiology tutor, WHY, the BLOCKS Tutor and the MENO-TUTOR) seem to use Socratic dialogues in equivalent forms (see [14]).

4 Consistency of Tutorial Dialogues

One of the most basic constraints imposed on formal languages is consistency. Natural languages, on the other hand, lack such a quality for their sentences usually include alternate meanings of words (ambiguity) and little ordering of ideas. Besides that, as humans, we are also capable of reasoning with inaccurate and incomplete knowledge. However, consistency can become a very important requirement if (pseudo-) natural language is to be used by computer tools like the GTM. This important characteristic, although extensively developed for the construction of knowledge bases, does not seem to be frequently approached by existing frameworks for tutorial dialogues. The only possible exception is UMFE [12], in which consistency rules can be designed to avoid implausible knowledge states while delivering instruction.

To enforce consistency of more elaborate tutorial dialogues, domain-specific teaching and protection rules are integral processing ingredients. Through the conditional clauses of such rules, the GTM computes which body of action is appropriate to be executed at the moment in order to propagate diagnostic information. Such information carries, in textual form, the reflex of an expert's experience, organised in well-defined knowledge units (production rules) located in specific nodes of a graph structure of anatomic components. After being refined during the design phase, the feedback provided to students through these rules tends to display rich information along with how well they are doing or how contradictory their statements are. However, the actual consistency check lies in the conditional clause of domain-specific teaching and protection rules.

Conditional clauses of teaching/protection rules are logic expressions in Predicate Calculus which have their truth values checked against the dialogue history as well as against the current sentence input by the student. The GTM then submits the conditional clause of candidate rules to its theorem prover for determining truth values. This logic proof mechanism is specifically adapted to work with the corresponding rule actions in the sense that, whenever existing interrelationships are violated by the student, some action is performed towards bringing the student's beliefs to a consistent state. In effect, it is actually this correspondence mechanism that carries the responsibility of linking the underlying formal proof of the logic expressions with the "natural" appearance of surface text, giving us the illusion that consistency resides in the interface language when in fact it emerges form a deeper knowledge structure.

5 Conclusion

The method outlined provides mechanisms for reasoning about symbolic image descriptions of abnormal features guided by a model of dialogue interpretation. Philosophical aspects of the method and mechanisms have been discussed, highlighting solutions for specific problems like dealing with over-general student beliefs and enforcing consistency of tutorial dialogues. The tools are fully implemented.

To substantiate generality claims about RUI, we have combined the evaluation of the software tools with the definition of knowledge bases for four different domains of expertise. The evaluation procedures have concentrated on the generality of the formalisms as well as on the usability of the tools. The positive results suggest that RUI is a suitable framework in the context of ITS evolution.

The RUI project keeps progressing in several research streams. Recent accounts of ITS architectures attribute a key role to interface design [14], claiming that knowledge should be communicated in different forms (e.g. applying a variety of tutorial styles) which can be achieved by incorporating knowledge about cognitive principles. On going work in RUI is devoted to explore and implement a number of classes of interface objects so that domain experts can create system-active and system-passive tutorial interactions in a flexible way by operating authoring tools for the interface of the Learning Tool.

References

1. Bonar, J., Cunningham, R., Schultz, J.: An object oriented architecture for intelligent tutoring. In Proceed. of OOPSLA'86. (1986) 269–276
2. Direne, A. I.: Methodology and tools for designing concept tutoring systems. Technical Report – 294, COGS - The University of Sussex - UK (1994)
3. Jeffery, N., Teather, B.A., Teather, D., Sharples, M., du Boulay, B., Direne, A.I., du Boulay, G.H.: Statistical modelling and intelligent tutoring of visual concepts for MR imaging of the head. In Proceed. of AIED'93. (1993) 562
4. Lesgold, A.M.: Acquiring expertise. In J.R. Anderson & S.M. Kosslyn (Eds.), Tutorials in Learning and Memory. W.H. Freeman (1984)
5. Mervis, C. B., Rosch, E.: Categorisation and natural objects. Annual Review of Psychology, 32 (1981) 89–115
6. Murray, T., Woolf, B.: Results of encoding knowledge with tutor construction tools. In Proceed. of AAAI'92. (1992) 17–23
7. Myles-Worsley, M., Johnston, W.A.: The influence of expertise on x-ray image processing. Journal of Experimental Psychology, 14 (1988) 553–557
8. O'Shea, T., Bornat, R., du Boulay, B., Eisenstadt, M., Page, I.: Tools for creating intelligent computer tutors. In A. Elithorn & R. Barneji (Eds.), Human and Artificial Intelligence. North-Holland (1984)
9. Parkes, A.P.: The prototype CLORIS system. Information Processing and Management, 25 (1989) 171–186
10. Rosch, E., Lloyd, B.B.: Cognition and Categorization. Lawrence Erlbaum (1978)
11. Sharples, M., du Boulay, B.: Knowledge representation, teaching strategy and simplifying assumptions for a concept tutoring system. In Proceed. of ECAI'88. (1988) 268–270
12. Sleeman, D.H.: PIXIE: a shell for developing intelligent tutoring systems. In R. Lawler & M. Yazdani (Eds.), AI and Education: Learning Environments and Intelligent Tutoring Systems. Ablex Publishing (1987)
13. Swett, H.A., Miller, P.L.: ICON: A computer-based approach to differential diagnosis in radiology. Radiology, 163 (1987) 555–558
14. Wenger, E.: Artificial Intelligence and Tutoring Systems: Computational and Cognitive Approaches to the Communication of Knowledge. Morgan Kaufmann (1987)

Acknowledgements. The author is grateful to M. Sharples and B. du Boulay for the discussions. The expertise in medical imaging has been provided by the MEDSYS group (De Montford Univ.–UK) and by T. Arvanitis (Sussex Univ.–UK). The research is supported by grant CNPq–Brazil–360984/93.2.

Knowledge Based Clustering of Partially Characterized Objects

Manuel L. Campagnolo[1], Helder Coelho[2] and Jorge H. Capelo[3]

[1] Dpt. Matemática. ISA. Un. Técnica de Lisboa. e-mail: mcampagnolo@isa0.isa.utl.pt
[2] Dpt. Informática. Faculdade de Ciências. Univ. de Lisboa. e-mail: hcoelho@inesc.pt
[3] Estação Florestal Nacional. DCRN. Tapada da Ajuda. 1300 Lisboa. Portugal.

Abstract. Cluster analysis can be generally described as a way to discover and identify concepts from a set of multicharacterized objects. In cluster analysis, each concept is described extensionally by a subset of objects called a class. Taking those concepts as reference, it is known, when the characteristics are not all available, that the cluster analysis procedure can lead to spurious class definitions, caused by the loss of information on the object descriptions. So, one of the possible techniques to handle this problem consists of incorporating more knowledge about the structure of classes of objects in this classification process. In this paper we propose and defend a new method for clustering partially characterized objects, by combining three approaches: 1) the use of probability theory to represent uncertainty on objects' description, 2) the adoption of a Bayesian network model to support and explore knowledge on dependence relations among the objects' descriptive variables, and 3) the introduction of a new similarity measure consistent with the used objects' representation. We also apply this method to a vegetation classification problem and we show that the achieved classification is less sensitive to data erosion than classifications obtained just from the known characteristics of the objects.

1   Introduction

In this paper we propose an extension of the classical clustering methods, in order to group partially characterized objects, *i.e.*, objects which characteristics are not all available, by taking into account techniques of Artificial Intelligence. In fact, in many applied sciences we have to deal with incomplete knowlegde.

Cluster analysis is a particular category in computational learning often called unsupervised learning because explicit examples of the concepts to be learnt are not provided ([10], [6]). We don't discuss here the quality of the concepts (classes) defined through classical clustering methods. The discussion of that important and controversial topic may be found, for instance, in [2], [1], or in [5]. We will be only concerned with the task of overcoming the incompleteness of data description. Instead of dropping out each unknown characteristic, as suggested in [2], or summing over the whole data set to estimate a likelihood for each unknown value, as implemented in AutoClass [6], we propose a method that uses aditional knowledge on data structure. Our basic contribution for this method consists in articulating diverse models and techniques from Artificial Intelligence and probability theory and in proposing a new similarity measure for the objects' representation we use. As a matter of fact, in most literature, a satisfactory measure is not available. As it will be shown in Sect. 5 for a real data application, the average performance of the proposed method is significantly better than each one of the performances obtained with those two more straightforward approaches.

The form of representation we use for expressing knowledge combines context representations and uncertainty. For the context representation, we follow an Artificial Intelligence approach which consists in structuring the problem domain through causal dependencies between the components of this domain. For the uncertainty representation, we decided to use the probability theory to support the uncertainty on the objects' characteristics because of its ability to process context-sensitive beliefs (see [9]) and because of its compatibility with the model of causal dependencies that we use for context representation.

The procedure that will be proposed for clustering partially characterized objects is a three step procedure. The first step consists in gathering some knowledge about the non-available characteristics. This will be done using a variable dependencies model called a Bayesian network, a computational model for human's inferential reasoning, that supports subjective, incertain and incomplete knowledge [7]. The second step involves the computation of a similarity measure for all the pairs of partially known objects. This measure depends on the similarity of the objects' characterization and depends, also, on the lack of knowledge about the description of objects. Finally, the last step is the hierarchical clustering of the objects through a classical similarity based method.

2 Formal statement of the problem

Let $X_1, ..., X_m$ be m random variables from the set of objects to m sets of quantitative or qualitative values. Let's suppose that each variable (X_k) can take a value of one of a finite number (n_k) of mutually exclusive modalities. The modality taken by X_k for an object will be called k-th characteristic of the object. Let p_{kj} represent the probability that X_k takes its j-th modality, i.e., $p_{kj} = P(X_k = x_{kj})$. Then, the k-th characteristic of the object is described through $(p_{k1}, ..., p_{kn_k})$, with $\sum_j p_{kj} = 1, \forall k$. The full probabilistic representation of an object is given by the vector $\mathbf{x}$:

$$\mathbf{x} = ((p_{11}, ..., p_{1n_1}), ..., (p_{k1}, ..., p_{kn_k}), ..., (p_{m1}, ..., p_{mn_m})). \tag{1}$$

In case we need to specify one particular object, we can do it explicitly. For instance, $p_{kj}(\mathbf{x})$ represents the probability p_{kj} for the object $\mathbf{x}$.

Using the probabilistic representation of the objects we can state that the k-th characteristic is unknown if all probabilities, $p_{k1}, ..., p_{kn_k}$, are equal and the k-th characteristic is known if one of these values is 1 and the others 0. Furthermore, the probabilistic representation allows us to represent partial knowledge about a particular characteristic. For instance, $(0.6, 0.1, 0.2, 0.1)$ could be the probabilistic representation of a four modality variable, meaning that the first modality has a 0.6 probability, the second a 0.1 probability, and so on.

Given an object, we will call the set of values of the known characteristics *evidence* of that object. For instance, $\varepsilon = (X_2 = 5, X_3 = 5, X_6 = 4, X_7 = 1)$ represents the evidence of an object for which the second, third, sixth and seventh characteristics are known.

We can now define formally the problem of clustering for which a new approach will be proposed in this paper. The partially characterized objects clustering problem is stated as follows: Given a set of n objects, $\Omega = \{x_1, ..., x_n\}$, with m characteristics, which are not all available, and a function S of similarity between two sets of objects, we are looking for N classes, $\mathcal{C}_1, ..., \mathcal{C}_N$, which are a partition of Ω such that

$$\forall x \in \mathcal{C}_i, \ \forall j \neq i, \ S(\{x\}, \mathcal{C}_i - \{x\}) \geq S(\{x\}, \mathcal{C}_j) \tag{2}$$

and maximize[4]
$$M_N = \frac{1}{n} \max_p \sum_{j=1}^{N} |\mathcal{C}_{p(j)} \cap \mathcal{C}_j^*|, \tag{3}$$

being p a permutation of $\{1, ..., N\}$ and $\mathcal{C}_j^*$ the j-th class of the reference classification (the classification that would be achieved if all the characteristics were available). M_N is an evaluating function. It is the maximum proportion of objects common to both the classes of the reference classification and the classes obtained with incomplete data. M_N takes its maximum value, 1, if the produced classification has the same classes than the reference classification.

3 Completion of objects' description

In this work we will assume that at least some variables are related by causal dependencies. Those dependencies will be described in a qualitative and quantitative way by a mathematical model called a *Bayesian network* or a *belief network*. This structure is, following [7], a directed acyclic graph in which the nodes represent propositions (or variables), the arcs signify direct dependencies between the linked propositions and the strengths of these dependencies are quantified by conditional probabilities. Therefore, we can represent a Bayesian network by a pair (G, p), where G is the graphical component (a directed acyclic graph) and p is the probabilistic component (a joint probability distribution of the variables $X_1, ..., X_m$). The graph, $G = (X, E)$, is defined by $X = \{X_1, ..., X_m\}$ and E as the set of directed arcs (X_t, X_s). The existence of (X_t, X_s) in E means that the variable X_t depends directly of the variable X_s. We will denote by $pa(X_k)$ the set $\{X_i : (X_k, X_i) \in E\}$, *i.e.*, the set of parents of X_k. Gathering information on an unknown characteristic of an object consists in estimating the marginal distribution conditioned by the existing evidence on that object, *i.e.*, estimating, for a variable X_k, $p(x_k/\varepsilon)$.

---

[4] $|A|$ denotes the cardinality of the set A.

In a Bayesian network, the joint distribution of $(X_1, ..., X_m)$ can be written as a function of probability distributions of subsets of variables. Formally, as proved in [8], we have

$$p(\mathbf{x}) = \Pi_{k=1}^{m} p(x_k/pa(X_k)). \tag{4}$$

Each one of the sets $\{X_k\} \cup pa(X_k)$ can be viewed as a processor and the graph as a modular computational architecture for evidency propagation.

The probability distribution (4) has $\sum_{k=1}^{m}(n_k \Pi_{i:X_i \in pa(X_k)} n_i)$ elements. Notice that this value increases exponentially with $\max_k\{|pa(X_k)|\}$ and the number of elements of the simple joint distribution increases exponentially with m. So, the Bayesian network model has less parameters than the simple joint distribution and this is crucial because: 1) it reduces the computational requirements for calculating the marginal distributions of the variables, and 2) it permits that the estimation of the required parameters of the model, from the data set, be considerably more reliable. As a matter of fact, this second property results, not only of the reducement of the number of the parameters, but also of the modularity feature of the Bayesian network model. This point will be further commented in Sect. 5.

We will call propagation of the evidence through the graph the estimation of the marginal distributions of all the variables of X that don't belongs to the evidence. Several methods of propagation have been developed. In the text book of Pearl ([9]) diverse algorithms for evidencies propagation that can be used for our purpose are described. We use one of those methods, called stochastic simulation, because it is acomplishable in polynomial time and because it is especially suited for tasks involving complex and nondecomposable models. The computation of probabilities of the marginal distribution is done by counting the fraction of time that events occur in a series of simulation runs.

As was pointed out at the begining of this section, the Bayesian network has two components, a graphical one and a probabilistic one, that have to be defined, for a given data set, in order that the evidence propagation can be done.

The graphical component can be induced from the descriptions of the objects and/or can be built by an expert on the problem domain. The first possibility is based on the correlations between variables (see [11] for details) or consists in the identification of the network which maximize a similarity between the simple joint distribution and the joint distribution of the Bayesian network model (see [9]). The second possibility consists in asking an expert to choose the fathers for each variable, *i.e.*, to decide which variables affect directly each one. The graphical representation can allow the expert to control easily his choice of variable direct dependancies (see Fig. 1, in Sect. 5, which ilustrates this point).

To define the probabilistic component of the variable dependancies model we need to specify each one of the probability values of the model, which are the conditional probabilities that appear in formula (4). Each one of those values is estimated from the set of objects and may be, eventually, revised by the expert. Since we have objects with unknown characteristics, the estimation for each processor of the Bayesian network will have to be based on subsets of objects for which all the characteristics associated to this processor are known.

4 Probabilistic objects clustering

A similarity measure for probabilistic objects. After having propagated the known characteristics through the Bayesian network we obtain a complete probabilistic description for each object and we may calculate a similarity measure for each pair of objects. In most literature, a satisfactory similarity measure for probabilistic objects is not available. Therefore, we will propose a measure and analyse its behaviour. Our proposal is based on a family of measures used for objects described by nominal variables which are called *matching coefficients* (see [2]).

The similarity measure for probabilistic objects will be defined by

$$s(\mathbf{x}_1, \mathbf{x}_2) = \sum_{k=1}^{m} \rho_k \, \delta_k(\mathbf{x}_1, \mathbf{x}_2), \qquad \delta_k(\mathbf{x}_1, \mathbf{x}_2) = D_k(\mathbf{x}_1, \mathbf{x}_2) \, [E_k(\mathbf{x}_1)]^{\frac{1}{2}} \, [E_k(\mathbf{x}_2)]^{\frac{1}{2}} \tag{5}$$

where ρ_k, $0 \leq \rho_k \leq 1$, are the weights that express the importance of the characteristics in the measure definition and $\delta_k(\mathbf{x}_1, \mathbf{x}_2)$, $0 \leq \delta_k \leq 1$, expresses the similarity between the k-th characteristic of the objects $\mathbf{x}_1$ and $\mathbf{x}_2$.

Each component δ_k depends on two features of the data. Firstly, the amount of knowledge on the description of the object, *i.e.*, the degree of certainty of the objects description[5]:

$$E_k(\mathbf{x}) = 1 + \frac{1}{\log n_k} \cdot \sum_{j=1}^{n_k} p_{kj}(\mathbf{x}) \, \log p_{kj}(\mathbf{x}) \tag{6}$$

This is evaluated by the simmetric of the entropy for the k-th characteristic (see [10] for the measurement of the overall uncertainty level of a set of messages based on the Shannon information theory). Secondly, the similarity of the k-th characteristic probabilistic description. The term $D_k(\mathbf{x}_1, \mathbf{x}_2)$ is defined as the symmetric of the euclidian distance between $p_k^*(\mathbf{x}_1)$ and $p_k^*(\mathbf{x}_2)$,

$$D_k(\mathbf{x}_1, \mathbf{x}_2) = 1 - \|p_k^*(\mathbf{x}_1) - p_k^*(\mathbf{x}_2)\|, \tag{7}$$

with $\|\mathbf{y}\| = (\sum_i y_i^2)^{\frac{1}{2}}$ and $p_k^*(\mathbf{x}) = \frac{1}{\sqrt{2}}(p_{k1}, ..., p_{kn_k})$, if X_k is nominal, and $p_k^*(\mathbf{x}) = \sum_{j=1}^{n_k} p_{kj} \, \sigma_{kj}$, if X_k is ordinal. We use a vector of weights of the modalities, $\sigma_k = (\sigma_{k1}, ..., \sigma_{kn_k})$ if the variable is ordinal to substitute the probability distribution of modalities by a score on the variable X_k. If we set σ_k such that $0 = \sigma_{k1} \leq \sigma_{kj} \leq \sigma_{kj+1} \leq \sigma_{kn_k} = 1$ then $D_k(\mathbf{x}_1, \mathbf{x}_2)$ will take values between 0 and 1.

From the previous definition it is easy to verify that δ_k takes the value 0 if and only if one of the k-th characteristics of $\mathbf{x}_1$ or $\mathbf{x}_2$ is unknown or if they are totally different. It's easy to prove, also, that $\delta_k = 1$ if and only if the k-th characteristics are known and are the same for $\mathbf{x}_1$ and $\mathbf{x}_2$.

---

[5] If $p_{kj}(\mathbf{x}) = 0$ we establish that $p_{kj} \log p_{kj}$ takes the value 0.

The clustering algorithm: We will use a conventional hierarchical clustering algorithm (HCA), to build the classes of objects. Nevertheless, the previous proposals are directly aplicable to the other clustering approaches. A HCA has as input a similarity matrix describing all pairwise similarities among objects and has as output n hierarchical partitions, of cardinalities n, $n-1$, ..., 1, of the set of objects, where n is the number of objects. That algorithm requires the definition of similarity measure between two sets of objects (called, in this context, linkage form). That linkage function, which we denoted by $S(\mathcal{C}_1, \mathcal{C}_2)$ in (2) is, in general, a function of all the similarities, $s(\mathbf{x}_1, \mathbf{x}_2)$, for every $\mathbf{x}_1 \in \mathcal{C}_1$ and every $\mathbf{x}_2 \in \mathcal{C}_2$. In the next section we will use three common linkage forms (see [2], [5]) - single linkage, complete linkage and average linkage[6] - to test the partially characterized objects clustering method proposed in this paper.

5 Test of the method with a real data example

Classification of vegetation data. Plant and plant community data are one of the classical types of data that have been used in cluster analysis and have motivated the development of cluster analysis methods. The reason for this is, perhaps, the fact that descriptive studies with plant or plant community data yield controversial results, in the sense that they can support or contradict theories of vegetation evolution and structure. Furthermore, the vegetation analists have to deal frequently with incomplete data, *i.e.*, with partially characterized objects. For those reasons, we chose a plant community data set for testing the proposed method.

Vegetation ecologists usually attempt to produce descriptive models of the natural vegetation cover. Due to selective habitat preferences most plant species form natural structures - plant communities or plant associations - which are represented by means of an hierarchical structure called syntaxomy. Syntaxonomies are produced by classification of a *ground plots* × *species* matrix (ground plots=objects; species=variables).

Although a given plant association describes an ideal stable situation in which all the characteristic species would be present, most vegetation data lack information on some of these species. However, in well-known territories, a professional (vegetation ecologist) can establish empirical relationships on the joint occurence of most species that would complete the matrix data. The traditional solutions include *a posteriori* subjective refinement of the classification. The proposed method can be used to attemps automatically the integration of both sources of ecological information in a unique framework. Thus, a stronger syntaxonomy is derived both from the actual data and expert knowledge and is, therefore, less sensitive to the incompleteness of the sampling process.

---

[6] In single or complete linkage the similarity of two sets is, respectively, the similarity between their closest or their most distant elements and in average linkage it is the mean of all pairwise similarities.

Case study: vegetation data from Southern Portugal. The plant community data has 74 plots × 24 species abundance from low-scrub *Cistus sp.* dominated communities from southern Portugal. The variables (species abundance) take as values four levels of percent cover of each species on the ground plot (absence, low, medium, high). The values were obtained by man direct observation and measurement of the plots.

The used data set is constituted by totally characterized objects, *i.e.*, the matrix represents complete, stable vegetation plots regarding the occurence of characteristic species. This choice of data enables the evaluation of our method. The procedure that was followed starts with the random erasing of a certain proportion of the objects characteristics, pursues with the application of the method described in this paper, and ends with the comparison of the clusters obtained with complete and incomplete data. The set of clusters obtained with complete data is used as the reference structure of the data. That procedure is repeated for several proportions of erased characteristics (10%, 20%, 30 % and 40%), for ten random choices of sets of characteristics to be erased, and for the three linkage forms referred in Sect. 4.

The large number of variables (24) envolved in this case study limits the *a priori* perception of all relations among them. However, we can perform a previous data exploration - the computation of variables' correlation coeficients (see [11]) - to help the expert in defining the relevant dependencies. So, the graphical component of the Bayesian network is built from the analysis of the variables' correlation matrix and is revised subsequently by an expert. The whole network for the used data has 31 directed arcs. We present in Fig. 1 the network of the ancestors of one variable (abundance of the species *Lavandula luisieri*) which was obtained with that approach. The same kind of representation could be build for other subsets of network nodes.

Fig. 1. Graphical representation of the dependencies among one variable's ancestors

Thymus	→	*Lavandula*	←	*Genista*		*Halimium*	←	*Stauracanthus*
mastichina		*sampaioana*		*polyanthos*		*ocymoides*		*boivinii*

$$\nearrow \qquad \downarrow \qquad \nwarrow \qquad \swarrow$$

Ulex	→	*Lavandula*	←	*Genista*	←	*Cistus*
argenteus		*luisieri*		*triacantos*		*populifolius*

The probabilistic component of the Bayesian network is estimated, for each random erasure, from the set of available characteristics. For the analysed vegetation data, the probabilistic component of the network still has a large number of parameters (3096) which is, yet, considerably smaller than the number of parameters (2.81×10^{14}) of the complete joint distribution. Although the expert cannot easily revise the conditional probabilities for large families of variables, he can analyse some reasonable sized conditional probabilities tables of the Bayesian network.

Results. As we said before, we perform ten random choices of subsets of the data set for proportions of 10%, 20%, 30% and 40% of erased data, obtaining forty incomplete data sets.

Then, we apply, on each of those forty data sets, the three following procedures, conducing each one of them to a 74 × 74 symmetric matrix of similarity measures: **P1**) The method proposed in this paper, that is, the completion of objects description with the marginal probabilities estimations (of the evidence propagation through the Bayesian network) obtained by Pearl's stochastic simulation algorithm[7] (see Sect. 3), and the calculation of the similarity measure proposed in Sect. 4; **P2**) The substitution of each unknown characteristic by an uniform probability distribution of the respective variable modalities, and the calculation of the same similarity measure; **P3**) The substitution of each unknown characteristic by the marginal probability distribution of the respective variable modalities, estimated just from the known characteristics of the respective variable, and, once more, the calculation of the proposed similarity measure. Notice that, in this last procedure, the existing evidence on an object is not used to estimate the probability distribution.

Finally, we execute the cluster algorithms associated to the three linkage forms referred in Sect. 5 and we obtain a hierachical classification tree for each one of the 10 × 4 × 3 × 3 analysed cases.

In order to be able to assess the global results, we use the evaluating function M_N (see Sect. 2) and we compute it just for the four last levels of the tree (corresponding to N=5, N=4, N=3 and N=2 classes) assuming that we are only interested in defining a small number of classes. The mean values of M_N, for the 10 random erased data sets, are presented in Tab. 1.

We realize a statistical test (based on the t distribution) on the difference between the results of the procedure which includes our proposals (P1) relatively to the results of the other applied procedures (P2 and P3). In the cases where P1 reveals to be significantly better than P2 or P3, that conclusion is pointed out in the P2 or P3 column of Tab. 1, respectively.

Looking at the results in Tab. 1, we can say that our method has a comparative good behaviour. In point of fact, for the three linkage forms, its mean performance is significantly better than the performance of the other procedures. The global results, relatively to the reference structure, vary substantially with the used linkage form and tend to decrease with the increase of the erased objects' proportion. Complete-link results are the ones for which that tendency is more clear. As it would be expected, M_N decreases while N increases, since the number of possible partitions of the set of objects increases exponentially with the number of classes.

Another important feature of the values in Tab. 1 is that the performance measure of P1 is much closer to P3 than to P2. This can be easily explained by the nature of the data set for two reasons: 1) the ground plots are relatively homogeneous and so it is acceptable to estimate the unknown characteristics

---

[7] We establish that the weights of the variables and the weights of the modalities are $\rho_k = 1$ and $(\sigma_{k1}, \sigma_{k2}, \sigma_{k3}, \sigma_{k4}) = (0.0, 0.33, 0.67, 1.0)$ for all variables X_k.

Table 1. Percentages of common objects relatively to the reference classifications.

e.p.	N	single-link			complete-link			average-link		
		P1	P2	P3	P1	P2	P3	P1	P2	P3
10%	5	93.0	87.3***	92.3***	65.4	54.2***	67.6	71.6	62.8***	65.8***
	4	98.2	92.3***	97.8***	65.5	53.5***	67.8	89.5	88.5***	92.0
	3	98.2	94.6***	97.4***	69.2	65.3***	64.9***	96.6	93.9***	97.0
	2	98.0	97.8***	98.6	89.2	87.8**	88.4	98.6	93.8***	97.8***
	mean	96.9	93.0***	96.6***	72.3	65.2***	72.2**	89.1	84.8***	88.2***
20%	5	90.7	86.4***	90.4***	67.3	46.4***	67.8	69.6	61.2***	66.6***
	4	96.5	91.9***	95.7***	63.1	47.7***	63.5	92.4	87.0***	91.2***
	3	98.2	94.3***	97.2***	63.4	56.9***	67.4	96.2	93.0***	96.9
	2	98.9	97.3***	98.4***	85.7	80.9***	87.8	98.4	94.1***	96.1***
	mean	96.1	92.5***	95.4***	69.9	58.0***	71.7	89.2	83.8***	87.7***
30%	5	89.1	85.0***	88.5***	63.0	42.8***	56.5***	65.5	59.9***	66.1
	4	94.7	91.1***	94.3***	59.9	44.2***	58.4***	91.1	85.8***	91.6
	3	96.5	93.5***	95.4***	62.0	58.1***	65.0	96.8	92.7***	96.4***
	2	97.4	97.6	98.1	80.4	76.8***	88.1	97.3	94.1***	95.5***
	mean	94.4	91.8***	94.1***	66.3	55.5***	67.0	87.7	83.1***	87.4***
40%	5	88.6	86.1***	87.6***	56.2	39.1***	52.2***	65.3	60.8***	64.9***
	4	94.6	91.6***	93.8***	57.0	41.4***	51.8***	90.0	86.9***	91.2
	3	95.5	94.3***	95.4	67.7	52.0***	64.6***	96.8	92.7***	95.4***
	2	97.6	97.3***	98.1	91.2	71.2***	88.2***	96.2	93.2***	95.7***
	mean	94.1	92.3***	93.7***	68.0	50.9***	64.2***	87.1	83.4***	86.8***
mean		95.4	92.4***	94.9***	69.1	57.4***	68.7***	88.2	83.8***	87.5***

e.p. - proportion of erased objects

N - number of classes

*** - P1 performs better at a significance level of 0.01

** - P1 performs better at a significance level of 0.05

of a plot from the analogous characteristics of the other plots; and 2) there is a modality (absence) which has a very large frequency for almost all variables. If the overall frequency distribution was more uniform than it is, then the marginal distribution of unknown characteristics estimated through P3 would have a smaller degree of certainty (E_k) (see Sect. 4) and, consequently, the results would be closer to the results obtained with P2. Notice than this proximity between the results of P1 and P3 cannot be expected for all kinds of data. If the set of objects is very heterogeneous, then the estimation of the distribution of an unknown characteristic just based on the corresponding variable (P3) can lead to important errors in the completion of each object description.

6 Conclusion

The data analysed in Sect. 5 have a single characteristic which is common to the generality of plant community data: high dimensionality of the objects representation space. This explains why the example didn't deeply illustrate how to make use of the method to integrate expert knowledge in the classification procedure but, at the opposite, showed how the use of the Bayesian network could reduce drasticaly the dimensionality of the objects' representation. With lower dimensionality problems the graphical representation of variable dependencies is clear and the expert revision of all conditional probabilities becomes feasible. For instance in [3] and [4], for eight and ten variables domains, it is shown that an expert is able to integrate his knowledge - even in the whole probabilistic component - using an approach similar to the one described in this work.

As we already stated we don't discuss here the quality of the structure of classes revealed by the classical linkage forms used in hierarchical clustering methods. We argue that the proposed method is able to recover, at least partially, the class structure when there is a loss of information on the objects description. This conjecture is supported by the two following arguments. First, the method allows to integrate other sources of knowledge (expert knowledge on causal dependencies among variables) than just the object characteristics, in the classification process. Secondly, the organization of the whole variable set as a multiprocessor architecture, and the consequent reduction of the dimensionality of the variables' joint distribution, leads to a more eficient use of the available data in the sense that it allows more reliable estimates of the parameters.

References

1. Aldenderfer, M.S. and Blashfield, R.K.: *Cluster Analysis*. Sage Publications. Beverly Hills. (1984)
2. Anderberg, M.R.: *Cluster Analysis for Applications*. Academic Press. New York. (1973)
3. Campagnolo, M.L., Coelho, C.: Classification of objects' with partially unknown characteristics. *Estudos de Economia*, **13**, 3, (1993) 275–292 (in Portuguese)
4. Campagnolo, M.L.: Proposal of a method for knowledge integration in classification. Unpublished M.Sc. Dissertation, Instituto Superior de Economia e Gestão, Universidade Técnica de Lisboa (1992) (in Portuguese)
5. Gnanadesikan, R., Blashfield, R.K., Breiman, L., Dune, O.J., Friedman, J.H., King-Sun Fu, Hartigan, J.A., Kettenring, J.R., Lachenbruch, P.A., Olshen, R.A., Rohlf, F.J.: Discriminant analysis and clustering. *Statistical Science*, **4**, 1 (1992) 34–69
6. Hanson, R., Stutz, J., Cheeseman, P.: Bayesian Classification with Correlation and Inheritance. In *Proceedings of the Eleventh International Joint Conference in Artificial Intelligence*, (1989) 692–698
7. Pearl, J.: Fusion, propagation and structuring in belief networks. *Artificial Intelligence*, **29**, (1986) 241-88
8. Pearl, J.: Evidential reasoning using stochastic simulation. *Artificial Intelligence*, **32**, (1987) 245–57
9. Pearl, J.: *Networks of Plausible Inference*. Morgan Kaufmann. San Mateo. (1988)
10. Thornton, C.J.: *Techniques in Computational Learning*. Chapman & Hall. London. (1992)
11. Whittaker, J.: *Graphical Models in Applied Multivariate Statistics*. Wiley. Chicester. (1988)

Constructing the Extensional Representation of an Intensional Domain Theory in Inductive Logic Programming

M.C.Nicoletti[1] and M.C.Monard[2]

[1] UFSCar-DC/ILTC, C.P. 676, 13565-905 - São Carlos, SP, Brazil
e-mail:carmo@icmsc.sc.usp.br
[2] USP-ICMSC-SCE/ILTC, C.P. 668, 13560-970 - São Carlos, SP, Brazil
e-mail: mcmonard@icmsc.sc.usp.br

Abstract. Inductive Logic Programming — ILP — is a new paradigm in the field of Machine Learning, which adopts the language of logic programs as a description language for the expression of instances, hypothesis and domain theory. Learning logical definitions requires the exploration of a very large space of hypothesis descriptions and, consequently, restrictions should be imposed on the hypothesis space to make learning a feasible task. In this work we discuss ways of confining the ILP hypothesis space by restricting the domain theory description language. Specifically we focus on the notion of generative clauses, which enable the construction of a restricted form of Horn clause program. In fact, the use of generative logic programs as description language allows for automatic transformation of the intensional expression of a domain theory into its extensional expression, as required by many existing ILP systems. We present an ILP environment which takes as input an intensional domain theory and, after verifying that all clauses in the theory are generative, automatically constructs the extensional expression of this domain theory. We illustrate the use of this implemented environment through the ILP system *GOLEM*.

1 Introduction

One of the most widely adopted and studied paradigm for symbolic learning is known as *inductive learning from examples*. In this paradigm the learning task consists in building a general concept description (or *hypothesis*) from a given set of examples (*positive examples*) and counterexamples (*negative examples*) of the concept. Generally machine learning systems employ formal languages for describing instances and concepts referred to as the *instance description language* and the *concept description language* respectively.

In order to represent instances — training examples — many of the existing inductive learning algorithms use an *attribute-based* language. Despite their success, attribute-based learning methods are constrained by the language used to describe examples and concepts, as well as by the limited and inexpressible role that domain theory plays in the learning process. Only concepts expressible in propositional logic may be learned by a system which uses an attribute-based language.

Owing to the representational limitations imposed by an attribute-based language, the use of more powerful representations, such as variants of first-order logic, has received attention recently. Nevertheless, the adoption of a more powerful language description gives rise to many difficulties that need to be overcome. Ways of confining the hypothesis space can be implemented by restricting instances, hypothesis and domain theory description languages [4,5]. By reducing the representative power of the languages employed, the search carried out by a learning system can be both better controlled and limited.

The subject of inductively inferring logic programs, named *Inductive Logic Programming* — ILP — is an attempt to integrate the techniques already available and established for logic programming in a framework of learning, aiming to induce first-order logic programs from examples, using domain theory. In ILP the system's knowledge consists of examples and domain theory expressed as a logic program. The expressiveness of logic programs and the use of domain theory have promoted ILP as a powerful inductive learning paradigm.

Since learning logical definitions requires the exploration of a very large space of hypothesis, restrictions must be imposed on the hypothesis space in order to make learning a feasible task.

This work focuses on ways of restricting the use of domain theory, for application in ILP systems. The intensional expression of a domain theory will be restricted to generative clauses only, since the use of generative clauses allows the construction of a finite model associated with a program. Having a finite model is a condition required by several well-known ILP systems.

The work is organized as follows: in Section 2 the task of empirical, single predicate learning using ILP is formally presented. Section 3 highlights and discusses the main concepts and ideas used in this work for limiting the domain theory. In Section 4 the transformation of an intensionally expressed domain theory into its extensional form is discussed. An algorithm to verify that the given domain theory consists only of generative clauses is described, as well as two algorithms for constructing its extensional expression. The ILP environment where these algorithms have been implemented, as well as an example to illustrate the way the environment can be used through the ILP system *GOLEM* is presented in Section 5. We conclude in Section 6.

2 The Learning Process in ILP

In an ILP framework the learning of a single concept can be viewed as the learning of a predicate definition. A predicate definition p is the set of all program clauses with the same predicate p in the head (and same arity). A predicate can be defined *extensionally* as a set of ground facts or *intensionally* as a set of database clauses [2]. For some ILP systems the learning of a predicate definition is restricted to the learning of a single clause, which can be formulated as follows. Given:

- a set of training examples $\mathcal{E}$ described in a language $\mathcal{L}_\mathcal{E}$ and consisting of positive examples ($\mathcal{E}^+$) and negative examples ($\mathcal{E}^-$) of an unknown predicate p (target relation),
- a concept description language $\mathcal{L}_\mathcal{C}$, specifying syntactic restrictions on the definition of predicate p,
- domain theory $\mathcal{K}$, described in language $\mathcal{L}_\mathcal{K}$, defining predicates q_i (other than p) which may be used in the definition of p and which provide additional information about the arguments of the examples of predicate p,
- a matching operator between $\mathcal{L}_\mathcal{E}$ and $\mathcal{L}_\mathcal{C}$ wrt $\mathcal{L}_\mathcal{K}$ that determines whether an example is covered by a clause expressed in $\mathcal{L}_\mathcal{C}$.

Find:

- a definition $\mathcal{H}$ for p, expressed in $\mathcal{L}_\mathcal{C}$, such that
  - $\mathcal{H}$ is complete, i.e., $\mathcal{K} \wedge \mathcal{H} \models \mathcal{E}^+$,
  - $\mathcal{H}$ is consistent, i.e., $\mathcal{K} \wedge \mathcal{H} \not\models \mathcal{E}^-$
  with respect to the examples.

In ILP the languages $\mathcal{L}_\mathcal{E}$, $\mathcal{L}_\mathcal{K}$ and $\mathcal{L}_\mathcal{C}$ used to represent examples, domain theory and concept descriptions respectively are typically subsets of first order logic, namely logic programs. For a great deal of available ILP systems those languages are the language of Horn clauses.

In order to deal with such complex hypothesis spaces, some representational aspects of the learning task should be analysed and ways of restricting the search process should be considered. One possible way of restricting the search process is restricting the domain theory as treated in this work.

3   Restricting the Domain Theory

The domain theory used in ILP systems should always be restricted otherwise the learning task in first order logic, approached as a search process, inherits the undecidability of the deduction process. The restriction to function-free ground domain theory (as well as to function-free ground unit clauses as examples) enables the use of $\theta - subsumption$ [6] as a complete inference procedure. Function-free knowledge has another positive effect on deduction. It has been proven that inferring ground domain theory can be done in time polynomial to the size of the domain theory $\mathcal{K}$ if $\mathcal{K}$ consists only of function-free generative Horn clauses (see Definition 3.5) and there is a fixed maximum arity of predicates in the domain knowledge [1], as discussed below.

3.1   The H-easy Model

A common restriction employed by ILP systems is to accept the domain theory only if it is expressed in its ground form and the examples only if they are expressed as ground unit clauses. If the logic program P which expresses the domain theory $\mathcal{K}$ consists of only ground facts, P itself can be chosen as a model

M. If the logic program P consists of arbitrary clauses, the model M for P can be infinite. In order to deal with situations like that and restrict infinite models to finite ones, the notion of h-*easiness* [3] was established and is presented next.

Definition 3.1 *Given a logic program P, an atom a is h-easy with respect to P, for a given natural number h, iff there exist a derivation of a from P involving at most h binary resolutions*

Definition 3.2 *The Herbrand h-easy model of P - M_h - is the set of all Herbrand instantiations of h-easy atoms of P.*

Theorem 3.1 *Given a logic program P, for any finite h, the number of h-easy atoms of P is finite.*

3.2 Generative Clauses

There follows a definition of a restricted form of Horn clause program P for which the Herbrand h-easy model is finite.

Definition 3.3 *The n-atomic-derivation set of program P, $D^n(P)$ is defined recursively as follows*[3]

- $D^0(P) =$ *set of unit clauses in P*

- $D^n(P) = D^{n-1}(P) \bigcup \{A\theta_1 \ldots \theta_n : A \leftarrow B_1, \ldots, B_m \in P$ *and for each B_i* $\exists B_i' \in D^{n-1}(P)$ *such that θ_i is the mgu (most general unifier) of B_i and B_i'*$\}$

The atomic-derivation-closure is defined as:

$$D^*(P) = D^0(P) \bigcup D^1(P) \bigcup \ldots$$

Definition 3.4 *The logic program P is said to be semantically generative iff every element of $D^*(P)$ is ground.*

The following syntactic constraint on logic programs corresponds to this semantic definition.

Definition 3.5 *The clause $A \leftarrow B_1, \ldots, B_m$ is syntactically generative whenever the variables in the head A are a subset of the variables in the body $B_1, \ldots, B_m$. The logic program P is syntactically generative iff every clause in P is syntactically generative.*

Theorem 3.2 *Every syntactically generative logic program P is semantically generative.*

It is important to notice that the Least Herbrand Model and the atomic-derivation-closure of a semantically generative logic program are the same.

Theorem 3.3 *For every syntactically generative logic program P and every h, $M_h(P)$ is finite.*

---

[3] Observe that with the definitions presented here, in fact $M_h = D^{h-1}(P)$.

4 Transforming Intensional Domain Theory into Extensional Domain Theory

Some ILP systems, such as $GOLEM$ [3] and $FOIL$ [7], require all domain theory to be given extensionally. The only way to use an intensionally specified domain theory P in $GOLEM$ or $FOIL$ is by using an extensional version of this knowledge. This version can be obtained by deriving ground atoms from the domain theory as a pre-processing step of the learning task.

Based on Theorem 3.3, it can be seen that after verifying that a given domain theory P consists only of generative clauses, it is possible to construct the finite model associated with it, by constructing its *atomic-derivation-closure*. For this, it is necessary to find all (up to a certain depth) possible conclusions of the program P.

This can be done in either of two directions of a clause: from body to head (forward) or from head to body (backward). The algorithm which verifies that a program P is generative is given next. It is followed by the forward and backward chaining algorithms used to construct the atomic-derivation-closure of a given program P.

4.1 Algorithm for Verifying if a Logical Program is Generative

Let a logical program P be defined as the set of clauses $\{C_1, C_2, \ldots, C_m\}$ of the form $C_i : A_i \leftarrow L_{i_1}, L_{i_2}, \ldots, L_{i_{n_i}}$ for $i = 1, \ldots, m$ and $n_i \geq 0$ and let $variables(L_{ij})$ be the set of variables occuring in literal L_{ij}.

```
function  generative(P) : boolean
    begin
        generative ← true
        for  k = 1 to m do
        begin
            B = ∅
            H = variables(A_k)
            for p = 1 to n_k do
                B = B ∪ variables(L_{kp})
            if  H ⊄ B then
                begin
                    generative = false
                    exit
                end
        end
    end
```

on exit, if *generative(P)* is *true* then the logical program P consists only of generative clauses.

4.2 Two Algorithms for Generating the Atomic Closure of a Generative Logical Program

In this section the two algorithms for generating the atomic-derivation-closure of a generative logical program P are presented. They are implemented using backward and forward chaining respectively. In both versions P is a logical program as defined in 4.1.

Version 1 - Backward Chaining

```
begin
input  P, HDepth
       begin  Model ← ∅
              repeat  let C be a clause of P
                      if  C is a unary clause
                      then  Model ← Model ∪ C
                      else
                            begin
                                  HDepth = HDepth − 1
                                  if  HDepth ≥ 0 then
                                  repeat the process for each Lᵢ of C and increment
                                  Model
                            end
                      until  all clauses of C have been considered
output  Model
end
```

The algorithm for model generation using forward chaining (or modus pones reasoning) has to consider the facts in order. For each fact F, it is necessary to find all clauses $A_i \leftarrow L_{i_1}, L_{i_2}, \ldots, L_{i_{n_i}}$ in which some of the literals L_{i_j} can be matched with the fact F. For each of these clauses a new clause is generated without this fact. Whenever a fact matches the unique literal in the body of a clause, the head of the clause has been proven as a new fact. One important point to consider is the order in which new facts are pursued. New facts can be added in front of those not yet considered, such that the fact just proven will be the next fact to be considered.

Although this method is useful when it is necessary to reach some conclusion as fast as possible, it is not appropriate if it is necessary to systematically find every possible conclusion from the facts. In the later case it is better to put new proven facts at the end of the set of facts, i.e., the fact list resembles to a queue.

Another point which should be considered is the presence of negated atoms in the body of a clause. The algorithm presented next follows the *closed-world assumption* under which if L cannot be proven, then $\neg L$ is assumed to be true. For this, the forward chaining algorithm must first assume that all negations are false, prove all possible facts and only consider to be true those negations which still are not facts. It should be noted that when those negations are held to be true, they can be used to prove new facts with new consequences.

Version 2 - Forward Chaining

begin
input P
unused_queue_fact ← queue of all facts
used_queue_fact ← ∅
queue_clauses ← queue of all clauses C (which are not unit clauses)
   repeat
       while *unused_queue_fact* ≠ ∅ **do**
         begin
           let F be the first literal in *unused_queue_fact*
           for each C in *queue_clause* which can match F with a literal in its
             body **do**
            begin
              create a new clause C' from C by removing the literal F after the
              necessary bindings for the variables in C have been done to make
              the match possible
              if C' is a unit clause
                then add C' as the last element of *unused_queue_fact*
                else add C' as the first element of *queue_clause*
           end
         end
         for each negated atom ¬B of clauses in *queue_clauses* such that B does
           not match any atoms in *used_queue_fact* add ¬B as the first element
           of *unused_queue_fact*
   until *unused_queue_fact* = ∅

These algorithms have been implemented as meta-interpreters in Sicstus Prolog and run on SUN Sparcstations. They are part of the ILP environment described next.

5   The ILP Environment

As commented earlier, some of the existing ILP systems, such as $FOIL$ and $GOLEM$, require an extensionally expressed domain theory. For those systems, if the available domain theory is expressed intensionally, in order to be of any use the theory should first be converted into its extensional form. If the conversion cannot be performed, the task of learning using those ILP system will not be feasible. Figure 1 shows the ILP Environment we are implementing, were the module that transforms the domain theory — noted by . — should always be utilized when the available domain theory is in its intensional form.

As there is not a unique pattern for expressing the input data for those ILP systems, the first order customizer module has the role of customizing the input to the input requirements of the ILP system currently being used.

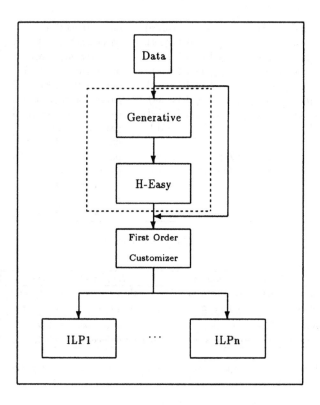

Fig. 1. ILP Environment

To illustrate the use of this environment, we present a simple example were the domain theory consists of some basic knowledge about sex and parenthood of individuals (given in their extensional forms), as well as a rule (given in its intensional form) which establishes the predecessor relationship among those individuals, as shown in Table 1.

Using the modules Generative and H-Easy, part of the ILP environment, the models M_2 (43 facts), M_3 (51 facts) and M_4 (55 facts, also the Least Herbrand Model) were generated. Each one of those models plus the positive and negative examples shown in Table 2, were input to $GOLEM$, aiming to learn respectively the concept of $female\_predecessor/2$ and $male\_predecessor/2$. The correct concepts

$$male\_predecessor(X,Y) : -predecessor(X,Y), male(X).$$
$$female\_predecessor(X,Y) : -predecessor(X,Y), female(X).$$

were learned when using the models M_3 and M_4. When using M_2 model, $GOLEM$ was not able to learn any concept. An interesting feature of the implemented ILP environment is that the new learned rules can be added to the intensional model and the process can be repeated to learn other new concepts.

male(fred).	female(jackie).	parent(fred,tim).
male(tim).	female(vicky).	parent(beth,tim).
male(ben).	female(kelly).	parent(ben,jackie).
male(ed).	female(vera).	parent(mary,jackie).
male(sean).	female(mary).	parent(tim,vicky).
male(john).	female(anna).	parent(jackie,vicky).
male(martin).	female(rachel).	parent(vicky,anna).
	female(beth).	parent(martin,anna).
		parent(rachel,vera).
predecessor(X,Z):- parent(X,Z).		parent(ed,vera).
predecessor(X,Z):- parent(X,Y),		parent(rachel,sean).
	predecessor(Y,Z).	parent(ed,sean).
		parent(sean,john).
		parent(kelly,john).

Table 1. Domain Theory $\mathcal{K}$

Positive Examples	Negative Examples
female_predecessor(beth,vicky).	female_predecessor(mary,vera).
female_predecessor(rachel,john).	female_predecessor(tim,anna)
male_predecessor(ed,john).	male_predecessor(fred,sean).
male_predecessor(tim,anna).	male_predecessor(rachel,sean)

Table 2. Positive and Negative Examples for learning *female_predecessor/2* and *male_predecessor/2*

6 Conclusions

In this work we have discussed ways of incorporating domain theory into the learning task, as well as restricting the domain theory description language in the field of ILP, so that the search space is limited, thus making the learning task feasible.

A restricted form of Horn clause program, named generative program, was discussed in detail, since if a domain theory $\mathcal{K}$ can be expressed as a generative logic program then there is a finite model associated with $\mathcal{K}$.

Based on this result, we described an ILP environment and the algorithms implemented. The environment verifies if a given domain theory $\mathcal{K}$ consists of generative clauses and constructs the finite model associated with it. A simple example of using this environment with the ILP system *GOLEM* was also presented.

Acknowledgements: This research has been partially supported by the National Research Council — CNPq. Special thanks to S.V. Warrick and S. Matwin for their valuable comments.

References

1. Kietz, J-U.: Some Lower Bounds for the Computational Complexity of Inductive Logic Programming. Lecture Notes in Artificial Intelligence 667, Pavel B. Bradzil (ed.), Springer-Verlag, (1993) 115–123
2. Lavrač, N., Džeroski, S.: Inductive Logic Programming: Techniques and Applications. Ellis Horwood, London, (1994)
3. Muggleton, S.H., Feng, C.: Efficient Induction of Logic Programs. In: S.H.Muggleton (ed.) Inductive Logic Programming, Academic Press (1992) 262–280
4. Nicoletti, M.C., Monard, M.C.: The Role of Description Languages in Inductive Concept Learning. I SBAI, Brazil (1993) 403–443
5. Nicoletti, M.C.: Expanding the Limits of Inductive Machine Learning through Constructive and Relational Approaches. (in Portuguese) Ph.D. Thesis, IFSC-USP-São Carlos, Brazil (1994)
6. Plotkin, G.D.: Automatic Methods of Inductive Inference. Ph. D. Thesis, Edinburgh University (1971)
7. Quinlan, R.: Learning Logical Definitions from Relations. Machine Learning 5 (1990) 239–266

A Generic Algorithm for Learning Rules with Hierarchical Exceptions

Tobias Scheffer

Technische Universität Berlin, Artificial Intelligence Research Group, Sekr. FR 5-8, Franklinstr. 28-29, D-10587 Berlin, email: scheffer@cs.tu-berlin.de

Abstract. An algorithm for learning ripple down rules, that is rules with hierarchical exceptions, is presented. The algorithm is generic with respect to the set of possible conditions; conditions are manipulated by an abstract generalization operator only. A specialization of the algorithm is shown that learns classification rules in real-valued attribute space; it is compared to other machine learning, neural network, and statistical algorithms. Learning algorithms for graphs or first order logics can be derived as well.

Keywords. Machine learning, classification, exceptions

1 Introduction

Since knowledge acquisition in expert systems is a major problem in AI, it is a central aim of machine learning to develop algorithms that gain knowledge from observations. With respect to expert systems or data mining systems, it is of special interest to develop learning algorithms that deliver *comprehensible* knowledge structures.

The most common representations for knowledge used in machine learning algorithms are *decision trees* [13, 16] and DNF rules [2, 6]; both, decision tree algorithms and rule extraction algorithms, can be used to inductively gain rule knowledge for expert or data mining systems.

Yet, with the amount of knowledge increasing, unordered sets of rules quickly loose much of their comprehensibility. There is need for structured knowledge representation schemes and corresponding inductive acquisition tools.

Ripple down rules (RDR) [3, 5], that is rules with exceptions (and exceptions of exceptions...), seem to be a promising representational scheme. A RDR is a list of rules where each rule may be associated to another list of more special rules: its exceptions. They were developed as a strategy for expert system maintenance and proved to be comfortable for human needs due to the implied principle of locality, since 'rough' rules can be described first and refined in the exception levels, with the exceptions effecting only the domain of the next-general rule.

Hierarchical rules were studied in several, slightly different variants [17, 14, 8, 7, 4], ripple down rules being the most general and most strongly structured scheme. For objects represented by discrete-valued attributes, a learning algorithm was proposed by Compton and Gaines [5], other learning algorithms for hierarchical rules are an algorithm for learning non-monotonic conclusions [4] and an algorithm that learns hierarchical rules with a fixed depth based on a string-representation of objects. The last two algorithms are based on ordering the samples by their "generality"; no explicit generalization is done. For less structured "nested differences", a learning algorithm was proposed [7] that learns intersection-closed training sets.

1.1 Structural and Numerical Learning

It is known, that an object representation based on attribute-vectors cannot be used in many problem domains. In first order logics, structured objects can be expressed adequate; although real-valued attribute vectors can be expressed as well, first order logics can not be considered adequate; neither are algorithms of *Inductive Logic Programming* [12] suited for learning in attribute spaces, because (1) the isomorphism problem unnecessarily increases the complexity and (2) in attribute space a completely different type of generalization is required.

In this approach, the domain-specific parts of the algorithm are separated strictly from the "pure" learning algorithm, the learning algorithm uses a domain-specific generalization operator to manipulate rules.

2 Domain Specification

A learning domain is characterized by a tuple $(O, C, (L, \Psi), \epsilon, +)$, where O is a set of object representations, C is a set of concept symbols. L is the condition language, i.e. the set of possible left hand sides of rules. Ψ is called the semantics of the rule language. $\Psi(l)$, $l \in L$ being a condition, is the set of objects characterized by the condition l. A condition *holds* for a given object o, if $o \in \Psi(l)$; e.g. the condition "low temperature" holds for the object "$0°C$" since "$0°C$" $\in \Psi($"low temperature"$)$, where $\Psi($"low temperature"$)$ is the set of all low temperatures.

$\epsilon : O \rightarrow L$ is called the elementary condition function and maps object representations to conditions, that characterize them ($o \in \Psi(\epsilon(o))$); e.g. $\epsilon(15°C) =$ "medium temperature".

The generalization operator $+ : L \times L \rightarrow L$ maps two conditions to a new condition that holds for at least every object characterized by either of the two conditions: $\Psi(l_1) \subseteq \Psi(l_1 + l_2) \supseteq \Psi(l_2)$, i.e. a generalization is assumed to be *at least a union* of the characterized objects; e.g. "low temperature" + "medium temperature" = "between low and medium".

A generalization $l_1 + l_2$ is called the least generalization, if any other generalizing condition characterizes more objects, i.e. is more general:

$$\Psi(l_1) \subseteq \Psi(l) \supseteq \Psi(l_2) \Rightarrow \Psi(l) \supseteq \Psi(l_1 + l_2)$$

The proposed learning algorithm uses the incremental case of the generalization only: A condition is only generalized with an elementary condition of an object, thus only $l + \epsilon(o)$ needs to be defined.

3 Ripple Down Rules

In this section, a formal definition of ripple down rules is given, that corresponds to the concept informally proposed in [3].

3.1 Syntax

Let L be a language for conditions, C a set of concept symbols. The set of ripple down rules is the smallest set R that satisfies

1. $\lambda \in R$
2. $\langle l \rightarrow r, X, N \rangle \in R$ iff $l \in L; r \in C; X, N \in R$

That is, a RDR may be empty or it may be a binary tree with a rule node, an X-branch, the exception tree, and an N-branch, the succeeding tree.

3.2 Semantics

A RDR r characterizes a classification function $\Phi(r) : O \rightarrow C \cup \{\star\}$, mapping objects to concept symbols or the unknown concept symbol $\star$.

1. $\Phi_\Psi(\lambda)(p) = \star$

2. $\Phi_\Psi(\langle l \rightarrow r, X, N \rangle)(p) = \begin{cases} \Phi_\Psi(N)(p) & \text{if } p \notin \Psi(l) \\ \Phi_\Psi(X)(p) & \text{if } p \in \Psi(l) \\ & \wedge \Phi_\Psi(X)(p) \neq \star \\ r & \text{else} \end{cases}$

When a RDR is applied to an object $p \in O$, it is first checked, if the rule at the root node holds ($p \in \Psi(l)$). If so, the exception tree ist recursively applied to the object. If the exception tree fails, i.e. returns $\star$, the rule is applied, else the result generated by the exception rule is returned. If the rule at the root node does not hold, the next tree N is applied. That is, an exception overrides a more general rule and each rule overshadows its successors.

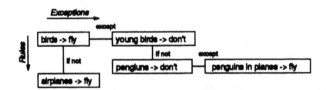

Fig. 1. A ripple down rule

Figure 1 shows an example for a RDR. "Birds fly" is the topmost rule, possessing a branch of exceptions labeled "except" and a succeeding rule "airplanes fly". The exception tree specifies two exceptions to the rule "birds fly": "Young birds don't fly" and "penguins don't fly", the last rule has yet another exception: "penguins in planes fly".

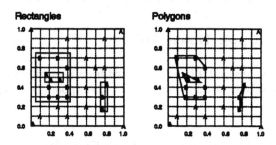

Fig. 2. A RDR in attribute space

Figure 2 shows two RDRs classifying objects in attribute space; the condition language being rectangles in the first and polygons in the second case. In the left example, the surrounding rectangle $([0,1][0,1] \rightarrow A)$ is the topmost rule with two exceptions: The small rectangle at the bottom right hand side $([.75,.85][.15.45] \rightarrow B)$ and the medium rectangle $([.05,.42][.25,.75] \rightarrow B)$ which in turn has another exception $([.15,.35][.45,.55] \rightarrow A)$.

3.3 A Node's Context

A node's context is the set of objects, that "reach" it, when being classified. If a rule has context *con*, then its exception node has context $con \cap \Psi(l)$, its succeeding tree has context $con \setminus \Psi(l)$. The context is needed for the definition of an admissible generalization and for the optimization of RDRs.

3.4 Acquisition of Rule Knowledge

In automatic knowledge acquisition and data mining, rules that describe the behavior of complex systems are to be learned. Classification is the underlying principle. The class of objects that are characterized by a rule is to be discriminated from their complementary class; the rules' scheme is "if concept then behavior". while the class of objects characterized by a rule is disjoint to its complementary class, different rules may overlap, that is, using ripple down rules to modularize knowledge, a set of rules is turned into a set of ripple down rules, each ripple down rule representing one concept, i.e. one rule.

3.5 Flattening Ripple Down Rules

Ripple down rules can be transformed into lists of rules automatically. This can be done by drawing the exception tree of each node in front of it and flattening it and the succeeding tree recursively. Thus, the example shown in fig. 1 becomes [young birds → don't, penguins in planes → fly, penguins → dont, birds → fly, airplanes → fly].

Turning flat rules into non-flat RDR sets up an optimization problem that cannot be solved syntactically, it depends on the semantics Ψ.

4 Learning Ripple Down Rules

This section shows, how a RDR can be learned from a set of samples $S \subseteq O \times C$, which is a finite subset of the world O with corresponding classes given by a teacher.

4.1 The CuT.2 Algorithm (CuboidTree Classification)

In each learning step, a new sample (p, c) is inserted into the RDR by the function "$\leftarrow_\beta$". A threshold $1 - \beta$ specifies an upper bound for the misclassification rate with respect to the training set. If the training set is separable (the available conditions are enough to separate objects of different classes) a classifier with an error rate of at most $1 - \beta$ is found [15].

1. $\lambda \leftarrow_\beta (p, c) = \langle \epsilon(p) \to c, \lambda, \lambda \rangle$
2. $\langle l \to r, X, N \rangle \leftarrow_\beta (p, c) =$
    (a) $\langle l \to r, X \leftarrow_\beta (p, c), N \rangle$, if the rule is applicable $(p \in \Psi(l))$ and $(r \neq c$ or X classifies p $(\Phi(X)(p) \neq \star))$.
    (b) $\langle l \to r, X, N \rangle$, if the rule is applicable, X does not classify p and $(r = c$ or the dominance threshold β is exceeded $(P(c|\Psi(l) \cap con) \geq \beta))$.
    (c) $\langle l + \epsilon(p) \to r, X, N \rangle$, if the rule is not applicable $(p \notin \Psi(l))$, the threshold is not exceeded for any other class and $r = c$ and $l + \epsilon(p)$ is an *admissible* and *useful* generalization.
    (d) $\langle l \to r, X, N \leftarrow_\beta (p, c) \rangle$ otherwise.

Applied to an empty rule node, the "$\leftarrow_\beta$"-function generates a new rule, that consists of the new object's elementary condition.

If the "$\leftarrow_\beta$"-function reaches a nonempty node with a condition holding for the inserted object but either the rule yields the wrong result or the exception tree already classifies the new object, then the object is an *exception* of the rule and it has to be inserted recursively into the exception branch. If the concept symbols are identical, then the rule is already correct; if the rule is not applicable but the concept symbols are identical, the rule and the new object have to be generalized or the object has to be inserted recursively into the successor branch.

A generalization is *admissible*, if:

1. The generalized rule is still more special than the next-general rule, i.e. the *context* is shrunk
2. The dominance threshold is not exceeded for any other class.

The *usefulness* of a generalization is checked a heuristic function; proposed heuristics are:

1. A generalization is always useful. This can be decided without reference to the training set, in this case the algorithm becomes incremental. It is always possible and has proven to be useful for the classification of graphs and in general is suited for discrete, binary domains, while the third heuristic is suited for continuately valued domains.
2. A generalization is useful, if the concept's probability is higher than the probability of any other class within the rule's domain. The algorithm has to refer to the complete training set in each learning step to calculate probabilities.
3. A generalization is useful, if the concept's variance is higher than the variance of any other class within the rule's domain. Instances of a class with a small variance are more local and can thus be modeled as exceptions. This heuristic was used in the instantiation to real valued attributes; it requires the definition of a metric.

The algorithm tries to include new samples into one of the early rules. A sample is passed to a succeeding node only if a generalization is not admissible or not useful. Thus, the topmost rules extend and overshadow the succeeding rules, which after being overshadowed can be removed. The resulting RDRs are simplified during the training.

For a special issue of the algorithm, CuT95, covering the instantiation for real valued domains and an instantiation for graphs and first order logics, correctness (a correct classifier is found, if the available conditions are sufficient to separate the training set) is proven formally [15].

If the training set is not separable, i.e. two isomorphic objects are assigned to different classes, this has to be trapped in (2a). In this case, there exists no exact classifier.

Based on this scheme, learning algorithms can be derived for various domains based on a condition language and a generalization operator.

4.2 Instantiation to Real-Valued Domains

The described algorithm can be used to learn classification functions in the real-valued feature space $\mathcal{R}^n$. Let O be the set of points in $\mathcal{R}^n$, let the condition language L be defined as

$$l \in L \Leftrightarrow l = [a_1, b_1][a_2, b_2] \ldots [a_n, b_n]$$

describing hyper-cuboides in $\mathcal{R}^n$. The semantics is defined

$$\Psi([a_1, b_1] \ldots [a_n, b_n]) = \{p | a_1 \leq p_1 \leq b_1 \wedge \ldots \wedge a_n \leq p_n \leq b_n\}$$

denoting the set of points within the hyper-cuboid. The elementary description is defined

$$\epsilon(p) = [p_1, p_1] \ldots [p_n, p_n]$$

which is the cuboid containing only p. The generalization operator $l + \epsilon(p)$ yields the smallest axis-parallel hyper-cuboid containing the hyper-cuboid l and the point p.

Figure 2 (left figure) shows a toy-problem example for a real-valued ripple down rule tree that has been generated by the algorithm CuT95.

Results The algorithm was compared to the *Induct*-algorithm [5], on two datasets with only discrete-valued attributes.

For both datasets – prescription of contact lenses [1] and a NASA landing control dataset [10]. Fig 3 shows the resulting RDR found for the contact lens problem. While 9 rules including 30 tests are extracted from an *ID3* decision tree, only 4 rules with 8 tests are required by a RDR. Because of the modularity and the reduced size, it is well comprehensible.

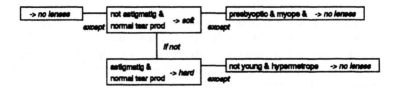

Fig. 3. A RDR for the contact lens problem

The algorithm was compared to several other machine learning, statistical and neural network learning algorithms on some "real-world" datasets. Decision tree and rule extraction algorithms were outperformed in various cases, statistical and neural network algorithms were outperformed on datasets with a multimodal class distribution. On the diabetes-dataset (e.g. [11]), CuT95 proved to be the best known symbolical algorithm; on the shuttle-dataset [11] with a strongly multimodal distribution, CuT95 yields the best known result (see fig. 4).

Learning time did not exceed 15 minutes for the largest dataset with about 60,000 samples on a sparc station.

4.3   Other Instantiations

Instantiations to other domains can be derived very easily. There are several domains with obvious condition languages and useful generalization operations. The following complete and consistent specializations give an outline of the possible application domains.

Another instantiation of the algorithm to real-valued attribute spaces uses convex polygons as conditions (see fig. 2, right figure). This approach is not bound to axis-parallel cuts, but the resulting RDR are less understandable.

An instantiation to first order logics can be derived easily.

Contact lens prescription			Diabetes			Shuttle diagnosis	
Algorithm	# Rules	# Tests	Algorithm	Test-err.	Rank	Algorithm	Test-err.
ID3	9	30	**Logdisc**	0.223	1	**CuT95**	**0.001**
Induct x.	**4**	**8**	Dipol92	0.224	2	NewId	0.01
CuT95	**4**	**8**	Discrim	0.225	3	Baytree	0.02
Shuttle landing			CuT95	0.231	4	Cal5	0.03
Algorithm		# Rules	SMART	0.232	5	CN2	0.03
RULEMASTER.		13	BackProp	0.248	7	ITrule	0.41
Induct exc.		7	C4.5	0.270	13	BackProp	0.43
CuT95		**5**	NewID	0.289	19	Discrim	4.83

Fig. 4. Some experimental results

Let the world O be the set of conjunctions of literals. The condition language L can be defined as the set of conjunctions of literals as well.

The semantics Ψ of the condition language is defined as follows: $\Psi(l)$ holds for p, if there is a substitution θ, such that $l\theta \geq p$. That is, the *granularity* of the resulting classifier is restricted to *isomorphism classes*. Since the predicate Ψ searches for a suitable substitution, it is not possible to distinct objects that differ only in the names of their variables, which is exactly the desired behavior.

The elementary description function ϵ is then trivial and the generalization function is defined as the largest match.

Fig. 5 shows a RDR that learned the toy-concept "arc". The topmost rule is very general and reads "anything is a non-arc". It has one exception: Two blocks that support another object set up an arc. This rule has another exception: If there is another block under the two supporting blocks, it is no longer an arc.

The first rule was set up by generalizing the second and the sixth sample, the second rule by generalizing the first and seventh sample. This match yields two unary attributes block(X), block(Y) and two support-relations sup(X,Z), sup(Y,Z); the upper element's attributes, block(Z) resp. wedge(Z) is not matched.

5 Conclusion and Further Research

The presented learning algorithm provides an advance in automatic knowledge acquisition since well comprehensible systems of rules can be generated from observations at any domain. A complete and consistent specialization of the algorithm for any set of objects can be derived, if the following items are available.

1. A condition language together with a function that maps single objects to conditions.
2. A generalization operation that maps a condition and a new object to a new condition that holds for at least for the new object, too.

189

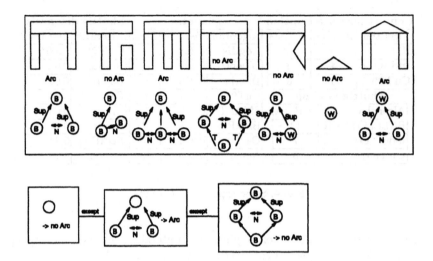

Fig. 5. A RDR for the arc-problem

Instantiations of the algorithm for real-valued attribute domains are of special interest to pattern matching, medical and technical diagnosis and many other practical issues, since good results have been achieved especially in complex and strongly multimodal distributed domains.

While the learning algorithm instantiated to real-valued attribute vectors yields good results on complex and multimodal datasets it is outperformed by statistical and neural network learning algorithms on approximately normal distributed datasets. For that reason, the algorithm is integrated with a statistical and neural network learning algorithm.

The domain-independency and the minimal specification of learning domains provides a new perspective on learning rules over domains with more complex object representation, like continuously attributed graphs or formulae of variable-valued logics [9].

References

1. J. Cendrowska. An algorithm for inducing modular rules. *International Journal for Man-Machine Studies*, pages 349–370, 1987.
2. P. Clark and T. Niblett. The cn2 induction algorithm. *Machine Learning*, 3:261–283, 1989.
3. P. Compton and R. Jansen. Knowledge in context: a strategy for expert system maintainance. In *Proceedings of the 2nd Australian Joint Artificial Intelligence Conference*, volume 406 of *LNAI*, pages 292–306, Adelaide, 1988. Springer.
4. Y. Dimopoulos and A. Kakas. Learning non-monotonic logic programs: Learning exceptions. In N. Lavrač and S. Wrobel, editors, *Machine Learning: ECML-95 (Proc. European Conf. on Machine Learning, 1995)*, Lecture Notes in Artificial Intelligence 912, pages 122 – 137, Berlin, Heidelberg, New York, 1995. Springer Verlag.
5. B. R. Gaines and P. J. Compton. Induction of ripple down rules. *5th Australian Conference on Artificial Intelligence*, pages 349–355, 1992.
6. R. M. Goodman and P. Smyth. The induction of probabilistic rule sets – the itrule algorithm. In B. Spatz, editor, *Proceedings of the Sixth International Workshop on Machine Learning*, pages 129–132, San Mateo, 1989. CA: Morgan Kaufmann.
7. D. Helmbold, R. Sloan, and M. K. Warmuth. Learning nested differences of intersection-closed concept classes. *Proceedings of the Workshop on Computational Learning Theory*, pages 41–56, 1989.
8. J. Kivinen, H. Mannila, and E. Ukkonen. Learning hierarchical rule sets. *Proceedings of the ACM Workshop of Computational Learning Theory*, 1993.
9. R. S. Michalski. Pattern recognition as rule-guided inductive inference. *IEEE Transactions on Pattern Analysis and Machine Intelligence*, 2(4):349–361, July 1980.
10. D. Michie. Problems of computer aided concept formation. In J. R. Quinlan, editor, *Applications of Expert Systems*, volume 2, pages 310–333, 1989.
11. D. Michie, D. J. Spiegelhalter, and C. C. Taylor. *Machine Learning, Neural and Statistical Classification*. Ellis Horwood, 1994.
12. S. Muggleton. *Inductive Logic Programming*. Volume 38 of A.P.I.C. series. Academic Press Ltd., London, 1992.
13. J. R. Quinlan. Induction of decision trees. *Machine Learning*, 1(1), 1986.
14. R. L. Rivest. Learning decision lists. *Machine Learning*, 2(2):229–246, 1987.
15. T. Scheffer. Induktion hierarchischer Regelsysteme. Master's thesis, Technische Universität Berlin, 1995.
16. S. Unger and F. Wysotzki. *Lernfähige Klassifizierungssysteme*. Akademie Verlag Berlin, 1981.
17. S. A. Vere. Multilevel counterfactuals for generalizations of relational concepts and productions. *Artificial Intelligence*, 14:139–164, 1980.

A Neural Model for the Visual Attention Phenomena

Luís Alfredo V. de Carvalho e Valéria L. Roitman

COPPE - Programa de Engenharia de Sistemas e Computação

Caixa Postal 68511, CEP 21945-970, Rio de Janeiro, Brazil

Abstract Two interesting and complex tasks are performed by the brain in the process of perception: The integration of characteristics leading to an easier recognition of a pattern as a whole (binding), and the extraction of properties that need to be detailed and analyzed (attention). Classically, binding is viewed as a process whereby sets of properties are gathered in representative entities, which are themselves linked to form higher level structures, in a sequence that culminates in the total integration of the pattern features in a localized construct. The convergent axonal projections from one cortical area to another would be the neurobiological mechanism through which binding is achieved. Attention comprises the selective excitation of neuronal networks or pathways that stand for specific pattern properties. We propose a computational model aiming at bringing together the main (and apparently diverging) ideas about binding and attention. Based on experimental data, a neuronal network representing cortical pyramidal cells is assembled, and its structure and function are related to the binding and attention phenomena. Computer simulations are shown which reproduce the electrophysiology of pyramidal cells and mimic some interesting experimental results in visual attention. We conclude by conjecturing that attention is ·a driven interruption in the regular process of binding.

1 Introduction

It is a fact in Neurobiology that different sensations, perceived by specific sensorial organs, are processed by distant and specialized brain regions. As a consequence, an object with many features, such as shape, color and smell, is fragmentarily represented in geographically distinct areas. The question of how the brain performs this integration or, in other words, how the brain stores several pieces of information in different places without confusing them later, is the so called "binding problem" [1]. Another interesting question is how the brain selects, from the several characteristics of an object or event, the one it wants to pay attention to, or how the brain shifts its attention from one feature to another of the the same object [2]. We may call this latter question the "attention problem," which seems to be a dual of the "binding problem."

A classical solution to the "binding problem" relies on the assumption that, at each stage of processing, some features are put together in order to form a "macro-feature," which is then recognized by a specific region of the cortex. This process of "macro-featuring" continues in a hierarchical and anatomically convergent way to the extreme case that a single cell is capable of recognizing a specific object [3]. In other words, what this theory states is that in some higher cortical areas, there could be "grandmother" neurons responding selectively to the precise features (Gestalt) of one's grandmother [1]. Some neuroanatomical and neurophysiological issues are compatible with this view [4,5], since primary cortices project to higher cortical areas in a sequence that enlarges their receptive fields.

Recently, a new solution to the binding problem was proposed [6], in which different features of one object are only transiently linked by some kind of coupled neural activity. Some authors [7, 8] have proposed that the reticular nucleus of the thalamus would be the binding entity, exciting through its thalamocortical projections the cortical areas representing each one of the characteristics of the object. Another view [9] is that the higher order anterior cortices store a binding code that enables the brain to reconstruct the whole object from different sources. Finally, some evidences suggest that the coupled neural activity is a kind of neural resonance where multiple brain regions, representing the different aspects of an object, oscillate synchronously [10, 11].

Actually, the two possible solutions just lead us to the old debate between opposite paradigms of neural data processing: Memory capacity (grandmother cell theory) or computational power (coupled oscillations). As experimental evidences favor both solutions, it seems plausible that binding is accomplished by a combination of them.

2 The Neocortex and the Visual Attention Phenomena

The largest brain structure in mammals is the neocortex, occupying in volume approximately eighty percent of the whole brain. This structure is responsible for performing high-level functions, like speech, reasoning, recognition, and many others [12]. In cortical neurons, action potentials are generated by a fast voltage-dependent sodium current I_{Na}, responsible for depolarizations, and a restorative and delayed voltage-dependent potassium current I_K. Another sodium current present in cortical neurons is persistent, fast and voltage-dependent, driving the membrane potential to the range where I_{Na} can be activated. The interval between spikes is controlled by outward and calcium-dependent potassium currents whose time constants are greater than the duration of an action potential. Different hyperpolarization phases are observed when the two calcium-dependent currents, the transient I_c or the slow I_{ahp}, are activated. Some experiments indicate that the fast inactivation of I_c is retarded by the intracellular calcium concentration, leading the cell to the phenomenon of adaptation [13, 14]. In contrast, the amplitude of I_{ahp} increases with the intracellular calcium concentration, which seems to be the basis of the burst spiking [15, 16]. At least three cortical pathways originate in the primary visual cortex (V1). One of them is directed into the temporal lobe [5], another into the parietal lobe [3] and a third one ends in the superior temporal sulcus [17]. Neurons in the parietal cortex appear to change their firing rates as the result of the localization of a stimulus [18]. Neurons in the superior temporal sulcus mediate the perception of visual motion [19]. Finally, the pathway projecting to the temporal lobe is responsible for object recognition, which makes it important to the mechanism of attention. Starting at V1 and passing through the visual cortical areas V2, V3 and V4 on its way to the inferotemporal cortex (IT), this pathway shows neurons hierarchically organized to recognize from simple features in small receptive fields to global properties in large visual fields [2]. This large receptive field is an economical way to encode great amounts of information in one IT neuron, but at the same time leads us to the question of how attention can be focused in a desired detail of the whole scene.

An interesting experiment in monkeys, trained to attend to one or another of two stimuli within the receptive field of one V4 and one IT neuron, showed that neuronal responses depend on the place of attention within the field [20]. A neuron was isolated and two sets of stimuli were selected: One that was effective in eliciting response by the cell and another that had no response at all. An effective and an ineffective stimulus were presented at the same time in different places in the receptive field and the monkey was trained to attend to one location and ignore the other. When the animal attended to the effective stimulus, the neuron responded with a tonic spiking behavior, as one would expect. But when the attention was directed to the ineffective stimulus, the neuron reduced its firing pattern even though the effective stimulus was still present in the receptive field. No similar effect was detected in areas V1, V2 and V3, indicating that area V4 is the first on the temporal pathway under control of the attentional effort. It is worth noting that if one stimulus was located within the visual field and the other outside, it made no difference which of the two was attended to by the animal. This result indicates that the mechanism of attention helps V4 neurons to decide between two possible responses when there are many stimuli present in the visual field. If only one stimulus is inside the receptive field, there is no decision to take and the neuronal behavior is determined solely by the effectiveness of the stimulus itself. Recently, some authors have reported about neuronal coupled oscillations in the neocortex of animals when attending to meaningful stimuli [11, 21]. Suggestions that phase-locked oscillations between cortical areas or columns are a mechanism of binding different features of the same object are also present in the literature [22].

3 The Model

In this work we wish to model the signal propagation through pyramidal neurons between the primary visual area V1 and the cortical area IT, considering the intermediate areas V2, V3 and V4. For this purpose, a neuronal network of pyramidal cells is assembled to represent each of the mentioned areas and with receptive fields that increase progressively from V1 to IT, as described in the literature [2]. We assume that the visual field is projected through these areas in stimulus-specific pathways [3]. In addition, the model allows only two kinds of stimuli, for example red and green lights. An important hypothesis of the model is the fact that two stimulus-specific pathways processing the same visual field inhibit each other in area V4 by the action of interneurons. Reports about connections between cortical areas located at the same hierarchical level are commonly found [19] and some authors strongly correlate these lateral interactions to functional consequences, such as the sensitivity of a cell response to the context in which the stimulus is embedded [23].

Assuming complete homogeneity of the electrophysiological properties of pyramidal cells in the areas considered, we define a simplified neuron model [24] with a single compartment where dendrites, soma and axon are concentrated, and whose electrical potential is V. The excitable membrane is modeled by an electric capacitor, with capacitance C, which integrates the ionic currents as

$$C\frac{dV}{dt} = I_c + I_{ahp} + I_K + I_{syn} + I_l, \tag{1}$$

where I_{syn} represents the dendritic current induced by synaptic action and I_l stands for leak currents not explicitly modeled. Considering a linear relation between the voltage across the membrane and the ionic currents, we have $I_c = g_c(E_K - V)$ (2), $I_{ahp} = g_{ahp}(E_K - V)$ (3), $I_K = g_K(E_K - V)$ (4), $I_l = g_l(E_l - V)$ (5), and $I_{syn} = g_{syn}(E_{syn} - V)$ (6) where E_K, E_l and E_{syn} are the reversal potentials for the K^+-dependent, leak and synaptic currents, respectively. The parameters g_c, g_{ahp}, g_K, g_l and g_{syn} stand for the conductances corresponding to the currents I_c, I_{ahp}, I_K, I_l and I_{syn}, respectively.

The voltage-dependent sodium current, I_{Na}, is not explicitly modeled but its ionic channel is represented by a step gating function s, whose unitary value represents the activation of the sodium gate: $s = \begin{cases} 1, & \text{if } V \geq \theta, \\ 0, & \text{if } V < \theta, \end{cases}$ (7) where θ is a constant voltage threshold for the opening of the gate. The response of the neuron is given by the function r that equals the membrane voltage V, except at instants when a spike is triggered ($s = 1$), assuming the peak voltage, V_{max}, of an action potential: $r = V + s(V_{max} - V)$ (8). The conductance g_c is hypothesized to increase linearly with the intracellular calcium concentration $[Ca]$ as $g_c = \bar{g}_c[Ca]$ (9), $\bar{g}_c$ being the proportionality constant. The calcium concentration increases with the frequency of spiking and decreases due to the action of calcium buffers and pumps:

$$\frac{d[Ca]}{dt} = \frac{s\beta_{Ca} - [Ca]}{\tau_{Ca}}, \tag{10}$$

where β_{Ca} is a calcium concentration constant rate and τ_{Ca} is a relaxation time constant. When the intracellular calcium concentration reaches a threshold value θ_{Ca}, the K^+ ionic channels of the current I_{ahp} are opened and the conductance g_{ahp} increases at a rate β_{ahp} with a time constant τ_{ahp}:

$$\frac{dg_{ahp}}{dt} = \frac{f\beta_{ahp} - g_{ahp}}{\tau_{ahp}}, \tag{11}$$

where f is the gating function $f = \begin{cases} 1, & \text{if } [Ca] \geq \theta_{Ca}, \\ 0, & \text{if } [Ca] < \theta_{Ca} \end{cases}$ (12).

The conductance g_K of the restorative current I_K increases quickly with a rate β_K after a spike is triggered as

$$\frac{dg_K}{dt} = \frac{s\beta_K - g_K}{\tau_K}, \tag{13}$$

where τ_K is the time constant associated with the channel.

The conductance g_{syn} of the synaptic current I_{syn} is a sum of alpha functions representing the rise and decay of neurotransmitter action for every one of the N presynaptic spikes that occurred at times t_i before time t, $1 \leq i \leq N$:$g_{syn} = \bar{g}_{syn} \sum_{i=1}^{N}(t - t_i)e^{-(t-t_i)/t_p}$ (14). The term $\bar{g}_{syn}$ is a maximal conductance that assumes a different value for each synapse modeled and t_p is the peak time of the alpha function. Finally, we note that the conductance g_l of the leak current is a constant adapted to the needs of the model.

5 Computer Simulations

Before simulating the whole neuronal network, it is interesting to show that the neuron model embodies the behavior of a typical pyramidal cell. For this purpose, an external depolarizing current of 4 μA was applied and the function r recorded. The response was a train of spikes of decreasing frequency, characterizing the adaptation of the pyramidal cell to the stimulus. This adaptive behavior was due to the increase in the outward potassium current I_c, since each sodium spike increases the intracellular calcium concentration. The spiking frequency gradually falls to a steady-state level that bounds the calcium concentration, precluding it from reaching the calcium threshold θ_{Ca}. The second simulation used a value of $\bar{g}_c$ equal to one tenth of its nominal value. In this way, the adaptation was greatly reduced, leading to a greater frequency of spiking. As a consequence, the intracellular calcium concentration reaches the calcium threshold and the ionic channels of I_{ahp} are opened, causing an afterhyperpolarization phase that takes the cell to the burst response. This calcium-controlled transition from adaptation to bursting was reported ealier [13] but instead of reducing the influence of the intracellular calcium concentration, the current I_c was entirely blocked. Finally, a third simulation was performed in which the calcium concentration constant rate β_{Ca} was clamped to zero, thereby impairing significant intracellular calcium accumulation. As one would expect, the resulting behavior was a tonic spiking pyramidal cell with no adaptation at all. This tonic or regular firing neuron is taken as the model for the inhibitory interneurons in area V4 and for the single IT neuron. Although bursting pyramidal cells are scarcely detected in the neocortex [14, 15], we assume that all pyramidal neurons in the network entrain in this behavior by the reduction of $\bar{g}_c$.

In a second set of simulations, a neuronal network composed of thirty-three model neurons was assembled in accordance to the topology already described. With the exception of three tonic spiking neurons, all model neurons are pyramidal cells, that is, have the dual behavior of accommodation and bursting. The visual field was stimulated in one spot with a constant spiking frequency of 300 Hz, representing red light, and in another spot with a constant spiking of 200 Hz, standing for green light. Initially, all pyramidal cells have their parameters $\bar{g}_c$ in nominal values and the red and green signals propagate through the cascade of neurons from V1 to V4. Considering the cell on the red pathway in area V4 as the neuron to be observed, the red light is, from now on, labeled as the effective stimulus and the green light as the ineffective one. Since the visual field is stimulated with the effective and ineffective stimuli, the responses elicited in the cells in both pathways are clearly an adaptive spiking, as can be seen in Fig. 1 for the red pathway (the neuronal response of the path V1 to IT is seen from Fig. 1a to Fig. 1e). The competition between the pathways in area V4 changes the response of their cells, that are further integrated in one signal by the single neuron representing area IT. Note that the IT neuronal response is the same for any position of the red and green lights in the visual field, since the convergence of the projections gave a large receptive field for the IT neuron. This unique and integrated signal would represent the binding of the two stimuli. As reported in the literature [2], the observed neuron in area V4 of the red pathway has a regular response since the effective stimulus is present in its receptive field.

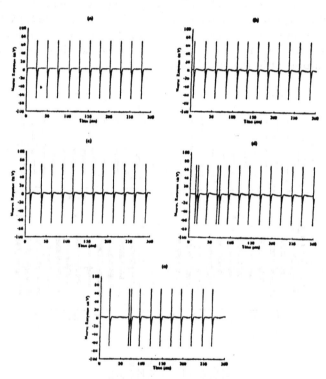

Fig. 1 — Initial Response in the Red Path from V1 (a) to IT (e)

In another simulation, the parameter $\bar{g}_c$ of the cell responsible for the processing of green light in area V2 was reduced. As shown in Fig. 2b, this cell, excited by V1 (Fig. 2a), entrains in a bursting behavior which propagates to V3 (Fig. 2c) and V4 (Fig. 2d). In area V4, the mutual inhibition between the bursting neuron and the accommodated one forces the latter to reduce the regular response it showed so far (Fig. 1d), albeit the effective stimulus is still present in the visual field, as depicted in Fig. 3. This figure shows the propagation from V1 (Fig. 3a) to V4 (Fig. 3d) through the cortical areas V2 (Fig. 3b) and V3 (Fig. 3c) highlighting the fact that the neuron in V4 is now silent.

The signal propagated to IT (Fig. 2e) is solely the one coming from the green pathway, that is, the ineffective stimulus. The normal binding of the two stimuli is interrupted and the IT neuron seems to shrink its receptive field around the green light spot, as it neglects the red light stimulating its visual field. In other words, if we associate the reduction of $\bar{g}_c$ in the cells of V2 to attention, some experimental facts can be better understood: When the two stimuli are present in the visual field, the large receptive field neurons of V4 have a response that reflects the global properties of the stimuli. Neurons in the red and in the green pathways show a strong and regular spiking because they are receiving meaningful stimulation. However, if attention is paid to the green light spot, that is, the parameter $\bar{g}_c$ of the cells in V2 processing the green light is reduced, the behavioral change from accommodation to bursting propagates to V4 and makes the green pathway the winner of the competition there established. Now, the red pathway neuron in V4 responds weakly, or not at all, even though the red light is still present in the visual field.

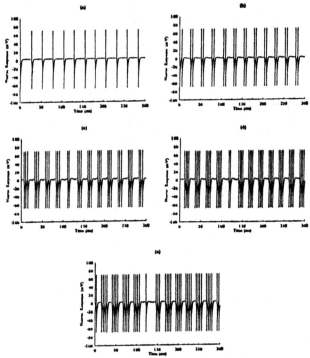

Fig. 2 — Response in the Green Path from V1 (a) to IT (e)

In an apparent paradox, the red pathway neuron seems to ignore the effective stimulus and ceases the transmission of information to IT, leaving it free to pay attention to the green light. The red pathway neuron responds as if the large receptive field had contracted around the attended stimulus, in this case the green light. Clearly, the neuronal substrate of attention — the reduction of the parameter $\bar{g}_c$ — must be triggered at the lower levels of the visual cortex or the effect of receptive field contraction would not be observed. There is no experimental evidence about where this attentional mechanism would operate, and for the model this location is indifferent. Finally, it is worth noting that the bursting activity that propagates through the visual areas when attention is being paid (Fig. 2b, 2c, 2d) would be the coupled or phase-locked oscillation reported by some authors [11, 22]. Indeed, some electrophysiological experiments [15] indicate that a kind of synchronized activity initiates, under certain circumstances, in cortical bursting neurons.

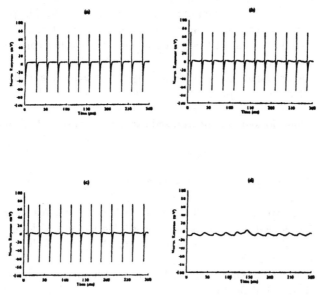

Fig. 3 — Response in the Red Path from V1 (a) to IT (e)

6 Conclusions

It was assumed that the projections from the primary visual area to the inferotemporal cortex are convergent, following the idea of binding by macro-featuring, and in accordance to neuroanatomical reports. As a consequence, neurons in the inferotemporal cortex would represent grandmother cells capable of recognizing visual patterns as a single entity. We postulate, with the support of experimental data, that the pathways from the primary visual area to the inferotemporal cortex are stimulus-specific, or else the selectivity observed in attentional efforts would not be possible.

When all the pyramidal cells are in adaptive spiking, the stimuli present at the visual field are transmitted to the inferotemporal cortex where they are integrated in a single pattern representing the binding entity. As cells at a lower level of the hierarchy (here assumed to be the area V2) change their behavior to bursting, the signal propagation to the inferotemporal cortex is altered due to the enhanced competition at V4. The pathway where the bursting signal propagates wins the competition, inhibiting the other pathway that carries the unattended stimulus. Attention is associated with the bursting activity of the neurons in V2 which is capable of winning the referred competition and reliably transmitting its stimulus to the inferotemporal cortex. Since the bursting neurons of V2 have a fine receptive field, the effect of attentional focus is produced, highlighting the features of the pathway in relation to the remainder of the scene. Concisely, attention can be thought of as an interruption in the normal process of binding caused by a change in the behavior of a class of pyramidal cells. The physiological mechanism that produces this change is open to discussion, but a good beginning would be the study of projections to V2 coming from other cortical or motor areas related to attention.

Finally, the propagating bursting activity of the pyramidal cells can be the alteration needed to the opening of the thalamic gateway that is commonly associated with the focus of attention. In addition, this activity can also be the source of the phase-locked or synchronized oscillations observed in some cortical regions.

7 References

[1] Stryker, M. P., Is Grandmother an Oscillation ?, Nature, Vol. 338, pp. 297 – 298, 1989.

[2] Desimone, R., Wessinger, M., Thomas, L., Schneider, W., Attentional Control of Visual Perception: Cortical and Subcortical Mechanisms, Cold Spring Harbor Symposia on Quantitative Biology, Vol. LV, pp. 963 – 971, Cold Spring Harbor Laboratory Press, 1990.

[3] Van Essen, D. C., Felleman, D. J., DeYoe, E. A., Olavarria, J., Knierim, J., Modular and Hierarchical Organization of Extrastriate Visual Cortex in the Macaque Monkey, Cold Spring Harbor Symposia on Quantitative Biology, Vol. LV, pp. 679 – 696, Cold Spring Harbor Laboratory Press, 1990.

[4] Gross, C. G., Rocha-Miranda, C. E., Bender, D. B., Visual Properties of Neurons in Inferotemporal Cortex of the Macaque, Journal of Neurophysiology, No. 35, pp. 96 – 111, 1972.

[5] Perrett, D. I., Rolls, E. T., Caan, W., Visual Neurones Responsive to Faces in the Monkey Temporal Cortex, Experimental Brain Research, No. 47, pp. 329 – 342, 1982.

[6] Malsburg, C., Schneider, W., A Neural Cocktail-party Processor, Biological Cybernetics, Vol. 54, pp. 29 – 40, 1986.

[7] Crick, F., Function of the Thalamic Reticular Complex: The Searchlight Hypotheses, Proceedings of the National Academy of Science of the U.S.A., Vol. 81, pp. 4586 – 4590, 1984.

[8] Carvalho, L. A. V., Modeling the Thalamocortical Loop, International Journal of

Bio-Medical Computing, 35, pp. 267 — 296, 1994.

[9] Damasio, A., The Brain Binds Entities and Events by Multiregional Activation from Convergence Zones, Neural Computation, No. 1, pp. 123 – 132, 1989.

[10] Gray, C. M., König, P., Engel, A. K., Singer, W., Oscillatory Response in Cat Visual Cortex Exhibit Inter-columnar Synchronization which Reflects Global Stimulus Projections, Nature, Vol. 338, pp. 334 – 339, 1989.

[11] Crick, F., Koch, C., Some Reflections on Visual Awareness, Cold Spring Harbor Symposia on Quantitative Biology, Vol. LV, pp. 953 – 962, Cold Spring Harbor Laboratory Press, 1990.

[12] Douglas, R. J., Martin, K. A. C., Neocortex, in The Synaptic Organization of the Brain, Ed. Shepherd, G. M., Oxford University Press, pp. 389 – 438, 1990.

[13] Berman, N. J., Bush, P. C., Douglas, R. J., Adaptation and Bursting in Neocortical Neurones may be Controlled by a Single Fast Potassium Conductance, Quarterly Journal of Experimental Physiology, Vol. 74, pp. 223 – 226, 1989.

[14] Schwindt, P. C., Spain, W. J., Foehring, R. C., Statfstrom, C, E., Chubb, M. C., Crill, W. E., Multiple Potassium Conductances and Their Functions in Neurons From Cat Sensorimotor Cortex in Vitro, Journal of Neurophysiology, Vol. 59, No. 2, pp. 424 – 449, 1988.

[15] McCormick, D. A., Connors, B. W., Lighthall, J. W., Prince, D. A., Comparative Electrophysiology of Pyramidal and Sparsely Spiny Stellate Neurons of the Neocortex, Journal of Neurophysiology, Vol. 54, 782 – 806, 1985.

[16] Connors, B. W., Gutnick, M. J., Prince, D. A., Electrophysiological Properties of Neocortical Neurons in Vitro, Journal of Neurophysiology, Vol. 48, No. 6, pp. 1302 – 1320, 1982.

[17] Bruce, C., Desimone, R., Gross, C. G., Visual Properties of Neurons in a Polysensory Area in Superior Temporal Sulcus of the Macaque, Journal of Neurophysiology, Vol. 46, No. 2, pp. 369 – 384, 1981.

[18] Wise, S. P., Desimone, R., Behavioral Neurophysiology: Insights into Seeing and Grasping, Science, Vol. 242, Nov. 1988.

[19] Boussaoud, D., Ungerleider, L. G., Desimone, R., Pathways for Motion Analyses: Cortical Connections of the Medial Superior Temporal and Fundus of the Superior Temporal Visual Areas in the Macaque, The Journal of Comparative Neurology, Vol. 296, pp. 462 – 495, 1990.

[20] Moran, J., Desimone, R., Processing in the Extrastriate Cortex, Science, Vol. 229, pp. 782 – 784, Aug. 1985.

[21] Gray, C. M., Singer, W., Stimulus-specific Neuronal Oscillations in Orientation Columns of Cat Visual Cortex, Proceedings of the National Academy of Science of the U.S.A., Vol. 86, pp. 1698 – 1702, 1989.

[22] Singer, W., Gray, C., Engel, A., König, P., Artola, A., Brocher, S., Formation of Cortical Cell Assemblies, Cold Spring Harbor Symposia on Quantitative Biology, Vol. LV, pp. 939 – 951, Cold Spring Harbor Laboratory Press, 1990.

[23] Gilbert, C. D., Hirsch, J. A., Wiesel, T. N., Lateral Interactions in Visual Cortex, Cold Spring Harbor Symposia on Quantitative Biology, Vol. LV, pp. 663 – 677, Cold Spring Harbor Laboratory Press, 1990.

[24] MacGregor, R. J., Neural and Brain Modeling, Academic Press Inc., 1987.

Learning Rare Categories in Backpropagation

Lucila Ohno-Machado and Mark A. Musen
Section on Medical Informatics, MSOB X-215, Stanford University
Stanford, CA 94305-5479
machado, musen@camis.stanford.edu

Abstract

Hierarchical systems of neural networks based on the backpropagation algorithm were used to test the hypothesis that rare categories could be learned more accurately and in shorter training times than in nonhierarchical neural networks also based on the backpropagation algorithm. In two artificial data sets, the problem of learning rare categories was quantified and an existing solution was shown to be inadequate. HNNs were compared to nonhierarchical neural networks. In both artificial examples, HNNs performed better than nonhierarchical neural networks in terms of sensitivity and time to train. Specificities were not significantly different. In two real-world examples, these results were confirmed.

1. Introduction

Classification, or pattern recognition, is one of the most common uses of neural networks. Usually, the output node that has the highest activation at the end of the training phase in feed-forward networks will indicate the predicted category. In a classification application, inputs are generally composed of the attributes of each instance in a data set, and outputs constitute classification categories. Even though researchers are often looking for low frequency data or rare patterns, the latter are difficult to recognize in certain types of machine learning methods, including backpropagation-based neural networks[1]. The difficulty is often due to the fact that the utility of a classification is not taken into account by the methods employed, and that the error that needs to be minimized is not weighted accordingly. The standard error function to be minimized in a backpropagation-based neural network is usually

$$E(w) = \frac{1}{2} \Sigma \left[\zeta_i - O_i \right]^2 \tag{1}$$

where w is the weight matrix, ζ_i is the expected output for pattern i, and O_i is the output provided by the network.[2] The changes in weights in the backpropagation algorithm are proportional to the first derivative of the error function. Since the error function is the result of the sum of squared errors of all patterns, the patterns with higher frequency will have a stronger influence in the weight changes. Utilities can be taken into account in the process of changing weights if the error function is changed to reflect the researcher's interest in detecting a given pattern. Utilities can be incorporated in the error function as follows:

$$E(W) = \frac{1}{2} \sum_{p1} \sum_i \left(\zeta_i - O_i \right)^2 I_1 + \frac{1}{2} \sum_{p2} \sum_i \left(\zeta_i - O_i \right)^2 I_2$$

modified error function

In the latter case, however, a different network will have to be trained each time the utilities change, and the recognition of a pattern cannot be disambiguated from the process of making an optimal decision. We tried to avoid mixing the process of classifying patterns according to their attributes with the process of making the optimal classification based on a decision-theoretic approach.

Backpropagation-based neural networks are able to perform classification reliably, provided that the frequency of the relevant patterns is not low. Traditional classification methods, such as linear-discriminant analysis, also have difficulties in detecting infrequent patterns.[3] If the variability of the most frequent classes is high, then a rare class may be considered just another instance of the most frequent class, and no discrimination will be possible. On the other hand, if all classes are equally represented and they are separable (linearly separable, if the simplest form of neural networks — the perceptron — is used), then the neural network should be able to make the distinction. Unless neural network applications address the problem of discriminating low frequency patterns, their use in real-world applications will not scale up to useful real-world applications.

2. Methods

Hierarchical classifiers can partition the outcome space according to multiple variables. There are several advantages to having an automatic classifier perform hierarchically. First, development and implementation of the model can be incremental; that is, detailed classification can be postponed to a later stage. Second, there is a potential for identifying where in the hierarchy the classifier starts to lose its discriminating power. Since the maximum number of examples is used in the highest level of the hierarchy, it is expected that this level will yield the most accurate predictions. Classifiers in lower levels use fewer examples, and their prediction ability is expected to be progressively worse. Third, the use of the full set of attributes may be unnecessary at different levels, so censored data may be used.

The hierarchical architecture of neural networks that we propose is depicted schematically in Figure 1. In hierarchical systems of neural networks, a triage network divides the sample into smaller groups, classifying the cases according to similarity and creating abstract groupings. The smaller groups constitute inputs to specialized networks that are able to discriminate certain patterns with enhanced accuracy and at enhanced speed.

Hierarchical neural networks do not imply a change in the backpropagation algorithm per se, but they provide a method for constructing and training neural networks incrementally. The backpropagation algorithm is utilized in its pure form in each of the various levels of the hierarchical system. There is no need to alter the weight update function for each output category. This method separates the process of categorizing using input features from that of assigning utilities for each correct classification to obtain the best decision boundary based on a decision-theoretic principle. In addition, the preprocessing of data to form abstractions used in the intermediate levels of the hierarchical system may provide a means to explain later the system's reasoning. Patterns are grouped by similarity, and the changes in prior probabilities are due solely to rearrangement of patterns in similar groups. There are no replications or deletions of data that change the prior probability of each output category in the system as a whole.

Fig. 1. Hierarchical neural network. A triage network is used to "filter" interesting cases from the whole training set. The filtered instances are further processed by specialized networks that provide the final classification.

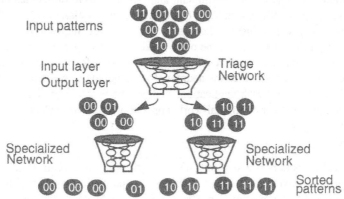

3. Example I: Deterministic Sorting of Binary Numbers

We demonstrate next the problem of learning infrequent patterns in a simple artificial example. Although meaningless from a practical point of view (since real-world problems tend to be much more complex), this example demonstrates the basic ideas underlying the recognition of infrequent patterns and current methods to minimize this problem. In order to evaluate the power of HNN in classifying low frequency patterns, and to compare it to a standard neural network, we created an artificial data set using a known distribution. In the artificial data set, four categories (Category 0, Category 1, and so on) have to be discriminated. There were two attributes for each pattern, which constituted the binary representation of the number assigned to each of the classes ("00" was the pattern that corresponded to Category "0," "01" corresponded to Category "1," "10" corresponded to Category "2," and "11" corresponded to Category "3"). Each input unit corresponded to one digit of the binary number. All the units were binary. Consider that the problem could be formulated as follows. There are two symptoms, S_1 and S_2, and four conditions, D_1, D_2, D_3, and D_4. If the patient has both symptoms S_1 and S_2, then he should be diagnosed as having disease D_4; if the patient has symptoms S_1 and $\neg S_2$, he should be diagnosed with D_3; if he has symptom S_2 and $\neg S_1$, he should be diagnosed with D_2; and finally, if he has symptoms $\neg S_1$ and $\neg S_2$, he should be diagnosed with D_1. The inputs patterns, frequency of each type of pattern, and the expected output categories are shown in Table 1.

Table 1. Distribution of patterns for Example I.

Pattern			Frequency	Output (Disease)	
00	$\neg S_1 \neg S_2$	●	44%	0	D_1
01	$\neg S_1 S_2$	◆	1%	1	D_2
10	$S_1 \neg S_2$	▲	5%	2	D_3
11	$S_1 S_2$	■	50%	3	D_4

Figure 2 shows how the patterns are distributed and the perfect classification that is achieved by defining categories in quadrants. The task of a machine learning method is to define the boundaries of such quadrants.

Fig. 2. Example I. Perfect classification of patterns in four categories. In this simple example, classification of diseases is deterministic: $\neg S_1 \neg S_2$ (00) corresponds to D_1, $\neg S_1 S_2$ (01) corresponds to D_2, $S_1 \neg S_2$ (10) corresponds to D_3, and $S_1 S_2$ (11) corresponds to D_4.

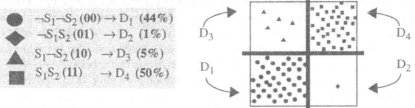

We tested the hypothesis that the HNN could discriminate low frequency patterns earlier (i.e., requiring fewer training cycles) than a standard neural network could, provided that the systems had the same number of weights. A standard feed-forward neural network that tries to classify the patterns in just one step was created for comparison. Classification in the HNN was done in a supervised manner in each step. The neural networks of the first-level (Triage networks) discriminate patterns 0 and 1 from patterns 2 and 3. The two networks for the second-level (Specialized networks), discriminate between patterns 0 and 1 and patterns 2 and 3, respectively. Note that the *total* number of weights in the HNN is the same as that of the standard neural network (i.e., the total number of parameters that needed to be estimated in each of the systems is controlled to be the same). Table 2 displays the number of parameters to be estimated (weights), the number of training cycles (epochs), and the average time that each system took to converge to a perfect solution.

Table 2. Comparison of systems for Example I.

System	Units	Weights	Epochs[†]	Time [‡]
Standard NN	10	24	148,791	50 min 53 sec
Hierarchical NN	18	24	14,623	2 min 37 sec
Perceptron	6	8	11,119	2 min 00 sec
Hierarchical Perceptron	12	12	6,437	36 sec

A perfect solution was defined to be achieved when the activation of the correct output unit was at least twice that of the other output units. No noise was added to the data. Training was done by epochs. We performed 10 simulations for each system, starting with different initial weights. All networks were trained with a fixed learning rate of 0.01 and no momentum term. The overall time spent for making the perfect classification was significantly reduced ($p < 0.01$) with the use of HNN. We did not run Specialized networks in parallel, even though by doing so time could be reduced even more. It must also be taken into account that one epoch in the non-hierarchical network takes longer than one epoch in any of the networks in the hierarchical system, given the smaller number of weights in each of the networks of the latter, and the smaller number of patterns in the Specialized networks

One might still argue that the pre-selection of subsets that were themselves linearly separable introduced a bias in favor of the hierarchical system. We also ran the same experiments dividing the subsets in a different way, such that patterns "00" and "11" would be separated from patterns "01" and "10" in the Triage network. This grouping would require that the Triage network would be able to solve a non-linearly separable problem first, and is by far the worst possible grouping: the Hamming distance between patterns in the same group is twice that of patterns in other groups. Furthermore, the proportions involved would require the Triage network to detect a subgroup that had a low frequency value itself (the patterns "01" and "10" constitute only six percent of the total number of patterns). The HNN exhibited a peculiar behavior: four of the ten networks converged to a solution after relatively few epochs (mean: 34,944), but the other six did not converge to a perfect solution even after 4×10^5 epochs. This result indicates that the groupings should be done by similarity of features, rather than be based purely on pattern frequencies. Therefore, merging rare patterns that do not share similarities into a group simply to increase their frequency in the training set does not help. Another experiment, in which the pattern distribution was changed to the one shown in Table 3, proved that the difficulties encountered by the Triage network were not related to the combined low frequency of the group "01" and "10", but to the fact that the similarities within the groups were low. None of the ten Triage networks built for this experiment converged to a perfect solution after 4×10^5 epochs.

Table 3. Another distribution of patterns for Example I.

Pattern	Frequency	Output (Category)
00	1%	0
01	45%	1
10	5%	2
11	49%	3

Pattern similarity seems to be the key factor in determining the success of HNN. Evaluation of a test set was not necessary in this artificial example because the categories were *defined* as being the decimal representation of the binary numbers. The systems would have exhibited the same performance on any test set composed of the same patterns, independent of their distribution. Overfitting was not a concern for exactly the same reason.

Although a replication method produced good results in Example I, there is an important limitation in the data set used there. All classifications in that example were deterministic and mutually exclusive (that is, once a pattern was known, its classification did not depend on any random factor and it belonged to just one category). We will demonstrate next that when random factors are involved in classification (that is, once a pattern is known, there is a certain probability—different from 1—that it belongs to a given class), the replication method does not work. In this example categories are still mutually exclusive, but the results apply to similar problems where categories are not mutually exclusive as well.

4. Example II: Probabilistic Sorting of Binary Numbers

We have shown in the previous example that backpropagation neural networks take a long time to recognize patterns that are infrequent. In that example, the categories were deterministically defined, and the replication method would work nicely to enhance the speed of learning. In this next example, however, categories are stochastic: the same pattern may appear in different categories, and the relative frequency of each pattern in a certain category will determine how that pattern should be classified. The distribution of the patterns and their categories is shown in Table 4.

Table 4. Distribution of patterns. Example II. Shaded cells show the best diagnosis for a pattern.

Input pattern	D_1 (%)	D_2 (%)	D_3 (%)	D_4 (%)	Total (%)
00 $\neg S_1 \neg S_2$ ●	24	2	3	15	44 (44%)
01 $\neg S_1 S_2$ ◆	0	1	0	0	1 (1%)
10 $S_1 \neg S_2$ ▲	1	0	3	1	5 (5%)
11 $S_1 S_2$ ■	12	6	12	20	50 (50%)
Total (%)	37(37%)	9 (9%)	18 (18%)	36 (36%)	100 (100%)

The shaded cells indicate the best diagnosis for each input pattern. For example, a patient with symptoms $S_1 S_2$ should be classified as having disease D_4, a patient with $S_1 \neg S_2$ should be classified as having D_3, a patient with $\neg S_1 S_2$ should be classified as having D_2, and a patient with $\neg S_1 \neg S_2$ should be classified as having D_1, because the posterior probability of these diseases is the highest, given the symptoms just mentioned. The posterior probability of a disease given the symptoms is of course not 100%. For example, a patient with $\neg S_1 \neg S_2$ has a probability of 24/44 (54.6%) of having D_1, 2/44(4.5%) of having D_2, 3/44 (6.8%) of having D_3, and 15/44 (34.1%) of having D_4. Figure 3 shows how patterns are distributed in the four output diagnostic categories.

Fig. 3. Example II. Distribution of patterns and output categories. In this artificial data set, classification of diseases is stochastic: each input pattern has a probability of belonging to a given disease category. For example, if pattern "00" is present, there is a probability of 55% that D_1 is present, 4% that D_2 is present, 7% that D_3 is present, and 34% that D_4 is present.

● $\neg S_1 \neg S_2$ (00) → D_1 (55%), D_2 (4%), D_3 (7%), D_4 (34%)
◆ $\neg S_1 S_2$ (01) → D_1 (0%), D_2 (100%), D_3 (0%), D_4 (0%)
▲ $S_1 \neg S_2$ (10) → D_1 (20%), D_2 (0%), D_3 (60%), D_4 (20%)
■ $S_1 S_2$ (11) → D_1 (24%), D_2 (12%), D_3 (24%), D_4 (40%)

The same network used in Example I, with the cross-entropy error function, was used to classify the patterns. It was again evident that patterns that were less frequent were more difficult to be recognized by the neural network.

Now consider the option of replicating some patterns (so that each output category is equally represented) in order to enhance the speed by which all categories are learned. Table 5 shows the distribution of patterns after replication of the most frequent patterns. Patterns are replicated in rare categories, but their proportions inside that category remain practically unchanged after this process. For example, patterns for category D_2 are replicated so that the initial proportion of input patterns — 2/9 (22%) for "00," 1/9 (11%) for "01," 0/9 (0%) for "10," and 6/9 (67%) for "11" are replicated to 8/37 (22%), 4/37 (11%), 0/37 (0%), and 25/37 (67%), respectively. Shaded cells correspond to the best diagnoses for each input pattern.

Table 5. Distribution of patterns for Example II, after replication. Infrequent patterns were replicated, so that all categories became equally represented (25% of the patterns of each category) in this example. Shaded cells correspond to the diagnosis that should be made for each pattern. Compare these shaded cells with the ones presented in Table 4.

Input pattern	D_1 (%)	D_2 (%)	D_3 (%)	D_4 (%)	Total (%)
00 $\neg S_1 \neg S_2$ ●	24	8	6	15	53(36%)
01 $\neg S_1 S_2$ ◆	0	4	0	0	4 (3%)
10 $S_1 \neg S_2$ ▲	1	0	6	1	8 (5%)
11 $S_1 S_2$ ■	12	25	25	21	83 (56%)
Total (%)	37 (25%)	37 (25%)	37 (25%)	37 (25%)	148 (100%)

5. Real-World Examples

Two real-world examples from the medical domain, reported in detail elsewhere, have confirmed these results. In classifying patients with thyroid diseases,[4] the use of neural networks proved to be faster and more accurate than the use of standard neural networks. In one example, patients were first classified as "hypothyroid," "hyperthyroid," or "normal," and the ones who were not normal were further classified as having "primary hypothyroidism," "secondary hypothyroidism," "primary hyperthyroidism," "secondary hyperthyroidism," and so on. In another example, prognosis of patients with AIDS was made easier by the use of hierarchical neural networks.[5]

6. Discussion

Several authors have dealt with the decomposition of complex problems inside and outside the field of neural networks. The reasons for developing the hierarchical models of neural networks were in general very different from the ones presented in this article. Sunil et al.[6] have use hierarchical neural networks to predict tool wear in the domain of machine conditioning monitoring. The authors used a top level network to extract features that would then be used in a more refined network. Their system differs from ours because the top level network, in our case, is not a mere feature extractor, but a search-space separator that tries to extract irrelevant cases from those that will be the focus of a specific specialized neural network.

The systems developed by Jordan et al.[7] and Curry and Rumelhart[8] bear the most similarity to the one described in this article. Jordan proposed a system where many networks of experts would receive the system's inputs and compete for providing the best solution. A gating network decided among the experts' solutions. The system proposed in this article is different. Even though we propose a system were Specialized networks refine the partial solutions proposed by the Triage network, the decision on which network to use is done first, so not all experts need to be overburden with all data.

Curry and Rumelhart's work on the Mass Spectrometry Network (MSNet) is closely related to the one presented here. In that system, categories of chemical compounds are determined in a Top level network. The probability of belonging to a given group, allied to the original input attribute vector were then used by Specialized networks to refine the solution and get a final diagnosis. The authors were concerned with the fact that low frequency patterns would cause the performance of the network to decay, and they solved the problem of dealing with infrequent patterns by using a different strategy: they trained the network to recognize low frequency patterns by assigning a higher utility to these patterns. This procedure was done by modifying the learning algorithm, and processing the final output to reflect the consequent changes in posterior probabilities. Our system, however, tried to disambiguate the process of diagnosing the categories from the process of using utilities while training to make an optimal decision based on a decision-theoretic approach. In our system, the diagnosis is based on the similarities between the patterns, and not on their relative utility. Once the diagnostic process is proven to be reliable and based mainly on the features presented by the inputs, the use of utilities and the decision on which category to choose should be straightforward. The selection of the best grouping at the Triage level may involve human participation, as in this study, or the clustering of examples by similarity-based algorithms, such as multidimensional scaling.[9]

As electronic data bases become more common, screening large data sets for unusual patterns may be greatly enhanced by the use of HNN. The unusual patterns detected by the neural networks can then be processed by a number of manual or computer-based decision-support applications. Database mining for knowledge discovery in large databases may also benefit from the power and simplicity of HNN.

7. Conclusion

The number of epochs required to train a neural network to detect patterns increases exponentially with the decrease in pattern frequency. To minimize this problem, a HNN can be used. Two examples, which used an artificial data set to classify binary numbers, indicate that hierarchical systems of neural networks can overcome the problem of low frequency pattern detection in backpropagation neural networks if the selection of groupings at each step is based on pattern similarity. Many real-world problems are amenable to such decomposition and should benefit from the use of HNN, especially if the detection of low frequency patterns is required. Furthermore, a rational choice of groupings may be useful for providing partial diagnoses and even for explanation purposes.

Acknowledgments

We thank Dr. Michael Walker, Prof. Edward Shortliffe, and Prof. Les Lenert for useful discussion in different stages and different aspects of the present work. This work has been funded by the Conselho Nacional de Pesquisa (CNPq), Brazilian Ministry of Education. Computing facilities were provided by CAMIS, through grant LM05305 from the National Library of Medicine.

References

1. Rumelhart DE; Hinton GE; Williams RJ. Learning internal representation by error propagation. In Rumelhart, D.E., and McClelland, J.L. (eds) *Parallel Distributed Processing*. MIT Press, Cambridge, 1986.
2. Hertz JA; Palmer RG; Krogh, AS. *Introduction to the Theory of Neural Computation*. Addison-Wesley, Redwood City, 1991.
3. Gray NAB. Constraints on "learning machine" classification methods. *Analytical Chemistry*, 1976, 48(14):2265–8.
4. Ohno-Machado L. Identification of Low Frequency Patterns in Backpropagation Neural Networks. *JAMIA Symposium Supplement*, 1994, 853–9.
5. Ohno-Machado L; Walker MG; Musen MA. Hierarchical Neural Networks for Survival Analysis. Proceedings of the *MEDINFO*, 1995.
6. Sunil EVT; Shin YC; Kumara SRT. Machining Conditioning Monitoring via Neural networks. *ASME Winter Annual Meeting, in Monitoring and Control of Manufacturing Processes*. SY Liang and TC Tsao (Co-eds), PED-VOL 44, ASME Publications, pp85-95, December 1990
7. Jordan RA; Nowlan SJ; Hinton SJ. Adaptive mixtures of local experts. *Neural Computation*, 1991, 3:79–87.
8. Curry B; Rumelhart DE. MSnet: A neural network that classifies mass spectra. *Tetrahedron Computer Methodology*, 1990, 3:213–37.
9. Shepard RN. Multidimensional scaling, tree-fitting, and clustering. *Science*, 1980, 210:390–8.

An Automatic Adaptive Neurocomputing Algorithm for Time Series Prediction

Emmanuel Passos[1] and Romildo Valente[1]

Instituto Militar de Engenharia
Departamento de Engenharia de Sistemas
Pós-graduação em Sistemas e Computação
e-mail: emmanuel@ime.eb.br

Abstract. This work proposes a new algorithm called KNNN (k-nearest neighbours network) and demonstrates its use in a prediction task. The algorithm constructs estimators arranged in layers, using cross validation and kernel smoothing to achieve function approximation. Here it is compared to the back-propagation (with weight-elimination) algorithm in the prediction of future behavior of the benchmark sunspot series. The results show that KNNN can be applied successfully as an estimator.

1 Introduction

In various situations, the desire to estimate the future is the guiding force behind the search for rules that explain the behavior of certain systems. Examples range from forecasting the rainfall in a chosen area to estimating currency exchange rates.

The effectiveness of an architecture for predicting the future behavior of a given system hinges on two types of knowledge. The first and most powerful one is knowledge of the laws underlying a given phenomenon. When this knowledge is expressed in the form of equations that can be solved, one can predict the future outcome of an experiment once the initial conditions are completely specified.

A second and less powerful method for predicting the future relies on the discovery of strong empirical regularities in observations of the system. However, there are serious problems with this approach. Periodic patterns are not always clear enough to be identified, and they are often masked by noise. Even worse, there are phenomena — although recurrent in a generic sense — that seem random, without apparent periodicities (deterministic chaos).

1.1 State-space Forecasting.

If an experimentally observed quantity arises from deterministic governing equations, it is possible to use time-delay embedding to recover a representation of the relevant internal degrees of freedom of the system from the observable. Although the precise values of these reconstructed variables are not meaningful (because of the unknown change of coordinates), they can be used to make precise forecasts because the embedding map preserves their geometrical structure.

Figure 1 is an example of the structure that an embedding can reveal. Notice that the surface appears to be single-valued; this, in fact, must be the case if the system is deterministic and if the number of time lags used is sufficient for an embedding. Differential equations and maps have unique solutions forward in time; this property is preserved under a diffeomorphic transformation and so the first component of an embedded vector must be a unique function of the preceding values $x_{t-\tau}, \cdots, x_{t-(d-1)\tau}$ once d is large enough. Therefore, the points must lie on a single-valued hypersurface. Future values of the observable can be read off from this surface if it can be adequately estimated from the given data set (which may contain noise and is limited in length).

Using embedding for forecasting appears to be very similar to Yule's original AR model: a prediction function is sought based on time-lagged vectors. The crucial difference is that understanding embedding reduces forecasting to recognizing and then representing the underlying geometrical structure, and once the number of lags exceeds the minimum embedding dimension, this geometry will not change. A global linear model (AR) must do this with a single hyperplane.

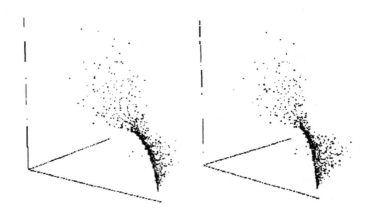

Fig. 1. Three-dimensional embedding of a data set with just 1000 points.

Early efforts to improve global linear AR models included systematically increasing the order of interaction (bilinear models [1]), splitting the input space across one variable and allowing for two AR models (threshold autoregressive models [2]), and using the nonlinearities of a Volterra expansion. Farmer and Sidorovich introduced local linear models for state-space forecasting, based on the simple idea that any manifold is locally linear (i.e., locally a hyperplane). The great advantage of local models is their ability to adhere to the local shape of an arbitrary surface; the corresponding disadvantage is that they do not lead to a compact description of the system. Global expansions of the surface reverse this tradeoff by providing a more manageable representation of the risk of large local errors.

1.2 Connectionist Forecasting

Neurocomputing techniques can be applied to the forecasting problem using adaptive algorithms for functional estimation. When both input and output are observable and usable by the algorithm, the learning process is called supervised since the output signal works as a teacher signal. A general form to represent systems, both linear and nonlinear, is the Kolmogorov-Garbor polynomial [3] shown below:

$$y = a_0 + \sum_i a_i x_i + \sum_i \sum_j a_{ij} x_i x_j + \cdots \tag{1}$$

where y is the output, and x is the input to the system.

Garbor et al [3] proposed a learning method that adjusted the coefficients of (1) by minimizing the mean square error between each desired output sample and the actual output. Lapedes and Farber [4] explored the hypersurface interpretation of the functional relationship in (1). Their work concentrated on the use of feedforward neural networks in which the node transfer function is the sigmoid, or the logistic function. The structure of the network is fixed, and the weights adjusted by the generalized delta rule algorithm. The elementary structure of the system is based on n nodes of the first connected to the nodes of the second layer, and the nodes of the second connected to the nodes of the third layer according to a particular connectivity pattern (Fig. 2). This substructure forms a hypersurface in $n + 1$ dimension, which they call a "bump" [4].

The approaches described above suffer from the rapid explosion of the possible combination of terms as the order of the polynomial increases. The number of samples needs to be much larger than the dimensionality of the hypersurface used, which for practical purposes can be difficult to achieve. They also require repeated presentation of the training data.

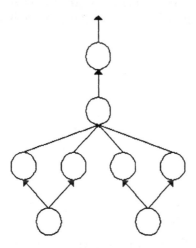

Fig. 2. The "bump" surface is formed by this simple structure

To address some of the difficulties described above, a heuristic algorithm called the group method of data handling (GMDH) was developed [5]. This method constructs a feedforward network as it tries to estimate the system function. The node transfer function consists of a quadratic polynomial of two variables, and its parameters are obtained through regression. At each stage of the algorithm, nodes are created pairwisely connecting the output of one layer to form a new layer, starting with the input nodes. This process is exhaustively done for all possible input pairs in each layer, and the connections are always in feedforward, n to $n + 1$ layer form. The GMDH method discards unpromising nodes using a selection process based on a performance criterion which evaluates how closely the new surface describes the output data in a least-mean-square sense, thus generating suboptimal estimates at each node output. The algorithm can be stopped at any point to obtain a model of the process, using a heuristic stopping criterion.

The approach proposed here resembles GMDH in the attempt to produce suboptimal estimates at each node output and in the Darwinian selection process in each layer, but not in the transfer function and in the network architecture.

2   The KNNN Algorithm

The KNNN algorithm is a method that mixes state-space reconstruction and connectionist forecasting. Like GMDH, it builds a network in which each output node is a suboptimal estimate of the system function. It starts with a first layer composed of d time-delayed neurons. Each subsequent layer is constructed taking pairwisely all possible pairs of neurons, the first from the last created layer and the second from any of the built layers, thus generating a non-hierarchical structure. The node transfer function is a k-nearest neighbor smoother applied through a neighborhood (chosen using a cross-validation scheme) around each of the training points, considered as l-dimensional vectors.

Figure 3 shows a typical network generated by the KNNN algorithm:

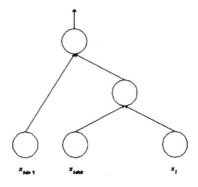

Fig. 3. A typical KNNN network

The algorithm can use validation or not, depending on the nature of the series to be predicted and on the amount of available data. In the general case, the cost function is chosen to be the total normalized mean square error (NMSE), for both the training (T) and validation (S) sets,

$$\frac{\sum_{k \in (T+S)} (observed_k - estimated_k)^2}{\sum_{k \in (T+S)} (observed_k - mean(k))^2} \tag{2}$$

where $target_k$ is the true value of the time series at time k, and $prediction_k$ is the output of the network for time k. Only the p best estimators in each layer remain in the network, avoiding a combinatorial explosion when building the layers of the network.

2.1 Kernel Functions

The k-nearest neighbor (k-NN) estimate is a weighted average in a varying neighborhood [6]. This neighborhood is defined through those training points which are among the k-nearest neighbors of the point under estimation in Euclidean distance. The k-NN weight sequence has been introduced by Loftsgaarden and Quesenberry [7] in the field of density estimation. The k-NN smoother is defined as

$$m_k(x) = n^{-1} \cdot \sum_{i=1}^{n} W_{ki}(x) Y_i, \tag{3}$$

where $\{W_{ki}(x)\}_{i=1}^{n}$ is a weight sequence defined through the set of indexes

$$J_x = \{i : X_i \text{ is one of the } k\text{-nearest observations to } x \}. \tag{4}$$

In this work three different kernel functions were applied as weight sequences to generate the estimate at each node:

constant
$$W_{ki}(x) = \frac{n}{k}, \quad \text{if } i \in J_x \text{ and } 0 \text{ otherwise} \tag{5}$$

linear
$$W_{ki}(x) = \frac{n R_i^{-1}}{\sum_{i=1}^{k} R_i^{-1}}, \quad \text{if } i \in J_x \text{ and } 0 \text{ otherwise} \tag{6}$$

gaussian
$$W_{ki}(x) = \frac{n \cdot \exp\left(\frac{1}{2}\left(\frac{R_i}{R_k}\right)^2\right)/\sqrt{2\pi}}{\sum_{i=1}^{k} \exp\left(\frac{1}{2}\left(\frac{R_i}{R_k}\right)^2\right)/\sqrt{2\pi}}, \quad \text{if } i \in J_x \text{ and } 0 \text{ otherwise} \tag{7}$$

where R_i is the Euclidean distance between the ith-nearest neighbor and the point under estimation in the reconstructed l-dimensional state-space.

The optimal *neighborhood x kernel* pair for each node is selected by means of a cross-validation scheme [6]. For each neighborhood in the pre-defined neighborhood grid and for each kernel function is calculated the value of the function

$$CV = \sum_{i \in T} (observed_i - estimated_i)^2, \qquad (8)$$

and the pair leading to the smallest error is chosen to estimate the system function for that node.

The KNNN algorithm can be summarized as follows :

a) define the lag-space d, the dimension of the reconstructed state-space l, the number of candidate nodes at each level p, and the neighborhood grid to be used;

b) construct the first layer with d time-delayed neurons and compute its error;

c) select the next node to be built and find the best neighborhood x kernel to estimate the system function at it;

d) if the layer is complete

```
   then
       if the error is reduced
       then
          go back to step c,
       else
          go to step e
       end
   else
       go back to step c
   end
```

e) compute the overall network performance as the performance of the best neuron in the last layer and eliminate all the nodes that do not contribute to the final result.

3   Example - The Sunspot Series

Sunspots, often larger in diameter than the Earth, are dark blotches on the sun. They were first observed around 1610, shortly after the invention of the telescope [8]. Yearly averages have been recorded since 1700. The series is shown in figure 4. The average time between maxima is 11 years. However, the time between maxima ranges from 7 to 15 years.

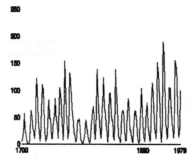

Fig. 4. The benchmark sunspot series

The sunspot series has served as a benchmark in the statistics literature. Within the time-delay or lag-space paradigm, different models differ in the specific choice for the primitives for the surface above the input space. In the simplest case, a single hyperplane approximates the data points. Such a linear autoregressive model is a linear superposition of past values of the observable.

$$x_t = c_1 x_{t-1} + c_2 x_{t-2} + \cdots + c_d x_{t-d} + \varepsilon_t \tag{9}$$

The sunspot series was the first time series ever studied with such a linear autoregressive model [9].

The evaluation of the KNNN model is carried out here by comparison to a modified backpropagation model (Weigend, Huberman, Humelhart [10]) and to the threshold autoregressive model (Tong and Lim [2]). The same data intervals for training (from 1700 through 1920) and evaluation (from 1921 to 1979) were used here, as well as the same input dimension (12) and error measure (arv). The average relative variance of a set S can be defined as [10]

$$\mathrm{arv}(S) = \frac{\sum_{k \in S} (target_k - prediction_k)^2}{\sum_{k \in S} (target_k - mean)^2}. \tag{10}$$

The following parameters were chosen before generating the KNNN model to predict the sunspot series:

> lag-space $= 12$
> dimension of the state-space $= 2$
> neighborhood grid $= \{3, 4, 5, 6, 10, 15, 20\}$
> number of candidates nodes per layer $= 3$

and the final network is shown bellow.

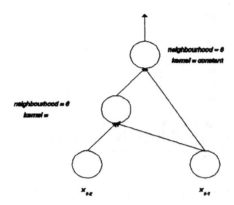

Fig. 5. The network generated by the KNNN algorithm to predict the sunspot series

The following table summarizes the results obtained and the comparison between KNNN, backpropagation and TAR single-step predictions using the average relative variance measure:

arv	KNNN	Backpropagation	TAR
train (1700-1920)	0.056	0.082	0.097
predict (1921-1955)	0.078	0.086	0.097
predict (1956-1979)	0.230	0.350	0.280

The following graph shows the multi-step prediction variance obtained by the three different methods:

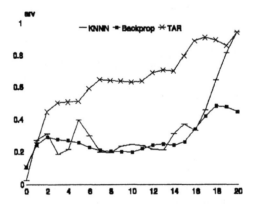

Fig. 6. Multi-step prediction error for the sunspot series, as a function of the predicted time (number of iterations). The KNNN performance is found to be similar to the BP one and better than the TAR one.

4 Conclusion

In summary, the KNNN method outperformed more traditional ones in forecasting the benchmark sunspot series in both the single-step and the multi-step prediction. The results obtained show potential for further research, using different kernel functions.

References

1. Granger, C.W.J. and Andersen, A.P.: An Introduction to Bilinear Time Series Models. Gottingen: Vandenhoek and Ruprecht, 1978.
2. Tong, H.: Nonlinear Time Series Analysis: A Dynamical Systems Approach. Oxford: Oxford University Press, 1990.
3. Garbor, D. et al.: A universal nonlinear filter, predictor and simulator which optimizes itself by a learning process. Proc. IEEE, **108B**, 422–438 (1961).
4. Lapedes, A. and Farber, R.: Nonlinear Signal Processing Using Neural Networks; Prediction and System Modelling, 1987.
5. Ivakhnenko, A.G.: Polynomial Theory of Complex Systems. IEEE TSMC, **SMC-1** (4), 364–378 (1971).
6. Härdle, W.: Applied Nonparametric Regression. Cambridge University Press, 1989.
7. Loftsgaarden, D.O. and Quesenberry, G.P.: A Nonparametric Estimate of a Multivariate Density Function. Annals of Mathematical Statistics, 1965.
8. Foukal, P.V.: The Variable Sun. Sci. Am, 1990.
9. Yule, G.U.: On a method of investigations periodicities in disturbed series with special reference to Wolfer's sunspot numbers. Philos. Trans. R. Soc. Lond. Ser. 1927.
10. Weigend, A.S. , Huberman, B.A. and Rumelhart, D.E. Predicting the future: a connectionist approach. International Journal of Neural Systems, 1990.

A Computational Approach to Situation Theory Based on Logic Programming to Design Cognitive Agents

Milton Corrêa

Serpro - Serviço Federal de Processamento de Dados

Sueli Mendes

Departamento de Enegenharia e Sistemas de Computação COPPE/UFRJ

Abstract

This paper describes a framework based on logic programming to provide computational instruments to design cognitive agents and systems in Situation Theory.

This framework provides a representation in Prolog for the Situation Theory objects: individuals, relations, infons, situations, parameters, anchors, types (object types and situation types) and for making inferences by using rules such as "supports" and "constraints". It provides also two mechanisms for inferences: based upon backward chaining and upon forward chaining. These inferences are situated in a particular or in a general context.

We conclude this paper giving examples of applications of this framework and showing how it can be used as a tool to build agents and systems having Situation Theory as their theoretical basis. We claim that this framework can be easily extended to include induction and belief systems.

Content areas: applications, agent-oriented programming, situation theory and logic programming

1. Introduction

Situation Theory makes possible to use partial description of knowledege and situated inferences, that is, inferences in a particular context (Barwise and Perry, 1983; Devlin, 1991; Aczel et al., 1993), so its become very atractive to design agents that interacts with the world and themselves through some formal or natural language (Devlin and Rosenberg, 1993; Poesio, 1993; Corrêa and Coelho, 1993 and Corrêa, 1994). Unfortunately we have no space in this paper to present even a brief introduction to Situation Theory. We remit the reader for an introduction to our bibliography.

Application of this theory to build agents and systems in a computational environment as computer and robots, for example, demands the development of programming instruments as, for example, presented in Nakashima et al. (1988) who advocated the use of logic programming paradigm for a computational approach to Situation Theory. They also have developed a programming language based on Situation Theory called PROSIT. Our approach is also based upon logic programming paradigm, but instead of a special programming language we define a set of Prolog's predicate to make possible the application of it to the building of agents and systems based on Situation Theory. This framework provides a practical and powerfull instrument to agents and intelligent system programming since Prolog is available and widespread used in computer systems throughout the world (Bratko, 1986; Sterling and Shapiro, 1986). The interested reader may have the source code of STPF by sending an e-mail to correa@rio.cos.ufrj.br (Milton Corrêa).

2. Situation Theory Prolog Framework

The primitive elements of Situation Theory are individuals, relations, temporal localizations (called time), spatial localizations (called space), parameters, infons, situations and types. These elements will be represented below with their respectives representations and applications into the context of Prolog. This set of tools we call Situation Theory Prolog Framework or STPF.

To make references to these objects in STPF, we use Prolog's alphanumeric constants beginning with lowercase alphabetic character, thus, for example, it is possible to make reference to the space l1, time t1, relation greater_then, parameter parm1 infon e2 etc. The other elements of STPF are numerical constants and character strings of the Prolog language.

Any element of a STPF program must be declared by a declaration type predicate as:

dcl_type(<term>, type-of-element), where

<term> is a term that make reference to an object and type-of-element is the object's type such as relation, individual, space, time, infon, situation and parameter. We will introduce other forms of type declarations in the paragraphs below.

Examples of type declaration:

dcl_type("John", individual).

dcl_type(e1, infon).

dcl_type(s1, situation).

2.1 Infons

The infons (units of information) are represented by a Prolog's structure:

infon(r,[a_1, a_2 ,..., a_n], i), where

r is a n-place relation ($n \geq 0$), a_1, a_2,..., a_n are objects (individual, space, time, situation, infon, parameter, type) and i (called polarity of the infon) is 1 if the objects a_1,a_2,..., a_n stand in the relation r, 0 if the objects a_1, a_2,...,a_n do not stand in relation r and u if it is undetermined that objects a_1, a_2,...,a_n do or do not stand in the relation r.

Note here that we are using Barwise and Perry (1983) distinction between the case where we know that a relation is or not is valid for a tuple of objects and the case where we don't know either. This last case they call an "open question". What we do is to apply this distinction to Devlin(1991) definition of an infon. We consider that these distinctions are essential for constructing models of cognitive agents.

Examples of representation of infons:

infon(greather-than, [10, 5], 1),

infon(plays, ["Pelé", football, "Maracanã" , 1969], 1).

To declare an object as an infon we write:

dcl_type(e, infon(r, [a_1, a_2,...,a_n], i)) where e is the term used to indicate the infon in this predicate.

Two infons: infon(r, [a_1, a_2,...,a_n], 1) and infon(r, [a_1, a_2,...,a_n], 0), which difference is only the opposite polarities (1 and 0) are called duals infons. We will use the notation e and ¬e to indicate that these infons are duals[1]. The Theory of Situations, distinguishes "abstract situation" from "real situation" (see Barwise and Perry, 1983 and Devlin, 1991). The former can be described as supporting any set of infons, can include also duals infons, and the second cannot include duals infons.

In this work we adopt from Barwise and Perry (1983) the distinction between "real world" and "ideal world". By doing this we are not ressurecting the old philosophical dispute between realism and idealism. Although Barwise and Perry (1983) explicitly embrace a realist philosophy we only adopt the above mentioned distinction to design an agent model where this can be expressed. This is necessary because it is undisputable that we have a conscious distinction between what we presume to be true of the world outside ourselves and what we think, believe and know about this world. Essentialy this distinction is expressed by the difference between the perception of an object x and the assumption that x is of type y, see Barwise (1993).

2.2 Compound infons

In STPF is possible to define compound infon by using the logical operators & (and), • (or) and # (exclusive or). For example:

---

[1] Note that infons are not true or false and e = ¬¬e.

$infon_1 \& infon_2 \& ... \& infon_n,$

$infon_1 \bullet infon_2 \bullet ... \bullet infon_m,$

infon(red,[bycicle, "Mary"], t)#infon(blue, [bycicle, "Mary"],1),

infon(brother, ["John", "Peter"],1)&infon(brother, ["John", "Alice"],1).

To declare an infon e as a compound infon we write:

dcl_type(e, <compound-infon>).

For example:

dcl_type(e, infon(red,[bycicle, "Mary"], 1)#infon(blue, [bycicle, "Mary"],1)).

2.3 Situations

The situations are, normally, incomplete and partially described by the agents, and it is not the case that different agents must have the same description of the same situation. The situations can be described by a set of infons. In STPF, to assert an infon to a situation description of an agent, is used the predicate:

supports(s, e), where s is a situation and e is an infon[2].

The presence of this predicate in the agent's model, that is, in an STPF model of an agent, means that, according to a particular description of this agent, the situation s supports the infon e. It does not mean that in the world this situation supports this infon, because it is possible that the agent changes it's description and asserts the predicate supports(s, ¬e) to its knowledge base.

To assert an infon e to a description of a situation s it is used the predicade include_infon(s, e) and to delete an infon e from a description of a situation s is used the predicate exclude_infon(s, e).

If the predicate supports(s, e) is not present in the agent's description of situations, this means that it is not the case that this situation supports the infon e in an agent's particular description of the situation s.

---

[2] supports(s, $e_1 \& e_2$) if and only if supports(s, e_1) and supports(s, e_2) .

supports(s, $e_1 \bullet e_2$) if and only if supports(s, e_1) or supports(s, e_2) .

supports(s, $e_1 \# e_2$) if and only if supports(s, e_1) and it is not the case that supports(s, e_2)

or supports(s, e_2) and it is not the case that supports(s, e_1) .

We note that, the information that the situation s supports (or does not) the infon e can also be given by infon(supports,[s, e], i), where i = 1 (or i = 0) if it is a fact that the situation s supports (or does not) the infon e, according to a particular description of the situation s.

This can be used, for example, when two agents transfer information between them. For example, if an agent want to tell another agent some information about the characteristics of birds it can send a message with the infons:

infon(supports, [bird, infon(has_feathers, [], 1)],1) and

infon(supports, [bird, infon(fly, [], 1)],1) and

infon(supports, [bird, infon(is-normal, [], 1)],1).

The definition of an infon permits that the polarity i can also be u (undetermined), but in the case of the relation supports, it is not possible the occurrence of this polarity, because the information is about an agent's particular description of a situation, and it is assumed that an agent is always sure about its description of the world although it may not be sure about the facts of the world.

For example, let an agent description of the situation s_room (a particular room) contain the predicates: supports(s_room, infon(has, [cushion], 1)) and supports(s_room, infon(has, [elephant], 0)). Then, according to this particular description of the situation s_room, the agent will answer "yes", to the question: 1) "In your description, has s_room a cushion?". It will answer "no" to the question: 2) "In your description, has s_room an elephant?". It will also answer "yes" to the question: 3) "Has s_room a cushion ?" and "no" to the question: 4) "Has s_room an elephant?". Note that these two last questions is about the facts of world and not about the agent's description of the world.

On the other hand it will answer "no" to the question: 5) "In your description, has s_room a cock-roach?". But if the question is: 6) "Has s_room a cock-roach?", the agent may answer "I don't know", that is, it is undetermined for this agent if, in the world, the s_room has or not a cock-roach, because, there is no information about cock-roach in its description of the s_room. We note also if there is no predicate supports for the situation s_room, then the agent will answer "no" to the questions 1 and 2 above, and will answer "I don't know" (it's undetermined), for example, to the questions 3 and 4.

These two kinds of questions to an agent: about it's world descriptions and about the facts of the world, can be made by the predicates:

- see_description(s, X), where s is a situation and X is variable (Prolog) that will be instantiated by an infon supported by the situation s, according the particular description of an agent. If X is instantiated by an infon before the activation of this predicate or this argument is an infon, the predicate will be true or false if agent's situation s is described as supporting this referred infon. The first argument can be also a variable that will be instantiated by a situation.

- get_information(s, e, V), where s is a situation and e is an infon and V is a variable that is instantiated by 1, if the situation s supports the infon e, 0 if the situation doesn't supports the infon e and u if it's undetermined, by the agent, if the situation s supports or not the infon e. Any arguments of this predicate can be a variable that will be instantiated by the correspondent object. More details about these predicates will be presented in paragraph 2.7.

It is possible that, after some interaction with the world, it's asserted to the agent's description of the situation s_room, the predicate:

supports(s_room, infon(has, [cock-roach], u)).

This assertion, can occur, for example, when the agent is asked about the existence of cock-roach in s_room. It searches for this insect in s_room and concludes that although it cannot find any cock-roach, at this moment, in s_room, it thinks that its possible that some may be in it.

2.4 Parameters

As defined in Situation Theory, parameters are used to make reference to arbitrary objects of a given type. To declare them we use the predicate:

dcl_type(<term>, parameter(<basic-type>)) where <basic-type> can be: individual, relation, infon, situation, space and time. For example:

dcl_type(p, parameter(individual)), means that p is a parameter for individuals.

dcl_type(l, parameter(space)), means that l is a parameter for space.

In Theory of Situation (Devlin, 1991), to assign values to parameters, we use functions called "anchors". Formally, an anchor for a set P, of basic parameters, is a function defined on P, which assigns to each parameter p_n in P an object of determined type, that is, $f(p_n) = x$, where the object x has the same type of the parameter p_n.

In STPF, a parameter can be anchored in a object by the predicate anchor(f, p, x), where f is a function that anchor the parameter p to the object x, that is this predicate is true if and only if the parameter p can be anchored in x by f. When the function is not specified (is a Prolog variable F) the predicate anchor(F, p, x) is true if and only if F is instantiated by a function f such that the parameter p can be anchored in x by f. We note that f is a Prolog atom to denote the function anchor, and this anchor is fixed by STPF unless the predicate free_anchor(f) is used. It is also possible to free all fixed anchors by the predicate free_anchor(all).

A parametric infon is an infon that has one or more occurrences of one or more parameters. So, if e' is a parametric infon and f is an anchor for some or all the parameters that occur in e', then e'[f] denote the infon that results by replacing each parameter p in the domain of f that occurs in e' by its value f(p).

If J is a set of parametric infons and f is an anchor for some or all of the parameters that occur free in infons in J, J[f] denote the set of infons e'[f], such that e' is a parametric infon in J, that is, J[f] = {e[f], e ∈ J}.

In STPF, the predicate anchor_infon(f, e', e), where e' is a parametric infon and e is the infon e'[f] is true, if the infon e can result by anchoring the parameters of e' by f.

We can also use the predicate anchor_situation(f, s', s), where s is a situation such that supports(s, e) is true and e = e' or e = e'[f], for all e' such that supports(s', e') is true. We say that the parameter situation s' is anchored in a situation s by anchor f.

2.5 Object Types

The object types are a more fine-grained discrimination of types by the agents than the basics types seen above. The object types are determined over some situation s, a parameter p that can be anchored in a collection of the objects, and an infon or a compound infon e which involves the parameter p. An object type x can be declared in STPF by the predicates:

dcl_type(p, parameter(<basic-type>)).

dcl_type(s, situation).

dcl_type(x, (p, (s, e))).

For example:

dcl_type(p,parameter(individual)).

dcl_type(s, situation).

dcl_type(brazilian_football_player, (s, infon(play, [p, football], 1) & infon(brazilian, [p], 1))).

These declarations means that p is a parameter for all Brazilian football players. That is, for example, if Pelé is an individual and there is an anchor f such that f(p) = Pelé then Pelé is a "Brazilian football player" and on the other hand is Pelé is a "Brazilian football player" then there is an anchor f such that f(p) = Pelé.

2.6 SituationTypes

The situation types are a higher order uniformities across situations that are discriminated by cognitive agents, in STPF they are declared by the predicates:

dcl_type(s, parameter(situation)).

dcl_type(sT, (s, e)), where s is a parameter for situation and e is a infon or a compound infon.

This means that sT is a type for all situations that supports infon e. We note that sT is another object of the theory: the situation type. So, a situation s1 is of type sT if and only if there is an anchor f such that s1 = f[s], supports(s1, h) and h = e or h = f[e]. For example:

dcl_type(s, parameter(situation)).

dcl_type(l, parameter(space)).

dcl_type(sT, (s, infon(smoke-present, [l, t], 1))).

These declarations means that sT is a type for all situations such that smoke is present in local l (that can be anchored in a specific local) at moment t (that can be anchored in a specific moment). So, the situation s1, such that supports(s1, infon(smoke-present, ["Mary's house", 12pm], 1)) is of type sT.

2.7 Inferences

In Barwise and Perry(1983) and Devlin(1991) to indicate that a situation can mean another is introduced the notion of constraint, which make possible the flow of information linking different situations types. Constraints may be natural laws, conventions, norms, analytic rules, linguistics rules etc. In STPF a constraint is represented by:

infon(involves, [sT1, sT2] , 1)   where sT1 and sT2 are situation types.

This constraint enables the agent infer that the situation type sT1 is part of a possibly larger situation type sT2. For example:

dcl_type(s3, parameter(situation)).

dcl_type(s4, parameter(situation)).

dcl_type(x, parameter(individual)).

dcl_type(y, parameter(individual)).

dcl_type(sT3, (s3, infon(kissing, [x, y], 1))).

dcl_type(sT4, (s4, infon(touching, [x, y], 1))).

These type declarations and infon(involves, [sT3, sT4], 1), represent the fact that "kissing means touching", that is, if, for example, "John" and "Mary" are individuals, and there is some situation sx such that supports(sx, infon(kissing, ["John", "Mary"], 1)), then there is also a situation sy such that supports(sy, infon(touching, ["John", "Mary"], 1)). On the other hand it is also possible to answer the question "is John touching Mary?" through inferences.

To make inferences in STPF it is used the predicate:

get_information(s, e, V), where s is a situation, e is an infon and V is a variable instantiated with the value 1 if the situation s supports the infon e, 0 if the situation s doesn't support the infon e and u if it is undetermined if the situation s supports the infon e (we note that any argument of this predicate can be, also, a variable). For example:

Using the declarations above, and the fact supports(s, infon(kissing, ["John", "Mary"], 1)). The predicate get_information(s, infon(touching, ["John", "Mary"], 1), V) returns V =1.

The mechanisms of inferences used by STPF are, normally, the backward chaining and, optionally, the forward chaining if the predicate for inferences is get_information_fw(s,e,v). The backward (or forward) chaining is a sound proof procedure as noted by Nakashima et all. (1988) and can be employed in Situation Theory such that the following are all possible:

1) supports(s, e),   2) supports(s, ¬e) and

3) its is not true that supports(s, e) nor supports(s, ¬e),

Therefore refuting the case supports(s, ¬e) doesn't entail that supports(s, e) is true. So, in STPF, if get_information(s, ¬e, 0) is true then it is not the case that get_information(s, e, 1) must be true.

The situations are partially defined so an inference can be valid at some moment and invalid at another moment.

Another relation between situations is defined and can be used to make inferences, particularly, in reasoning by inheritance. This is the relation "part_of" which means, in infon(part_of, [s1, s2], 1), that the situation s1, viewed as a set of infons, constrains all the infons in s2, that is, all constraints in s1 also apply to infons in s2. That is, the relation "part_of" occurs between two situations s1 and s2, if and only if, for every infon e such that supports(s1, e) is true, then supports(s2, e) is true.

 Let s be a situation and e an infon, the inference by backward chaining is defined by the following rules:

A) the predicate get_information(s, e, 1), is true, get_information(s, e, 0) is false and get_information(s, e, u) is false if and only if :

1a) supports(s, e) is true or

2a) supports(s, e') is true and there is a anchor f such that $e = e'[f]$ or

3a) there is a constraint infon(involves, $[sT_1, sT_2]$, 1) supported by situation s and if there is a situation s_2 of type sT_2 such that supports(s_2, e) or supports(s_2, e'), where $e = e'[f]$ for some anchor f, then s is of type sT_1.

4a) there is a chain of constraints infon(involves, $[sT_1, sT_2]$, 1), infon(involves, $[sT_2, sT_i]$, 1),..., infon(involves, $[sT_j, sT_n]$, 1), supported all by situation s and if there is a situation s_n of type sT_n such that supports(s_n, e) or supports(s_n, e'), where $e = f[e']$ for some f, then s is of type sT_1.

5a) if there is a situation s_1 such that get_information(s_1, e, 1) is true then supports(s, infon(part_of, $[s_1, s]$, 1), 1) is true.

6a) if there is a situation s_1 such that get_information(s_1, e, 1) is true then there is chain of infons: infon(part_of, $[s_1, s_2]$, 1),infon(part_of, $[s_2, s_i]$, 1),..., infon(part_of, $[s_j, s]$, 1) supported by situation s.

B) The predicate get_information(s, e, 1) is false, get_information(s, e, 0) is true and get_information(s, e, u) is false if and only if <u>no one</u> of the conditions 1a to 6a above holds for s and e, and <u>one</u> of these conditions (1a to 6a) holds for s and ¬e.

C) Otherwise, get_information(s, e, u) is true and get_information(s, e, 1) and get_information(s, e, 0) are both false, that is, it is undetermined if the infon e can be inferred or not from situation s.

As the backward chaining, the forward chaining is also defined by a set of rules that are similar the rules above.

Example of inference:

dcl_type(tweety,situation).

dcl_type(bird,situation).

dcl_type(canary,situation).

dcl_type(fly,relation).

dcl_type(color_yellow,relation).

supports(canary, infon(part_of,[bird,canary],1)).

supports(tweety, infon(part_of,[canary,tweety],1)).

supports(bird,infon(fly,[],1)).

supports(canary,infon(color_yellow,[],1)).

The predicate get_information(tweety, infon(fly,[],1), V) will return V=1 and the predicate get_information(tweety, INFON, V), can return INFON = infon(color_yellow,[],1) and V = 1. In this example canary and bird are situations from which infons are inherity through a chain of relations part_of by the situation tweety.

We note that in Situation Theory inferences are supposed to be situated. So, these inferences are dependent on the situation and their rules are applied only into the situation, such that they can be more efficient than if these rules were applied in the set of every situation described by the agent. For example, to prove that get_information(tweety, infon(fly,[],1), 1) is true (as in example above), it is used inheritance rules only in the context of the situation tweety. On the other hand, it is also possible to extend the space for inferences defining situations as, for example, supports(s, infon(part_of,[gs, s], 1)) where gs is a parameter for situation. Then the space for inferences will include any situation such that gs can be anchored.

Sometimes can be desirable to include in a description of a situation all the infons that can be inferred from this situation. A procedure with rules as in the forward chaining is used by the application of the predicate expand(s), where s is the situation expanded with these new infons.

As a facility to program in Situation Theory we also introduce a change in the sintax of constraints (as Nakashima et al., 1988): an infon in a situation can include another infon in that situation if this situation supports an infon(involves, [e_1, e_2], 1) where e_1 and e_2 are infons, that is is e_1 holds in the situation s then e_2 also holds in s. For example:

infon(involves, [infon(kissing, [x, y], 1), infon(touching, [x, y], 1)], 1)

This was made only for convenience of the representation because this can be seen as a particular case of the definition presented in Barwise e Perry (1983) and Devlin(1991), when the situation s supports the constraint infon(involves, [sT_1, sT_2], 1) and there is a situation s_1 of type sT_1 such that supports(s_1, e1) and there is a situation s_2 of type sT_2 such that supports(s_2, e2). So, writing that a situation s supports an infon(involves, [e_1, e_2], 1) means that it is implicit that these conditions holds.

These inferences in a context of logic programming can also be made by introducing local Prolog variables in a situation and additional symbolic objects as Prolog lists or Prolog structures (this is also an extension of the Situation Theory, as presented in Barwise an Perry, 1983, 1993 and Devlin, 1991, 1993). For example:

supports(member_of_list, infon(member, [X, [X|L]], 1)).

supports(member_of_list, infon(involves, [infon(member,[X, L], 1),

infon(member, [X, [Y|L]],1)).

The predicate get_information(member_of_list, infon(member, [b, [a,b,c]], 1), 1) is true.

This example shows that Prolog's lists are another type of object (a symbolic object) of this framework. Another symbolic objects are the Prolog's structures as, for example, sentence(subject(article(X), noun(Y)), predicate(verb(Z))).

We observe that in this framework, as in Nakashima et al.(1988), the variables are local, that is the unification algorithm is applied (a Prolog's unification algorithm is used in our framework) only in the scope of one STPF predicate, and they can be unified with any data structure or objects. This is a very useful feature of this framework to design agents which can transfer knowledge among themselves.

The predicate see_description(s, e), where s is a situation and e is an infon is true if and only if, one of the backward chaining conditions 1a to 6a above is true, otherwise see_description(s, e) is false. We also can use see_description(s, X) where X is a Prolog variable, in this case, X is instantiated by an infon such that one of the conditions 1a to 6a is true.

2.8 Conclusion

We presented in this paper a framework to make possible Situation Theory programming. Our objective was to get together the advantages of the semantic representation and the informational approach of this theory, with the powerful computational capacities of Prolog, to build intelligent agents and human-machines interfaces. This framework has a basic set of predicates and rules from which is possible to implement the fundamentals of Situation Theory in the paradigm of logic programming. It also has, as an extension of this theory, the inclusion of the undeterminated infon and simbolic elements as variables, lists and structures. By this way the reasoning itself can be represented as a simbolic situation.

This framework can be extended with new features to approximate more to the structure of Situation Theory and it is also a base for our future works in Situation Theory programming of agents as, for example, the inclusion of belief systems and induction.

Bibliography

Aczel, P. Israel, D., Katagiri, Y. and Peters, S.(Eds), Situation Theory and its Applications, Vol 3, CSLI Lectures Notes N° 37, 1993.

Barwise, J. and Perry, J., Situations and Attitudes. Bradford Books, MIT Press, 1983.

Barwise, J., Constraints, Channels and the Flow of Information. In Aczel, P. Israel, D., Katagiri, Y. and Peters, S.(Eds), Situation Theory and its Applications, Vol 3, CSLI Lectures Notes N° 37, 1993.

Bratko, I., Prolog programming for Artificial Intelligence. Addison Wesley Publishing Company, 1986.

Corrêa M. and Coelho H., Around the architectural approach to model converstations. In Proceedings of Modelling Autonomous Agents in a Multi-Agent World (MAAMAW), Nêuchatel, Swiss, 1993.

Corrêa, M., The Architecture of Dialogs of Distributed Cognitive Agents, D.Sc. Thesis, (in portuguese). Federal University of Rio de Janeiro, 1994.

Devlin, K., Logic and Information, Cambridge University Press, Cambridge, 1991.

Devlin, K., and Rosenberg, D., Situation Theory and Cooperative Action. In Aczel, P. Israel, D., Katagiri, Y. and Peters, S.(Eds), Situation Theory and its Applications, Vol 3, CSLI Lectures Notes N° 37, 1993.

Nakashima, H., Suzuki, H., Halvorsen, P. and Peters, S., Towards a Computational Inerpretation of Situation Theory. Proceedings of the International Conference on Fifth Generation Computer Systems, 1988.

Poesio, M., A Situation-Theoretic Formalization of Definite Description Interpretaiton in Plan Elaboration Dialogues. In Aczel, P. Israel, D., Katagiri, Y.

and Peters, S.(Eds), Situation Theory and its Applications, Vol 3, CSLI Lectures Notes N° 37, 1993.

Sterling, L. and Shapiro, E., The Art of Prolog: Advanced Programming Techniques. The MIT Press, 1986.

Measuring Agreement and Harmony in Multi-Agent Societies: A First Approach

Flávio M. de Oliveira

Instituto de Informática - PUCRS
Av. Ipiranga, 6681 - prédio 16 - sala 160
Bairro Ipiranga
90619-900 PORTO ALEGRE - RS
BRAZIL
fax.: +55-51-339-1564
e-mail: flavio@music.pucrs.br

Abstract

The existence of independent goals is a natural and often desirable characteristic in societies of autonomous agents. Depending on the application, some societies might be more tolerant to independence than others. Nevertheless, agents must have means for negotiate their goals gracefully and efficiently. Indeed, we find in the literature some proposals of *goal negotiation strategies*. At the present state of the art, there is a need for frameworks under which one can compare such strategies and study their influence in the social behavior of the agents. We present here some analytical tools to measure the negotiation characteristics in a society. The underlying notions in these tools are the ideas of *agreeability* and *harmony*. By agreeability we mean the ability of an agent to adopt the goals of another agent and/or induce their own goals on another agent. Harmony is the global agreeability in a society. We give mathematical definitions for these notions and illustrate how the definitions can be applied to the study of societies at various levels.

Keywords: Distributed AI, Multi-Agent Systems, Logic Programming

1. Introduction

The field of Distributed Artificial Intelligence is traditionally divided in two main approaches: *distributed problem-solving (DPS)* and *Multi-agent systems (MAS)* [BON 88, DEM 90, SIC 92]. In the first approach, there is some problem to solve, or a task to be executed, and the developer designs a system composed of multiple agents to accomplish it. In the second approach, there is a *society* of autonomous agents that will organize themselves to solve the problem; the existence of the society is independent of any particular problem or task. In both cases, the notion of agent is fundamental: an agent can be defined as an entity capable of perceiving its environment and executing actions that cause changes in the environment and/or in the agent's internal state.

In this paper, we focus on societies of *rational, autonomous agents*. An autonomous agent has (implicit or explicit) goals, which may be not the same goals of the other agents or of the society as a whole. A rational agent has some explicit representation of its goals, and chooses its actions according to them. The existence of independent goals is thus a natural and often desirable characteristic in societies of autonomous agents. Depending on the application, some societies might be more tolerant to independence than others; Galliers [GAL 90] pointed out the potential benefits of conflicts for societies. Nevertheless, agents must have means for negotiate their goals gracefully and efficiently. Indeed, we find in the literature some proposals of *goal negotiation strategies* [WER 90, KHE 94]. At the present state of the art, there is a need for frameworks under which one can compare such strategies and study their influence in the social behavior of the agents. We present here some analytical tools to measure the negotiation characteristics in a society. The underlying notions in these tools are the ideas of *agreeability* and *harmony*. By agreeability we mean the ability of an agent to adopt the goals of another agent and/or induce their own goals on another agent. Harmony is the global agreeability in a society. By means of the mathematical apparatus of metric spaces, we give precise definitions for these notions and suggest applications of these definitions to the study of societies and of individual agents.

In this paper, we consider that agents have their goals represented as sets of first-order clauses (logic programs); we call such sets *goal theories*, in the sense that they are composed of basic goals (ground facts) and rules to derive secondary goals from the basic ones. Intuitively, the priority of a goal is inversely proportional to the number of steps needed to derive it. Societies are finite sets of agents. Strategies for goal negotiation may be defined locally (one for each agent) or globally (one for the society). In the first case, we represent strategies by functions from goal theories to goal theories and, in the second case, by functions from sets of goal theories to sets of goal theories. The section 2 gives some general definitions that establish the basis for organizing metric spaces of agents and societies. The section 3 presents the definition of (dis)agreement and agreeability. In the section 4, we develop the notion of harmony. In the section 5 we discuss some directions for future work, specially the possibility of extending our approach to other types of goal languages.

2. Distance Between Clause Theories

The ideas described in this paper are variations over one central theme: how can we measure the "proximity" between the goal theories of agents in a society? Oliveira, Viccari and Coelho [OLI 94] presented a way of organizing taxonomies of attribute-values pairs into a metric space. Such a topological setting yields a consistent framework for the idea of proximity. Following this approach, we define here a distance (which we call *model distance*) for theories represented by sets of first-order Horn clauses [LLO 84]. Then, in the next sections, we develop the definitions of agreeability and harmony in terms of model distance. The first step is to define a metric for sequences of finite sets.

Definition. Let S be the set of all (finite and infinite) cumulative sequences of finite sets, i.e., sequences with the form $S = \{\, C_1, C_2, C_3, ... \}$, where $C_i \, \mu \, C_{i+1}$ for all i. The distance $d\colon S \times S \rightarrow [0,1]$ is defined by

$$d(S_1, S_2) = 0 \qquad\qquad\qquad \text{if } s_1 = s_2$$

$$d(S_1, S_2) = 1 - \#(C_{1n} \cap C_{2n})/\#(C_{1n} \cup C_{2n}) \qquad \text{if } s_1 \neq s_2$$

Where

n is the least index such that $C_{1n} \neq C_{2n}$;
C_{1n} is the n-th element of S_1 and C_{2n} is the n-th element of S_2;
$\#C$ is the cardinality (number of elements) of C.

It can be shown that the set S with the distance d is a *metric space*, i.e., d satisfies the properties [LIP 65]

(i) $d(x,y) \geq 0$
(ii) $d(x,y) = 0$ implies $x = y$
(iii) $d(x,y) = d(y,x)$
(iv) $d(x,z) \leq d(x,y) + d(y,z)$

The complete proof is a little complex, and was not included here only for reasons of space.

Equipped with this general result, we now apply it to the case of clause theories - more precisely, to models of clause theories. The natural approach to compare two sets of first-order Horn clauses would be to define a distance function between their meanings, which, in model-theoretic semantics, are defined by their least Herbrand models [LLO 84]. Unfortunately, such models are often infinite; even when they are finite, it may be computationally expensive to build them. We adopt a compromise solution: to compare the (partial) process of computation of the models. As defined in Lloyd [LLO 84], the least Herbrand model of a clause theory is known to be the least fixed point of the *immediate consequence mapping*: given a clause theory P (or a logic program P), we define a mapping on interpretations Tp: $I \rightarrow I$ as:

Tp(I) = $\{\, A \in B(P) \mid A \leftarrow B_1, B_2, ..., B_n, n \geq 0$, is a ground instance of a clause in P, and $B_1, B_2, ..., B_n \in I \, \}$

To compute the least Herbrand model of a clause theory P, we apply iteratively the T_p mapping, starting with the empty interpretation:

$$T_P^0(\{\}) = T_P(\{\})$$

$$\mathrm{T_P^1(\{\}) = T_P(T_P^0(\{\})) \cup T_P^0(\{\})}$$

$$\mathrm{T_P^2(\{\}) = T_P(T_P(T_P^0(\{\}))) \cup T_P^1(\{\})}$$

...

$$\mathrm{T_P^n(\{\}) = T_P(T_P^{n-1}(\{\})) \cup T_P^{n-1}(\{\})}$$

In $\mathrm{T_P(\{\})}$ we generate the facts in P (clauses of the form A ←); in $\mathrm{T_P(T_P(\{\}))}$ we generate the consequences of facts, and so on. The least Herbrand model of P is

$$M(P) = T_P^\omega(\{\}) = \lim_{n \to \infty} \bigcup_{i=0}^{n} T_P^i(\{\})$$

We can think of $\mathrm{T_P^n(\{\})}$ as a partial model of P, and the whole process as a sequence of partial models $S_p = \{\}, \mathrm{T_P^0(\{\})}, \mathrm{T_P^1(\{\})}, ..., \mathrm{T_P^n(\{\})}, ...$, which is in fact an element of S as defined above. In other words:

Definition. Let L be a language of Horn clauses. Let $Sp \, \mu \, S$ be the set of all sequences of the form S_p above, where $P \, \mu \, L$. We define the *model distance d*: $\wp(L)$ x $\wp(L) \to [\,0,1\,]$ by

$$d(P_1, P_2) = 0 \qquad\qquad \text{if } P_1 = P_2$$

$$\mathbf{d}(P_1, P_2) = 1 - \frac{\#(T_{P_1}^n(\{\}) \cap T_{P_2}^n(\{\}))}{\#(T_{P_1}^n(\{\}) \cup T_{P_2}^n(\{\}))} \qquad\qquad \text{if } P_1 \neq P_2$$

Where
n is the least index such that $\mathrm{T_{P1}^n(\{\})} \neq \mathrm{T_{P2}^n(\{\})}$.
$(\wp(L),d)$ is a metric space, since $\mathrm{T_p}$ is a function.

Example: Let us see a quite simple example of comparing concepts represented in logic programs. Consider the following three programs:

c1:

```
is_a(A,bird):-
        atrib(A,has_wings,yes),
        atrib(A,has_feathers,yes).

atrib(tweety,has_wings,yes).
```

atrib(tweety,has_feathers,yes).
atrib(birdy,has_feathers,yes).

c2:

is_a(A,bird):-
       atrib(A,flies,yes),
       atrib(A,has_feathers,yes).

atrib(A,flies,yes):- atrib(A,has_wings,yes).

atrib(tweety,has_wings,yes).
atrib(tweety,has_feathers,yes).
atrib(birdy,has_feathers,yes).

c3:

is_a(A,bird):-
       atrib(A,has_feathers,yes).

atrib(tweety,has_wings,yes).
atrib(tweety,has_feathers,yes).
atrib(birdy,has_feathers,yes).

is_a(I,C) means that *I* is a member (instance) of class *C*. *atrib(I,A,V)* means that instance *I* have value *V* for attribute *A*. The three programs are implementations for the concept of *bird*. All of them have finite models: the model of *c1* is:

{ atrib(tweety,has_wings,yes), atrib(tweety,has_feathers,yes),
atrib(birdy,has_feathers,yes), is_a(tweety,bird) }

the model of *c2* is

{ atrib(tweety,has_wings,yes), atrib(tweety,has_feathers,yes),
atrib(birdy,has_feathers,yes), atrib(tweey, flies, yes), is_a(tweety,bird) }

the model of *c3* is

{ atrib(tweety,has_wings,yes), atrib(tweety,has_feathers,yes),
atrib(birdy,has_feathers,yes), is_a(tweety,bird), is_a(birdy,bird) }

The difference in $c2$ appears in the second step of application of Tp, when *atrib(tweey, flies, yes)* is generated by the corresponding rule, and *is_a(tweety,bird)* is generated by $c1$. Thus the distance between $c1$ and $c2$ is

$$d(c1,c2) = 1 - \frac{\#(T_{c1}^{n}(\{\}) \cap T_{c2}^{n}(\{\}))}{\#(T_{c1}^{n}(\{\}) \cup T_{c2}^{n}(\{\}))} =$$

$$1 - \frac{\#(atrib(tweety, wings, yes), atrib(tweety, feathers, yes), atrib(birdy, feathers, yes))}{\#(T_{c1}^{n}(\{\}) \cup T_{c2}^{n}(\{\}))}$$

$$= 1 - \frac{3}{5} = 0.4$$

The difference in $c3$ appears just in the third step of application of Tp, when *is_a(birdy,bird)* is generated, which is not generated by $c1$. Thus the distance between $c1$ and $c3$ is

$$d(c1,c3) = 1 - \frac{\#(T_{c1}^{n}(\{\}) \cap T_{c3}^{n}(\{\}))}{\#(T_{c1}^{n}(\{\}) \cup T_{c3}^{n}(\{\}))} =$$

$$1 - \frac{\#(atrib(tweety, wings, yes), atrib(tweety, feathers, yes), atrib(birdy, feathers, yes), is\_a(tweety, bird))}{\#(T_{c1}^{n}(\{\}) \cup T_{c3}^{n}(\{\}))}$$

$$= 1 - \frac{4}{5} = 0.2$$

An algorithm for calculating d halts for theories with finite models and for theories with distinct infinite models, since in that case there exists n such that $Tp_1^{n}(\{\}) \_ Tp_2^{n}(\{\})$. It does not halt, however, for theories with equal, infinite models. It is computationally less expensive than comparing directly the models, because it stops as soon as it finds a difference. In practice, however, there may be situations where n is too high. Implementations might consider some maximum value for n: by default, if no difference appears in n iterations, the theories are considered equivalent. The default is reviewed when some conflict arises.

3. Agreeability: the Agent-Level Case

Let us consider a simple society composed of two agents A1 and A2, with their goals represented as clause theories[1].We could say that two agents are "agreeable" if and only if the model distance $d(A1,A2) = 0$. However, this is too restrictive. For

---

[1]In this paper, we use the terms "clause theory" and "logic program" interchangeably.

example, the two agents below do not satisfy that condition, although their goal theories are logically equivalent:

A1:
a(t).
b(X):- a(X).
c(X):- b(X).

A2:
a(t).
c(X):- a(X).
b(X):- c(X).

There *is*, in fact, a conflict: both A1 and A2 have the goal $b(t)$, but not for the same reasons (recall that the priority of a goal is inversely proportional to the number of steps needed to derive it). Nevertheless, a simple negotiation strategy might be able to detect the equivalence and solve the conflict. The point here is that we want to think of agreeability not as the *equality of goals*, but rather as the *ability to negotiate* - which means that their goal theories are compatible somehow. Such an ability is what distinguishes a society from a chaotic set of isolated individuals. These considerations led us to formulate the following definition:

Definition. Let A be an agent equipped with a goal theory $G_A \in \wp(G)$, where G is the a language of Horn clauses, called the *goal language*, and a negotiation procedure $f: \wp(G) \times \wp(G) \to \wp(G)$. We say that A is *agreeable* to some agent B if and only if the sequence

$$<G_A^n> = G_A, f_B(G_A), f_B(f_B(G_A)), ..., f_B^n(G_A),..., \text{ where } f_B(G_A) = f(G_A, G_B).$$

is *convergent* in $(\wp(G), d)$, i.e., exists Q in $\wp(G)$ such that $\lim_{n \to \infty} f_B^n(P_A) = Q$.

We call d the *degree of disagreement* of A and B. The idea here is that, if A *needs* to negotiate with B, it is able to do it by successive applications of f. If A is not agreeable to B, its negotiation procedure can not guarantee a consensus, since it can be applied over and over again, and never reach stability. The agreeability expresses an inclination of an agent; agreement is a position taken by it, it is an attitude. The degree of disagreement is a measure of the intensity of this attitude.

The definition of agreeability is individual, relative to a particular agent: A being agreeable to B does not imply that B is agreeable to A. Moreover, it is a property of a particular *state* of an agent, in relation to other agent, also in a particular state, as is the distance between A and B. We can thus study the variation over time of these characteristics, and make comparisons among different negotiation strategies and/or goal theories. If we wish to implement systems with automatic control of agreeability, we can relax the definition: an agent A is agreeable to B if $d(f_B^n(G_A), G_B) \leq \delta$, where n and δ are pre-defined, application-dependent values.

Of course, we could define "A and B are agreeable to each other if A is agreeable to B and vice-versa"; that sounds good for two agents, but what if we wish to extend it to *n* agents? We should say "a set of agents S = { $A_1 \cdot A_2 \cdot ..., A_n$ } is agreeable if A_i is agreeable to A_j for every i,j ≤ *n*, i ≠ j". This is too restrictive and, even worse, much more expensive. In the next section, we discuss an alternative definition, developing the global notion of *harmony*.

4. Harmony: the Society-Level Case

In the preceding section, we presented an agent-level definition of agreeability. We will now define a corresponding notion for the society level, by treating the whole society as having a single goal theory, which is defined, at each application of T_P, by the intersection of the partial models of all goal theories in the society. Also, instead of considering a separate negotiation procedure for each agent in the society, we consider that the society has a global negotiation strategy *F*. That would be the case of having a special agent (a "moderator") with the responsibility of managing disagreements among the members of the society. First, let us define a metric for societies:

Definition. Let *S* be the set of all societies of agents S = { $A_1 \cdot A_2 \cdot ..., A_k$ } [2], $k \in N$. Let SA = { $A_1 \cdot A_2 \cdot ..., A_p$ } and SB = { $B_1 \cdot B_2 \cdot ..., B_q$ } be two societies in *S*. The model distance $d: S \times S \rightarrow [0,1]$ is defined by

$$d(SA,SB) = 0 \qquad \text{if } SA = SB$$

$$\mathbf{d}(P_1, P_2) = 1 - \frac{\#(T_{SA}^n(\{\}) \cap T_{SB}^n(\{\}))}{\#(T_{SA}^n(\{\}) \cup T_{SB}^n(\{\}))} \qquad \text{if } SA \neq SB$$

where $T_{SB}^n(\{\}) = \bigcap_{i=1}^{q} T_{Bi}^n(\{\})$ and $T_{SB}^n(\{\}) = \bigcap_{i=1}^{q} T_{Bi}^n(\{\})$. (*S*,*d*) is a metric space. The proof is the same as in the single-agent case, *mutatis mutandis.*

Now for the definition of harmony:

Definition. Let S = { $A_1 \cdot A_2 \cdot ..., A_n$ } $\in$ *S* be a society equipped with a negotiation function $F : \wp(G)^n \rightarrow \wp(G)^n$. We say S is *harmonic* if and only if the sequence

$$<S^n> = S, F(S), F(F(S)), ..., F^n(S),...$$

is convergent in (*S*,*d*).

---

[2] As there is no ambiguity, for simplicity of notation we denote the goal theory of an agent Ai by the same symbol Ai, and not by G_{Ai} as in the preceding section.

If F is a contraction (a contraction in a metric space (X,d) is a function f such that $d(f(x),f(y)) \leq d(x,y)$ for all x and y in X [LIP 65]), then every sequence of the form $<S^n>$ above is Cauchy-convergent. If the metric space (S,d) is complete, then every contraction F has a unique fixed point, which is the limit of every sequence $<S^n>$. Thus, completeness of (S,d) is an interesting safety condition for negotiation functions.

With the notion of harmony, we characterize formally the ability of a society to deal of its internal conflicts. As the agent-level definition of agreeability, harmony is relative to the state of the society. As in the agent-level case, we can study the behavior of different negotiation strategies, observing the variation of harmony over time in the society.

5. Future Work

The ideas presented here are applications of a general approach: using the mathematical apparatus of metric spaces to formalize the notion of *approximation* for theories, by means of convenient metrics. The resulting framework can be easily adapted to implementations with limited computational resources, by considering finite sub-sequences of $<G_A^n>$ or $<S^n>$. The representation chosen for goals - sets of Horn clauses - is simple and has a well-known denotational semantics, with a little loss of generality. Our motivation in this case was our interest in studying the application of Inductive Logic Programming (ILP) techniques [LAV 94] to negotiation in Multi-agent systems. Nevertheless, goal theories do have some limitations: for example, they are closed under logical implication, which may lead to some non-intuitive behavior, as Wainer remarks [WAI 94]. We are presently studying ways to extend our approach to other types of representations. All we need is a model-theoretic semantics for the representation, and an incremental definition of the models. The knowledge structures defined by Fagin, Halpern and Yardi [FAG 91], seem to be an interesting candidate for further investigation .

Acknowledgments

The ideas described in this paper were developed thanks to many fruitful and pleasant discussions with Dr. Antônio Carlos da Rocha Costa e Dr. Rosa Maria Viccari, from UFRGS (Brazil), and Dr. Helder Coelho, from INESC (Portugal). Their comments and criticisms were very important.

This work has financial support from CNPq.

References

[LAV 94] LAVRAC, N. Inductive Concept Learning Using Background Knowledge. In: Pequeno, T.; Carvalho, F. (eds.) *Proceedings of the XI Brazilian Symposium on Artificial Intelligence.* Fortaleza, Universidade Federal do Ceará, 1994. p. 1-16.

[BON 88] BOND, A.H.; GASSER, L. (eds.) *Readings in Distributed Artificial Intelligence.* San Mateo, California: Morgan Kaufmann, 1988.

[DEC 87] DECKER, K.S. Distributed Problem-Solving Techniques: a Survey. *IEEE Transactions on Systems, Man and Cybernetics,* 17(5):729-740, September/October 1987.

[DEM 90] DEMAZEAU, Y.; MULLER, J.P. (eds.) *Decentralized Artificial Intelligence.* Morgan Kaufmann, 1990.

[FAG 91] FAGIN, R.; HALPERN, J.Y.; YARDI, M.V. A Model-Theoretic Analysis of Knowledge. *Journal of the ACM,* 2:382-428, April 1991.

[GAL 90] GALLIER, J.R. The Positive Role of Conflict in Cooperative Multi-Agent Systems. In: DEMAZEAU, Y.; MULLER, J.P. (eds.) *Decentralized Artificial Intelligence.* Morgan Kaufmann, 1990.

[KHE 94] KHEDRO, T.; GENESERETH, M.R. Modeling Multiagent Cooperation as Distributed Constraint Satisfaction Problem Solving. In: Cohn, A. (ed.) *Proceedings of the 11th European Conference on Artificial Intelligence.* New York, J. Wiley & Sons, 1994. p. 249-253.

[LIP 65] LIPSCHUTZ, S. *General Topology.* McGraw-Hill, 1965.

[LLO 84] LLOYD, J.W. *Foundations of Logic Programming.* Berlin, Springer-Verlag, 1984.

[OLI 94] OLIVEIRA, F.M.; VICCARI, R.M.; COELHO, H. A Topological Approach to Equilibration of Concepts. In: Pequeno, T.; Carvalho, F. (eds.) *Proceedings of the XI Brazilian Symposium on Artificial Intelligence.* Fortaleza, Universidade Federal do Ceará, 1994. p. 527-523.

[SIC 92] SICHMAN, J.; DEMAZEAU,Y.; BOISSIER, O. When can Knowledge-based Systems be Called Agents? In: *IX Simpósio Brasileiro De Inteligência Artificial,* Rio de Janeiro, RJ, Out. 1992. *Proceedings.* Rio de Janeiro, SBC, 1992.

[WAI 94] WAINER, J. Yet Another Semantics of Goal and Goal Priorities. In: Cohn, A. (ed.) *Proceedings of the 11th European Conference on Artificial Intelligence.* New York, J. Wiley & Sons, 1994. p. 269-273.

[WER 90] WERNER, E. Distributed Cooperation Algorithms. In: DEMAZEAU, Y.; MULLER, J.P. (eds.) *Decentralized Artificial Intelligence.* Morgan Kaufmann, 1990.

Detecting the Opportunities of Learning from the Interactions in a Society of Organizations

Marcos Augusto Hochuli Shmeil & Eugénio Oliveira

Faculdade de Engenharia da Universidade do Porto
Rua dos Bragas, 4099 Porto Codex, Portugal
{shmeil, eco}@fe.up.pt

Abstract. Organizations, as any complex and inherently distributed entities, are characterized by their internal and external interactions. Generally, and as a result of the continuous interactive process, the involved organizations become more efficient. This performance increase, achieved through resources optimization, can be seen as the outcome of a know-how acquired from previous interactions.

In broad terms, the work presented in this paper can be classified as a contribution to the study and modeling of the behavior of organizations. In particular, we are concerned with a specific inter-organization relation: the selection process that leads to the establishment of contracts between organizations. This selection process can be characterized as an iterative loop composed of an evaluation phase followed by a negotiation phase. During the selection activity, conflicts may occur imposing further negotiation as a mean for conflict resolution. According to the diverse selection methodologies that can be adopted, different learning opportunities can also be detected.

The computational system under development, which supports the above mentioned interaction processes, is called ARTOR (ARTificial ORganizations), and is based on the Distributed Artificial Intelligence - Multi-Agent Systems (DAI-MAS) and Symbolic Learning (SL) paradigms. Each component, or agent, is provided with the needed observation, planning, coordination, execution, communication and learning capabilities to perform its social role.

Keywords. Distributed AI, Organizations Integration and Modeling, Distributed Learning.

1 A Society of Organizations

Human being, either as the protagonist of the natural world[1] or as the creator of an artificial world[2], has been constantly modifying the real world (natural and artificial world).

The real world changes inflicted by human being are based on his own perceptions and conceptual models (Fig. 1) of the reality. These changes are conceived and performed according to their natural capabilities and limitations (both cognitive and physical), and are usually described as human behaviors. Cognitive capabilities are the result of three components: perception, memory and thinking [2]. The ultimate human goal is to satisfy human being's basic needs, desires and intentions. Due to the cognitive and physical limitations presented to the individual, human being soon realized the advantages that came from joining efforts with other individuals. This gregarious attitude introduced new concepts like social interaction and society. Internally, these societies were, and still are, structured in organizations, where each human being contributes with his capabilities and expertise, exhibiting an intelligent behavior. In this social scenario, an intelligent behavior may be characterized by the following features: (i) environment perception; (ii) decision

---

[1] Objects and phenomena studied by natural science.

[2] Man-made artifacts [1].

making; (iii) social interactions, (iv) action coordination; (v) planning and (vi) learning. The previous individual goals are shaped and enriched in light of the new organizational and social needs. "The modern and industrialized society is a society of organizations, on which human beings rely on to born, live and die"[3].

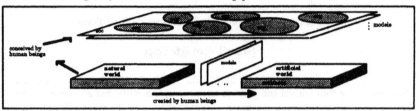

Fig. 1. The real world

2 The Organizations

As a social entity, an organization can be characterized in terms of its interactions within the society. The internal capabilities of the organization or *inner*, are not, in this context, as relevant as its interactions with its external counterparts or *outer*. Our aim is to study and analyze the interface [1] between the *inner* and the *outer* worlds of the organizations.

The inner/outer interactions can be either passive (observation) or active (sending/receiving information both by request or spontaneously). They provide the organizations with the means to achieve, modify or create goals, that lead the real world into new states. An organization inner resources are composed of human and non-human resources (e.g., raw material from natural world, technological and financial resources from artificial world). The inner world contains: (i) a physical structure (the resources location), (ii) a conceptual structure (concepts generated from the internal and external interactions), and (iii) two basic sets of tasks: support tasks (maintenance, logistics, etc.) and main tasks (business goals). In order to become operational, the organization components have to be adequately managed. This management activity consists of the following actions: (i) planning, (ii) eventual physical and conceptual restructuring, (iii) decision making and (iv) action coordination. As in other complex systems, hierarchical decomposition was the methodology chosen for the detection of the different functionalities and associated levels of responsibility within an organization. This hierarchical decomposition refers, not only, to the authority structure, but also to the decomposition of higher level functions into lower level functions.

An organization can be pictured as a three-layered cake [4]. The top layer is characterized by higher level decision-making capabilities, triggered by the interactions either with the outer world or with the remaining inner layers. The top layer views the organization as a whole. The intermediate layer is responsible for guaranteeing the execution of the tasks communicated by the higher layer: pre-defined and *ad hoc* tasks. The lowest layer executes the tasks received from the intermediate layer.

An organization's local perspective of the outer world is composed of what it knows and learns about the outer world facts and conceptual models (concepts about the society, etc.). The organization's "survival" depends on the inner's capabilities of perceiving and adjusting to the outer. This is achieved through the continuous analysis of the inner/outer interactions.

3 A Scenario for a Society of Organizations

The goods and services market is composed of two types of economics agents, the organizations and the individuals, related by their interactions. They can, dynamically, assume productive, distributive and consumptive basic roles. The interactions play a decisive part in the behavior of the organizations and individuals, and are used to: (i) decide what and how to produce, (ii) indicate where and how to distribute the production and (iii) determine how to promote and validate the products. In our scenario proposal (Fig. 2), the involved organizations are conceived as goods and services producers, consumers or distributors (suppliers), depending on the role they play in each interaction. In this scenario individuals are consumers. To model this domain, the computational system ARTOR (ARTificial ORganizations) uses Distributed Artificial Intelligence-Multi Agent System (DAI-MAS) and Symbolic Learning (SL). Its goal is, to create, maintain and provide an adequate setting where organizations and their interactions are simulated (Fig. 3).

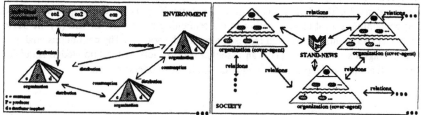

Fig. 2. The scenario proposal   **Fig. 3.** The Multi-agent society

In this setting each organization acts as a cognitive agent with the capability of performing any of the following economic roles: production, distribution (supplying), and consumption . These roles or behaviors are dynamically enabled/disabled by the established interactions. The agents that map such organizations are referred as *cover-agents* (Fig. 4). Cover-agents are semi-autonomous agents that need to establish and maintain interactions in order to "survive". Cover-agents are implemented as a set of fine-grained agents. The inter-cover-agent communication can be of three types: (i) point to point, when a cover-agent addresses its message or observation to another cover-agent, (ii) point to multi-point, when a cover-agent addresses its message or observation to more than one cover-agent, and (iii) newspaper-like, when a cover-agent wishes to make public some data. The latter is built using a blackboard [5] called *stand-news*, where the data is posted and kept for public consultation. From the society point of view, the cover-agents are distributed agents, that act in conformity with their cognitive capabilities.

3.1 An Overview of the Inner of a Cover-agent

The adopted cover-agent architecture is based on the three layered hierarchical structure decomposition. The top and intermediate layers are composed of cognitive, homogeneous, semi-autonomous agents, while the bottom layer contains cognitive, heterogeneous, semi-autonomous agents. The number of agents per layer depends on the layer's hierarchical level: (i) the top level layer has exactly one agent, (ii) the intermediate layer number of agents is problem-domain dependent - there can be further in layer hierarchical decomposition, both horizontal and vertical, according to the complexity of the domain being mapped and (iii) the bottom layer number of agents is also problem-domain dependent - there is no hierarchical decomposition, and the amount of agents varies horizontally, based on the needs imposed by the problem-domain.

Time-sharing, agent performance, resources similarity and process nature are some of the criteria used for establishing the composition of the intermediate and bottom layers.

The required capabilities of the agents of the top and intermediate layers are planning, action coordination, communication and learning. These agents are called *administrator-agents*. The required capabilities of the agents of the bottom layer are task execution (domain expertise), communications and learning. These agents are called *executor-agents*. From the cover-agent point of view, the intermediate and bottom set of inner agents are distributed and centralized.

There are two different sets of knowledge present in an organization: the corporate knowledge (CK) or the cover-agent knowledge, and the individual knowledge (IK) or the administrator/executor-agents knowledge. The CK and IK are acquired, transformed and learnt by the inner agents during their interactions with the other cover-agents inner agents. The CK can be divided in two classes [6]. The first knowledge class, known as self model (SM), represents the styles, missions, resources, processes, etc., of the inner world. The second knowledge class, denominated acquaintance model (AM) represents the outer or external world. The AM is divided in two sub-models: (i) the cover-agents sub-model (CS) containing a local representation of the remaining cover-agents, and (ii) the society sub-model (SS) containing a local representation of the society. The continuous analysis of the cover-agents interactions plays an essential role: it acts as the knowledge acquisition interface that enables learning. Consequently, both sub-models are dynamic.

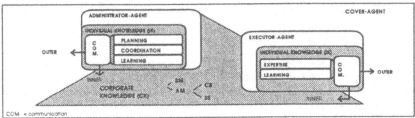

Fig. 4. A cover-agent

4 Cooperative Interactions between Producers and Suppliers

Our work is focused on a well defined type of interaction: the interactions that occur between cover-agents acting as producers and cover-agents acting as suppliers. The producers intent is to find the most adequate supplier[3] of a good or service. A cooperative action is established when a supplier is contracted by a producer. This contracting is the result of a selection process. The selection process (Fig. 5) consists in sending an invitation (posted in the stand-news by the producer) to the society, followed by the evaluation of the received offers. Negotiation is invoked when conflicts arise. The contract will be celebrated with the first supplier that satisfies the producer's constraints. In the specific setting of our approach we assume that the selection process is undertaken by the bottom layer executor-agents of the involved cover-agents. However, and depending on the importance and complexity of the product's specification, the selection process has sometimes to be attributed to higher layer agents. The communication is based on the contract net protocol [7]. The cover-agents engaged in a cooperative mission have well-defined roles [6]: (i) the producers, or *organizers* are the cover-agents which are searching for cooperative partners, and (ii) the suppliers, or *respondents*, are the cover-agents that wish to participate in the proposed cooperative activity.

---

[3] The most adequate supplier is the one that satisfies the constraints imposed by the producers.

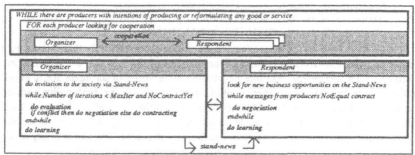

Fig. 5. The selection process

The evaluation process for each good or service to be contracted is based on the analysis of the existing local constraint list (CL). A CL is a conjunction of units denominated evaluation constraints (EC). They are used by the organizer to validate the respondents proposals according to three criteria: (i) an organizational criterion that validates organizational attributes (structural, financial , etc.), (ii) a technical criterion that validates the characteristics of the good or service (color, dimension, etc.) and (iii) a commercial criterion that validates commercial attributes (price, quantity, etc.). The ECs have the following structure:

```
Each EC is a 5-tuple where:
   EC_i = (id_i, vd_i, va_i, pr_i, sm_i) where:
       id_i     is the constraint identification
       vd_i     is the constraint default value
       va_i     is represented by a 2-tuple (vac_i, fed_i) where:
            vac_i  represents the EC_i domain
            fed_i  is the most favorable evolution direction within the domain:
                   right    when it is advantageous to move towards the right;
                   left     when it is advantageous to move towards the left;
                   none     when there is no preference among the any of the
                            possible values (vac_i).
       pr_i     EC_i is the value of the agent's utility(pr_i ∈ Dcardinal)
       sm_i     represents the agent's state of mind (open or close minded):
                   grounded  the first EC_i offer will be posted specifying a defined
                             value;
                   free      the first EC_i offer will be posted without any value
                             specification.
```

Trees have been the adopted data structure to represent the taxonomy of the constraints (Fig. 6).

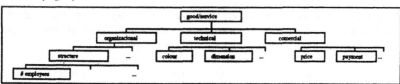

Fig. 6. Evaluation of the constraints

This sort of CL is called *default_CL*. As an example,a default_CL is presented, involving three constraints: color, price and payment_period.

```
{(color, blue, ((black, green, blue), right), 2, ground),
 (price, 30, (([0, 33], left), 5, free),
 (payment_period, 60, (([30, 60, 90], right), 2, ground)}.
```

Alternative CLs can be provided representing, either alternative constraint values or pre-defined constraint values relaxation, which define the alternative bids. These new CLs are called *alternative_CLs*. As an example, is presented an alternative_CL, involving the same three constraints: color, price and payment_period.

```
{(color, blue, ((black, green, blue), right), 2, ground),
 (price, 34, ([34, 36], left), 4, ground),
 (payment_period, 120, ([120, 150], right), 3, ground)}.
```

The union of the cartesian product of the domains of the ECs that belong to the default_CL with the cartesian product of the domains of the ECs that are specified in the alternative_CLs, define the plausible negotiation state space of an agent for a good or service. Every EC has two different utility parameters: (i) the first utility parameter denominated pr_i represents the EC's importance within the CL; and (ii) the second utility parameter expresses the most favorable evolution direction (fed_i) of the concept within its domain (left, right, none) as it was shown in the ECs structure. The global utility of a CL is given by the sum of the individual ECs utility parameters (pr_i and fed_i).

The respondents have, internally, the same CL representation data format. There is, however, one exception: the respondents do not communicate their states of mind. The selection process is started and ended by the organizers. It starts when the organizer sends the invitation to the stand-news using the following data type:

```
(idorg, datli, list of constraints, qty), where:
        idorg is the identification of the organizer;
        datli is the answering deadline;
        list of constraints is a list of constraints represented by (id, vd,
        negotiation) where:
                id is the constraint identification;
                vd is the constraint default value;
                negotiation is y when vac contains other values than vd;
                negotiation is n, otherwise;
        qty is the maximum number of iterations per negotiation
```

Example:

```
(agentₙ, 12, ((color, blue, y), (price, _, y), (payment_period, 60, y)), 10)
```

In our setting, the economic principles that guide the behavior of the organizations make them eager to cooperate.

Every cover-agent that has available resources continuously, poles the stand-news in search of new business opportunities. The invitations posted in the stand-news are analyzed by every one of these potential respondents. Those who have the necessary resources send their first offer to the organizer.

4.1 The Evaluation Process

The evaluation process is exclusively performed by the organizers. The goal of this process is to measure the distance between the specified demand and the received offers. In order to calculate these distances values two filters are applied:

a) Filter 1 is applied to the ECs that contain only default values;

b) Filter 2 is applied to the remaining types of ECs. It computes the distance between the default and answered values for each remaining EC and for each respondent ($dist = default\_value - answered\_value$).

Three situations may arise:

(i) there is only one respondent such that dist $\leq$ 0 (this means that either the respondent offer satisfies (dist = 0) the CL specified by the organizer, or that it may contain more attractive values (dist < 0). Negative distances (dist < 0) occur when the offered values are more advantageous than the proposed ones;

(ii) more than one respondent has presented attractive offers (dist $\leq$ 0);

(iii) there are no respondents that, totally or partially, fit into the initially specified default values (dist > 0) for any or all ECs.

4.2 The Negotiation Process

The negotiation process is a decision making process, which helps the agents to satisfy their goals. The organizers look for respondents such that, $\forall$ EC, $dist \rightarrow$ Z, $(Z \leq 0)$. The respondents' aim, while trying to satisfy the organizer's CL, is to be contracted. In their effort to satisfy the organizer bids they make use of the available EC utilities. Organizers use the conflict resolution for further negotiation. Conflicts occur when the distance calculated in the evaluation phase is either negative or positive, giving rise to the positive and negative conflict types [6].

The selection process has diverse halting conditions:

(i) Through the celebration of a contract when only one respondent has met the bid's requisites.

(ii) After a pre-defined number of evaluation-negotiation interactions. This value is defined by the organizer. This condition is met when: (a) more than one respondent has made tempting offers $(dist \leq 0)$; (b) no agent is making offers, and (c) none of the respondents' offers are sufficiently close to what the organizer has specified $(dist > 0)$.

Before beginning the negotiation phase each involved agent selects one strategy (Fig. 7), among those available in its strategies set. This choice is made based on the consultation of the following agent's knowledge: the self model (SM) and the acquaintance model (AM). In the case of the self model, the agent's style is what is more relevant. The agent's style is a meta-knowledge that characterizes the agent inner and outer behavior. This style may be classified as win/win or win/lose. A win/win agent governs its activities with reciprocal advantage concepts towards its partners. It is characterized for taking into account, totally or partially, the answered values. A win/lose agent directs its activities in an egocentric fashion, solely moved by his own advantage. It is characterized for disregarding the answered values. The acquaintance model helps the agent to select its strategy based on what it knows about the involved cover-agent (CS) as well as about the society (SS) as a whole. At startup, ARTOR's cover-agents have empty acquaintance models. As a result of the established interactions, the AMs are, incrementally, built and refined.

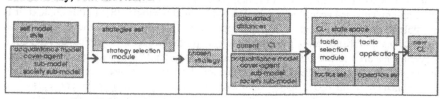

Fig. 7. Strategy choice   **Fig. 8.** Counter-proposal generation

Once chosen the strategy, organizer and respondent, have to select the most adequate tactics. Each strategy has an associated number of tactics and operators that are applied to the current CL in order to create the new CL (Fig. 8). The organizer selects the most appropriate tactics according to: (i) the current CL (ECs values), (ii) the calculated distances - when the offer exceeds the values of the previous demand $(dist \leq 0)$, the organizer employs the tactics that maximize its benefits. Otherwise it applies tactics that provide alternative_CLs and (iii) acquaintance model.

The respondent chooses the tactics that try to meet the organizers demand, based on the current CL and acquaintance model.

Each iteration (Fig. 9) is composed of an evaluation of the proposals (CL_n), followed by the generation of a counter-proposal (CL_{n+1}) and the subsequent sending of the new counter-proposal (CL_{n+1}) to the involved agent(s). The generated values or counter-proposal (e.g., CL_{n+1}) is the result of the application of the strategy, tactic and operator chosen.

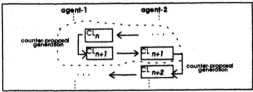

Fig. 9. An interaction

The set of styles, the strategies, the tactics and the operators of an agent are represented as frames (Fig. 10). Each style has an associated set of concept frames defining it. The set of applicable strategies is defined by the style. Associated to each strategy there are frames representing tactics which support the strategy enforcement via specific operators. Operators can increase, decrease or maintain the EC values.

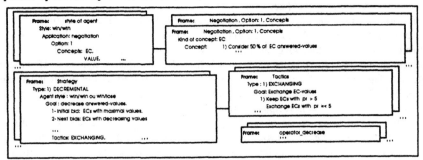

Fig. 10. Knowledge representation

4.3 Interactions and Learning Opportunities

The model chosen for the study of the discussed segment of the goods and services market is being implemented according to the DAI-MAS methodologies [8]. In this context, it is possible to detect a number of learning opportunities, solely based on the analysis of the interactions established among the cover-agents (organizations). In particular, ARTOR's cover-agents are focused on two specific learning opportunities: (i) learning organizational concepts - The conceptualization of the behavior of other cover-agents or the construction and refinement of the cover-agents sub-model (CS) and (ii) learning social concepts - The conceptualization of the behavior of the society, as a whole, or, simply, the construction and refinement of the society sub-model (SS).

In the ARTOR's model, the learning capabilities lay on the individual inner agents. The learning capabilities of a cover-agent, as a whole, is the sum of the individual inner agents capabilities. The aforementioned opportunities process is only bounded by the number and diversity of the established interactions. The inter-agent exchanges that occur during the evaluation and negotiation steps, constitute the set of examples used for learning. Each example is a triplet (P_{r1}, CL_{n+1}, CL_{n+2}) (Fig. 11). P_{r1} is the internal transformation process used to generate the new constraint list from the current CL (CL_n). The CL_{n+1} is the new internal constraint list that will be generated once P_{r1} is applied to CL_n. The CL_{n+2} is the constraint list that will be externally produced upon the reception of CL_{n+1}. The learning will be concentrated on the virtual consequence dependency that can be established between the internally generated CL_{n+1} and the externally generated CL_{n+2}.

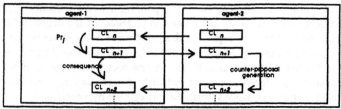

Fig. 11. An inter-agent exchange

The purpose of the individual learning activity is to hypothesize assumptions regarding the behavior of others. This type of learning is based on the analysis of the CLs changes that exist during the selection process. From the comparative analysis of consecutive CLs (CL_{n+1} and CL_{n+2}) a classification of the experienced EC changes emerges. The calculated deltas, or variations are catalogged in three possible classes: (i) null delta or = class - when the ECs have remained unchanged, (ii) positive delta or ↑ class - when the ECs have experienced an incremental alteration and (iii) negative delta or ↓ class - when the ECs have suffered a decremental variation.

The calculated deltas represent the difference between the desired and offered EC values. In Fig. 12 a default_CL which contains three constraints (EC) denoted by a, b, c is presented. The default ECs values are in the central line of the first column (CL_i) which are expected by the organizer. The other columns represent posterior states which were generated by respondent and organizer during the selection process.

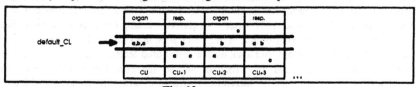

Fig. 12. An example

In this case the calculated deltas are:

CL	a	b	c		a	b	c
CL_i	initial	initial	initial	CL_{i+1}	↓, [value]	=	↓, [value]
CL_{i+2}	=	=	↑, [value]	CL_{i+3}	↑, [value]	=	↓, [value]

⇒　　　　　　organizer　　　　　⇐ ⇒　　　　　respondent　　　　　⇐

The learning process has two phases: (i) example analysis and (ii) submission of the new example set to the learning algorithms. The analysis of the example consists in establishing for each constraint (EC) the extremes of the negotiated values. The applied algorithm uses both inductive and deductive reasoning. The agents involved in a selection process (the organizer and the respondent agents) will have, by the time it finishes, a more accurate internal model of its counterpart. The quality of the model created depends on the quantity of information made available during the selection process, or in other words, the richness of the set of examples provided. The inductive and deductive learning methodologies are applied over the same set of examples but distinct complementary concepts are obtained. Through the application of: (i) the inductive learning paradigm [9], higher level knowledge about the behavior of the CLs during the selection process is produced and (ii) the deductive learning algorithm based on (EBL, mEBG) [10], higher level knowledge concerning the style of the agents involved in the selection process, is generated.

In the first case (i), the organizer and the respondent not only learn new organizational concepts concerning the evolution and relative importance[4] of the negotiated constraints, but also learn social concepts regarding their respective social roles/behaviors. In the second case, the agents use as background knowledge (BK) the knowledge present in each agent style, strategies and tactics slots to deduce new social perspectives. However, when the background knowledge does not support deductive reasoning, deductive learning is not possible. In such circumstance specialized concepts are hypothesized.

Generically, the learnt assumptions concerning the organizational concepts are represented in the cover-agent sub-model (CS) by a $\langle id\_ag, assumptions\rangle$ slot, while the social concepts are represented in the society sub-model (SS) using a $\langle assumptions\rangle$ slot, where id_ag is the identification of the counterpart agent, and *assumptions* are the learnt assumptions (rules, propositions, etc.). As a trivial example, and according to the interaction described in Fig. 12, the organizer (agent$_1$) has learnt about the respondent (agent$_2$), that in those specific circumstances EC_b remains constant:

```
<agent_2, EC_b = default_value when EC_a ⊂ [t_1, t_n] and EC_c ∈ {c_1, c_i}>.
```

5 Conclusions

The work we have described in this paper aims at contributing to the computer simulation of the interacting of organizations. Recently, several different approaches for modeling the goods and services market as well as its organizations have been attempted and implemented. The work of Wellman [11] and the research of Barbuceanu and Fox [12] are some good examples of the currently undergoing investigation on this subject. Conflict resolution via negotiation in multi-agent systems is also based on previous work by Oliveira [13] and by Sycara [14], while cooperative learning has been explored in Sian [15] and others. The main contribution of our work lays, not only, on the model proposed for the society of organizations, but also, on the distributed learning methodology applied to the established partnerships, in particular, and to the community, in general. The combination of the three layered hierarchical structure with the in-layer multi-agent architecture provides a rich and adequate setting for the representation of complex organizations. The inherent modularity of the presented architecture allows the representation of organizations with different levels of complexity, by means of social grouping. In particular, our efforts are concentrated on the analysis of a specific type of interaction: the cooperative interaction between producers and suppliers. The producers intent is to find the most adequate supplier, according to a set of specified constraints. The supplier's aim is to be contracted while trying to meet every producer's demand. The mechanism used to select the most adequate partner is based on a selection process which is composed of evaluation, negotiation and conflict resolution phases. Once an interaction is established, every exchanged constraint list is collected. The set of collected constraint lists constitutes a cooperative example, which can be used by the learning algorithms to generate assumptions about the behavior of the involved organizations, as well as about the society as a whole.

Many questions regarding the proposed scenario remain open. Issues like how to validate the learnt assumptions and how to use the acquired low-level knowledge to guide future high level interactions are some examples. In a near future, we hope to provide quantitative results concerning ARTOR's performance.

---

[4] The importance of a constraint can be measured in terms of its weight in the final sucess or failure of the selection process: hard constraints are non relaxable and soft contraints are relaxable.

Acknowledgments

The first author's current research is being supported by PUC-Pr and CNPq-Conselho Nacional de Pesquisa, Brasil, Grant Number 200413/92-9. We are specially grateful to Benedita Malheiro for her useful comments during the revision of this paper.

References

[1] Simon, H.A., The Sciences of The Artificial, Massachusetts, The M.I.T. Press, 1968. p.1-22.

[2] Gopnik, M., Cognitive Sciences. In: Encyclopedia of Physical Science and Technology. Academic Press, Inc., 1987. p.123-139.

[3] Chiavenato, I., Introdução à Teoria Geral da Administração. São Paulo, Editora McGraw-Hill Ltda, 1993. p.473-479.

[4] Simon, H.A., Decision Making and Organizational Design. In: Pugh, D.S.ed. Organizational Theory. Penguin Books. p.189-212.

[5] Engelmore, R., Morgan, T., Blackboard Systems. Addison - Wesley Publishing Company, 1998.

[6] Oliveira, et.al., Negotiation and Conflict Resolution within a Community of Cooperative Agents. In: Proceedings of The First International Symposium on Autonomous Decentralized Systems, Kawasaki, Japan, March 1993.

[7] Smith, R.G., The Contract Net Protocol: High-level Communication and Control in a Distributed Problem Solver. In: Readings in Distributed A.I., Edited by Alan H.Bond and Les Gasser, Morgan Kaufmann Publishers, 1998.

[8] Gasser, L. Huhns, M.N., Distributed Artificial Intelligence, vol.II, Pitman Publishing, London 1989.

[9] Michalski, R.S., Learning Flexible Concepts: Fundamental Ideas and a Method Based on Two-Tired Representation. In: Machine Learning - An Artificial Intelligence Approach, vol. III, Edited by Yves Kodratoff and Ryszard Michalsky, Morgan Kaufmann Publishers, Inc, 1990.

[10] Kodratoff, Y., Learning Expert Knowledge by Improving the Explanations Provided by the System. In: Machine Learning - An Artificial Intelligence Approach, vol. III, Edited by Yves Kodratoff and Ryszard Michalsky, Morgan Kaufmann Publishers, Inc, 1990.

[11] Wellman, M.P., A Market-Oriented Programming Environment and its Application to Distributed Multicommodity Flow Problems. In: Journal of Artificial Intelligence Research, 1 (1993) 1-23, AI Access Foundation and Morgan Kaufmann Publishers, 1993.

[12] Barbuceanu, M., Fox, M.S., The Information Agent: An Infrastructure for Collaboration in the Integrated Enterprise. In: Proceedings of the 2nd International Working Conference on Cooperating Knowledge Based Systems, Editor S.M.Deen, University of Keele, June 1994.

[13] Oliveira, E., Mouta, F., Distributed AI Architecture Enabling Multi-Agent Cooperation. In: Industrial and Engineering Applications of Artificial Intelligence and Expert Systems, Edited by Paul W.H. Chung, Gillian Lovegrove and Moonis Ali, Gordon and Breach Science Publishers, 1993.

[14] Sycara, K.P., Multiagent Compromise via Negotiation. In: Distributed Artificial Intelligence, vol.II, Edited by Les Gasser and Michael N. Huhns, Pitman Publishing, London 1989.

[15] Sian, S.S., Adaptation Based on Cooperative Learning in Multi-Agent Systems. In: Decentralize A.I. - 2, Edited by Yves Demazeau and Jean-Pierre Muller, Elsevier Science Publishers B.V., 1991.

Exploiting Social Reasoning to Enhance Adaptation in Open Multi-Agent Systems

Jaime Simão Sichman * and Yves Demazeau **

LIFIA/IMAG
46, avenue Félix Viallet
F-38031 Grenoble Cedex, France

Abstract. This paper shows how a *social reasoning mechanism* can be used by an agent in order to *enhance his adaptation in an open multi-agent system*. By open multi-agent system, we mean that new agents can dynamically enter and leave the agency and that some of them can change their current knowledge during execution time. We call *adaptation* the fact that due to these changes, the agents may be led to make different choices regarding the way to achieve their goals, particularly to whom they will propose/accept to collaborate in order to achieve these goals. Precisely, an agent can reason about his dependence situations in order to choose which are the most appropriate partners for achieving a certain goal, when he cannot achieve it alone. We present briefly both our agent model and the theory of dependence on which our social reasoning mechanism is based, and illustrate how such an adaptation can be achieved using a very simple example of the blocks world.

Keywords: agent-oriented programming, distributed AI, open systems.

1 Introduction

Academic research in Distributed Artificial Intelligence (DAI) has started in the late seventies [1], and one of its more recent research axes is known as Multi-Agent Systems (MAS) [7]. The idea behind MAS is to define *agents* able to provide complex services. Agents can define their own goals and plans, and can perform complex interactions with the others, using high level domain independent communication primitives. They are independent of a particular problem solving organisation: indeed, they can define or even change this organisation as the problem solving activity goes on. In order to do that, they must be able to perceive the changes and to act on the environment they are immersed in. They are also able to take into account other agents' skills and goals, in order to solve a problem cooperatively. In this paper, we address this last point.

We are particularly interested to show how a *social reasoning mechanism* can be used by an agent in order to *enhance his adaptation in an open multi-agent system*. By open multi-agent system, we mean that new agents can dynamically

---

* On leave from PCS-EPUSP, Brazil, and supported by FAPESP, grant number 91/1943-5.
** Research Fellow at CNRS, France.

enter and leave the agency and that some of them can change their current knowledge during execution time. We call *adaptation* the fact that due to these changes, the agents may be lead to make different choices regarding the way to achieve their goals, particularly to whom they will propose/accept to collaborate in order to achieve these goals. Precisely, an agent can reason about his dependence situations in order to choose which are the most appropriate partners for achieving a certain goal, when he cannot achieve it alone.

In the next section, we introduce the agent model we are adopting. The theory of dependence on which our social reasoning mechanism is based is briefly presented in section 3. In section 4, we illustrate how this mechanism can help an agent to adapt himself in an open multi-agent system, using a very simple example of the blocks world. Finally, in section 5 we present our conclusions and further work.

2 Agent Model

Due to the lack of space, we are not going to present here the complete model of the cognitive agent which we are adopting, a more detailed description may be found in [10]. An agent has some domain dependent problem solving capabilities, he is able to perceive the external environment and act on it, and he is able to communicate with the other agents. An internal mechanism we claim as essential is *social reasoning*: an agent must be able to reason about the other agents' activities, which is accomplished by an internal representation of the other agents' attributes (capabilities, reasoning mechanisms, restrictions, performance, etc). A control policy establishes when an agent should perceive, communicate, plan or act.

In this paper, we want to limit our analysis to a very particular issue: how agents decide to achieve a certain goal together. We suppose that this process happens as follows:

1. First of all, an agent chooses the goal to be achieved and a plan to achieve it. Planning may be carried out dynamically or the agents may select the most appropriate plan using case-based reasoning. Both of these activities are out of scope of this paper, we simply assume that an agent can do so;
2. If the agent can perform all the actions needed in the plan alone, he does so. Otherwise, he activates his social reasoning mechanism to select the other(s) agent(s) that can perform the needed action(s) of the plan which he cannot perform;
3. Once this selection has been done, the agent starts an interaction protocol [6] with the others in order to form a *coalition*[3] for achieving the selected goal [13]. In the case that the other(s) accept(s) to collaborate, a coalition is formed and the agents start executing the actions needed in the plan. At the end of this process, if the actions have been done correctly, the goal is achieved;

---

[3] We have borrowed this term from the game theory community, in order to express this notion of an organisation which is formed dynamically, during execution time.

4. In the case where the the coalition is not formed (because the others are not willing to collaborate), the agent starts to look for another possible partner(s);

5. If there are no more possible partners available, he decides that the current goal can not be achieved and selects another one.

One way to choose which are the more appropriate partners to be addressed is by using a social reasoning mechanism based on dependence theory, as described next.

3 Theory of Dependence

In this section, we briefly present the main features of the model we are adopting. This model is based on Social Power Theory [2], mainly on the notion of dependence relations between agents [3]. A more detailed formal description of this model can be found in [11, 10].

As we have said in last section, we consider that an essential building block of an autonomous agent is a *social reasoning mechanism*. We call social any reasoning mechanism that uses *information about the others* in order to infer some conclusions. This information about the others is stored in a data structure called *external description*. In our model, an external description is composed of goals, plans, actions and resources, where plans are meant to be some sequence of actions that may eventually use some resources. Every agent has his *own private external description*, where information about all the agents are stored.

Using this external description, an agent may infer his *dependence relations* regarding the other agents. Intuitively, an agent is *autonomous* for a given goal, if there is a plan that achieves this goal for which he can perform all needed actions and has control on all needed resources. If an agent is not autonomous, he *depends on others* for the considered goal. An agent depends on another one for a given goal, if there is a plan that achieves this goal, he is not autonomous for it and at least one action/resource appearing in this plan belongs to the other agent's action/resource set[4]. Once defined these dependence relations, an agent can construct a *dependence network* to represent in a same structure all of his action/resource dependences regarding the others.

We have defined the notions of *mutual* and *reciprocal* dependence. Intuitively, a mutual dependence (MD) expresses the fact that an agent infers that he and another agent depend on each other for a *same goal*, while a reciprocal dependence (RD) expresses that they both depend on each other but for *different goals*. A more detailed discussion about the relation between both mutual and reciprocal dependence and some social behaviours, like cooperation and exchange, may be found in [5].

Obviously, an agent can always access his own set of plans. On the other hand, as he has in his external description a representation of the plan(s) of the others, he can use both his own plans and those of the others in order to

---

[4] In this paper, we will restrict our analysis to action dependences.

infer his dependence relations. In this latter case, we may consider that an agent does a kind of simulation of the others' reasoning mechanism, an approach that is similar to the one proposed in [12]. We say that an agent *locally/mutually believes* a certain dependence if he uses exclusively his own plans/his plans and those of the others in order to reach such a conclusion.

By using these definitions, we have built a preliminary taxonomy of *dependence situations*[5]. This notion relates two agents and a goal, and we have defined 6 possible different cases:

1. *Independence (IND):* using his own plans, an agent infers that he does not depend on another for a certain goal;
2. *Locally Believed Mutual Dependence (LBMD):* using exclusively his own plans, an agent infers that there is a mutual dependence between himself and another agent;
3. *Mutually Believed Mutual Dependence (MBMD):* using both his own plans and those he believes the other one has, an agent infers that there is a mutual dependence between them;
4. *Locally Believed Reciprocal Dependence (LBRD):* using exclusively his own plans, an agent infers that there is a reciprocal dependence between himself and another agent;
5. *Mutually Believed Reciprocal Dependence (MBRD):* using both his own plans and those he believes the other one has, an agent infers that there is a reciprocal dependence between them;
6. *Unilateral Dependence (UD):* using his own plans, an agent infers that he depends on another one for a certain goal, but this latter does not depend on him for any of his goals.

These dependence situations may be used for establishing some *decision criteria* to help an agent to choose his partners when he is not able to achieve a certain goal alone. In fact, it is shown in [10] that we can mathematically construct a partially ordered set by defining a relation $\prec$ on DS^2, where $DS = \{$IND, UD, LBRD, LBMD, MBRD, MBMD$\}$ is a set composed by the possible dependence situations. This partial order is based on two complementary criteria, which are based on:

- *the nature of the dependence:* it is always better for an agent to choose a partner who has the same goal (*MD*), because in this case the other would reciprocate. A second best choice is to choose a partner who has a *RD*, since in this case the agent can propose an exchange ("if you help me to achieve my goal, I'll help you to achieve yours"). A *UD* is the worst choice, since the agent has nothing to offer in return;
- *the locality of the dependence:* it is always better for an agent to choose a partner who has a mutual believed dependence (*MBMD* or *MBRD*), since in this case the agent would not need to convince the other that his plan is better, which would be necessary to do if there is a locally believed dependence (*LBMD* or *LBRD*).

---

[5] Concerning only action dependences.

The combination of these criteria establishes the following partial order: $IND \prec UD \prec LBRD \prec \{LBMD, MBRD\} \prec MBMD$. According to this partial order, the best choice of partners for an agent are those whose dependence situation is a *MBMD*, followed by either a *LBMD* or a *MBRD*, then by a *LBRD* and finally by a *UD*. The two dependence situations *LBMD* and *MBRD* are incomparable according to the combination of the two above criteria.

Finally, we would like to remark that we are aware that the meaning which we have associated to our notions of plans, actions and resources are somewhat restrictive in the general context of AI, but we need to adopt such notions in order to investigate the effects of our social reasoning mechanism, which is the particular point we are concerned about in our research.

4 Social Reasoning for Enhancing Adaptation

In order to illustrate how the notions defined in the last section may be exploited by an agent, let us consider a very simple example of the blocks world. The agency is composed of three agents, *jaime*, *yves* and *olivier*, and neither of them can achieve their own goals by themselves. We will analyse the evolution of this agency by supposing small changes in it, and these changes will be considered to happen in different instants of time. For each of these instants, we will present the current dependence relations, as well as the dependence situations. The items represented in shaded boxes are those which have changed since the previous instant. We will consider also that (i) all agents become aware of these changes when they happen, and (ii) all agents have the same external description entries of each other.

4.1 Scenario at t=0

The external description, dependence relations and dependence situations for the initial scenario are presented in example 1. As an example of a dependence network, the one of agent *olivier* would look like:

```
olivier
---------- on(A,B)
       |---------- on(A,B):=clear(C), put_on(A,B).
              |---------- put_on
                     |---------- jaime
                            |----------
```

Each line of the tables presented in this example corresponds to the point of view of the agent of the first column, designed as "me". For instance, the dependence just presented above is represented in the third line of the table describing the dependence relations.

In this scenario, no agent has a plan for any other goal, except for his own. Everyone infers a *UD*, even if this is not what would be inferred by an external observer. Supposing that at t=0 agent *olivier* chooses to achieve his goal, he could possibly start an interaction with agent *jaime* like this: *"I need your*

Agent	Goals	Actions	Resources	Plans
jaime	on(C,table)	put_on	B	on(C,table):=clear(C).
yves	on(A,B)	—	C	on(A,B):=clear(C), put_on(A,B).
olivier	on(A,B)	clear	A	on(A,B):=clear(C), put_on(A,B).

External Description

DEP	others		
me	jaime	yves	olivier
jaime	—	—	clear
yves	put_on	—	clear
olivier	put_on	—	—

Dependence Relations

D-SIT	others		
me	jaime	yves	olivier
jaime	—	—	UD
yves	UD	—	UD
olivier	UD	IND	—

Dependence Situations

Example 1. Scenario at t=0

action put_on in order to achieve my goal on(A,B). Could you help me?" As from agent *olivier*'s point of view there is a *UD*, he can not offer anything that could interest agent *jaime*, so his chances to obtain the needed help will strongly depend on what agent *jaime* is currently doing, if this latter has a benevolent behaviour etc. Moreover, agent *olivier has not any other choices* in order to accomplish his selected goal.

4.2 Scenario at t=1

The new external description and dependence situations at t=1 are now represented in example 2.

Agent	Goals	Actions	Resources	Plans
jaime	on(C,table)	put_on	B	on(C,table):=clear(C).
yves	on(A,B)	—	C	on(A,B):=clear(C), put_on(A,B).
olivier	on(A,B)	clear	A	on(A,B):=clear(C), put_on(A,B). on(C,table):=clear(C).

External Description

D-SIT	others		
me	jaime	yves	olivier
jaime	—	—	UD
yves	UD	—	UD
olivier	LBRD	IND	—

Dependence Situations

Example 2. Scenario at t=1

At t=1, agent *olivier* learns the plan of how to put a block on the table, even if he does not have this goal. The way this knowledge can be acquired is out of scope for the moment, we have only to suppose that he has stored this information in his external description. As we have neither added a new agent nor changed the actions and resources of the existing ones, the current dependence relations remain the same as presented in example 1.

One can observe that now agent *olivier* infers a *LBRD* regarding agent *jaime*, and therefore he can offer something in exchange for getting help. For instance, if agent *olivier* had to start an interaction at this time with agent *jaime*, he could say: *"I need your action put_on in order to achieve my goal on(A,B), but I suppose that you also need my action clear to achieve your goal on(C,table). If you help me, I promise that I'll help you too."* The strategy of agent *olivier* is to first convince agent *jaime* that this latter needs him to accomplish the goal *on(C,table)*, which is quite easy, as agent *jaime* is aware of this dependence. However, what agent *jaime* does not know for the moment is that agent *olivier* also depends on him for achieving goal *on(A,B)*.

4.3 Scenario at t=2

At t=2, agent *jaime* also learns the plan of how to put a block on another. The new external description and dependence situations are now summarized in example 3. Once more, the current dependence relations remain the same as presented in example 1.

Agent	Goals	Actions	Resources	Plans
jaime	on(C,table)	put_on	B	on(C,table):=clear(C). on(A,B):=clear(C), put_on(A,B).
yves	on(A,B)	—	C	on(A,B):=clear(C), put_on(A,B).
olivier	on(A,B)	clear	A	on(A,B):=clear(C), put_on(A,B). on(C,table):=clear(C).

External Description

D-SIT	others		
me	*jaime*	*yves*	*olivier*
jaime	—	—	MBRD
yves	UD	—	UD
olivier	MBRD	IND	—

Dependence Situations

Example 3. Scenario at t=2

We can notice that now both agents *olivier* and *jaime* infer a *MBRD* regarding one another, and therefore both of them can offer something in exchange for getting help since the beginning of the interaction. This fact leads to a possibly easier and faster collaboration, since neither of them needs to reason about whether it is advantageous to engage in such a common activity. Moreover, as it is clear for both of them that the other one is dependent on himself, the chances of reciprocation are higher. In the previous instant, for instance, as agent *jaime* didn't have a plan for goal *on(A,B)*, he could think that agent *olivier* was cheating. The interaction is similar to that presented in t=1, with the difference that the receiver is currently aware of the situation, and therefore is more willing to give and receive help.

4.4 Scenario at t=3

At t=3, agent *michel* arrives, with both a plan and a goal to put block A on block B. This new scenario is summarized in example 4. As the agency has a new member, which has an action that interest the others, the dependence networks change. For instance, the new dependence network of agent *olivier* would look like:

```
olivier
---------- on(A,B)
        |---------- on(A,B):=clear(C), put_on(A,B).
                |---------- put_on
                        |---------- jaime
                        |----------
                        | michel
                        |----------
```

Agent	Goals	Actions	Resources	Plans
jaime	on(C,table)	put_on	B	on(C,table):=clear(C). on(A,B):=clear(C), put_on(A,B).
yves	on(A,B)	—	C	on(A,B):=clear(C), put_on(A,B).
olivier	on(A,B)	clear	A	on(A,B):=clear(C), put_on(A,B). on(C,table):=clear(C).
michel	on(A,B)	put_on	—	on(A,B):=put_on(A,B).

External Description

DEP	others			
me	*jaime*	*yves*	*olivier*	*michel*
jaime	—	—	clear	—
yves	put_on	—	clear	put_on
olivier	put_on	—	—	put_on
michel	—	—	—	—

Dependence Relations

D-SIT	others			
me	*jaime*	*yves*	*olivier*	*michel*
jaime	—	—	MBRD	—
yves	UD	—	UD	UD
olivier	MBRD	IND	—	LBMD
michel	—	—	—	—

Dependence Situations

Example 4. Scenario at t=3

One may notice that now, agent *olivier has a choice* for obtaining the action *put_on*, either from agent *jaime* or from agent *michel*. On the other hand, for the moment, agent *michel* believes he can achieve his goal alone.

Agent *olivier* infers now a *LBMD*, i.e., that according to his own plan agent *michel* and himself depend on one another to achieve the same goal. If he decides to start an interaction at this moment, he may choose to interact with agent *michel* instead of agent *jaime*, like the following: *"I know you have also the goal on(A,B) as I do, and I suppose that you need my action clear to accomplish it. As I cannot perform the action put_on, do you want to help me so we can achieve it together?"*

On the other hand, as stated before, now agent *olivier* has two options to get the action *put_on* done, as the option of doing a social exchange with agent *jaime* remains. As these two dependence situations are incomparable referring to the criteria defined in section 3, an additional decision criterion must be introduced.

It is out of scope of this paper to discuss how this additional criterion should be, but one may think that an agent can also maintain in his social reasoning mechanism a history of past collaborations, and chooses the partner which has a higher rate in past successful interactions. We could also associate a measure of cost to the actions performed by the others, so that an agent should choose the partner which offers the same action at a lower cost.

4.5 Scenario at t=4

In this last scenario, agent *michel* learns that his plan was incomplete and adds the action *clear(C)* to his plan. This new scenario is shown in example 5. Once more, agent *michel*'s dependence network will change:

```
michel
---------- on(A,B)
        |---------- on(A,B):=clear(C), put_on(A,B).
              |---------- clear
                    |---------- olivier
                          |----------
```

Agent	Goals	Actions	Resources	Plans
jaime	on(C,table)	put_on	B	on(C,table):=clear(C). on(A,B):=clear(C), put_on(A,B).
yves	on(A,B)	—	C	on(A,B):=clear(C), put_on(A,B).
olivier	on(A,B)	clear	A	on(A,B):=clear(C), put_on(A,B). on(C,table):=clear(C).
michel	on(A,B)	put_on	—	on(A,B):=clear(C), put_on(A,B).

External Description

DEP	others			
me	jaime	yves	olivier	michel
jaime	—	—	clear	
yves	put_on	—	clear	put_on
olivier	put_on	—	—	put_on
michel	—	—	clear	—

Dependence Relations

D-SIT	others			
me	jaime	yves	olivier	michel
jaime	—	—	MBRD	—
yves	UD	—	UD	UD
olivier	MBRD	IND	—	MBMD
michel	—	IND	MBMD	—

Dependence Situations

Example 5. Scenario at t=4

We can observe that now both agents *olivier* and *michel* infer a *MBMD* regarding one another, and therefore both of them can offer something to the other and start the interaction. This situation is similar to the scenario corresponding to time = 2, the difference is that the goal to be achieved now is the same for both agents. The discussion made about reciprocation also holds here, but reciprocation is now more probable, as both agents have the same goal. Finally, regarding agent *olivier*'s choice regarding whom to ask for help, it can be observed in section 3 that a *MBMD* is better than a *MBRD*, so he chooses to interact with agent *michel*.

4.6 Discussion

The main cognitive assumption adopted in this work is that dependence relations can explain some social behaviours as *cooperation*. If two or more agents are committed to achieve a same goal, and each of them needs the other(s) to perform a certain action needed in a plan that achieves this goal, one can explain why cooperation arises, and why agents decide/accept to form a coalition dynamically. However, our approach is slightly different from the ones based on game theory, like [8, 9]. In these approaches, agents are homogeneous and self-sufficient, and they decide to cooperate with the others either to maximize their expected utility or to minimize harmful interferences, due to goal conflicts. We instead consider heterogeneity as a ground basis for cooperation.

On the other hand, we have shown another important aspect regarding the stability of the process of coalition formation: *depending on the beliefs which the agents have about the others, they may adapt themselves to new situations, by choosing different partners, if they believe that the chances of obtaining a cooperative behaviour from these latter are higher.*

5 Conclusions and Further Work

In this paper, we have shown how a *social reasoning mechanism* can be used by an agent in order to *enhance his adaptation in an open multi-agent system.* We have presented some decision criteria based on *dependence situations*, which are exploited by the agents in order to select the more appropriate partners, when they try to form a *coalition* dynamically in order to achieve their goals, and we have illustrated the usage of these criteria by using a simple example of the blocks world. We intend to improve our work basically in the following directions:

1. regarding the *dependence situations*, we intend to take into account resource dependences in order to extend the proposed taxonomy. There are some interesting situations that may arise involving three-party dependences, as described in [4]. This extension will have a direct impact on the proposed decision criteria, which will have to be extended;
2. we also intend to establish a notion of *quantification of dependence*. Our first idea is to quantify the dependence relations according to the importance of a given goal, number of actions and resources involved in a plan and number of plans to achieve a certain goal. As a consequence, this quantification will also have to be taken into account by the decision criteria;
3. we are also currently developing some *interaction protocols*, whose general model is presented in [6], in order to implement the exchange of messages between agents that we have presented in our examples.

Acknowledgements

The authors would like to thank Dr. Uma Garimella (LIFIA-IMAG) and the anonymous reviewers for their useful comments during the revision of this paper.

References

1. Alan H. Bond and Les Gasser, editors. *Readings in Distributed Artificial Intelligence*. Morgan Kaufmann Publishers, Inc., San Mateo, CA, 1988.

2. Cristiano Castelfranchi. Social power: A point missed in multi-agent, DAI and HCI. In Yves Demazeau and Jean-Pierre Müller, editors, *Decentralized A. I.*, pages 49–62. Elsevier Science Publishers B. V., Amsterdam, NL, 1990.

3. Cristiano Castelfranchi, Maria Micelli, and Amedeo Cesta. Dependence relations among autonomous agents. In Eric Werner and Yves Demazeau, editors, *Decentralized A. I. 3*, pages 215–227. Elsevier Science Publishers B. V., Amsterdam, NL, 1992.

4. Rosaria Conte. Three-party dependence and rational communication. In Rosaria Conte and Sila Fiorentino, editors, *Atti del 2do Incontro del Gruppo AI*IA di Interesse Speciale su Inteligenza Artificiale Distribuita*, pages 105–114, Roma, Italia, November 1992.

5. Rosaria Conte and Jaime Simão Sichman. DEPNET: How to benefit from social dependence. *Journal of Mathematical Sociology (Special Issue on Sociological Algorithms)*, 1995. Forthcoming.

6. Yves Demazeau. From interactions to collective behaviour in agent-based systems. In *Pre-proceedings of the invited lectures of the 1st European Conference on Cognitive Science*, St. Malo, France, March 1995.

7. Yves Demazeau and Jean-Pierre Müller, editors. *Decentralized A. I.* Elsevier Science Publishers B. V., Amsterdam, NL, 1990.

8. Piotr J. Gmytrasiewicz and Edmund H. Durfee. Reasoning about other agents: Philosophy, theory and implementation. In Khaled Ghedira and François Sprumont, editors, *Pre-proceedings of the 5th European Workshop on Modelling Autonomous Agents in a Multi-Agent World*, Neuchâtel, Switzerland, August 1993.

9. Jeffrey S. Rosenschein and Gilad Zlotkin. *Rules of Encounter: Designing Conventions for Automated Negotiation among Computers*. MIT Press, Cambridge, MA, 1994.

10. Jaime Simão Sichman. *Du Raisonnement Social Chez les Agents: Une Approche Basée sur la Théorie de la Dépendance*. Thèse de doctorat, Institut National Polytechnique de Grenoble, Grenoble, France, 1995. A paraître.

11. Jaime Simão Sichman, Rosaria Conte, Yves Demazeau, and Cristiano Castelfranchi. A social reasoning mechanism based on dependence networks. In Tony Cohn, editor, *Proceedings of the 11th European Conference on Artificial Intelligence*, pages 188–192, Amsterdam, The Netherlands, August 1994. John Wiley & Sons Ltd.

12. Jacques Wainer. Reasoning about another agent through empathy. In *Anais do 11° Simpósio Brasileiro em Inteligência Artificial*, pages 17–25, Fortaleza, Brasil, October 1994. Sociedade Brasileira de Computação.

13. Michael Wooldridge and Nicholas R. Jennings. Towards a theory of cooperative problem solving. In Yves Demazeau, Jean-Pierre Müller, and John Perram, editors, *Pre-proceedings of the 6th European Workshop on Modelling Autonomous Agents in a Multi-Agent World*, pages 15–26, Odense, Denmark, August 1994.

A System for Aiding Discovery: Mechanisms for Knowledge Generation

Edilson Ferneda, Mário E. de Souza e Silva, and Hélio de Menezes Silva

Universidade Federal da Paraíba
Departamento de Sistemas e Computação
Caixa Postal 10.090, 58.109-970 Campina Grande - PB, Brazil
{edilson,ernesto,hmenezes}@dsc.ufpb.br

Abstract. This paper proposes a computer aided discovery system which may also be seen as a knowledge acquisition environment. It uses a knowledge representation (the Semi-Empirical Theories) to formulate, to experiment, and to communicate that knowledge. The system's objective, rather than producing an exact knowledge, is yielding a knowledge which may present a high-level, convincing rationale on its validity and may also be improved via a dialog protocol. Emphasis is given to the proposed (abductive and inductive) mechanisms for efficiently generating knowledge. The paper proposes what seems to be good heuristics (based on measures of simplicity and of coverage) for better traversing both the hypotheses and the conjecture spaces, during the inductive step of the learning mechanisms.

1 Introduction

An informal specification of the learning mechanisms for a Rational-Agent machine is proposed in this paper. A Rational Agent is an autonomous system that appears to the user as having reasoning abilities, because it is capable of common sense reasoning and of handling intentions, beliefs, and knowledge that is tolerated to be, to some extent, evolutionary, incomplete, imprecise, and erroneous.

From an Artificial Intelligence vantage point, this work may be seen as lying in the confluence of the streams of Knowledge Acquisition and Machine Learning. According to the definition proposed in [2]:

The domain of Knowledge Acquisition for Knowledge Based Systems (KBS's) is characterized by the identification and management of the processes necessary to the elaboration (conception, evaluation, and evolution) of a KBS from heterogeneous sources of knowledge (documented, human, and experimental). The result expected ... is to furnish the future system with the knowledge that will be the foundation of its expertise. The conductor of the process of knowledge acquisition is the knowledge engineer: he orchestrates the intervention of the different processes, actors, and agents.

While Knowledge Acquisition uses the machine as a mere tool for helping the knowledge engineer to elicit the expert's knowledge, Machine Learning studies the set of mechanisms that gives the machine the faculty of building the knowledge base by analyzing data, explanations, criticisms to solutions, etc.

Several works have shown the necessity of making Machine Learning and Knowledge Acquisition to synergetically work together for modeling the control component of the learning process.

Learning proficiently is not enough if the expert is left without proper ammunition to efficiently check and validate the information acquired by the machine. This information has a too large volume and the expert needs a tool capable of helping him to efficiently criticize his decisions, particularly the choice of the description language (which implies the choice of the learning tool) and of the selected sample of examples.

Our System for Aided Discovery (SAID) is a synergetic combination of Machine Learning and Knowledge Acquisition. It follows principles (summarized in [20]), such as those for data acquisition, for abstraction based on information about a conceptual model, for particularization of this model, etc.

The study of expert systems has shown a pervasive dichotomy between deep knowledge (characterized by having theoretical justification and by being found in scientific books, articles, etc.) and shallow knowledge (which is characterized by being situational, empirical, and not found in conventional scientific writings). Both kinds of knowledge are used by novices and experts, but what gives these a leading edge over those is the better quality and greater extension of their shallow knowledge. SAID discovers shallow knowledge by taking advantage of both some deep (theoretical) knowledge made available and a set of incomplete, partially erroneous data. The knowledge base is assumed to be revisable (by error correction) and evolutionary (by making the knowledge more precise, broader, deeper, more structured, more understandable,... or, in short, by improving the knowledge, in any sense).

Here, scientific discovery is seen as being the result of examining and revising a modeling process over which both theoretic models and experimental data intervene.

A first effort for conceptualizing an artificial apprentice generated a conceptual framework: the Semi-Empirical Theories (SETs) [17, 18]. That effort established the elementary concepts which allow building (modeling) an apprentice's knowledge and studying its evolution. SETs, however, being focused on the structures and mechanisms of an apprentice, neglected a fundamental learning aspect: the environment for the interaction between the apprentice and the external world. Therefore, [15] proposed a learning environment, as well as a description of a learning protocol, named MOSCA. [6] shows how this protocol can be merged with the SETs framework.

Since concepts formulated by an apprentice can be erroneous, an intervening agent should be able to determine counter-examples (and also examples likely to be close to or beyond the frontier of the apprentice's current knowledge), testing and exercising him to the limits of his capabilities, hopefully embarrassing him by exposing his deficiencies, therefore stimulating him to revise and improve his knowledge. The goal is not to have an apprentice capable of acquiring a perfect (exact and complete) knowledge, but rather to have an apprentice capable of acquiring a knowledge which will be considered as quite adoptable (because the apprentice can yield a high-level and convincing rationale of its correctness and adequacy) and may also be corrected/improved via a dialog protocol.

2   Rational agents

There are active entities which display behavior conventionally considered as being intelligent. These entities will hereafter be named *agents*.

Researches for the conceptualization and design of artificial systems (or agents) capable of exhibiting behavior accepted as intelligent must take into consideration the several characteristics presumed as necessary for that behavior to be classified as being intelligent. Among these attributes, we are here particularly interested in the one of *rationality* [12]. The notion of rationality, more specific than the one of intelligence, is related to the treatment of a well delineated class of problems.

A *Rational Agent* is defined as being any (human or artificial) system capable of producing and controlling its own knowledge in a certain domain, in such way that the system will be able to proficiently perform some classes of complex tasks (such as deciding, classifying, diagnosing, predicting, simulating, restricting, conceiving, and planning) conventionally considered as requiring intelligence.

Many works [16, 13, 5] show the possibility of constructing systems that: *a)* interpret symbolic structures; *b)* know their limitations; *c)* act in logical accordance with their beliefs; and *d)* adapt their actions to the changes in their knowledge. These systems, therefore, are capable of improving their representation of the external world and of better interacting with this world.

Next, we will describe the behavior of an apprentice rational-agent (*apprentice*, for short) whose knowledge is the result of communicating with other agents. This agent builds and controls the evolution of its knowledge. It has reasoning mechanisms such as those of the Semi-Empirical Theories.

3   Semi-Empirical Theories

Lakatos introduced the notion of SETs when he formulated [8]:

> [The objective of this work] *is formulating the question that the non-formal, semi- empirical Mathematics does not advance by means of monotonic growth of the number of incontrovertibly established theorems, but by means of the unceasing improvement of opinions resulting from speculation and criticism, and from the logic of the proofs and refutations.*

SETs, conceived for conducing to a theoretic formulation, are neither completely axiomatic (since they do not forcefully have to rely on any initial knowledge), nor completely empirical (since they do not mandatorily rely on any once-forever data analysis, but they rather evolve from their study). This explains the title Semi-Empirical. [18]

The model adopted by SETs aims at determining both the validity and the relevance of conjectures. It does so by respectively determining the conjectures power to correctly answer questions and convincingly explaining how it arrived to the answers. SET's are a form of knowledge representation which expresses a conjecture by means of relationships among sentences of a language. [17]

It was deemed convenient that the rational agent which is in charge of discovering knowledge in a certain domain, will formulate only the kind of knowledge which may be criticized by another agent, the domain expert. Therefore, in order to conceive and design a rational agent, it is necessary that we first arrive to an agreement on the heuristics which will define the forms of the knowledge. These forms will allow the building of a system able to elaborate a SET, since they determine how the sentences of the language will be interpreted.

It was also deemed convenient that the rational agent will be able to yield decisions acceptable as being rational. For this, it is necessary that this agent adopt a form of communicating with all other involved agents, in such way that it can offer arguments and receive criticisms about the understanding of the proposed problem, thus identifying new facts, formulating and examining new conjectures, controlling the building and the evolution of its knowledge.

In this setting, a rational agent may be defined as a system capable of constructing and controlling the evolution of a SET.

T. Addis [1] proposed a taxonomy of the terms used for expressing knowledge in SETs:

- *Data*, represented by expressions to be generated and evolved. This knowledge is captured in one of the three following forms: *Facts* (statements to which a degree of validity can be attributed); *Hypotheses* (statements to which a degree of relevance can be attributed); and *Heuristics* (defining the forms that facts and hypotheses may take on).
- *Mechanisms* for creating knowledge (by *abduction*, proposing new facts), organizing them (by *induction*, suggesting new hypotheses and new heuristics) and propagating restrictions on them (by *deduction*, determining the logical consequences of the knowledge).
- *Methods* related to the interactions with an external agent that plays the role of criticizing or the role of proposing a statement to be proved. Methods examine the adequacy of information such as *being a lemma, being an objection, being a proof, being a conjecture*, etc.

All the ideas above are still being polished. See details in [17, 18].

We will hereafter focus on an illustrative application of the above introduced concepts to the well known domain of Euclidean Geometry. More specifically, we chose the problem of discovering how a square is constructed.

4   The learning mechanisms

This section presents the mechanisms that allow building the knowledge of a rational agent according with SETs' principles.

The first step, previous to the learning process, is the definition of the language terms (and the concepts already learned) which will play an active role in that learning. The learning calculus may, therefore, be reduced.

Figure 1 illustres the kinds of objects composing the training set of examples and counter-examples. Figure 2 is a translation of this object description to an adequate representation.

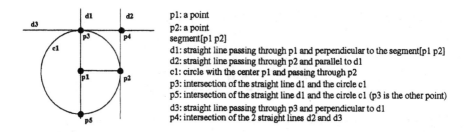

p1: a point
p2: a point
segment[p1 p2]
d1: straight line passing through p1 and perpendicular to the segment[p1 p2]
d2: straight line passing through p2 and parallel to d1
c1: circle with the center p1 and passing through p2
p3: intersection of the straight line d1 and the circle c1
p5: intersection of the straight line d1 and the circle c1 (p3 is the other point)
d3: straight line passing through p3 and perpendicular to d1
p4: intersection of the 2 straight lines d2 and d3

Fig. 1. An element of the sample composed by examples and counter-examples of the concept Square

The following sections describe the mechanisms responsible for generating new knowledge by looking for similarities among the objects composing the sample.

4.1   Abduction

Here, abduction is seen as aiming at enriching a model by proposing new facts [1]. In the current problem, an object is represented by a graph, and a fact is a subgraph representing a statement which is *dominantly valid* [18] with respect to a sample. The abduction method should be able to extract (or discover) regularities (facts) from the representation of the sample.

Abduction, in INNE method [9], extracts subgraphs each one representing a similarity which is both frequently found in a set of conceptual graphs named *Examples* and rarely found in another set of graphs named *Counter-Examples*. Here, abduction will generate two sets of subgraphs: one of *assimilation*, computed from the whole sample, and the other of *discrimination*, computed by considering of the distinction between examples and counter-examples. The problem can be seen as follows:

Let E be a set of conceptual graphs named examples, and C be a set of conceptual graphs named counter-examples. The objective is to find an

obj1
    is-a [geometric-figure]
    <external-name,[ ]>
       value <"Example 1">
    <composed-by,[ ]>
       value <[o1p1,o1p2,o1p3,o1p4,o1p5,o1d1,o1d2,o1d3,o1c1,o1s1,o1s2,o1s3,o1s4]>

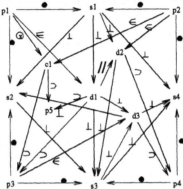

Fig. 2. Example of a graph representing one of the objects of the sample. The nodes are objects, the arcs are the relations between those object. p*, s*, d* and c* represent, respectively, points, segments, straight lines and circles. The symbols representing the types of relations (attributes) are: • is end-of; ⊥ is perpendicular-to; ˙ is center-of; ⊃ is superset-of, ∈ is is-element-of; // is parallel-to

    equivalence class of conceptual graphs such that their graphs are facts dominantly valid with respect to the sample E ∪ C.

    An object may be perceived as an oriented, labeled, bipartite graph, where the set of nodes is partitioned in two subsets, the first one composed of classes labels or object values (their types), and the second one composed of labels of relations (attributes) among the objects. The abduction mechanism here proposed extracts regularities directly from an object oriented representation, where the triple *<object, attribute, value>* verified over a sample object will be named an *elementary fact*.

    Abduction yields a set of assimilating statements and a set of discriminating statements. These sets are built by using certain heuristics for determining the form that the statements will take (for example, statements will take the forms of paths in the graph, minimal and maximal depth, etc.). *Point ∈ Straight Line ⊥ Segment ⊥ Segment* is an example of a path representing a fact, since it occurs in the majority of the examples and occurs only in a few counter-examples.

4.2 Induction

Induction aims at enriching a model by proposing new hypotheses and new heuristics.

Induction is performed in three steps: *(a)* the generation of a rule for each relevant fact; *(b)* the pattern matching of these rules, in order to build more general rules (the hypotheses); and *(c)* the pattern matching of hypotheses in order to form a conjecture.

First inductive step: generation of rules. A rule is built for each subgraph generated by induction. This operation is a kind of induction, since it yields rules having a generalizing character with respect to the sample.

Second inductive step: generation of hypotheses. Several learning systems were defined aiming at learning concepts from a set of objects (examples or counter-examples). What mostly distinguishes a learning method from the other ones is the manner it represents and builds its knowledge.

LEGAL (LEarning with GAlois Lattice). E. Mephu Nguifo [11] conceived a learning system which, starting from a set of objects (examples and counter-examples) of a concept, generates another set of objects (standing for regularities found in the first set) by using a generalizing method. This structuring follows from the use of the notion of Galois lattices [21] in the inductive mechanism. LEGAL's major advantage is its exaustiveness, which gives the system the maximum regularity space to be explored.

LEGAL uses a propositional logic approach to describe the objects and the regularities. This description is originally accomplished by means of a finite set of binary attributes characterizing the concept to be learned, which is initially represented by means of a triple $<O,A,I>$, where O is a set of objects, A is a set of attributes, and I is the binary relation from O to A.

An object is described as a finite set of attributes. LEGAL constructs a semi-lattice containing no valid regularities, which are described by attributes which characterize A. A fundamental property of LEGAL is the fact that all the objects are described by the same set of attributes.

Our proposal, built upon LEGAL. The second inductive step of the system here proposed does not characterize objects by using attributes, but rather by using dominantly-valid statements (facts generated by the abduction mechanism) over the initial sample.

The choice of heuristics that will define the traversing of the hypotheses space should have a way of evaluating the "goodness" of each hypothesis. Here, two measures of this goodness will be considered:

- Simplicity. The number of facts composing a hypothesis should not be so large that it will make difficult the judgement of its relevance. Since LEGAL does not support this kind of restriction, the mechanism proposed in this article uses some heuristics to impose a limit on the number of facts allowed to compose a hypothesis. This way, a single, complex hypothesis generated by LEGAL may derive a set of hypotheses, each one having now its relevance more easily evaluated. Notice that the next step may compose again this set of hypothesis yielding again a single hypothesis, simpler than the original one, and with its relevance established by construction.

– Coverage. To assure that only the most relevant hypotheses are generated, the number of object components which are covered by each hypothesis should be minimal. In other words, in this step the number of unification of the free variables of the terms representing the facts should be the greatest possible.

Obviously, the hypotheses generated should themselves be dominantly valid. $\{Point \in Straight\ Line \supset Point \bullet Segment,\ Point \in Straight\ Line \supset Point \bullet Segment,\ Segment \perp Straight\ Line \supset Point \bullet Segment\}$ represents a hypothesis proposed by the system.

Third inductive step: generation of conjectures. Starting with the set of the assimilating hypotheses and the set of the discriminating hypotheses, the current step generates conjectures about the proof of the concept to be learned.

For the same reasons already explained in the second inductive step (generation of hypotheses), the system here proposed will obey the simplicity and the coverage criteria. Here, however, the coverage criterion will look for maximal coverage, rather than minimal. This follows from the obvious advantage of having the conjectures the closest possible to the sample objects (thus making use of all the facts already known about the objects), and of having the apprentice agent the least silent possible over new objects offered for being classified.

Figure 3 represents the elements which compose a conjecture.

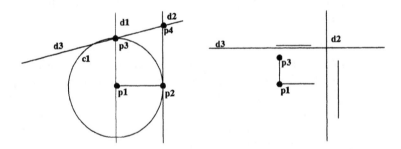

Fig. 3. Geometric representation of a conjecture by means of the composition of assimilating and discriminating hypotheses.

A protocol for communication (see [6]) will be used for assuring the evolution of the conjectures towards an empirical proof [8].

5 Conclusions

A learning environment whose learning mechanisms generate easily criticizable knowledge has been presented. This environment was studied within a conceptual framework, SETs, supporting the expression of both the reasoning and the structure of the apprentice.

Under the light of both theoretical and practical Machine Learning current results, integrating high level argumentation techniques into the learning system was deemed necessary to get the expert's validation, approval, and confidence in the acquired knowledge.

Experience has shown that most of the currently available learning tools do not fully satisfy the expert's expectations and needs. More than interested in a system that merely has the capability of learning correctly, experts are looking for systems able to go beyond that by understandably and convincingly explaining what and how they have learned. One of the major reasons for this is that the explanations may hint what should be changed in order to improve the knowledge base. All of this grows in importance when the expert uses the machine as an aid for scientific discovery (of course this involves modeling a phenomenon).

This approach has been corroborated by some applications to other domains, characterized by more numerous and larger-scale experiments, like Musical Analysis [7], Chemistry [14], Genetic Engineering [10]. However, it still has to fully establish itself as a really useful learning framework. In spite of this, the way the proposed system solves learning problems may be seen as an advancement at least as a methodologically and didactically relevant concept, in as much as it sees the learning problem in a way understandable and profitable to both the application domain expert and the Artificial Intelligence expert. It should be noticed that it was assured the possibility of refuting the learned knowledge. For accomplishing that, it is necessary that all heuristics involved in the knowledge acquisition may be reevaluated. This justifies the adoption of SETs for knowledge representation.

The paper proposed what seems to be good heuristics (based on measures of simplicity and of coverage) for better traversing both the hypotheses and the conjecture spaces, during the inductive step of the learning mechanisms.

6 Acknowledgements

The major part of this work was undertaken in the *Laboratoire d'Informatique, Robotique et Microelétrocnique de Montpellier*, under the direction of Jean Sallantin, with the collaboration of Phillipe Reitz, and with the support of CAPES.

References

1. Addis, T. R.: Knowledge organization for abduction. Interdisciplinary Information Technology Conference. Bradford University, England (1988)

2. Aussenac-Gilles, N., Krivine, J.-P., Sallantin, J.: L'acquisition des connaissances pour les systêmes à base de connaissance. Revue d'Intelligence Artificielle (Editorial). 6(1-2) Paris (1992) 87-127

3. Barbut, C., Monjardet, B.: Ordre et Classification, Algèbre et Combinatoire. Hachette, Paris (1970)

4. Bratman, M., Konolige, K., Israel, D. J., Pollack, M. E.: Rational behavior in resource-bounded agents. SRI, NSF Project Proposal (1989)

5. Ferneda, E., Py, M., Reitz, Ph., Sallantin, J.: L'Agent Rationnel SAID: une application en géométrie. Proceedings of the First European Colloquium on Cognitive Science. Paris (1992)

6. Ferneda, E., Silva, C. A. P. da, Teixeira, L. de M., Silva, H. de M.: A system for aiding discovery in musical analysis. Proceedings of the First Brazilian Simposium on Computer Music. Caxambu (1994)

7. Lakatos, I.: Logic of Mathemathical Discovery: Proofs and Refutations. Cambridge University Press (1976)

8. Liquière, M.: INNE (INduction in NEtworks): A structural learning algorithm for noisy exemples. Proceedings of the Fourth European Working Session on Learning. Morik K. (Ed), Pitman and Morgan Kaufmann Publishers Inc. London (1990) 111-123 1

9. Mephu N'guifo, E., Sallantin, J.: Prediction of primary spline junction gene sequences with a cooperative knowledge acquisition system. Proceedings of the First International Conference on Intelligent Systems for Molecular Biology. Washington (1993)

10. Mephu N'guifo, E.: Galois Lattice: a fremework for concept learning. Design, evaluation and Refinement. Proceedings of the T.A.I.'94 Conference - Tools for Artificial Intelligence. Louisiana (1994)

11. Newell A.: The knowledge level. Artificial Intelligence. 18 (1982) 87-127

12. Nilsson N.: Intelligent communicating agents. Stanford University, Project Proposal (1986)

13. Py M.: Analogical reasoning: an organic chemistry application. 8th International Conference on Applications of Artificial Intelligence in Engineering. Toulouse (1993)

14. Reitz Ph.: Contribution à l'étude des environnements d'aprentissage. Conceptualisation, Spécification et Prototypage. Doctorate Thesis. Université de Montpellier (1992)

15. Sallantin, J.: Logiques et comportements des systèmes rationnels - une esquisse d'épistémologie. In: Moigne J.-L. (Org). Intelligence des mécanismes, mécanismes de l'intelligence", Fayard / Fondation Diderot, Paris (1986)

16. Sallantin, J., Szczeciniarz J.-J., Barboux C., Lagrange M.-S., Renaud M.: Théories semi-empiriques: conceptualisation et illustrations. Revue d'Intelligence Artificielle (Editorial). 5(1) Paris, France (1991) 9-67

17. Sallantin, J., Quinqueton J., Barboux C., Aubert J.-P.: Théories semi-empiriques: éléments de formalisation. Revue d'Intelligence Artificielle (Editorial). 5(1) Paris (1991) 69-92

18. Wielinga, B., Boose, J., Gaines, B., Screiber, G., Someren, M. van (Eds): Current trends on knowledge acquisition. Proceedings of the European Knowledge Acquisition Workshop (1990)

19. Wille, R.: Concept lattices and conceptual knowledge systems. Computers Mathematic Applications 23(6-9) (1992) 493-515

This article was processed using the LaTeX macro package with LLNCS style

On a Composite Formalism and Approach to Presenting the Knowledge Content of a Relational Database

M. M. Fonkam

Universidade Federal do Maranhão, CT, De. E. E., CEP: 65080-400, São Luis, MA, Brasil,
Tel./Fax: +55 98 221 3530, Email: mmfonkam@fapema.br

Abstract

In this paper we present a graphical technique that combines in one formalism both the *structural* and *semantic integrity constraints* of a relational database (RDB) to produce a conceptual model, and then shows in the same formalism the connection between the conceptual model and the underlying logical model of the database, as represented within the database system (DBS). The broad aim is to offer to the increasing numbers of inexperienced users of these relational database systems a tool which they can use to quickly examine the knowledge content of the database and understand how these database semantics are actually modelled within the system, thus facilitating the user's task of framing queries to the system using the database query language. We borrow ideas from both the extended entity relationship (EER) and the ENIAM models in creating a graphical conceptual model for a RDB that combines both its structural and semantic integrity constraints and then introduce new concepts in the diagram that show how various relationships in the model are realised internally within the database logical model.

Keywords

conceptual model , presentation model, database semantics.

1. Introduction

The increasing numbers of inexperienced database (DB) users and the increasing complexity of DB technology exerts the demand on any database system (DBS) to be able to explain to its users what a database (DB) in it represents; i.e. the knowledge content or semantics of its databases. This is particularly relevant in the face of distribution and the need for inter-operability with other disparate technologies. A flurry of ongoing research activity has focussed on how to capture as much of the real-world semantics of an application domain as possible in a database. This has resulted in a plethora of proposed database conceptual models of the semantic, object-oriented or even logic types. The *conceptual model* of a database is an acceptable approximation of the description of the application domain being modelled. Usually however, there is not a one-to-one correspondence between this conceptual model of the database and the logical model of the same database within the database system (DBS). Much semantics is usually lost in the process of mapping from the former to the latter or only implicitly handled in the latter. This is particularly the case with the predominant relational database systems since the relational model cannot capture most types of real-world application semantics. Thus, there is now an important need to clarify what an existing database represents. A *presentation model,* as we denote it, is needed to tie the conceptual and implementation models together thus, making it easier for the users to understand the semantics or knowledge content of the database or that part of it of interest to them. Such a *presentation model* is necessary because most of the intended semantics captured by the conceptual model are lost or only implicitly handled in an actual implementation.

With respect to the predominant relational systems, a review of previous attempts to address the problem of clarifying the semantics of their existing databases reveals two main weaknesses:

(1)   the lack of a composite approach for presenting the two main types of constraints in relational databases. That is, the structural and semantic integrity constraints, and

(2)   little or no attention paid as to how the final model is presented to the user in order to aid rapid understanding.

These constitute the two main objectives of this paper.

In the next section we review some works that have been done with the broad aim of eliciting and presenting to database end-users the intended semantics of a relational database. We then follow in sections 3 and 4 with brief overviews of the ER and ENIAM models respectively, which form the basis of our proposed composite presentation model discussed in section 5. In section 6 some implementation aspects are discussed and some important techniques are suggested for presenting the final model to the end-user. Section 7 concludes the paper explaining further aspects of the work still being carried out.

2.   Existing Attempts at this Problem

The past approaches to the broad goal of eliciting and presenting to database end-users the semantics of a database can be put in three main camps: *structural constraint presentation tools, semantic integrity presentation tools* and *tools for presenting both structural and semantic integrity constraints.*

The *structural constraint presentation tools,* as the name suggests, are aimed at revealing to database users the structure of the database, as would typically be captured in an entity-relationship (ER) diagram or a variant of it. Indeed most of the existing works that have adopted this approach [ELM85 , DAV87, JOH89, FON92a] have used a variant of the ER-model as the target model for expressing and presenting the semantics of the database to its users.

The *semantic integrity constraint presentation tools* on the other hand have been exclusively focussed on capturing the logic assertions of the database, typically of a view of the database specified in the user's query, and presenting these constraints in some easy to understand format; typically some natural language-like format. Much of the research works that have adopted this approach have been in the deductive database domains [IMI87] and have used logical inference as the technique to deducing the applicable constraints. The work of Motro [MOT89] revealed the applicability and usefulness of the same idea for presenting the semantic integrity constaints applicable to a view defined in the user's query.

Tools that have been proposed for handling both the structural constraints and the semantic integrity constraints of the database go a long way in attempting a solution to this problem, if only by their acknowledgement that both types of constraints contribute to the semantics of the database. However, these past works have either treated both types of constraints separately as in [FON92] or else are inappropriate for the predominant relational systems as in [CRE89].

3.   The Entity-Relationship (ER) Model

Chen's ER-model [CHE76] can be seen as an extension of the relational model with more semantics. The model has a very rich and simple diagrammatic appeal. Like the relational model it recognises the concepts of *entity* (object), *attribute* (property) and *relationship*, with additional facilities for the representation of a limited number of *constraints*. Entities with their properties are represented by *entity relations* while relationships between entity types are represented by *relationship relations*. Thus, we may have ER-relations for some DB as in Figure 3.1:

DEPT(DNO DNAME)
EMP(ENO ENAME SAL)
PROJECT(PNO PNAME PBUDGET)
MACHINE(MNO MNAME)
Entity Relations

EDN(DNO ENO)
EPM(ENO PNO MNO HOURS-WORKED)
Relationship Relations
Figure 3.1   Relations of a Company Database

All *one-to-many* and *many-to-many* relationships are represented the same way; the way that many-to-many relationships are typically represented in the relational model. This allows 1:n relationships such as EDN to evolve into m:n relationships. EPM represents a *relationship relation* amongst three entities; *employee, project* and *machine*. Generalisations are represented in variants of this model, such as the extended entity relationship (EER) model described in [ELM85], by using new concepts. In most graphical presentations of ER only maximum and minimum cardinalities of relationships are shown while the roles of the entities is generally suppressed although its importance was emphasised in Chen's original work. This importance is given added weight when we seek to elicit the intended semantics of a DB to users unfamiliar with it. We are assuming in this work the EER model described in [ELM85] with the relationship cardinalities shown enclosed in brackets in the role that each entity plays in the relationship. Figure 3.2 then represents the ER-model for the concepts in Figure 3.1.

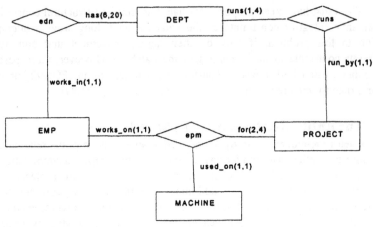

igure 3.2   ER-Model for a Company Database

4.   The ENIAM Model

ENIAM [CRE89] extends the NIAM model [HAB88] with existential graph constraints augmented with the inequality operators giving a powerful but simple knowledge representation scheme with a graphical appeal. By including existential graphs the full power of FOPL is used to express constraints with few symbols. In the ENIAM model depicted in Figure 4.1 (adopted from [CRE89]), people are scheduled to visit countries. Each country has certain vaccination (immunisation) requirements and each person is recorded as having certain vaccinations.

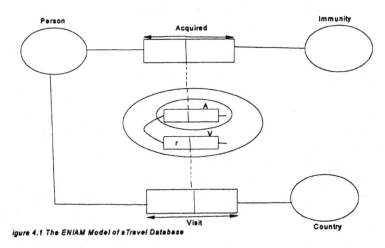

igure 4.1 The ENIAM Model of a Travel Database

The constraint that *anyone visiting a country must have a vaccination* is captured in this figure by taking a copy of the fact-types *Acquired* denoted by *A* and *Visit* denoted by *V* and using the ENIAM concepts of a *cut* and *line of identity*. The cut is a single line, with no crossings, drawn around a graph to indicate its negation while the line of identity, such as the one connecting A and V, is used to represent an individual. The constraint is essentially expressed in the double negative and can be equivalently read as: *no one who does not have an immunization may visit a country.* Figure 4.2 expresses the constraint that *no one needs a visa to visit their own country.*

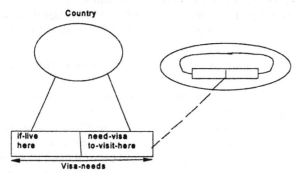

Figure 4.2 A Set Exclusion Constraint in ENIAM

5. A Composite Formalism for Presenting the Semantics of a Relational Database

5.1 Justification

As noted earlier, for the inexperienced or casual users of a DB, there is a special need for a quick approach to view the complete semantics of the database or that part of it of interest to them. Any such system must portray both the structural and the logical constraints that limit the data population abstracted in the database intension. The intension, and hence knowledge content, of a database is composed to a large extent of both these *structural specifications* and the *semantic integrity constraints (SICs)*. The latter constraints are logical restrictions on the values of the data and/or how the data may be related. It is noted in [DAT83] that as much as 80 percent of the intension of some commercial databases can be composed of these logical restrictions on data, representing for example company policy.

Most earlier attempts at eliciting and presenting the knowledge content of a relational database [see section 2] have either not dealt with both types of constraints or have treated them separately. The ENIAM model makes an important contribution in this regard but as a model for presenting the knowledge content of a relational database, two obvious difficulties emerge:

(1). there is more often than not far too many concepts to be included in the presentation;

(2). the model lacks a direct relationship (even a conceptual one) with the underlying logical model of the database. The users must understand this link to query the system using the database query language (DBQL).

Too many concepts in a diagram defeats the renown advantage of a diagram allowing users to see immediately the objects and relationships between them. This means the output from such a model may also overwhelm the user. This latter requirement becomes even more important if we consider that we are working with a fixed size user view device (the monitor) whereas the sizes of the intensional parts of different DBs would be different and perhaps large. Lack of a direct relationship with the underlying logical model leaves the user with the difficult task of working this out. The ER-model on the other hand bears a close relationship with the logical model of the predominant relational databases but cannot capture all the logical constraints of the database which often form a large part of the bulk of the database intension.

5.2   Main Goals of a Composite Approach to Presenting the Semantics of Relational Database

In summary then, a composite approach must capture in the same diagram both the structrural and logical constraints of the database or that part of it of interest to the user. It is important to express in the graphical model the relationship between itself and the underlying logical model of the database. The graphical model of the database must make explicit semantics of the database that are only captured implicitly in the database. The user needs to know how these semantics are modelled implicitly in the system before they can query the system using the query language.

5.3   The Composite Approach: ERESIC (ER Extended with Semantic Integrity Constraints)

The ER-model cannot capture most of the logical constraints of a database but it bears a close relationship with the relational model on which most commercial databases are based. ENIAM on the other hand can capture both types of constraints diagrammatical but lacks the other advantages of the ER-model [see 5.1]. We define our ERESIC model as an extension of the ER-relationship model to capture the semantic integrity constraints and its relationship with the underlying logical model of the DB. The *existential graph constraints* augmented with the *inequality operators* is the principle new feature that is introduced to the ER-model. We will use the example database intension of Figure 5.1 to demonstrate the mechanism of our ERESIC formalism.

In this diagram six relations describe the DB structure; *Emp* for *Employee, Dept* for *Department, Course, Student, Enrolmt* for *Enrolment* and *Activity*. Each relation has a number of attributes which will be explained as the need arises. The logical or semantic integrity constraints (SICs), are all expressed first in English then, where possible, as first-order predicate (FOPL) formulae. SIC6, SIC10 and SIC11 in the figure all require second-order logic for their expression as they involve quantification over predicates.

Figure 5.2 portrays the ER-model of this database intension. As can be seen some of the SICs (SIC6, SIC8, SIC9, SIC10 and SIC11) are captured by this traditional ER formalism but the others are not represented. In particular, single relation attribute logical constraints and those involving n-ary relations (for n>2) are not expressible in this traditional ER model. In Figure 5.2 the introduced relation, *Person* captures the generalisation of *Student* and *Employee* which is only implicitly shown in the logical model of Figure 5.1 through their common *ssn* (denoting social security number) *candidate keys*.

Our purpose then is to extend this presentation to capture the remaining types of logical constraints adopting the technique of the ENIAM model. We introduce the notion of *named-parts* to the *line of identity* concept of ENIAM in order to capture the attributes of an entity and extend the notion of *fact-types* to <u>range</u> over <u>both</u> *entities* and *relations*. The corresponding images of entities and relationships are used to capture logical constraints. A relationship image captures constraints between entities whilst an entity image captures constraints on the named parts of an entity. To enable expression of the generic n-ary relationship logical constraints we restrict the direction of entry of the line of identity into the image of the relationship to correspond with the entry point of the line connecting the entity to the relationship.

Thus, constraint SIC1 between entities Dept and Emp is shown in the portion in Figure 5.3. Figure 5.4 represents SIC2 (SIC3, SIC4 and SIC6 are similarly expressed) while Figure 5.5 represents SIC5.

6. On Presenting the Final Graphical Model to the End-User: Important Aspects of an Implementation

To show the relationship between the ERESIC model and the logical model we adopt the techniques proposed in our earlier work [FON93]. This involves introducing a few more concepts in the diagram that show how certain relationships are modelled at the logical level. For example, one-to-many relationships are usually represented at the logical level by using foreign keys while new relations are used for many-to-many relationships. An FK appearing in the relationship symbol means it is represented at the logical level as a foreign key.

As noted before, over complication of a diagram defeats the simplicity and the ease-of-understanding that a diagram offers. So it becomes imperative to find ways of reducing the number of concepts in the output whilst maintaining as far as possible the semantics of the model. We assume here firstly, that full graphics functions (pixel-level) are provided by the implementation tool rather than graphics based on the character set. Even with such full graphics capabilities it cannot be assumed that the full image would fit the user view device nor that it would be easy for the user to understand the graph, so there is both the need to provide for *scrolling* in order to see hidden parts of the figure and the need to reduce the number of concepts in the figure without losing important semantic links.

> Emp(emp#, ssn, qual, working_wk, status, salary, dept)
> Dept(dept#, location, budget, head)
> Course(cou#, name,size, hour, room)
> Student(stu#, ssn, sname, address, age, status)
> Enrolmt(stu#, cou#, date, mark)
> Activity(dept#, cou#).

Figure 5.1 (a) Structure of a University Database

SIC1: No Employee of a department may earn more than the head of that
department

$\forall(r,s,t,t1,u1,.....,z1)\ \exists(u2,w2,......,z2)\ \{Emp(t1, ..., z1) \wedge Dept(z1, r, s, t)\}$
$\Rightarrow \{Emp(t, u2, ..., z2) \wedge (y1 < y2)\}$

SIC2: All Visiting lecturers earn at least $16.000 and hold a Ph.D.

$\forall (t, ..., z)\ \{Emp(t, u, ..., z) \wedge (x = visiting)\} \Rightarrow \{(y \geq 16.000) \wedge (v = Ph.D.)\}$

SIC3: No employee may work more than 40 hours a week

$\forall(t, u, ..., z)\ Emp(t, u, ..., y, z) \Rightarrow (w \leq 40)$

SIC4: Part-timers work less than 20 hours a week

$\forall(t, u,......,z)\ \{Emp(t, u, ..., y, z) \wedge (x = part\text{-}timer)\} \Rightarrow (w < 20)$

SIC5: No two courses may be run at the same time in the same room

$\forall(v1,.....,z1,v2,....,z2)\{Course(v1,.....,z1) \wedge course(v2, ..., z2)\}$
$\Rightarrow \{(y1 \neq y2) \wedge (z1 \neq z2)\}$

SIC6: Every student must enrol for at least four courses and at most six.

SIC7: All student employees are part-timers and post-graduates.

$\forall(t1,...., z1,s,w2,....,z2)\ \{Emp(t1, ..., z1) \wedge student(s,u1,w2, ..., z2)\}$
$\Rightarrow \{(x1 = part\text{-}timer) \wedge (z2 = PG)\}$

SIC8: Every course is run by exactly one department

$\forall(u, v1, ..., z1)\ \exists(w2 ... z2)\{course(v1, ..., z1) \wedge Activity(u, v1)\}$
$\Rightarrow dept(w2, ..., z2) \wedge (u = w2)$

SIC9: No employee works in more than one department

$\forall(s, t, u,......, z)\ \{Emp(t, u, ..., z) \wedge Emp(t, u, ..., y, s)\} \Rightarrow (z = s)$

SIC10: Every course must take between 6 and 20 student.

SIC11: No department may run more than 6 courses

(b) The Semantic Integrity Constraints in English and FOPL Forms

Figure 5.1 The Intension of a University Database

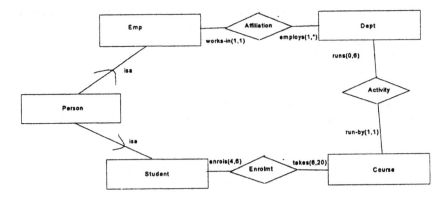

Figure 5.2 An ER-Diagram for the University Database

282

A good implementation of the graphical model should thus be based on a programming tool within a *Windows-type operating system* environment that could automatically handle scrolling in both the horizontal and vertical directions to reveal hidden parts of a figure. We then propose the provision of *user-controllable abstraction* and *elaboration* as important features to include in the implementation to facilitate user understanding.

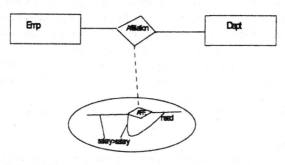

Figure 5.3 Graph of SIC1

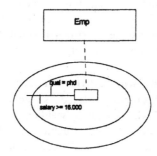

Figure 5.4 Graph of SIC2

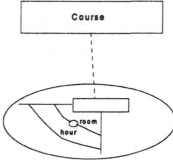

Figure 5.5 Graph of SIC5

6.1   Abstraction

Abstraction is the technique of suppressing (sometimes unnecessary) details, and focussing on concepts at a higher level. For example the process of generalisation abstracts from subtype objects to supertypes while that of aggregation abstracts from parts to the whole. Abstraction has a conceptual appeal and helps the user, essentially to *"see the wood from the trees"*, and thus can also enhance understanding. Suppression of the basic type definitions (domains) of attributes is a common abstraction practice of ER-model users. Even the attributes themselves are often suppressed in ER-diagrams showing only the entities and their relationships (aggregation). Subtype entities can also be suppressed in favour of the supertypes. Perhaps the semantic integrity constraints (SICs) are aspects of the figure requiring the greatest trimming down. Intuitively, the single relation SICs would be suppressed in favour of the relationship SICs while single attribute constraints would be suppressed before those involving more than one attribute of an entity.

6.2   Elaboration

Another important feature worth incorporating in the implementation is the ability of expansion, meaning that the user should be able to select certain objects (which are most likely abstractions) and then be able to see more details of these particular objects. This can be used hand in hand with abstraction, Some type of elaboration hierarchy can be constructed which the user can *"walk through"* to see lower level details of chosen concepts.

7.   Conclusions and Future Directions for Research

We have in this paper presented a suitable presentation model that derives from both the ER and ENIAM models yielding a convenient means of eliciting and presenting graphically both the structural and logical constraints of a relational database to its end-users. This is a difficult but increasingly important problem within the database community due not only to the widespread proliferation and complexity of the technology but also to the increasing numbers of inexperienced or casual users of it that need to be supported. The ERESIC model proposed bears a close relationship with the underlying logical model and can capture graphically both types of constraints in a relational database. In this regard, ERESIC is a more powerful technique for meeting the goals of this paper than either ENIAM or a version of the ER-model.

In our discussion on aspects of an implementation we proposed user-controlled abstraction as a technique of reducing the number of concepts in the output graph and elaboration as a way of seeing more details of chosen concepts in the graph.

Implementation of an ERESIC graphical display system is currently underway and is adopting as a basis the work in [FON93] which describes an algorithm for mapping from the logical model to a variant of the ER model. It is envisaged that more approaches to user-controllable abstraction would be discovered and included in the implementation.

References

[BRO84]   M.L. Brodie et al, *"On Conceptual Modelling: Perspectives from Artificial Intelligence, Databases and Programming Languages"*, Springer-Verlag, - 1984.

[CHE76]   *"The Entity Relationship Model -- Towards a Unified View of Data"*, ACM TODS Vol. 1, NO. 1, pp 9-36, - March, 1976.

[CRE89]   Peter Creasy, *"ENIAM: A More Complete Conceptual Schema Language"*, Procs. of the 15th Int. Conf. on Very Large Databases (VLDB) - Amsterdam, 1989.

[DAT83]   C.J. Date, *"An Introduction to Database Systems Volume II"*, Adison-Wesley, Reading, Mass. - August, 1983.

[DAV87]   K.A. Davis & A.R. Arora, *"Coverting a Relational DB Model into an Entity-Relationship Model"*, - Procs. 6th Int. Conf. on Entity Relationship Analysis - 1987.

[ELM85]   R. Elmasri et al, *"The category Concept: An Extension to the Entity-Relationship Model"*, in Data and Knowledge Engineering, Vol. 1, NO. 1, June, 1985.

[FON92a]   M.M. Fonkam & W.A. Gray, *"An Approach to Eliciting the Semantics of Relational Databases"*, in Procs. of the 3rd Int. Conf. on Advance Info. Systems Eng. (CAiSE), - 1992.

[FON92b]   M.M. Fonkam & W.A. Gray, *"Using Integrity Constraints for Query Modification and Intensional Answer Generation in a Multidatabase System"*, - Procs. of the 10th British National Conference on Databases - Aberdeen, -1992.

[FON93]   M.M. Fonkam, *"Knowledge Location in Relational Multidatabases"*, Ph.D. thesis submitted to the University of Wales, College of Cardiff, April, 1993.

[HAB88]   Henri Habias, *"Le Modéle Relationnel Binaire, Mathode I.A."*, Eyrolles - Paris, 1988.

[IMI87]   L. Imiellinski, *"Intelligent Query Answering in Rule Based Systems"*, Journal of Logic Programming, 4(3): 229-258 - Sept., 1987.

[JOH89]   P. Johannesson & K. Kalman, *"A Method for Translating Relational Schemas into Conceptual Schemas"*, 8th Int. Conf. on Entity-Relationship Approach, - 1989.

[KEN79]   W. Kent, *"Limitations of Record-Based Information Models"*, ACM TODs,   - 1979.

[MOT89]   A. Mitro, *"Using Integrity Constraints to Provide Intensional Answers to Relational Queries"*, Procs. of the 15th Int. Conf. on VLDBs, Amsterdam, - 1989.

Acknowledgements

I would like to thank *Foundação Soussandrade* and *Fapema* for their continuous assistance in my research activities.

Method for Knowledge Acquisition from Multiple Experts

Sofiane Labidi[1,2] and Mohamed Mohsen Gammoudi[2,3]

(1) INRIA Sophia Antipolis, ACACIA Project, BP. 93, 06902 Sophia Antipolis Cedex, France. Phone: (+33) 93.65.76.45, Fax: (+33) 93.65.77.83, email: labidi@samy.inria.fr

(2) Universidade Federal do Maranhão. Grupo da Ciência da Computação, 65080-040 São Luis-MA, Brasil. Phone: (+55) 98.235.31.71, Fax: (+55) 98.232.18.26, email: gammoudi@fapema.br

(3) Université de Tunis II, Faculté des Sciences de Tunis, Campus universitaire, Belvédère, Tunisie.

Abstract: In this paper, we present a method for knowledge acquisition from several experts. This method is based on a set of generic models which serve as a template to the knowledge engineer when acquiring knowledge from multiple experts. Experts are described as a society of interacting cognitive agents by instantiating the models. Our work can be viewed as an extension of KADS (Knowledge-based system Analysis and Design Structured methodology) [Schreiber &al. 94] to the multi-expertise.

1 Introduction

Knowledge acquisition is now seen as a modelling activity. Research in this domain aims at defining and developing techniques, tools and methods in order to help the knowledge engineer to perform this activity when developing a Knowledge Based System (KBS). Generally, works in this area deal with knowledge elicited from a single source of expertise (usually one human expert). At present, many projects in Artificial Intelligence (AI) need the use of several experts in the knowledge acquisition stage: experts can have the same speciality and use different problem solving methods, or cooperate to solve a common problem (each expert focus on a more specific sub-problem). However, conventional knowledge acquisition methods and techniques are inappropriate to manage the multi-expertise [Liou 90]. If knowledge acquisition is seen as the *bottleneck* of the life cycle of a KBS, the knowledge acquisition from several experts is described as a *log jam* [McGraw &al. 87].

There is an increasing interest in the problem of knowledge acquisition from multiple experts [Mittal &al. 85]. In fact, main research projects in this domain focus on the elicitation aspects [McGraw &al. 88] (study of the group dynamics [Shaw 76], etc.). Unfortunately, only a few projects deal with knowledge engineering of several experts [Murray &al. 90] [Dieng &al. 94] [Gaines &al. 89] and the methodological aspects [McGraw &al. 87] [Wolf 89] [Jagannathan &al. 85].

Few methods are proposed for knowledge acquisition from multiple experts. For example, MEKAM (Multiple Experts Knowledge Acquisition Methodology) [McGraw &al. 87] developed and used in AI laboratory of Texas Instrument in USA. This method is composed of six steps: (1) deciding of the use of several experts,

(2) defining the manner of work of the knowledge engineer with experts, (3) defining the group of experts, (4) preparing the expert group for knowledge elicitation sessions, (5) using knowledge elicitation techniques from multiple experts and (6) debriefing session. This method is very related to knowledge acquisition step when developing a KBS but it does not handle the problem of multi-expertise modelling. In [Jagannathan &al. 85], the MEDKAT (Multiple Expert Delphi-based Knowledge Acquisition Tool) method which is supported by a tool, is proposed. MEDKAT is based on the DELPHI technique [Linstone &al. 75] which is specific to knowledge acquisition from multiple expert. This method propose the integration of the knowledge of different experts to obtain the domain model.

Methods developed for knowledge acquisition from multiple experts, such as those presented above, present limitations particularly in modelling. In this paper, we propose a set of models which will be used for the definition of our method for knowledge acquisition from multiple experts. We will define an agent model which will be instantiate by the knowledge engineer to create a set of agents which are the base of the experts modelling in our approach. Thereby, we represent the experts by a set of agents. In order to describe the interaction in the group, we defined three other models: the cooperation model, the task model and the communication model. The implementation of these models constitutes the kernel of our knowledge acquisition tool which support our method. This implementation is in progress.

In the following, we first present our models (the agent model, the cooperation model, the task model and the communication model). Then, we show how we use these models to define our method for knowledge acquisition from multiple experts. We conclude by giving some results and perspectives of our work.

2 Agent Model

The definition of our agent model stems from the work on Distributed Artificial Intelligence (DAI) and multi-agent systems [Bond &al. 88] [Demazeau &al. 90] [Labidi &al. 93]. Still, our model is rather oriented for knowledge acquisition (expert modelling at a conceptual level) than towards development of multi-agent systems.

In order to define the agent model, we make a distinction between multiple viewpoints for representing experts. We see an agent as an *organizational, communicational, cooperative, specialist* and *rational entity*. This is with respect to the definitions given in the DAI literature [Ferber &al. 88], etc. The distinction between these viewpoints allow us to clarify and reduce the complexity of the model by focusing on certain aspects. In addition, an agent has some intrinsic characteristics such as a *name*, a *type* and a set of *status*.

2.1 Intrinsic characteristics of agent

Name

An agent has a *name* which serves to its identification, for example in a communication). All agents created would be assigned a name.

Type

Agents in our approach enable the knowledge engineer to model a group of experts. The obtained conceptual model is an input for developing the design model (in the sense of KADS) of the KBS. Users of the system can participate in the cooperative problem solving activity and then they may be modelled in the same way as agents. Moreover, experts can be assisted by other existing systems during problem solving. These particular systems may also be modelled as other kinds of agents. Therefore, we distinguish three types of agents: the *expert agent* which models the experts, the *user agent* which models the users and the *system agent* which models some existing systems. In this case, we join here the notion of compound system (heterogenous system) [AAAI 91].

Status

In a society of experts, each has a position in the group. The term position is used in social psychology to designate the power and the site of an individual in a group. Generally, each time an individual acts, he does it mostly from one position in the group. Thus, we use the term of status [Linton 77] to denote all social positions of an agent in the group. We distinguish two kinds of status: the *present* status which means the status occupied by the agent at a given time and the *latent* status which expresses all other status that an individual temporary occupies in the group. We characterize an agent by a set of status represents manages its authority in the organization (leader, managed, etc.).

2.2 Organizational structure of the agent

In real life, many experts can be grouped to perform a task which needs cooperation. This group of experts can be represented by a compound agent. A compound agent is obtained by aggregation of agents called sub-agents. Sub-agents that constitute a compound agent may be simple or compound. A compound agent is described by its *sub-agents*. A sub-agent has a father called the *super-agent* and which is unique. The particular super-agent which is the root of the tree is composed by all the agents of the tree and is called the *society agent*. It is super-agent of itself.

Social organization types

The compound agents adopt dynamically a kind of social organization according the kind of the problem to solve. According the research work on the group dynamics [Shaw 76] [Mintzberg 86] many kinds of social organization are possible: the community, the simple hierarchy, the uniform hierarchy, the multi-divisional hierarchy and the collective organization. We think that two distinctions can summarize all these social organization types: the *community* and the *hierarchy*.

The social organization in our model is dynamic. We describe the dynamics by a set of relations (cf. figure 1).

> **r-grouping** (*agt1, agt2, ... agtn, compound-agent, context*)
> **r-decomposition** (*compound-agent, context*)
> **r-reorganization** (*compound-agent, new-organization, representation, context*)

Fig.1: Dynamic relations

According to the context, which is in general the task to perform, the knowledge engineer describes the evolution of structure and the social organization of the agents using these relations. This is the result of his observation of the problem solving by the set of experts.

Inter-agent relations

A set of inter-agent relations achieves the description of the agent organization such as the *influence* relations and the *coordination* relations (called the *control* relations). Some other classes of relations expressing interaction relations between agents are defined, but are out of the scope of this paper.

2.3 Speciality of the agent

The description of an agent as a specialist entity is one of the most important of its characteristics. This outlines the ability of the agent which is described by the set of resources he has. These resources are the tools which are necessary for its reasoning and actions on its environment. We focus on the cognitive resources which represent the reasoning ability (the expertise knowledge or competencies). To model this kind of knowledge, we can use for example the commonKADS expertise model [Schreiber &al. 94] or another model from another approach. A compound agent is described by the set of the expertise models related to each sub-agent.

2.4 Rational characteristics of the agent

A cognitive agent is an intelligent agent which constitutes a rational and intentional entity (in the sense of Newell [Newell 81]) which has some believes and a control knowledge to manage its functioning.

2.4.1 Believes

The believes of an agent are constituted by a set of models of acquaintances. Acquaintances designate the other agents with which an agent can interact. The models of acquaintances of an agent represent its vision of these agents.

The *vision* notion indicates for an agent the accessible slots of its acquaintances. This is allows us to model the concept of *collaborators* in a group of experts. The models of acquaintances are updated according to the agent perceptions and interactions with other.

2.4.2 Control Knowledge of the agent

This includes goals and intentions, roles, planes and some strategic knowledge. This knowledge governs the involvement degree of the agent in the group life and it may be local or global (i.e. individual or shared by the set of agents).

Goals/Intentions

When participating to collective problem solving, an agent tries to reach some goals. Intentional agents are agents which are guided by goals. The knowledge engineer, when analyzing the cooperative activity of the experts, should detect their goals and their other characteristics for describing agents modelling experts.

Roles

During the running of the application, an agent can take the responsibility to perform a task if it is able to do it. In this case, we say that it plays a role in the group. The notion of role is a very important in our model. In fact, defining role of agents is one of the steps of our method for knowledge acquisition from multiple experts which is based on the identification of roles played by the experts when resolving the problem. We describe the agent roles by the set of tasks which they are able to perform. These tasks cannot belong to the same expertise model. Then, we represent a role by a set of pairs (task, expertise model of the task).

Plans

A plan is defined by the succession of actions needed to reach a goal. Plans deals with tasks performing. Note that one goal can be reached in different manners.

Strategic knowledge

The strategic knowledge of an agent is described by the *decision making* knowledge enabling the agent to select goals and plans for reaching its goals (heuristics, evaluation functions, etc.), and some *constraints* which express its limits to perform tasks which are allowed for him.

In order to solve a problem, agents must be able to interact, i.e. to cooperate and communicate within a group. The agent model presented here is static and don't enable us to model the interaction aspects. In the following, we present models to describe cooperation and communication between agents.

3 Cooperation model

The modelling of the cooperation is very important for an agent society modelling. However, there is no yet a clear theory for supporting the modelling of cooperation between agents. Different approaches have been defined for cooperation modelling. In our approach, we describe the cooperation by these three aspects:

1. the allocation of tasks to agents;
2. for each task, we describe the cooperative behavior adopted by agents to perform it;
3. delegation constrained.

The description of cooperative behavior is the main aspect for describing cooperation in our model. These are the behaviors we have defined:

Competition: it indicates that the same task is allocated to agents group (a compound agent). Each agent tries to perform this task in the place and before the others.

Coaction: same as in competition, except that in coaction there is no conflict and concurrence on the resources, etc.

Assistance: the task is allowed to one agent which is assisted when needed by others.

Dependence: the agents perform different tasks which are complementary.

Cohabitation: the agents perform independent tasks. This annotates the absence of a specific behavior.

An agent who cannot perform a task, delegates it to another agent. For this, it has to communicate with them. The delegation possibility constitutes a cooperative characteristic for agents which can be very important for a given application. Several modes of delegation are possible, e.g.: the *command* mode, where an executable agent is designed, or the *call for offer* mode, where agents which are interested in sending their demands for the agent who is in charge to delegate to make its choice. The possibility of delegation is described by the *constraints* characteristic in the agent model.

The description of the allocation and cooperative behavior adopted by agents to perform tasks is realized by the task model. It can also be described at the agent level by the class of relation *r-cooperation-mode* (*compound-agent, Behavior, Task*).

4 Task modelling

In CommonKADS (for example), a task is specified by some components such as: name, goal, input, output and sub-tasks, etc. We call the intrinsic characteristics. In order to take into account multi-expertise and to complete the description of cooperation we extend the task model by new components: the cognitive characteristics and the cooperative characteristics. The cognitive characteristics specify explicitly the expertise model in which the body of the task is described. Here is a description of the cooperative characteristics:

Task range: it indicates if the task is *local* (the task is allocated to only one agent) or *global* (several agents are interested in the task performance). Note that only the global (or collective) tasks need the specification of the cooperative behavior.

Allocation: this slot specifies the agent(s) to which the task are assigned.

Behavior: if the task is global, this slot specifies the cooperative behavior adopted by the agents performing the task (cf. the slot *allocation*).

5 Communication model

To interact, agents should be able to communicate. The communication is an important support for the interaction between agents in the group life. We describe the communication as a *transaction* between two agents: The *sender*, who initializes the communication and the *receiver* (one or several agents). A transaction is described by a *message* which has a goal which generally denoting an intention. Using the *speech acts* theory [Searle 79], this intention can be explicitly expressed by the *type* of an *illocutoire* act. We distinguish the following five acts: the *request, information, suggestion, expression* and *declaration*. Of course, the knowledge engineer can refine this classes depending on the studied application. The message is the propositional content of the transaction. It is expressed using a common language which is defined by the knowledge engineer. A transaction may be selective and needs some *criteria* for selecting the receivers (selection by name, by speciality, etc.) or a diffusion. It has necessary some *preconditions* for their release. All the transactions exchanged within the group may be governed by some *protocols*.

Then we represent a communication by the class of relation **r-intervention** (*sender, receivers, preconditions, type, message*). The knowledge engineer should describe all the possible transactions by instantiating the communication model.

6 Method for knowledge acquisition from multiple experts

As we mentioned earlier, we model the experts by a society of interacting cognitive agents. We have defined for it an agent model, a cooperation model and a communication model. The method which we propose is based on the definition of these models. Such models are useful for the knowledge engineer during the steps of knowledge acquisition. The method consists of the following seven steps.

1. Identification of roles and tasks for the definition of the global task model

The knowledge engineer, analyzing the activity of the experts resolving the problem, tries to define the task hierarchy (the *global task model*). The task model constitutes an abstract description of this activity. An expert can play different roles according to the set of tasks he is able to perform.

2. Identification of the adequate agents

Agent identification is a difficult issue. A simple solution is to associate agents to the experts. This approach can be compared to a «geographic distribution» of the knowledge and seems simple to apply. However, an expert can play several roles in the group and can have several functionalities. Thus, he could be described by a set of agents. This approach is compared to the «functional distribution». The knowledge engineer can alternate functional distribution and geographic distribution.

Artificial agents which represent experts will be identified and built progressively. Thus, an agent could partially or completely represent an expert. In another way, an expert could be represented by a compound agent where there are sub-agents which are common to all experts and one sub-agent representing only its specificities.

3. Instanciation of agent model (creation of the relevant agents)

Once agents have been identified, the knowledge engineer should create them by instantiating the agent model and by giving them their characteristics (filling the slots) according the model.

This is done during the whole process of knowledge acquisition by eliciting relevant knowledge from the corresponding human experts: information on their organization, information on their expertise, etc.

4. Expertise modelling

Expertise modelling is based on the CommonKADS expertise model. This implies the organization of the knowledge into three levels: the domain level, the inference level and the task level. The body of the tasks from the global task model will be described at this level [Schreiber &al. 94].

5. Cooperation modelling

The knowledge engineer instantiates the cooperation model by describing the task assignments, the cooperative behavior adopted by the agents when performing global tasks and the delegation aptitudes of agents.

6. Communication modelling

The knowledge engineer should identify all the possible transactions exchanged between experts for the problem resolution. A transaction is an instance of the communication model. The knowledge engineer should try to define communication protocols if they exist and try to define the common language of communication between the agents.

7. Refinement of agent modelling

The knowledge engineer may have to compare the acquired knowledge from several experts (expertise knowledge) for detecting their common parts and their incompatibility and to refine the model. The knowledge engineer can define a common expertise model shared by some experts and some specific sub-models or try to generate a unique consensual expertise model. For that the definition of some techniques of knowledge engineering are needed. These techniques depends on the used representation formalism. The comparison between expertise models expressed in CommonKADS, for example, requires a comparison between the three levels (*domain, inference* and *task*) that constitute the expertise model. In the domain level, knowledge is represented by graphs and production rules. In previous works we have proposed a method for comparing and generating consensus between conflicted knowledge using these formalisms [Gammoudi &al. 94] [Dieng &al. 94].

Note that there is no strict order between steps defined in the method, and the whole process needs some feedback between all the steps. The identification of agents is the result of the study of the organization where the agent acts.

7 Conclusion

We have presented in this paper a method for knowledge acquisition from multiple experts. The originality of our work is expressed by the use of techniques from DAI and multi-agent systems, for knowledge acquisition from multiple experts. The adoption of the agent notion is new in knowledge acquisition. However we denote its use by the ESPRIT Project KADS in its second part (KADS II) [Schreiber &al. 94] for representing the user and the system as two different interacting agents [Wærn &al. 93], but it is not used for the multi-expertise. Our work could then be seen as an extension of the CommonKADS methodology to the multi-expertise.

We are now studying the cohesion between these models. We also study their operationalization aspects and the way that the *conceptual model* is used when implementing an artifact, e.g. how the different cooperative behaviors that we have defined in the cooperation model will be implemented. Note that the artifact will constitute an implementation of the identified agents during the knowledge acquisition step and the cooperation process between agents. Then the artifact could be based on a multi-agent architecture.

A strong attention was also given to the definition of the common language in the communication model. Our tool assists the knowledge engineer in the instantiation of these models and the description of the different instances. The tool should give help to the knowledge engineer when instantiating models.

At present, we apply our method to the design of a system of help for analyzing road accidents in the objective of prevention. The types of experts which are involved in the case of a road accident are a psychologist, two vehicle engineers and two infrastructure engineers.

8 Acknowledgments

We are grateful to the FAPEMA, CNPQ and INRIA for their financial support. We are also grateful to M. Fankam and Philippe Martin for their proof reading.

9 References

[AAAI 91] Proceedings of the AAAI Spring Symposium on *Design of Composite Systems*. Stanford, CA. March 1991.

[Bond &al. 88] A. Bond and L. Gasser Editors. *Readings in Distributed Artificial Intelligence*. Morgan Kaufmann. 1988.

[Bond 90] A. H. Bond. *Distributed Decision Making in Organisation*. IEEE Transactions on Systems, Man and Cybernetics Conference. November 1990.

[Demazeau &al. 90] Y. Demazeau and J.-P. Muller. *Decentralized Artificial Intelligence*. In Decentralized A.I., **1**. Editors Y. Demazeau and J.-P. Muller. North Holland Elseiver Science Publishers. pp 3-13. 1990.

[Dieng &al. 94] R. Dieng, O. Corby and S. Labidi. *Expertise conflicts in Knowledge Acquisition*. In Proceedings of the Banff workshop on knowledge acquisition (KAW'94). Banff, Canada. January 30-February 4, 1994.

[Ferber &al. 88] J. Ferber et M. Ghallab. *Problématiques des univers multi-agents intelligents*. Actes des journées nationales PRC-GRECO Intelligence Artificielle. pp. 295-320. Toulouse. Mars 1988.

[Gaines &al. 89] B. R. Gaines and M. L. G. Shaw. *Comparing the Conceptual Systems of Experts*. Proceedings of the 11th IJCAI (IJCAI'89). pp. 633-638. Detroit. 1989.

[Gammoudi &al. 94] M. Gammoudi and S. Labidi. *An automatic generation of consensual rules between several experts using the rectangular decomposition method of a binary relation*. Proceedings of the XI Brazilian Symposium on Artificial Intelligence (SBIA'94). Fortaleza. October 17-20, 1994.

[Jagannathan &al. 85] V. Jagannathan and A. S. Elmaghraby. *MEDKAT: Multiple Expert Delphi-Based Knowledge Acquisition Tool*. In Proceedings of the ACM NE Regional Conference, Boston, MA. pp. 103-110. October 1985.

[Labidi &al. 93] S. Labidi et W. Lejouad. *De l'intelligence artificielle distribuée aux systèmes multi-agents.* Rapport de recherche INRIA. N° 2004. Août 1993.

[Linton 77] R. Linton. *Le fondement culturel de la personnalité.* Paris, Dunod. 1977.

[Linstone &al. 75] H. A. Linstone and M. Turoff. *The Delphi Method: Techniques and Applications.* Addison-Wesley. 1975.

[Liou &al. 90] Y. I. Liou, E. S. Weber and J. F. Nunamaker. *A methodology for knowledge acquisition in a group decision support system environment.* Knowledge Acquisition. 2. june 1990.

[McGraw &al. 87] K. L. McGraw and M. R. Seale. *Multiple experts knowledge acquisition methodology: MEKAM.* In 3rd Australian Conference on Expert Systems. pp. 165-197. 1987.

[McGraw &al. 88] K. L. McGraw and M. R. Seale. *Knowledge elicitation with multiple experts: considerations and techniques.* Artificial Intelligence Review. (2):31-44. 1988.

[Mintzberg 86] G. H. Mintzberg. *Structure et dynamique des organisations.* Les édition d'organisation, Paris. Les éditions Agence d'ARC Inc. Montréal. 1986.

[Mittal &al. 85] S. Mittal and C. L. Dym. *Knowledge acquisition from multiple experts.* Artificial Intelligence Magazine. pp. 32-36. 1985.

[Murray &al. 90] K. S. Murray and B. W. Porter. *Developing a tool for knowledge integration: initial results.* International Journal of Man-Machine Studies. (33):373-383. 1990.

[Newell 81] A. Newell. *The Knowledge Level.* Artificial Intelligence. 18:87-127. 1981.

[Schreiber &al. 94] G. Schreiber, B. J. Wielinga, H. Akkermans, W. Van de Velde and R. de Hoog. *CommonKADS: a Comprehensive Methodology for KBS Development.* IEEE Expert. 6(9). December 1994.

[Searle 79] J. R. Searle. *Expressions and Meaning. Taxonomy of illocutionary Acts.* Chapter 1. Cambridge University Press. 1979.

[Shaw 76] M. E. Shaw. *Group Dynamics: the psychology of small group behavior.* (2nd edition) New York. McGraw-Hill Book Company. 1976.

[Wærn &al. 93] A. Wærn and S. Gala. *The Common KADS Agent Model.* Technical Report. University of Amsterdam. Deliverable Id. KADS-II/M4/TR/SICS/002/ V.1.1. May 21, 1993.

[Wolf 89] W. A. Wolf. *Knowledge acquisition from multiple experts.* Sigart Newsletter. (108):138-140. April 1989.

A Conceptual Model for a Knowledge Base Homogeneously Stored in a Database Environment

Emmanuel Passos[1]; Alberto Sade Jr.[23]; Cícero Garcez[1] and Asterio Tanaka[1]

[1] Instituto Militar de Engenharia, RJ, Brazil
[2] Laboratório Nacional de Computação Científica, RJ, Brazil
[3] Coordenação dos Programas de Pós Graduação em Engenharia, RJ, Brazil
e-mail: emmanuel@ime.eb.br

Abstract. This paper proposes a conceptual approach as a way for storing Knowledge Bases in a Database Environment. The evolution of the model happened with the use of Entity-Relationship (ER) diagrams, Venn diagrams, Object-Oriented (OO) models and State Transition diagrams. With that model we are working in the construction of a Knowledge Server homogeneously stored in a Database environment and speculate about the possibility of that database to be shared in an heterogeneous environment. This research is an integration effort between the areas of Software Engineering (SE), Artificial Intelligence (AI) and Databases (DB) at Instituto Militar de Engenharia (IME).

1 Previous Research

The theory developed here is an initial result of the work in three different areas of research and it evolved from a number of MSc dissertations [6], [9], [1] and the core dissertation [8] of the model. More recently the Ph.D. thesis [11] provided the highlights of the possibilities involved. There is current work in development (MSc dissertations) in both areas AI (Development Environment for Expert Systems with Knowledge Bases that Support Inheritance) and DB (Methodology for Generation of Active Components in Databases).

2 Knowledge Base Architectures

When studying Expert Database systems one can get from [5] a summary and a taxonomy that classifies these systems in the following way:

- Enhanced Expert System;
- Enhanced Database System;
- Interdependent Expert and Database System; and
- Knowledge Base Management System.

The Enhanced Expert System can be performed by an internal or external enhancement. The first one extends the programming language or the environment in which the expert system is written. This in effect gives the expert system its own internal DBMS. In the second one the inference engine of the expert system is provided with direct access to a general-purpose, external DBMS.

The Enhanced Database System can be performed by embedded deductive routines, and acts as one additional facility of the DBMS. Another option is the use of the system when the user and application program queries are directed through a deductive component before being processed by the DBMS. In this sense, the deductive component acts as an interface between the DBMS and the user or application programs. There is a third possibility called interaction in which the DBMS, rather than user or application programs, interacts with the deductive component.

The Interdependent Expert and Database System allows the expert system and the database to exist as independent systems that communicate down a common data channel. We have had an actual experience using Power Builder to make windows (client) and Sybase or Oracle as a Database (server) with this architecture. The inference engine is written in C and is compatible with the model we are presenting, but it is not completely homogeneous.

A Knowledge Base Management System (KBMS) is a target still not modeled nor implemented in its plenitude yet. Our goal is to make our model the starting point for an architecture of a full-fledged KBMS.

3   A Knowledge Base Concept

Knowledge is a broad subject. Our focus is to represent knowledge in terms of facts and rules. The first part of knowledge is fact. This is a clause that can be true or false. The second part of the knowledge is the rule. A rule is made of two parts: the premise(s) and the conclusion(s).

When facts and rules are combined, one can reach conclusions. When the set of the premises of a rule is true then the conclusions of that rule are true.

The process of combination of facts and rules is called inferencing. In an OO view, one can see a knowledge base like a class of knowledge where its static part is a set of facts and rules and its dynamic part is composed of two methods: forward chaining and backward chaining (and in our focus also a third method called "reorganize base").

If we choose a relational environment the methods can be implemented through a third generation language that supports recursion and embedded SQL call. With an OO environment the model will be directly represented and persisted. A knowledge base can receive messages. The usual message is a hypothesis that can be proved or rejected (or perhaps the knowledge base neither prove nor reject the hypothesis).

4   A Knowledge Base Model

Now we will represent the model in terms of the ER diagrams, Object Oriented model, a State Table and Venn Diagrams.

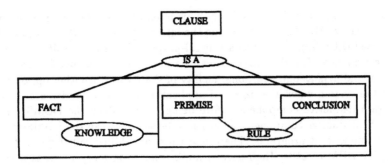

Fig. 1. An ER diagram that represents a knowledge base

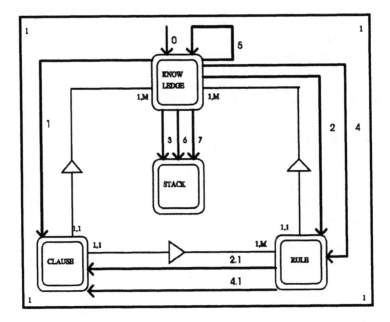

Fig. 2. An OO diagram that represents a knowledge base with backward chaining (knowledge base subject)

The development of this model evolved from an ER diagram [2] to a Venn diagram that represents the static body of our interpretation of the knowledge concept. In the later research we had used [7] and finally we used [3], [4].

The annotation of the message passing in the diagram will help the understanding of the following algorithm for the backward chaining resolution method.

```
BEGIN
Know.InfeBack(Hipo)
| repeat
| | if Clse.Comp(Hipo,1,0,0)  /* 1 */
| | |   then return 1
| | |   else I=0
| | |           while(Rule.Comp(Hipo,0,1,0))  /* 2 */
| | |           | I=I+1
| | |           | R[I]=#Rule
| | |           end-while
| | |           I=1
| | |           if R[I]
| | |           | then GoodRule=1
| | |           |    while(R[I] & GoodRule)
| | |           |    | Stck.Push(Hipo)  /* 3 */
| | |           |    | Rule.GetPrem(R[I],0,0,1,P[])  /* 4 */
| | |           |    | J=1
| | |           |    | while(P[J])
| | |           |    | | Hipo=Clse.Get(P[J])
------------------------result=Know.Infe(Hipo)  /* 5 */
    | |           |    | | if result=0 then P[J]=0
    | |           |    | | J=J+1
    | |           |    | end-while
    | |           |    | Stck.Pop(Hipo)  /* 6 */
    | |           |    | if result=1 then GoodRule=0
    | |           |    | I=I+1
    | |           |    end-while
    | |           | else return 0
    | |           end-if
    | end-if
    until Stck.Empt  /* 7 */
END
```

Fig. 3. A simple algorithm for backward chaining

From the static view of the ER diagram we evolved to a Venn diagram and an Object model. Then another kind of relationship became clear, a dynamic one, which reflects a possible active behavior. This lead to the enumeration of the possible states of a clause from its hypothesis state to its fact state.

From the assertion: "generalization is an OR relationship" [7], one can deduce that the set of the clauses is made by *hypothesis U facts U premises U conclusions*. But the point is that a clause can be simultaneously in two or even three of these states. There are eight possible states represented below:

CLAUSES STATE TABLE	
000	**Hypothesis** in its initial state. When the knowledge base receives a message this state must change or the inferencing cannot happen. There is no knowledge.
001	Exclusive **premise**. In this case this premise will never be fired, if the clause does not change its state.
010	Exclusive **conclusion**. In this case this conclusion will never be reached, if the clause does not change its state.
100	Exclusive **fact**. This is a truth. If this is an initial hypothesis, it is proved.
011	**Premise and conclusion**. It must change its state, or the clause can't be proved.
101	**Fact and premise**. The clause is proved. The knowledge base must be reorganized.
110	**Fact and conclusion**. The clause is proved. The knowledge base must be reorganized.
111	**Fact and premise and conclusion**. The clause is proved. The knowledge base must be reorganized.

Table 1

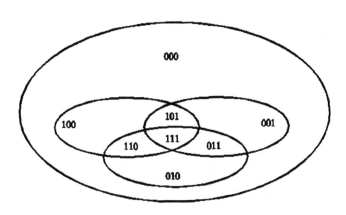

Fig. 4. A Venn diagram that represents a knowledge base

5 A Toy Example

This is an example from [10]. We use it to work with the conceptual model and the algorithm listed before. The rules are: 1) $F, B \rightarrow Z$; 2) $C, D \rightarrow F$; 3) $A \rightarrow D$. The facts are: A, B, C, E, G, H. The hypothesis is Z.

The initial state of the knowledge base:

FACT		PREMISE		CONCLUSION	
100	E,G,H	001		010	Z
101	A,B,C	011	D,F	011	D,F
110		101	A,B,C	110	
111		111		111	

Table 2

Z is not in the fact base. Z is a conclusion of rule 1. It is necessary to prove all premises of rule 1, to prove Z. Push (Z). Now the hypothesis is F (the first premise of 1). F is not in the fact base. F is a conclusion of rule 2. It is necessary to prove all premises of rule 2 to prove F. Push (F). Now the hypothesis is C (the first premise of 2). C is in the fact base. C is true. Now the hypothesis is D (the second premise of 2). D is not in the fact base. D is a conclusion of 3. It is necessary to prove all premises of rule 3, to prove D. Push (D). Now the hypothesis is A (the first premise of 3). A is in the fact base. A is true. Pop (D). D is true, changed its state:

FACT		PREMISE		CONCLUSION	
100	E,G,H	001		010	Z
101	A,B,C	011	F	011	F
110		101	A,B,C	110	
111	D	111	D	111	D

Table 3

Pop $(F) \cdot C$ and D are true. F changed its state:

FACT		PREMISE		CONCLUSION	
100	E,G,H	001		010	Z
101	A,B,C	011		011	
110		101	A,B,C	110	
111	D,F	111	D,F	111	D,F

Table 4

Now the hypothesis is B (the second premise of 1). B is in the fact base. B is true. Z changed its state. Pop (Z). Z is proved.

FACT		PREMISE		CONCLUSION	
100	E,G,H	001		010	
101	A,B,C	011		011	
110	Z	101	A,B,C	110	Z
111	D,F	111	D,F	111	D,F

Table 5

6 The Future: A Client-Server Perspective

Once the Knowledge Base is homogeneously stored our next challenge is to model a Client-Server version. In this case, another complexity issue must be clarified: the distribution of data happens in an organizational environment where there exist business units that can make local decision.

However, in general, these business units conform their decisions to the major policies of the organization. So there exists (or should exist) an organizational knowledge, a repository that we call a "Knowledge Server" that must be shared and (we hope) cannot contradict the local knowledge.

So if the central knowledge will be stored in the "Knowledge Server" and the local knowledge in the client place, we must design which parts of the software will run in each place, and the adequate interface.

7 Conclusions

This work is an interdisciplinary effort between three main research areas but each area follows a priority.

The AI contribution is in the development of environments for the knowledge use. The DB contribution is in the development of database engines that supports that use. The SE contribution is to create and follow all the software system life cycle determining the models that integrate OO, Client-Server architecture, Databases and Expert Systems.

There are two prototypes of this work. The first one is implemented using C++. The second one is implemented using DB2/2.

References

1. Amaral Filho, W. H. do: Object-Oriented Client-Server Architecture. MSc Dissertation, IME, 1993.
2. Chen, P.: The entity-relational model toward a unified view of data. ACM Transactions of Database Systems 1 (1976) 9–36.
3. Coad, P., Yourdon, E.: Object-Oriented Design. Yourdon Press, 1991.
4. Coad, P., Nicola, J.: Object-Oriented Programming. Yourdon Press, 1993.
5. Beynon-Davies, P.: Expert Database Systems, a Gentle Introduction. The MacGraw-Hill International Series in Software Engineering, 1991.
6. Lorenzoni, E.J.F.: Expert System Development Tool. MSc Dissertation, IME, 1987.
7. Rumbaugh, J., Blaha, M., Premerlani, W., Frederick, E., Lorensen, W.: Object-Oriented Modeling and Design. Prentice Hall Inc, 1991.
8. Sade Junior, A.S.: Intelligent Decision Support System Environment for Demographic and Statistic Applications. MSc Dissertation, IME, 1992.
9. Silva, A.T. da: Work Planning and Control Object-Oriented Environment. MSc Dissertation, IME, 1992.
10. Passos, E.L.: Artificial Intelligence and Expert Systems. LTC, 1989.
11. Tanaka, A.K. - On Conceptual Design of Active Databases. Ph.D. Thesis, Georgia Institute of Technology, 1992.

A Hierarchical Description of the Portuguese Verb

Paul McFetridge
Department of Linguistics
Simon Fraser University
Burnaby, British Columbia
Canada V5A 1S6
mcfet@cs.sfu.ca

Aline Villavicencio
Instituto de Informática
Universidade Federal do Rio Grande Sul
Porto Alegre, RS
Brazil
alinev@inf.ufrgs.br

Keywords: natural language understanding, nonmonotonic reasoning

Abstract

This paper presents an analysis of the Portuguese using DATR, a language designed for lexical representation by nonmonotonic inheritance hierarchies. The analysis shows that the verb has a consistent structure and that variations can be organized into subclasses that are themselves regular. The default inheritance rule of DATR permits and economical description of the structure of the verb while also retaining sufficient information that exceptions can be described in the appropriate points of the grammar.

1.0 Introduction

Increasingly, linguistic theories concentrate information in the lexicon. Head Driven Phrase Structure Grammar ([2],[3]) is an example of a theory that localizes information in the lexicon that was previously described in syntax. The increase of information and the need to structure this information has fostered research in the use of inheritance hierarchies to organize lexical information and represent classes that crosscut the lexicon.

This paper presents a grammar that relates grammatical descriptions of verbs to their orthographic representation. The primary goals are to explicitly represent facts about the structure and form of the Potuguese verb and express appropriate generalizations about the regularities found in the conjugation system of Portuguese and their exceptions. The grammar is written as a nonmonotonic inheritance hierarchy. The representation language is DATR designed by Evans and Gazdar for lexical representation.

A nonmonotonic inheritance network is an appropriate representation scheme for such a grammar for several reasons:

(1) It is *declarative*, generalizations of the language can be expressed directly;

(2) It permits subclassification so that verbs can be classed together according to their exceptional behaviour;

(3) Nonmonotonicity permits description of exceptional behaviour of a verb while retaining as defaults its regular participation in the conjugation system of the language.

1.1 Preliminaries

As a Romance language, Portuguese is characterized by a verbal structure that includes a thematic vowel that determines in large part how that verb is conjugated. The description presented here retains this feature by representing facts about inflection as either general facts about the Portuguese verb or facts about a particular thematic class or subclass. In general, a verb will inherit all information necessary for inflection through the node describing its thematic class. In some cases, a verb may inherit from more than one thematic class: for example, *estar* forms the imperfect *estava* as an a theme but the subjunctive *esteja* as an e or i theme. Only in the case of the truly irregular are facts about inflection represented as facts about an individual verb.

2.0 Hierarchy Construction

The syntax of DATR is patterned on that of PATR [4]. A node in a DATR hierarchy or theory consists of path/value pairs. A value is either stated explicitly or is inherited in one of several ways from other sources. These sources include another path in the same node, the same path in another node and a different path in another node.

A query to a DATR hierarchy consists of a node and a path. The hierarchy describing the Portuguese verb is constructed so that queries will have the following forms:

(4a)   <mood tense person number>
(b)   <nominal (infl)>
(c)   <imperative polarity>

For purposes of presentation, we focus on those of the form in (4a).

The value returned is determined by the rules of inference and conventions for matching the query path against those in the node. A partial example is the definition of *vender*.

Vender: $\diamondsuit$ == E_tema
            <raiz> == v e n d.

Figure 1

The statements define a node *Vender*[1] . The conventions for matching a query against the paths in a node select the longest path in the node that matches (left-to-right) that of the query. For example, any query path that begins with raiz will return *v e n d*.

This convention for matching a query against paths in a node is a consequence of the default rule of inference by which a path/value pair in a node implicitly represents the value for all possible extensions of that path not explicit in the node. For example, from the node in figure 1 it is possible to infer at least the following:

(5a)   Vender:<raiz ind> == v e n d
(b)   Vender:<raiz ind pres> == v e n d
(c)   Vender:<raiz ind pres pri sg> == v e n d

---

[1] A term beginning with an uppercase character is interpreted as the name of a node in the hierarchy.

(d)   Vender:<raiz sub> == v e n d

The default rule of inference provides for nonmonotonic inference which in turn provides a mechanism for description of regularities and subregularities. Consider the verb *perder* which inflects just as *vender*, except that it has the root *perc* instead of *perd* in the first person of the present indicative (and by extension all persons of the present subjunctive). These facts are expressed in figure 2.

Perder: <> == E_tema
            <raiz> == p e r d.
            <raiz ind pres pri sg> == p e r c.

Figure 2

A query to the node Perder that begins with raiz will always return *p e r d* unless the path is explicitly <raiz ind pres pri sg>. Because the longest path is selected over shorter paths, the query Perder: <raiz ind pres pri sg> will return *p e r c*. The analysis implicit in the nodes in figures 1 and 2 is that vender and perder are members of the same inflectional class, but that perder is slightly irregular.

A query to the nodes in figures 1 and 2 that does not begin with raiz will match the path <>. This is a consequence of the default rule of inference: <>, the null path, can be extended to any path. In the network including the nodes in figures 1 and 2, a query such as Vender:<ind pres pri sg> will result in the new query E_tema:<ind pres pri sg>. The new query is a consequence of 2 facts:

(6) E_tema on the right side of the path/value pair is an abbreviation for E_tema:<>;

(7) When the left-hand side of a statement is extended, the right-hand side of the statement is extended by the same subpath.

As a consequence on (6) and (7), the statement Vender:< >: == E_tema:<> implicitly describes the following theorems, among many others:

(8a) Vender:<tema ind pres> == E_tema:<tema ind pres>

(b) Vender:<vogal> == E_tema:<vogal>

(c) Vender:<pes sub pres tri pl> == E_tema:<pes sub pres tri pl>

Another consequence of the default rule of inference is that very general statements about the structure of the Portuguese verb can be made in nodes high in the hierarchy without reference to details about mood, tense or person and number. As illustration, a preliminary and partial definition of the Portuguese verb is given in figure 3.

Verb: < > == <tema> <af> <pes>
            <tema> == <raiz> <vogal>.

Figure 3

This node describes the Portuguese verb as consisting of a stem which itself consists of a root and thematic vowel, an affix that marks mood and tense, and a person/number marker. For example, the structure assigned to the imperfect subjunctive vendêssemos is [[vend + e] + sse + mos].

As a consequence of (7) above, implicit in the first statement of *Verb* are the following statements, among many others:

(9a)   <ind pres ter sg> == <tema ind pres ter sg> <af ind pres ter sg> <pes ind pres ter sg>

(b)   <ind pret ter pl> == <tema ind pret ter pl> <af ind pret ter pl> <pes ind pret ter pl>

By default, a path on the right side of a statement in a node refers to the value in the path/value pair of the same node. For example, Verb:<tema> == <raiz> <vogal> is an abbreviation for Verb:<tema> == Verb:<raiz> Verb:<vogal>. This is clearly not what we wanted since the root referred to by *<raiz>* is not that of *Verb* but that of the verb originally queried. DATR provides a rule of inference by which a query is interpreted in the global context instead of the context local to the node. According to this rule of inference, quoted paths are interpreted in the context of the node to which the original query was posed. With this in mind, the definition in figure 3 is revised.

Verb: < > == "<tema>" " <af>" "<pes>"
<tema> == "<raiz>" "<vogal>".

Figure 4

To illustrate the global interpretation of the path "<tema>", we consider how the relevant path of the query Vender:<ind pres ter sg> is evaluated. It is first necessary to create a node between *Verb* and *Vender*. This node describes just what is peculiar about verbs in the E_tema class, namely that the thematic vowel is *e*.

E_tema:< > = =Verb
<vogal> == + e

Figure 5

The path <ind pres ter sg> can only be the extension of the path <> in the Vender node (figure 1). Consequently, a new query E_tema:<ind pres ter sg> is posed. Again, this can only be the extension of <> and the query Verb:<ind pres ter sg> (figure 4) is posed. Since this is the extension of <>, the three paths on the right side are evaluated. Since each path is quoted, they are interpreted in the context of the original query and are extended with <ind pres ter sg>. In effect, 3 new queries are evaluated:

(10a) Vender:<tema ind pres ter sg>

(b) Vender:<af ind pres ter sg>

(c) Vender:<pes ind pres ter sg>

The first of these is an extension of <> at both the *Vender* and the *E_tema* nodes, but is an extension of <tema> in the *Verb* node. Since the paths on the right side of this statement are quoted, they are again interpreted in the context of the *Vender* node.

(11a) Vender:<raiz ind pres ter sg>

(b) Vender:<vogal ind pres ter sg>

The first of these is an extension of the path <raiz> in the *Vender* node and evaluates as *v e n d*. Note that if the query was Perder:<raiz ind pres ter sg> it would evaluate as *p e r d*. The second is an extension <vogal> in the *E_tema* node and returns + *e*. Thus the query in (10a) evaluates as *vend* + *e*.

In summary, the nonmonotonic character of the DATR hierarchy follows from the rule of inference by which paths implicitly represent all possible extensions of themselves. Fully specified paths take precedence over underspecified paths because they need not to be extended to match that of the query. A natural way to exploit this property is to use underspecified paths to express general properties of the language and highly specified paths to express exceptions to these general statements.

3.0 A Grammar of the Portuguese Verb

In this section, we present a fragment of the grammar of the Portuguese verb. We consider particularly the present, imperfect preterite, future and perfect preterite in the indicative and the present, imperfect preterite and future in the subjunctive. Singly and in combination, these grammatical categories illustrate several problems that are adequately solved in a DATR framework.

3.1 Structure

As described in the preceding sections, the structure of the Portuguese verb is [stem + af + pes]. We distinguish two stems: that formed from the root and theme vowel, and that formed from the infinitive. Examples of the latter are of course the personal infinitive (where person/number markers are suffixed to the infinitive), but additionally the future indicative and the future subjunctive. Thus, the structure of cantarás and cantares is [[cantar] + a + s] and [[cantar] + $\mathscr{F}$ + s], respectively. Since the infinitive is formed by suffixing the infinitival marker to the stem, the complete structure of these forms is [[[cant + a] + r] + a + s] and [[[cant + a] + r] + $\mathscr{F}$ + s]. These structural facts are described in the node *Verb*.

Verb: < > = = "<tema>" "<af>" "<pes>"
    <tema> = = "<raiz>" "<vogal>"
    <tema $modo fut> = = "<inf>"
    <inf> = = "<tema>" + r

Figure 6

DATR permits variables in the left-hand side of a path/value pair, and on the right-hand side if a variable of the same name appears on the left-hand side. Variables are represented as a term prefixed with "$". Thus, the third statement in the Verb node describes the stem of the future tense regardless of the mood as identical with the infinitive of the verb in question. The infinitive is built off the stem formed in the usual way (unless overridden by a lower node).

3.2 Affixation

As part of the definition of the verb, the regular tense/mood and person/number affixes are specified in the Verb node. Where there is a variation, it is often the case that the statistically frequent variant is taken as default and less frequent is specified as exceptional. For example, since the first person is unmarked in most tenses, the unmarked is taken as the default and the -*o* of the present indicative and *i* of the perfect indicative are exceptions.

Occasionally, there are better arguments for selecting a variant as default case. For example, the default imperfect indicative is taken to be *ia* as in *vendia* "he sold". This form is common to both *e* and *i* thematic classes. In the *a* thematic class, the imperfect indicative is marked with *va* as in *comprava* "he bought". On this analysis, the *verb* node contains the statement

(12) <ind impf> == + i a

and the node *A_tema* overrides this statement.

$$A\_tema: <> = = Verb$$
$$<vogal> = = + a$$
$$<ind\ impf> == + v\ a$$
$$<sub\ pres> = = + e$$

Figure 7

The alternative is to declare *va* the default. But in this case, the exceptional case must be stated in both the definitions of the *e* and *i* theme classes. In terms of a simplicity measurement, the original analysis is preferable. A similar argument holds for describing the regular subjunctive present marker as *a*, but *e* in *a* thematic verbs. The regular affixes are defined as:

(13a) <af ind> = =

(b) <af ind impf> = = + i a

(c) <af ind fut> = = + a

(d) <af sub pres> = = + a

(e) <af sub fut> = =

(f) <af sub impf > = = + s s e

Exceptional behaviour of affixes is identified in several parts of the grammar. Some exceptional cases such as the imperfect indicative are systematic and predicted by the conjugation class of the verb. Others are predicted in the combination of mood, tense, person and number. The case of the first singular marker in the perfect indicative is an example of this class. A final class are those defined by the verb itself. The second class is represented in the grammar by a node intermediate between the general definitions of structure and affixation in the *Verb* node and the nodes defining thematic classes. The definitions of the *A_tema* and *E_tema* should be considered amended so that they inherit directly from a node *Exceptions* rather than *Verb*.

Where *Verb* contains statements such as

(14a) <pes $modo $tempo pri sg> = =

(b) <pes $modo $tempo seg sg> = = + s

(c) <pes $modo $tempo ter sg> = =

(d) <pes $modo $tempo pri pl> = = + m o s

(e) <pes $modo $tempo seg pl> = = + i s

(f) <pes $modo $tempo ter pl> = = + m

The node Exceptions contains statements such as

(15a) <> = = Verb

(b) <pes ind pres pri sg> = = + o

(c) <pes ind pret pri sg> = = + i

(d) <pes ind pret seg sg> = = + s t e

(b) <pes ind pret ter sg> = = + u

These override those of Verb.

3.3 Thematic Classes and Subclasses

The node defining a thematic class describes the vowel that is added to form a stem and any exceptional formations that are common to the class. We have seen tense/mood markers specified in the description of the thematic class. The definition of the i thematic class includes the description of the thematic vowel in the second singular and the third person present indicative. Notice that the path <ind pres ter> can be extended to both <ind pres ter sg> and < ind pres ter pl>.

> I_tema: <>== Exceptions
> <vogal>= = +i
> <ind pres ter>= = +e
> <ind pres seg sg>= = +e
> **Figure 8**

Within a thematic class, there may be subclasses that generally behave as members of that class but have idiosyncratic behaviour. We consider one of the subclasses of the *i* themes. This class is exemplified by *dormir* and is characterized by a raised vowel in the first person present indicative: e.g. *durmo*. The description of this class uses a finite state transducer to raise the root vowel. A finite state transducer is emulated in DATR by considering path on the left-hand side of a path/value pair as the input tape, the right-hand side as the output tape. A transducer for raising the root vowel *o* is given in figure 9. The boundary symbol is "&". The second line will match any segment. The null path on the right-hand side is an abbreviation for Raise:<>. When <$seg> is extended to match the query, the subpath that is not matched is concatenated to Raise:<>. For example, if the path is <d o r m &>, then the new query is Raise:<o r m &>.

> Raise: <&> = =
> <$seg> = = $seg<>
> <o &> = = u
> <o $cons &> = = u $cons
> <o $cons $cons2 &> = = u $cons $cons2.
> **Figure 9**

Using this transducer, it is possible to define the subclass of *i* theme verbs that raise the vowel in the first person present indicative as in the figure 10. In this node, the first person stem is built up by creating a query consisting of the node Raise and a path consisting of the root and the boundary symbol.

> I_tema_raise: <> = = I tema
> <tema ind pres pri sg> = = Raise <"<raiz>" &>+ <vogal>.
> **Figure 10**

Other subclasses of *i* theme verbs that are treated similarly include those that lower the root vowel in the singular and the third person of the present indicative (e.g. subir), those that raise the root vowel in the singular forms and the third plural form of the present indicative (e.g. partir).

3.4 Paradigmatic Transfer

Occasionally, portions of a paradigm are built up from structure created elsewhere. We have described the future tense this way, basing it on the infinitive.

A particularly striking instance of this is the present subjunctive which with 7 exceptions is based on the first person present indicative. This is evident in forms from the *i* thematic class with irregular first person forms. For example, in the class exemplified by *dormir* and *servir* where the root vowel raises in the first person (*durmo* and *sirvo*) all forms of the present subjunctive have the raised vowel.

Indicative	Subjunctive	Indicative	Subjunctive
durmo	durma	sirvo	sirva
dormes	durmas	serves	sirvas
dorme	durma	serve	sirva

Table 1

The account for this is in the node *Verb* which contains the statement

(16) <tema sub pres> = = "<tema ind pres pri sg>"

This statement ensures that a query for the stem in the present subjunctive is replaced with a query for the first singular stem in the present indicative.

3.5 Phonology/Orthography

The structure of [[root + theme] + af + pes/num] predicts classes of exceptions that have not yet been discussed. There are instances where the thematic vowel is not present as in the first person present indicative: e.g. *vendo*, not **vendeo*. In other cases, the thematic vowel appears changed: e.g. *comprei*, not **comprai*. In addition, there are predictable changes to the orthography signalling the correct pronunciation of root final consonants (e.g. *chegar*, but first person perfect *cheguei*).

These are treated as phonological and orthographic operations rather than morphological. The actual phonological or orthographic spellout is transparent to morphological functions. It is a classical linguistic theorem that there is economy to describing variants phonologically rather than morphologically. For example, the thematic vowel *a* raises to *e* before *i* in the first singular perfect *comprei*. However, the vowel *a* from other sources raises to *e* before *i* as well: cf. first person singular imperfect *comprava*, but second person plural *compraveis*.

Interestingly, the network for converting the structure built up by the morphological functions to the orthographic form must itself be arranged hierarchically. This is evident when considering the raising rule discussed above and the rule responsible for deleting the thematic vowel when it occurs before any of *a*, *e*, *o*. The latter rule applies in the first person present indicative, deriving *vendo* from *vend + e + o* and the present subjunctive, deriving *venda* from *vend + e + a*. In the categories where the latter rule applies, the raising rule does not. The second person plural present indicative is *comprais* not **compreis*. The grammatical categories to which these two rules apply are mutually exclusive. The deletion rule applies in the present indicative and subjunctive; the raising rule does apply in these grammatical categories but in all others (though in some vacuously).

There are also rules that apply regardless of category. One is the rule that reduces two instances of *i* to one. The morphological structures of the second person plural in the present indicative *partis* and the first person singular in the perfect preterite indicative *parti* are [[part + i] + ∅ + is] and [[part + i] + ∅ + i] respectively. This indicates that the phonological/orthographic rules must be organized hierarchically as in figure 11.

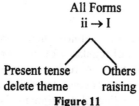

All Forms
ii → I

Present tense   Others
delete theme   raising

Figure 11

The hierarchy is implemented by prefixing the input tape with a name signifying the node in the hierarchy that contains the rule and a variable that records that will be queried next if the rule succeeds. An example of a small network is:

(17a)   <word $start &> ==
(b)   <word $start +> ==
(c)   <word $start $seg> == $seg <word $start>
(d)   <mono $start> == <word $start>
(e)   <mono $start a + o> == o
(f)   <raise $start> == <word $start>
(g)   <raise $start a + i> == e i <word $start>

If this network starts at the node labelled "mono" it will delete *a* when it appears before *o*, but it will not raise *a* to *e* before *i*. Thus, it will create *compro* from *compr+a+o* and *comprais* from *compra+is*. If the network starts at the node labelled "raise", then it will convert *a+i* to *e+i* and will create *comprei* from *compr+a+i*. In addition, it will delete any "+" in the input sequence. A larger network is given in the appendix.

Since the phonological/orthographic component of the grammar is itself a network, it is necessary to determine where a form is inserted into the network for each grammatical category. For the grammar defined here, it is necessary to state only that the any form in the present tense is inserted at the "mono" node, that others are inserted at "raise".

Phonology: <> == raise raise
                    <$modo pres> == mono mono.

Figure 12

Finally, it is necessary to amend the description of the structure of the verb from the node *Verb*. Where previously it was

(18) Verb: <> == "<tema>" "<af>" "<pes>"

it is now

(19) Verb: <> == Phon_hierarchy:<Phonology "<tema>" "<af>" "<pes>">

The effect of this change is to take structure that was originally create and prefix it with the name of the node in the phonological hierarchy relevant to that grammatical category. Recall that paths on the right-hand side are concatenated with the subpath that the left-hand side was extended with. Thus, if the original query was Verb:<sub pres pri sg>, the path used to extend <> will be appended to Phonology to form Phonology:<sub pres pri sg>. The sequence of the node name with the morphological structure form the path of the query evaluated in the *Phon_hierarchy*.

4.0 Irregularity

The inheritance hierarchy defined here provides measurements of irregularity. The relative degree of regularity of two verbs can be measured by the number of lines in their definitions. A regular verb will contain two lines: one describing the shape of the root and another describing its thematic class. Irregular verbs will of necessity contain additional descriptions. For example, *vender* is more regular than *perder*.

A second measurement of irregularity is distance from the root. Regular verbs inherit directly from the node defining the thematic class. Irregular verbs will have intervening nodes between them and that defining the thematic class. For example, *partir* is more regular than *dormir*.

5.0 Conclusions

The default inference rule of DATR permits concise descriptions of the structure of the Portuguese verb. It is not necessary to specify the structure of each of the various inflectional forms that the verb can take. Instead, the general skeleton is specified by underspecified paths in the highest node of the hierarchy. Because the subpaths that were required to fill out these underspecified paths are concatenated to subsequent queries, the information necessary to select affixes, select exceptions to general grammar statements or even override the general skeleton is retained.

A phonological component that applies after morphological structure is built up removes classes of putative exceptions, retaining morphological regularity.

6.0 References

[1]Evans, R. and G. Gazdar. **The DATR Papers, Volume 1**. Brighton, School of Cognitive and Computing Sciences, The University of Sussex, 1990.

[2]Pollard, C. and I. Sag. **Information-based Syntax and Semantics: Fundamentals**. CSLI Lecture Notes. Stanford, Center for the Study of Language and Information, 1987.

[3]Pollard, C. and I. Sag. **Head-Driven Phrase Structure Grammar**. Chicago, Chicago University Press, 1994.

[4]Shieber, Stuart M. **An Introduction to Unification-Based Approaches to Grammar**. Chicago: University of Chicago Press, 1986.

TALISMAN: A Multi-Agent System for Natural Language Processing

Marie-Hélène STEFANINI

stefanini @ stendhal.grenet.fr

Yves DEMAZEAU

demazeau @ lifia.imag.fr

CRISTAL-GRESEC

Université Stendhal

BP 47- 38040 GRENOBLE

CEDEX 9 FRANCE

LIFIA / IMAG / CNRS

46, avenue Félix Viallet

38031 GRENOBLE CEDEX

FRANCE

Abstract :

Natural Language Processing raises the problem of ambiguities and therefore the multiple solutions resulting from them. Architectures based on sequential levels, in which each module corresponds to a linguistic level (preprocessing, morphology, syntax, semantics) have shown their limitations. A sequential architecture does not allow a real exchange between different modules. This leads to the unavailability of the linguistic information needed for the reduction of ambiguities. Due to the necessity for cooperation between different modules we consider the use of a new architecture which stems from the techniques in Distributed Artificial Intelligence. This paper presents a general Natural Language Processing system called TALISMAN. One of the originalities of this system is the distributed treatment of sentence analysis (as opposed to a classic sequential treatment) and the introduction of linguistic laws which handle the communication between agents, without central control. At the implementation level, the system brings openness to dictionary modification, grammars and strategies of analysis, as well as the necessary mechanisms for the integration of new modules.

Keywords :

Natural language processing, the understanding of written French, distributed artificial intelligence, multi-agent systems, law governed systems, communication protocols.

1. Introduction

Natural Language Processing (NLP) is situated at the crossroads of several disciplines : Linguistics, Artificial Intelligence and Statistics. Undoubtly these disciplines have all contributed to the progress made in the field, notably in text analysis. The main goal is to derive from all the possible solutions, only those solutions which conform to language. However, because of these diverse origins, system designers are today faced with problems like interactions between different knowledge types, their integration into one an NLP system [Sag 91], and the elaboration of a real solving strategy able to take all encountered phenomena into account.

Faced with accuracy constraints of the interpretation, sequential level architectures are limited although largely adopted. In fact, each step of the analysis performed at a given level is executed on the basis of some decision criteria that are local to that particular level. This is due to the very limited, and sometimes even non existent, information exchange between modules. This drawback leads to difficulties since the removal of certain ambiguities often relies on various criteria (e.g. morphological and syntactical) involving the cooperation of several expert modules. In order to deal with this problem, this work includes our proposal of a model issued from Distributed Artificial Intelligence (DAI) techniques [Bon 88] which allows cooperation between specialized modules for text analysis. In particular, we will use a Multi-Agent System (MAS) paradigm which emphasizes modules and their interactions[1]. Such an approach distributes intelligence among agents, autonomous entities which are able to act rationally given on the one hand, the perception of the environment and the state of their knowledge and on the other, their interactions with each other. [Dem 90].

In our application, agents correspond either to classical levels in linguistics (morphology, syntax, semantics) or to complex language phenomena (coordination, ellipsis, negation etc.). By contributing to the search for solutions that are syntactically correct, agents facilitate the resolution of certain ambiguities that are inherent to the language. The framework of Law Governed Systems (LGS) as introduced [Min 91] will form the basis for the management of the interactions between agents. The contribution of our paper is that, as far as we know, it is the first time that direct communication is used between agents for general NLP. Moreover we introduce in the MAS domain the concept of laws.

The next section describes the limitations of sequential architecture in NLP. Section 3 briefly describes the conceptual model of MAS and why we choose to use them. We will propose in section 4 our distributed architecture for NLP named TALISMAN. For both conciseness and clarity purposes, we will focus on the morpho-syntactic analysis of French.

2. Limits of sequential architecture in NLP

2.1. An example of sequential architecture: the CRISTAL system

Most of NLP systems use a sequential architecture with classical linguistic levels (pretreatments, morphology, syntax, semantics, pragmatics): for example, English systems as ASK [Tho 85], LOQUI [Bin 88], TEAM [Pei 85], or French systems as SAPHIR [Erl 87] or LEADER [Ben 88]. First, the sequential architecture of the system is detailed to show its different limitations (as for as linguistics and information processing). The CRISTAL system was applied within a European Esprit project, entitled MMI2[2] (Multi-Mode Interface for Man-Machine Interaction) [Bin 89]. The system is thus broken down into three levels, each corresponding to an analytical level (Fig. 1).

---

[1] Focusing on MAS rather than on Distributed Problem Solving (DPS) is natural, since in DPS it is often necessary to know in advance how the system has to be split up, which seems to be unsuited in the framework of Natural Language.

[2] Its aim was to build an interactive user interface for an "expert system" computer application. The interface includes several different modes of expression : Natural language (English, Spanish, and French), Graphic mode, Gestual mode and a command language.

The first level is that of morphological analysis. The character strings provided by the user are converted into one or more sequences of pairs ("lexical entry", "grammatical category + values of variables"), which correspond to sentences.

The second level is that of phrase structure grammar. The analyser constructs sentence structures from the sequence produced at the preceding level. The last level is that of logical expression. A sentence constituent structure is converted into an "operator-operand" structure.

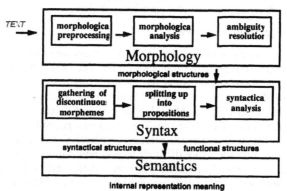

Fig. 1: A sequential architecture: The CRISTAL system

The **morphology module** consists of three stages:

• *Preprocessing*: the characters are standardized and the text is cut into forms.

• The text forms are then processed individually by the *morphological analyser* which attributes one or more interpretations to each in terms of a pair (lexical entry, category).

• *Ambiguities resolutions* (Markov model): Finally, by looking at the context, the number of multiple interpretations is reduced by removing ambiguities.

The **syntax module** involves two stages:

• *Splitting up into propositions*: The first stage cuts complex sentences into clauses while at the same time building up the structure. Clauses are complete syntactic units and are easier to analyse than sentences.

• The aim of *syntactic analysis* is to build up the syntactic structure of the clause.

Using the syntactic structure : the **semantics module** constructs a logical structure within which various operations are carried out.

2.2. Issues in linguistics

In NLP, there are different cases of ambiguities when one works with a general language and not with a sublanguage.

2.2.1. Examples of ambiguities at different levels

• Preprocessing : punctuations can be ambiguous: a full stop can indicate the end of the sentence or an abbreviation : *M. Clavier* (proper noun/ common noun).

• Morphology: Indicators of grammatical structure are words belonging to a grammatical category whose function is to indicate precisely the start of a phrase: for example, the determiners (D) but in some cases nouns or adjectives (F) which allow us to identify the beginning of a noun phrase (SN).

• Syntax : A general grammar has rules which interfere with others rules: for example :

N" -> N" N" enables to build N" resulting from the concatenation of two N". (*Alger* F(NOM, PPR) *la blanche, le lycée Louis* F(NOM, PPR)*Le Grand*).

The introduction of local grammars allow to apply this rule only when proper noun F(NOM, PPR) is detected, and avoids "parasite" solutions.

2.3. Issues in computer science

The sequential approach separates the analysis process into different stages, each of them corresponding to a specific linguistic model. The sequential architecture uses a fixed and constant data-flow between the different modules constituting the system without the possibility of some kind of backtracking. Furthermore, such a system should keep track of all the possible solutions without deleting an eventual solution from the entire list of possible solutions. This leads to a possible risk of combinatorial explosion and the usage of erroneous solutions ("parasite" solutions) not validated by the linguistic laws. It is therefore difficult to add new modules corresponding to an evolution in the treatment of linguistic problems, as the architecture of the system is fixed (i.e. the links between the different modules). Knowledge (e.g. dictionaries) and control are centralized, which necessarily increases the complexity and the size of the system given the diversity of the knowledge involved.

3. Multi-Agent Systems

3.1. Introduction

3.1.1. The use of a MAS approach for Natural Language Processing

Blackboards [New 72] have been applied in linguistics to Speech Understanding Systems [Erm 80] and more recently to the analysis of written French (HELENE [Zwe 89], CARAMEL [Sab 90]) and documentary research [Mek 91]. Global control of these systems is fully centralized: the distribution of reasoning capabilities enforces the maintenance of a global representation which is coherent and thus requires the use of belief revision mechanisms. Architectures based on direct communication between agents, allow complete distribution of both knowledge control and partial results. In fact, they make use of stronger local control in spite of global control. Each agent has a specific task and representation of knowledge that is not necessarily coherent with those of the others. Moreover, the reasoning and decision abilities in each agent enable it to act autonomously.

3.2. The model

We will briefly report on the agent and agent society concepts as they are defined [Dem 90]. We will limit ourselves to the internal description of both agents and society without getting into the detail of the external description of these MAS components.

3.2.1. The agent model

The Talisman agent model is a simplified instance of a generic agent as defined by Demazeau [Dem 90]. An agent can be divided into two main parts: its knowledge representation and its knowledge processing [Ber 92]). Knowledge and goals can be given or acquired through communication with other agents (perception is not defined within linguistic agents).

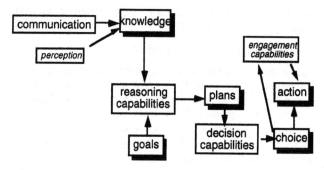

Fig. 2 : Agent model

3.2.2. The society model

We use the same description scheme for the society model. Knowledge representation defines the norms of the society and what is allowed within it, and knowledge processing defines the manner for using the network according to the society's rules.

3.2.3. Introducing Laws in a MAS

The MAS that we propose will make use of the concept of *laws* as defined by N. H. Minsky. This notion allows the imposition of protocols over open, heterogeneous, evolving, distributed systems [Min 91]. A new architecture named Law Governed Architecture for Distributed Systems (LGAD) enables enforcement of protocols, under which all interactions between agents are governed by an explicit set of rules called the laws of the system. Laws are global in the sense that all the agents must obey them, but can also be local to the agents. Laws are easily updated by modifying the rules which describe them. LGAD is currently being applied in Software Engineering and provides MAS with a new way to regulate the exchange of messages between autonomous agents. The flexibility of the LGAD model is a consequence of the explicitness of the law which enables one to implement a behaviour for a specific application . It is also due to the controlled mutability of the law which provides flexibility over time and allows law adaptation with regards to the evolution of the system. For each agent, we introduce local linguistic laws which are private and correspond to the local control of the agent. On the society level, global laws regulate communication. For every message-sending act, there is a law providing a rule for that act. This rule can deliver the message to its intended destination or block it, modify it, or reroute it to a new destination. Different types of TALISMAN laws such as initial and coordination laws (blocking, rerouting, transforming, priority etc.) are introduced in order to deal with conflicts.

4. TALISMAN System

4.1. TALISMAN Agents

At present, the society in the TALISMAN application is represented by the following linguistic agents and global laws: PRET for preprocessing, MORPH for morphological analysis, SEGM for splitting into clauses, SYNT for syntactic analysis,TRANSF for transformations of utterances (interrogatives, imperatives, etc...) in declarative clauses, STAT for statistics ambiguities resolution, COORD for coordinations, NEGA for negations and ELLIP for ellipses. All these agents are described in detail in [Ste 93]. There are different types of decomposition: Knowledge decomposition by abstraction

(PRET, MORPH, SEGM, SYNT...), task decomposition by type of input (COORD, NEGA), task decomposition by type of output (ELLIP).

4.1.1. An example of a TALISMAN's Agent: The SYNT agent

The SYNT knowledge representation includes, among other components, verb dictionaries, grammars, indicators of the lexical structure and indicators of the grammatical structure and prepositions introducing adverbial sentences. SYNT buildsup syntactic structures of the sentences. This predicts the structure of a string on the basis of syntactic schemes to which it can be applied. In order to do this, this agent has access data stored in a lexicon of fixed expressions such as adverbial phrases and compound words. It also uses an expert system including Earley's algorithm. It can inform the other agents on agreement with gender, number, verbs choices, etc. Its acquaintances (a set of other agents it knows and to whom it can speak) are MORPH, SEGM, COORD and TRANSF. The SYNT agent informs the other agents on agreement with gender, number and verbs choices, or proposes solutions for ambiguous sequences, etc. Its local memory holds its internal state and information about its acquaintances.

4.2. The interaction language

The interaction language [Dem 95] is divided into three parts : the communication language, the multi-agent language and the application.

<interaction> ::=**<communication>** translates the message from a pure distributed systems point of view,**<multi-agent>** refers to the multi-agent domain knowledge, encompassing the intention of the sender and the desired result of the utterance, **<application>** is here the application language for natural language.

4.2.1. The communication language

The syntax of communication language is defined by:

<communication> ::=**<from>** refering to the sender,**<to>** refering the receiver (agent entity or broadcast), **<id>** identity of the message,**<via>** channel (direct message passing,)**<mode>** mode (synchronous, asynchronous).

4.2.2. The multi-agent language

The syntax of multi-agent language is defined by :

<multi-agent> :: =**<type>** present, request, answer, inform, **<nature>** refering to the control layer of the receiver's agent model (decision-goal, adaptation-plans, command-actions, observation-hypotheses),**<strength>** refering to the priority of the message (information seeking, informing, warning, advising, bargaining, persuading, commanding, expressing) from commanding to informing.

4.2.3. Basic features for communication and society laws

We are currently studying a communication protocol for TALISMAN [Kon 95]. We will illustrate it through an example in the next section. Such a protocol regulates the exchange of messages from different types. Message types are inspired by Sian [Sia 91]. For example : ASSERT represents a non-modifiable assertion, PROPOSE allows to propose a new hypothesis, MODIFY gives a modified version of a previously proposed hypothesis, AGREED changes the status of a hypothesis from proposed to agreed, DISAGREE indicates disagreement with a hypothesis, CONFIRM confirms hypothesis, ACCEPT causes acceptance of a previously agreed hypothesis.

4.3. System Control

4.3.1. Initialization of the system

A priority law (L1) initializes the system. The sentence is dispatched to the agents using a broadcast message. PRET modifies the first data structure into a preprocessed sentence, sends its result by broadcast (law L2).

```
L1: send (ASSERT(_[ph),_)) ->deliver(ASSERT(_(ph), PRET)).

L2: send(<PRET> <all> [<asynchone> <inform> <accept> <ph(_ph_input,
_phpret>])->deliver(<PRET> <all> [<asynchone> <inform> <accept>
<ph(_ph_input, _phpret>]).
```

4.3.2. Cooperation and determination of the solution

All the agents are now able to cooperate or enter into conflict with other agents when difficulties at the level of linguistic phenomena are encountered. Interactions are based on exchanges of both *safe information* (not ambiguous), for example information about syntactical structures, morphological category, clauses, verb diagrams, decision choices, etc. and *uncertain information* or linguistic heuristics according to the level of the agent's comprehension. When new knowledge is validated by an agent, it modifies its local memory and restarts its resolution process. The system stops by itself when no further updating of the interpretation is to be done.

5. Examples

We will illustrate this with an example of interaction between PRET, MORPH, TRANSF, SEGM, NEGA and SYNT. The linguistic foundations of our analytical strategy are based on the indicators of a lexical structure (ILS) and the indicators of a grammatical structure (ISG). ILS covers all the words contained in the language which have a predicative function and therefore govern complements (verbs, nouns and adjectives derived from verbs and some adverbs). The typology of complements governed by the verb is based on the value of the pronoun which is substituted in its place whenever possible [Berr 90]. Thus :

In order to transform interrogative sentences into a canonical order, it is necessary to know the nature of complements which are governed by verbs. Thus, TRANSF and SYNT (which calculate verb diagrams) must cooperate.

After execution of laws L1 and L2, every agent becomes operational. But, when TRANSF recognizes an interrogative sign it transforms the sentence into a declarative and informs the others (L3). The priority law (L3) obligate all the agents to work now on declarative sentences named QTO (for total question) and not on the pretreatments (ph_pret).

```
L3: send[<TRANSF> <all> <asynchone> <inform> <accept> <ph(_ph_pret,
_phtransf(QTO)>]-> deliver <TRANSF> <all> <asynchone> <inform>
<accept> <ph(_phtransf(QTO)>]
```

est-ce que la machine ne garde en mémoire que la trace des programmes ? (Does the machine keep only the trace of programs in memory?)

Classical morphological analysis alone produces 576 possible combinations:

est-[3]*ce que la*[4] *machine* [5]*ne garde*[6] *en*[7] *mémoire* [8]*que la trace des programmes* [9]*?*

`<PRET>` `<all>` `<asynchone>` `<inform>` `<accept>` `<ph(_ph_input,` `_phpret["des" =(de=P, les=D)], _)>` {PRET informs all the agents that the sentence (ph_input) is pretreated (phpreat) and it has found reliable categories}

`<MORPH>` `<SYNT>` `<asynchone>` `<request><propose>` `<"programmes"=F>` {The other category is a verb: V}

`<SYNT>` `<MORPH>` `<asynchone>` `<request><confirm>` `<"programmes"=F>` {it can construct a noun phrase : <des programmes=SN>}

`<SEGM><MORPH, SYNT>` `<asynchrone>` `<inform>` `<accept><ph(nb_verb=2)>`

{it thinks that it has found a clause indicator [que=Q] and asks to seek verbs in the two clauses.}

`<SEGM><MORPH, SYNT>` `<asynchrone>` `<request>` <seek_verbs `["La...mémoire"/` `"la trace...opération"]>,_)`

`<SYNT>` `<all>` `<asynchone>` `<inform>` `<accept>` `[que=Wn],_)` (negative restriction)

`<NEGA>` `<all>` `<asynchone>` `<inform>` `<accept>` `[ne=deb_neg],_)`

`<NEGA>` `<MORPH>` `<asynchone>` `<request><propose>[fin_neg]`

{it asks to find the other half of the negation formula fin_nég "pas, plus jamais..."}

`<MORPH>` `<NEGA>` `<asynchone>` `<answer><disagree>[fin_neg]`

`<MORPH>` `<NEGA>` `<asynchone>` `<answer><withdraw>[fin_neg]`

There is a conflict between SEGM and SYNT resolved by a global law:

`send((SEGM,assert [que=Q]& (SYNT,assert [que=Wn],_)`

`& withdraw(_, fin_neg, NEGA)) -> deliver((SYNT, ASSERT[que=Wn],_))`

`<SEGM><MORPH,SYNT>` `<asynchrone>` `<inform>` `<accept>[nb_verbe` `"La...mémoire", 1 / "la trace...opération",0>],_)` (first clause contains 1 verb, second clause contains 0 verb)

`<MORPH > <SYNT>` `<asynchone>` `<request><propose>` `< ["trace"=F]>` {trace is also a verb }

`<SYNT > <MORPH>` `<asynchone>` `<request><confirm>` `< ["trace"=F]>`

{it can construct a noun phrase : <la trace=SN=C1(accusative SN)>}

---

[3]*est* is either the noun *east* or the verb *to be* :(F/V)

[4]*la* is either a preverbal, a determiner or the noun (a musical note)

[5]*machine* is either the verb (to plot) or the noun (machine) (V/F)

[6]*garde* is either the verb (to keep) or the noun (guard): (V/F)

[7] *en* is eitehr a preposition or a preverbal (P/V)

[8] *trace* is either the verb (to draw) or the noun (V/F)

[9] *programmes* is either the verb or the noun (V/F)

<MORPH>   <SYNT>   <asynchone>   <request><propose><["la"=D, "machine"=F]>{machine can be a verb}

<SYNT > <MORPH> <asynchone> <request><confirm><["la"=D, "machine"=F]>

{it can construct a noun phrase : <la machine=SN>}

<MORPH>   <SYNT>   <asynchone>   <request><propose><[seek_verbs, ["La...mémoire" =garder]>

<SYNT><MORPH><asynchone><request><confirm><[seek_verbs ["La...mémoire" =garder]> {it can construct a subject noun phrase : <la machine=C0>}

<SYNT><SEGM><asynchone><inform><accept><[seek_verbs,["La...mémoire" =garder]>

<MORPH><SYNT><asynchone><inform><accept><["mémoire"=F]>

<MORPH > <SYNT> <asynchone> <request><propose>["en"=P]>

{the other category is the preverbal called   (Y)}

<SYNT > <MORPH> <asynchone> <request><con,firm>["en"=P] {SYNT can construct the functional structure : C0= "la machine" V="garder" C1="la trace de les programmes", Circ. "en mémoire").

Detection and management of conflicts suppose more complex examples as detailed in [Ste 93].

6. Implementation

We are currently implementing a prototype. Application support is entirely implemented in ProLog by Bim (version 3.0) running on a Sparc station. An other version is implemented in Prolog II+. Most of the agents encapsulate CRISTAL modules written in C and Prolog. Communication acts between agents use the two primitives *send* and *deliver* :

send (E, M, D) where E is the sender, M is the message and D is the receiver. The message M and the receiver D can be modified during the act of sending.

deliver (E, M, D)   allows the effective delivery of the message M to receiver D.

Given a message send (E, M, D), the rule associated to this Law for this act is performed by evaluating the target message deliver (E, M, D).

7. Conclusion

We have presented a distributed approach for NLP able to resolve ambiguities by cooperation of different linguistic agents. One of the advantages in linguistics is a restriction of ambiguities through the cooperation between expert agents. Each agent activates its own knowledge at exactly the right moment. Another advantage lies in the fact that the linguistic models have been conceived in a thorough manner in order to cover several application fields (Human-Computer Communication in the project MMI2 [Bin 89], computational documentation SYDO [An 88]). Structures become less complex in nature by using local grammar rules.

Our system can operate with partial analyses at different classical levels of analysis, change strategies according to the applications or the corpus in question, use linguistic laws which are easily modifiable. Implementation of NLP in a MAS completed by laws should allow the flexibility needed to integrate new agents without transforming all of the system components.

Our long term research strategy will be to focus on their mutual interactions in order to obtain a better formalisation of the whole system.

References

[Ant 88] G. Antoniadis, G. Lallich-Boidin, Y. Polity & J. Rouault,"A french linguistic model for an information retrieval system". *ACM SIGIR*, Grenoble, june 1988.

[Berr 90] A. Berrendonner , "Grammaire pour un analyseur : aspects morphologiques", *Les Cahiers du CRISS, N° 15*, November 1990.

[Ben 88] P. Benoit, Ph. Rincel, P. sabatier, D. Vienne: "A User-Friendly Natural Language Interface to Oracle", *Proceedings of the European Oracle Users' group Conference*, Paris 1988.

[Bert 92] S. Berthet, Y. Demazeau, O. Boissier., "Knowing Each Other Better ." *in 11 th International Workshop on DAI*, An Arbor, Michigan, February 1992.

[Bin 89] J. L. Binot et al.,A Multi-Mode Interface for Man-Machine Interaction. "Literature review and general architecture". Esprit P2474, Deliverable d1. Bruxelles, 1989.

[Bon 88] A.H. Bond & L. Gasser, "Readings in Distributed Artificial Intelligence". Morgan Kaufmann, 1988.

[Dem 90] Y. Demazeau & J.P. Mueller, eds (+ Introduction) "Decentralized A.I.". Demazeau & Muller eds., North-Holland, Elsevier, 1990 .

[Dem 92] Y. Demazeau & J.P. Mueller, eds (+ Introduction) "Decentralized Artificial Intelligence II". Demazeau & Muller eds., North-Holland, Elsevier, 1992.

[Dem 95] Y. Demazeau "From Cognitive Interactions to Collective Behaviour in Agent-Based Systems". *European Conference on Cognitive Science*, Saint Malo, Avril 1995.

[Erl 87] Erli, SAPHIR, Manuel de description du logiciel, Société Erli 1987.

[Erm 80] L. D. Erman, F. Hayes-Roth, .R. Lesser, D.R. Reddy, "The Hearsay-II speech understanding system : integrating knowledge to resolve uncertainty". *A CM Computing Surveys 12*, 1980.

[Kui 91] E. Kuijpers, G. Lallich-Boidin & J. Rouault,"French System : From a Syntactic Structure to a CMR Expression". ESPRIT P2474 MMI2 Deliverable d20 for st.3.3.2. Grenoble, CRISS, April 1991.

[Mek 91] A. Mekaouche, J.C. Bassano,"Analyseur linguistique multi-expert pour la recherche documentaire". Avignon, Mai 1991.

[Min 91] N.H. Minsky, "The imposition of protocols over open distributed systems". IEEE Transactions on Software Engineering February 1991.

[New 72] A. Newell & H.E. Simon, "Human problem solving". Englewood Cliffs, 1972.

[Bin 88] J. L. Binot, B. Demoen, K. Hanne, L. Solomon, Y. Vasiliou, W. von Hahn, T. Wachtel: "LOQUI: A logic oriented approach to data and knowledge bases supporting natural language interaction", Proceedings of ESPRIT 88 Conference, North-Holland, 1988.

[Bin 89] J. L. Binot et al., A Multi-Mode Interface for Man-Machine Interaction "Literature review and general architecture" Esprit P2474, Deliverable d1, Bruxelles, 1989.

[Kon 95] J.L. Koning, M.H.Stéfanini, Y. Demazeau, "DAI Interaction Protocols as Control Strategies in a Natural Language processing System", *IEEE International Conference on Systems*, Man and Cybernetics, October, Vancouver.

[Ple 92] "Vers une Taxinomie du vocabulaire pour les Systèmes Multi-Agents", *1ère journée Nationale du PRC-IA sur les Systèmes Multi-Agents*, PRC-IA, Nancy 1992.

[Pei 85] F. Pereira, "The TEAM Natural-Language Interface System", Final Report, *SRI International*, Menlo Park, 1985.

[Sab 90] G. Sabah, "Caramel : A Computational Model of Natural Language Understanding using Parallel implementation". *Proceedings of 9th European Conference on Artificial Intelligence*, Stockholm, August 90.

[Sag 91] I.A. Sag, "Linguistic theory and natural language processing". Basic Research Series. E. Klein & F. Veltman (Eds). *Symposium Proceedings "Natural language and speech"*. Bruxelles, November 1991.

[Sia 91] S. Sian, "Adaptation based on Cooperative Learning in Multi-agent Systems", in *Decentralized A.I. 2*, Demazeau & Müller, eds., North Holland Elsevier, Amsterdam 1991.

[Ste 93] M.H. Stéfanini "TALISMAN : un système multi-agent pour l'analyse du français écrit", *Thèse de Doctorat*, Jan. 1993.

[Zwe 89] P. Zweigenbaum,"Hélène: Compréhension de compte-rendus d'hospitalisation". *Deuxième Ecole d'été sur le Traitement des Langues Naturelles*. L'ENSSAT, Lannion, Juillet 1989.

[Tho 85] B. Thomson, F. Thompson: "ASK is Transportable in Half a Dozen Ways". *ACM Transactions on Office Information Systems*, Vol 3, N° 2, April 1985.

Part-of-Speech Tagging for Portuguese Texts

Aline Villavicencio[†]
alinev@inf.ufrgs.br
CPGCC - Federal University of Rio
Grande do Sul

Nuno M. C. Marques[‡]
nmm@fct.unl.pt
FCT- CRIA/UNINOVA - New
University of Lisbon

José Gabriel P. Lopes[‡]
gpl@fct.unl.pt
FCT- CRIA/UNINOVA - New
University of Lisbon

Fabio Villavicencio[†]
fabiov@inf.ufrgs.br
CPGCC-Federal University of Rio
Grande do Sul

Content Areas: Natural Language Processing, Part-of-Speech Taggers, Probabilistic Models

1. Abstract

In this paper we will describe the work that is being cooperatively done by Portugal and Brazil. It uses Statistical Methods for Natural Language Processing. Namely, we will focus on the problem of Part-of-Speech (POS) Tagging. POS Tagging is a recent and successful technique for assigning each word in a sentence its correct POS tag. This technique can achieve more than 96% of accuracy, even with unseen untagged texts. All steps involved in this process will be described as well as the problems faced. Besides, we will present the stochastic approach to POS Tagging, which treats the generation of tag alignments as a probabilistic problem. Finally, we will report the results achieved by using these kinds of techniques for Portuguese texts.

2. Introduction

A Corpus is defined as a collection of texts written in a given language. When it has some linguistic features associated with its constituents, for instance, their part-of-speech tags, it is called a Tagged Corpus. This kind of annotation can help to show the patterns that occur in that corpus.

In the project being developed, we are using two Portuguese Corpora: the Lusa Corpus, which contains news from Lusa Agency from Portugal and the Radiobras Corpus, that contains news from the Radiobras Agency from Brazil. But the results presented in this paper were obtained using only the Radiobras Corpus.

One of the uses of a Tagged Corpus is to train a Part-of-Speech Tagger. A Part-of-Speech Tagger is a program that "learns" automatically the linguistic patterns from a given Corpus. It is done through the computation of the probabilities of

[†] Curso de Pós Graduação em Ciência da Computação- Universidade Federal do Rio Grande do Sul
Av. Bento Gonçalves, 9500 - Porto Alegre - Brasil - 91501-970 Phone/Fax: +55-51-3428687
[‡] Faculdade de Ciências e Tecnologia- CRIA/UNINOVA - Universidade Nova de Lisboa
Quinta da Torre,2825 - Monte da Caparica - Portugal Phone:+351-1-350-0281
Work partially suported by a PhD Scholarship by JNICT-PRAXIS XXI/BD/2909/94

word-tag alignments. After finishing the learning process, the Tagger is ready to use its acquired knowledge to tag any unseen untagged Corpus. Thus the work of the tagger is, given an input word sequence, to assign each word its corresponding part-of-speech tag. Hence its output is a sequence of tags.

These programs have been presenting very good results (see [5], [7] and [14 among others). They can tag at least 96% of the words correctly, with minimal restrictions on the input text. And they achieve this performance using only modest resources of space and time.

In this paper we will briefly explain the process of Part-of-Speech Tagging using stochastic methods. After that, we will comment on some tag sets commonly used and mainly on the tag set we used. We will also explain the architecture of the system developed. Finally, we will present some preliminary results of this work.

3. Part-of-Speech Tagging

Given a sentence W, which can be defined as a string of words, composed of $w_1, w_2, ..., w_n$. Part-of-Speech (POS) Tagging can be described as the process of assigning each word w_i of W a corresponding tag t_i from the T set of tags. These tags must be previously defined by the user. For each sentence W we get an alignment:

$(W,T) = w_1 t_1, w_2 t_2, ..., w_n t_n.$

However, because there might be more than one tag for each word, the sentence can have more than one alignment [2], [14]. But, from all possible alignments for a sentence only one should be considered correct. And the tagging process should select this correct alignment (the most probable one).

For example, consider the following English sentence[1]:

He can	can	a	can.
ProN	Mod	Mod	Det	Mod
	Nn	Nn		Nn
	Vb	Vb		Vb

Figure 1 - POS tag alignments

There are 27 possible alignments, but the correct one is:

He can	can	a	can.
ProN	Mod	Vb	Det	Nn

Figure 2 - Correct alignment

The performance of a tagging procedure can be measured by using two functions, following the ideas described by [14]:

- the first function computes the percentage of sentences correctly tagged in a given Corpus;
- the other one determines the percentage of words correctly tagged in the Corpus.

The first measure will always produce a lower result than the second one, because a sentence will only be tagged correctly if all the words in this sentence have the correct tag.

---

[1]ProN - Personal Pronoun, Mod - Modal Verb, Det - Determiner, Nn - Noun and Vb - Verb.

In this paper we will use the second measure, which has been adopted by the majority of researchers in this area [5], [7], [14] among others.

4. Statistical methods for Part-of-speech tagging

There are two main approaches for part-of-speech tagging: the rule-based [1], [16] and the statistical approach [14], [5], [7], [11], [10]. In the first one, the traditional method, the linguists encode their ideas about the language. This process is labour-intensive, since it requires skill and effort to write an exhaustive grammar. Brill, in his recent PhD thesis [1] presented a way of automatically estimate the grammar rules from tagged corpora. But the only way to perform this grammatical learning is using tagged corpora.

In the second approach, the pieces of information required for the tagging procedure are also automatically estimated. However, in this approach, the estimation can be performed using either tagged corpora or untagged corpora. The statistical approach tries to solve the ambiguity problems of a sentence through the determination of its most likely interpretation. In this approach, the generation of the alignments for a sentence W is considered to obey a probabilistic distribution $p(W,T)$. Therefore, the most likely alignment for a sentence will be considered the correct one.

Both, the rule-based and the statistical approach have presented very good results. However, in this work we will only present the statistical approach for part-of-speech tagging.

4.1 Finding the Most Likely Alignment

In order to find the most likely alignment for a sentence there are two algorithms that may be used: the Viterbi Algorithm and the Maximum Likelihood Estimation (MLE) [14].

The Viterbi Algorithm computes, for each sentence, the alignment that presents the most probable sequence of tags, while the MLE estimates the most probable tag for each word of the sentence. Merialdo in [14] presents a good comparison of these two methods. He concluded that the Viterbi is easier to implement and requires less computation while producing the best interpretation for a sentence. Besides, the MLE has the disadvantage of allowing the production of tag sequences that are grammatically impossible. Due to all these facts we have chosen to work with the Viterbi algorithm.

4.2 The n-gram model

When a word is ambiguous it can be fully disambiguated by just looking at its neighbourhood. Humans tend to follow this procedure in order to disambiguate a sentence. So analysing the sentence 1, it is easy to discover that "casa" is more likely to be a noun (house) than a verb (to marry).

Sentence 1: "Aquela casa está a venda" (That house is for sale)

This concept of "neighbourhood" can be found in the n-gram model. This model defines that the probability of a given tag is dependent on the probability of its "neighbouring" tags. From all n-gram models one of the most commonly used is the bigram (n=2). In the bigram model, the probability of a tag is dependent only on the probability of the previous tag.

Merialdo [14] defines the probabilities for the bigram model as:

$$p(t_i|w_it_i,...,w_{i-1}t_{i-1})= h(t_i|t_{i-1}),$$
$$p(w_i|w_1t_1,...,w_{i-1}t_{i-1}t_i) = k(w_i|t_i).$$

We have chosen to work with bigrams because they can easily produce reliable estimates. Consider, for example, the bigrams "art-noun" "noun-adj" and "adj-verb": these bigrams will occur hundreds of times in a Corpus, having frequencies higher enough to result in reliable estimates. However the trigrams "art-noun-adj" and "noun-adj-verb" will be a little bit more difficult to find and the quadrigram "art-noun-adj-verb" could have such a lower frequency that cannot be reliable. Consequently working with a bigger "n" (trigram or quadrigram) would require larger texts to produce reliable estimates. And even working with bigrams, one must be careful, because there may be some correct bigrams that never occurred in the training Corpus. These bigrams will be assigned a zero probability. It means that if such bigrams happen to occur in some other corpus, the tagger will not conceive it as a correct occurrence. To avoid such a situation, there are some smoothing techniques, such as the Good-Turing method and the Deleted Estimation [6].

4.3 Hidden Markov Models

A Hidden Markov Model can be defined as a tuple $<S,s_1,W,T>$ where S is a set of states (s_1 is the initial state and $s_1 \in S$), T is a set of transitions and W is a set of symbols. Associated with each transition there is an initial probability. From each state there might be more than one transition leaving it with the same symbol. Thus for each input string there might be more than one state sequence.

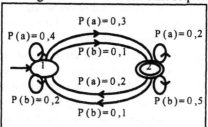

Figure 3- A Two State HMM

In the example above we have: $S = \{1,2\}$ and $s_1=1; W=\{a,b\}$;
$$T = \{1 \xrightarrow{a} 1 = 0,4; \ 1 \xrightarrow{b} 1 = 0,2; \ 1 \xrightarrow{a} 2 = 0,3; \ 1 \xrightarrow{b} 2 = 0,1; \ 2 \xrightarrow{a} 2 = 0,2;$$
$$2 \xrightarrow{b} 2 = 0,5; \ 2 \xrightarrow{a} 1 = 0,2; \ 2 \xrightarrow{b} 1 = 0,1 \}$$

Where $s_i \xrightarrow{w_k} s_j = n$ denotes the probability n of a transition from s_i to s_j while generating w_k. For POS tagging we define that the POS tags are the states of the HMM and the equivalence classes are the W symbols. As it can be seen, we implemented the bigram model through the use of HMMs. Thus the probability of a state is dependent only on the probability of the previous state [V1]and on the equivalence class used.

Training with Tagged or Untagged Text?

There are two approaches used to train a part-of-speech tagger: training with tagged texts or with untagged texts.

The first approach uses large amounts of tagged texts as input to the tagger to be trained. The probabilities of the parameters of the model are easily obtained from the tagged training Corpus. The tagger is trained by observing the occurrences of the pairs ($word_i$-tag_i) and (tag_{i-1}-tag_i) in the training Corpus. This approach was used by [5] and many others with very good results. Church reported an accuracy that varies from 95% to 99,5%. The only problem with this approach is its necessity of a large tagged Corpus to obtain reliable results (Church used the tagged Brown Corpus, which has about 1,000,000 words). And for many languages, like Portuguese, such a large amount of text is not available yet, even because of its costs and because of the time and difficulty to manually tag such a big Corpus.

A recent solution to this problem is found in [7]. This approach uses untagged text to train the tagger. [V2] Despite the fact that it does not need a tagged text, it needs a big dictionary to determine the possible POS tags for a given word in the Corpus. To train these taggers there are algorithms that reestimate the parameters of the tagger in order to maximise the likelihood of the training corpus. Cutting et all [7] used this approach obtaining more than 96% of accuracy using Hidden Markov Models.

Training an HMM with Untagged Text

The initial probabilities are guessed by the user. After that there is an algorithm, the Forward-Backward (FB) or Baum-Welch algorithm, that must be applied in order to refine these probabilities. The FB algorithm works by recursively processing the untagged training corpus and recomputing its probabilities. At each iteration, a new set of probabilities will result from this reestimation and they will be used to recompute better parameters. This process continues until either the pre-defined number of iterations is executed or the set of probabilities starts to present a decrease in the performance with the training corpus. The expected result is a set of probabilities that maximises the likelihood of the corpus being tagged.

However, one of the limitations of the FB algorithm is that it is only guaranteed to reach a local maximum. So, depending on how good the initial probabilities are,-it will achieve a better result or not. On the other hand, if these guessed probabilities are good enough, this reestimation procedure would not improve the tagging accuracy noticeably and can even deteriorate it ([8] and [14]). According to Merialdo, [14]: "*ML training, is a theoretically sound procedure, and one that is routinely and successfully used in speech recognition [...]. Although ML [using the FB algorithm] training is guaranteed to improve perplexity, perplexity is not necessarily related to tagging accuracy, and it is possible to improve one while degrading the other. Also, in the case of tagging, the relations between words and tags are much more precise than the relations between phonemes and speech signals (where the correct correspondence is harder to define precisely). Some characteristics of ML training, such as the effect of smoothing probabilities, are probably more suited to speech than to tagging.*".

Although Cutting et all [7] report 96% of accuracy using the FB training it's not described in the paper if this accuracy was obtained by using the FB algorithm or because the initial values were already good.

The solution we found to solve that was to use a tagged text just to set the initial parameters of the model. Until now, we just used the first estimation method, but we still intend to experiment the effects of the forward-Backward procedure on our model. The problem now was to find a tagged corpus.

5. The Tag Set

When defining the tag set, there are many aspects that must be considered, among them the amount of linguistic information needed for a specific task and the number of parameters of the model being used (in this paper an HMM). This last item must be carefully considered, because the number of parameters to be estimated depends cubically on the number of tags.

The linguistic aspect varies from language to language and has to do with having a more or less specific tag set. Thus the tag set can be defined taking into account some features like gender, person and number, among others, if they are relevant to the final result. Kempe in [11] presents a POS tagger that uses feature-structures; he also shows that more linguistic information increases the accuracy of the data. This way a word like 'homem' (man) would be tagged as N-SG-MASC[2]. Chanod and Tapanainen in [4], claim that for French texts, the number and the person aspects are very important. However, the gender is not used for nouns, adjectives and determiners, because they state that *"ignoring it at the level of part-of-speech tagging has no measurable effect on the overall quality of the tagger"*. Elworthy [9], present some interesting experiences with tag sets for Swedish, English and French, where the author tries to find out which aspects are worth being modelled and which are not.

An Open Class tag can also be clearly defined, including all open classes, which are those classes for which the set of elements cannot be completely described. For instance, Proper Noun is an open class, because many of its elements remain unknown, on the other hand Preposition is a closed class, because all its elements are known. Thus the Proper Noun class will be one of the elements of the Open Classes tag. This tag will be the most likely tag for unknown words. Thus when a word is not recognised by any means, it is assigned the default tag from the Open Class tag.

We will mention some tag sets reported in literature, to give an idea of how varied the size of tag sets is: the PennTrebank has 48 different tags, the Brown Corpus has 87 tags that could be combined into 187 tags, the LOB Corpus has 135 tags and the SUSANNE has 425 different tags. The tag set used in [4] has 88 tags and 353 possible combinations (6525 if the words joined with clitics are considered), [3] presented 46 regular tags and 11 special tags for Chinese, while [7] had 38 tags.

Our approach follows the ones presented in literature. This way, in Lusa Corpus we used the 45 tags. Due to some differences presented in the Portuguese from Portugal and the Portuguese from Brazil, this tag set was further reduced in Radiobras Corpus to 34 tags. However, until now we have not covered any

---

[2]N-SG-MASC is the tag used to express a masculine (MASC) singular (SG) noun (N)

morphological information. The tag we are assigning contains only part-of-speech information.

Another thing to mention is the fact that each word in the Corpus is treated separately in this work. For example, the foreign word "MacDonald's" is treated as: macdonald/NP '/CH s/NP - two Proper Nouns and a punctuation sign.

6. Equivalence classes

There is a great number of words that have more than one part-of-speech tag. For example, the word 'casa' can be a noun (house) as well as a verb (to marry) and there are many other words that equally follow some pattern. So Kupiec, cited in [3], introduced the concept of equivalence classes (or ambiguity classes), used by [7] and [3] among others. It states that words that have the same set of possible parts-of-speech belong to the same equivalence class. Thus, in this case, the word "casa" belongs to the "noun-verb" equivalence class. However, only one of the tags of the equivalence class is correct in a given context. Hence, in sentence 1, "casa" is a noun rather than a verb.

It is an important concept because, if well chosen, the equivalence classes, can reduce the number of parameters of the model to be estimated, without a relevant reduction in the performance of the tagger.

Rare words used to be a problem, because their frequency was too small. So to obtain more reliable estimates it was necessary to train the tagger using a huge Corpus. But, by using the concept of equivalence classes it is possible to combine the frequency of all words belonging to that class and to obtain a better estimate. Now the tagger can be reliably trained using smaller Corpora.

However, the most common words can still be represented individually, as they have a higher frequency and consequently they can produce a reliable estimate.

Another use for equivalence classes is to smooth lexical probabilities. Lexical probability is the probability of a give word occurring with one of its possible tags, e.g., "a" - ART - 63%, "a" - PREP - 25%, "a" - PPOA - 12%[3]. It's well known that lexical probabilities estimated from limited amounts of texts are not reliable. A good solution to this problem is to use equivalence classes to smooth word-based probabilities. Schmid in [15] presents a more detailed description of this idea.

In our approach, the use of equivalence classes is presenting good results. It revealed to be very useful. Indeed we managed to conjugate a more general set of classes derived from Porto Editora's Dictionary into the ones we needed to use in the Corpus. Several ambiguous classes in a dictionary search, such as verbs, are classified as auxiliary verbs or intransitive verbs.

Our corpora, both Radiobras and Lusa, have no diacritic. So the ambiguity problem tends to increase, as there are many words that are unambiguous with their graphical stresses, but become ambiguous without them. For example, the word 'e' (and) is a conjunction and the word 'é' is the 3rd person of the indicative present of the verb to be (is) and they are completely different with stresses, but become equal without stresses and consequently ambiguous.

---

[3]ART- article, PREP - preposition, PPOA - personal pronoun, object case.

7. The Architecture

We wanted to build a system capable of tagging Portuguese sentences. This POS tagger, was defined as being composed of three main modules (indicated by circles in Figure 4).

In the first module, we have the so called Build_HMM. We have a tagged corpus as input and we infer a first order HMM from this corpus, thus implementing a bigram model. In the HMM, as explained before, the POS tags are represented by the states and the equivalence classes by the symbols. The training process is executed and the probabilities of the parameters are reestimated. Some of these probabilities might be too small to be reliable, so they must be smoothed. The smoothing technique we are using is the Good-Turing method [6].

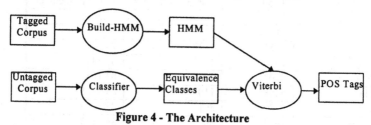

Figure 4 - The Architecture

The second module, the classifier, is responsible for reading a sentence from the Corpus, tokenising it and assigning each word its equivalence class, according to its dictionary definition. The dictionary used is based on a standard on-line Portuguese dictionary[4](with 120,000 entries-singular noun forms, infinitive verb forms, etc) that encapsulates knowledge allowing the lexicon recognition/generation of inflected forms (a total of 738,076 words).This dictionary has a graphical interface, the POLARIS System, described in [13], and it can deal with the morphological richness of the Portuguese Language [12].

After classifying each sentence, there is a disambiguation process. Each sentence is disambiguated using the Viterbi algorithm. As already explained, this algorithm finds the most likely path through the Hidden Markov Model, for a sentence. In other words, in this module, given the output of the classifier (the equivalence classes) and the generated HMM, using the Viterbi algorithm, we select the most appropriate sequence of parts-of-speech tags.

8. Results

Because there was no tagged corpus for Portuguese, we started tagging texts at the Federal University of Rio Grande do Sul, Brazil. But this is a time consuming task, and in order to make it easier, we passed our corpus through a dictionary using the classifier program to get the ambiguity classes and then we manually disambiguated it.

---

[4]The Porto Editora's Electronic Dictionary - produced by a consortium composed by UNINOVA, Heurística and Porto Editora. It was partially funded by project D (STRD/TIT/0060) from Portugal.

331

Until now we have 14,244 words tagged in the Radiobras Corpus and 2,316 words tagged in the Lusa Corpus. The tagged corpus used in our test was the Radiobras Corpus. This version of the corpus contains 559 sentences tagged with part-of-speech information. This corpus was divided in a training corpus and a test corpus according to the following division method: the test corpus contains the N first sentences and the training one contains the other M sentences of the corpus.

The training corpus was used to estimate the parameters of a first-order hidden Markov Model, through the use of an automatic HMM builder. As expected, the more words we used to train the tagger the better the results were. It can be seen in Table 1, which compares the size of the training and of the test corpus and the resulting accuracy.

Training Corpus	Test Corpus	Number of Errors	Tagging Accuracy
706	13538	4025	70.2689
1254	12731	3299	74.0502
2474	11512	2422	78.9611
3782	10250	1893	81.5317
5066	9005	1606	82.1655
7485	6548	1108	83.0788
8798	5189	861	83.4072
10008	3920	607	84.5153
11262	2731	397	85.4632
12658	1317	205	84.4343
13475	413	64	84.5036

Table 1 - Relation Between The Training Set, the Test Set and Tagging Accuracy

Due to the reduced amount of tagged text available by now, we can only show preliminary results. But one aspect that is already noticeable are the effects in the accuracy of the results produced by the decrease of the test size. No evaluation of this accuracy has yet been done and clearly we need a better test method.

As we have already said, these results presented here are still preliminary. They are similar to the ones presented in literature for training sets of this size. We are still far from the state of the art 96,6% accuracy, presented in most literature. But we are only using a 14,000 word hand-tagged Corpus. And we believe that with a larger tagged Corpus these results should certainly improve.

Moreover, until now, we are not using the FB algorithm, although we intend, in a near future, to test if it is worth applying it to our model or not.

9. Conclusion

In this paper we have described a system that is able to robustly suggest the best set of tags for an unrestricted Portuguese sentence. The approach chosen diverges from the traditional one (the rule-based) used in natural language processing. Besides it is integrated in a relatively new field in this area: the use of statistical methods.

The use of statistics brings the ever lasting problem of the data to estimate those statistics. In the English Language, this problem has been overcome by the creation of multi-million word tagged corpora. But tagging is expensive and even though the English community can have several corpora available, in other languages the problem remains. In our approach this problem also exists and it is not completely solved yet. The first results we present, still reflect this problem.

Despite these problems, due to the lack of data, we think the results are already relevant. Indeed, the advantages of the use of statistics become evident after using the system: instead of working with limited domains we are now starting to parse real unrestricted texts. And the results are encouraging.

The system performed remarkably well for the data available, both in terms of speed (it is capable of parsing hundreds of sentences in just a few seconds), and in terms of its robustness. We already have enough data to do the first experiments, and more text are still being tagged. We now want to investigate how to improve the data we have. To do this we intend to incorporate more linguistic information: we intend to supply the system with morphological information, and with the capability of handling that kind of information. We also intend to reduce the number of errors, not only by increasing the size of the training corpus but also, whenever possible, by correcting the results and by using the currently available grammars.

10. Bibliography

[1]BRILL, E.; **A Simple Rule-Based Part of Speech Tagger.** In Proceedings of the DARPA Speech and Natural Language Workshop, 112-116, 1992.

[2]BRISCOE, E.J.B.; CARROL, J.; **Robust Parsing - Advanced Course.** ESSLLI'94.

[3]CHANG, C.H.; CHEN, C.D.; **HMM-based Part-of-Speech Tagging for Chinese Corpora.** In Proceedings of the Workshop on Very Large Corpora: Academic and Industrial Perspectives, p. 40-47, 1993.

[4]CHANOD, J. P.;TAPANAINEN, P.; **Creating a tagset, lexicon and guesser for a French tagger.** CMP-LG, 1995.

[5]CHURCH, K. W.; **A Stochastic Parts Program and Noun Phrase Parser for Unrestricted Text.** In Proceedings of the Second Conference on Applied Natural Language Processing (ACL), p 136-143, 1988.

[6]CHURCH, K. W.; GALE, W.A.; **A Comparison of the Enhanced Good-Turing and Deleted Estimation Methods for Estimating Probabilities of English Bigrams.** In Computer Speech and Language, 5:19-54, 1991.

[7]CUTTING, D.; KUPIEC, J.; PEDERSEN, J.; SIBUN, P.; **A practical part-of-speech tagger.** In Proceedings of the 3rd Conference on Applied Language Processing, Trento, Italy, 133-140,1992.

[8]ELWORTHY, D.; **Does Baum-Welch Re-estimation Help Taggers?** In CMP-LG 1994.

[9]ELWORTHY, D.; **Tagset Design and Inflected Languages.** In CMP-LG 1994.

[10]KEMPE, A.; **A Stochastic Tagger and an Analysis of Tagging Errors.** Internal Paper. Institute for Computational Linguistics, University of Stuttgart.

[11]KEMPE, A.; Probabilistic Tagging with Feature Structures. IN CMP-LG 1994.

[12]LOPES, J.G.P., SANTOS, A.M.M.; **Portuguese Lexicon Acquisition Interface (PLAIN).** In Eurolex 8~90, Proceedings, Biblograf VOX, 1992, 105-107.

[13]MARQUES, N. M. C.; LOPES, J. G. P.; **POLARIS: A Portuguese Lexicon Acquisition and Retrieval Interactive System.** In Proceedings of the Conference on Practical Applications of Prolog , 1994.

[14]MERIALDO, B.; **Tagging English Text with a Probabilistic Model.** In Computational Linguistics, v. 20 ,n. 2, p. 155-171, 1994.

[15]SCHIMID, H.; **Part-of-Speech Tagging with Neural Networks.** CMP-LG 1994.

[16]VOUTILAINEN, A.; **A syntax-based part-of-speech analyser.** In CMP-LG 1995.

Quantification and Cognitive Constraints in Natural Language Understanding

Walid S. Saba[1,2] and Jean-Pierre Corriveau[2]

[1] AT&T Bell Laboratories, 480 Red Hill Rd. Middletown, NJ 07748 USA
walid@eagle.hr.att.com
[2] Carleton University, School of Computer Science, Ottawa, ON, K1S-5B6 CANADA
jeanpier@scs.carleton.ca

Abstract. Quantification in natural language is an important phenomena as it relates to scoping, reference resolution, and, more importantly, to inference. In this paper we argue that the reasoning involved in quantifier scoping and reference resolution is highly dependent on the linguistic context as well as time and memory constraints. Time and memory constraints are not only physical realities that an intelligent agent must cope with, but, as we shall argue, they play an important role in the inferencing process that underlies the task of language understanding.

1 Introduction

According to Micheal Dummet (1973), Frege's discovery of the notation of quantifiers and variables for expressing generality "resolved, for the first time in the whole history of logic, the problem which has foiled the most penetrating minds that had given their attention to the subject." To appreciate the expressive power of quantifiers and variables, consider the task of expressing the mathematical fact that "every natural number multiplied by 2 is an even natural number". This expresses a property of objects in an infinite domain, namely the domain of all natural numbers. Such properties can not be proved by deduction, but are typically established using an axiomatic system (e.g., algebra and number theory), and mathematical induction. Surprisingly, however, induction is a problematic phenomena since it requires us to have faith in a general principle stating that "regularities of the past will continue to into the future." (Goertzel, 1993). In mathematical reasoning, such regularities are accepted since a mathematical object, such as "2", for example, can not be expected to exhibit a different behavior, or take on different properties in different contexts. In everyday common sense reasoning, and in particular in language understanding, however, such regularities are not accepted so easily. Unlike properties attributed to mathematical objects, properties of "objects of thought" are context-dependent, and subject to revisions, exceptions, and other irregularities. In fact, whatever inductive generalizations we often make, must always involve some sort of "jumping to conclusions" (Flach, 1992). This problem, which has been termed by McCarthy (1987) as the problem of "generality in artificial intelligence" is central to the study of common sense reasoning and natural language understanding.

2 Context and Quantification

In computational linguistics, it has often been assumed that quantifiers have a fixed truth-functional meaning as suggested by the theory of generalized quantifiers (Barwise and Cooper, 1981), and Richard Montague's (1974) "proper treatment of quantification" (henceforth, PTQ). Such models are usually characterized by "compositionality", which states that the meaning of a compound phrase is a function of the meanings of the parts. Although it facilitates a systematic and elegant approach to semantic analysis of recursive syntactic structures, compositionality is generally at odds with context-sensitivity. Model-theoretic semantics with strict (Frege-style) compositional semantics are said to inherently suffer from the open-ended contexts problem (see Pereira and Pollack (1991) for a detailed discussion of this problem).

While model-theoretic semantics were able to cope with certain context-sensitive aspects of natural language, the intensions (meanings) of quantifiers, however, as well as other functional words, such as sentential connectives, are taken to be constant. That is, such words have the same meaning regardless of the context (see Forbes (1989)). In such a framework, all natural language quantifiers have their meaning grounded in terms of two logical operators: $\forall$ (for all), and $\exists$ (there exists). Consequently, all NL quantifiers are indirectly modeled by two logical connectives: negation and either conjunction or disjunction. In such an oversimplified model, quantifier ambiguity has often been translated to scoping ambiguity, and elaborate models were developed to remedy the problem, by semanticists (Cooper, 1983; Le Pore and Garson, 1983; Partee, 1984) as well as computational linguists (Harper, 1992; Alshawi, 1990; Pereira, 1990; Moran, 1988). However, the problem remains largely unresolved, and in our opinion, this is due in-part to the following:

1. the scope of quantifiers, as argued by Zeevat (1989), is usually given by "the linguistic context rather than by the linguistic rule that is responsible for their appearance in a sentence."
2. unlike objects in mathematical domains, properties of objects of thoughts are context-dependent, subject to exceptions, revisions, etc.
3. we are often forced to make decisions based on few examples, and using the, often incomplete, knowledge at hand.
4. Quantifiers, since they are used to refer to entities in large domains, must trigger inferences that are highly dependent on time and memory constraints.

Accordingly, the analysis of quantification in natural language must involve two types of analysis at two different levels. First, scope ambiguities are resolved using the linguistic context, a procedure that relies on background knowledge. This could be related to what Allen Newell (1980) calls the *knowledge level*. On the other hand, problems of quantification over large and potentially infinite domains are issues that are handled at a different level, namely at the *implementation level*, since these "performance" issues are directly related to requirements on time and memory resources (Kuipers, 1979, Johnson-Laird, 1994). Surprisingly, an adequate analysis that is "quantitative" in nature can be done at both levels without the need to devise *ad hoc* syntactic rules and without resorting to the use of complex semantic structures.

In this paper, we suggest a general strategy for dealing with quantification at two levels: (i) at the conceptual level scope ambiguities are resolved using *minimal* background knowledge, and (ii) at the implementation level, we will consider quantification over large and potentially infinite domains in a time- and memory-constrained model.

3 Quantifier Scope Ambiguity

The problem of scope ambiguity is a logical counter-part of the general phenomena of ambiguity in the meaning of quantifiers. To illustrate, consider the following:

(1a)   *Every student in CS404 received a grade.*
(1b)   *Every student in CS404 received a course outline.*

The syntactic structures of (1a) and (1b) are identical, and thus according to Montague's PTQ (Montague, 1974) would have the same translation. Ignoring an intensional derivation, the above sentences are translated in PTQ into the following:

(2a) $\forall x[Student(x) \wedge InCourse(x,CS404) \Rightarrow \exists y[Grade(y) \wedge Received(x,y)]]$

(2b) $\forall x[Student(x) \wedge InCourse(x,CS404) \Rightarrow \exists y[Outline(y,CS404) \wedge Received(x,y)]]$

Hence, (2b) incorrectly state that students in CS404 received different course outlines. Instead, the desired reading is one in which "a" has a wider scope than "every" resulting in the translation:

(2b') $\exists y \forall x[Student(x) \wedge InCourse(x,CS404) \wedge Outline(y,CS404) \Rightarrow Received(x,y)]$

that asserts that there is a single course outline for the course CS404, an outline that all students received. Clearly, such resolution depends on general knowledge of the domain: typically students in the same class receive the same course outline, but different grades. This "quantifier scoping ambiguity" problem can alternatively be viewed as an ambiguity problem in the meaning of quantifiers themselves. For example, "a" in (1a) can be read as "some", while "a" in (1b) refers to "the" (which is an anaphor referring to the "course outline of CS404). Due to the strict compositionality requirement, PTQ models can not cope with such inferences. Consequently a number of syntactically motivated rules for resolving such scoping ambiguities were suggested. In general, these rules suggest an ad hoc semantic ordering between functional words (see Moran (1988)), that is, an ordering fitted to a particular set of examples. While such techniques could adequately account for certain types of constructions (basically those that were used as data to these rules), the problem of dealing with open-ended contexts remains largely unresolved.

In recent years a number of suggestions have been made to enrich the context model so as to resolve such scoping ambiguities. The discourse representation theory (DRT) suggested by Kamp (1981), and the use of what Cooper (1995) calls the "background situation", in the general framework of situation semantics, are two such examples. However, both approaches have major shortcomings since the available context is still "syntactic" in nature, and no suggestion is made on how relevant background knowledge can be made available for use in a model-theoretic model.

4   Inferences in Resolving Scope Ambiguities

4.1   A Hierarchical Organization of Quantifiers

Before suggesting a general strategy for resolving scope ambiguity we briefly discuss some of the assumptions taken in our model. First, we assume a hierarchy of quantifiers along the following lines:

(3) $every \rightarrow most \rightarrow many \rightarrow some \rightarrow few \rightarrow the$

Furthermore, in this paper we will consider three[1] quantifiers with the following notation: $every: \forall$, $some: \exists$, $a(unique): \exists!$. The intended interpretation of the hierarchy of quantifiers given in (3) is that if "every P is Q" is true, then *under the same conditions*, "some P is Q" must be true, and, similarly, "there is a P that is Q", and so on. A quantified term phrase can be represented as $Q\ X$, where Q is a quantifier, and X is a set representing the extension of some concept. The simplest logical form which

---

[1] For simplicity, we will not discuss numeric and complex quantifiers (*three students*, *every one of the ...*).

could potentially involve scope ambiguities however is one where there are at least two quantifiers Q_1 and Q_2, a binary relation R, and two sets (extension of two concepts) X and Y. This can be represented as:

(4) $\qquad R(Q_1X, Q_2Y)$

For example, the proposition "every man loves a woman" is represented using (4) as $Love(\forall\ Man,\ \exists\ Women)$. In many instances we are interested in the scope of the two quantifiers, rather than the two concepts X and Y or the relation R. In such cases we will write (4) as Q_1Q_2. A quantifier Q_1 is "replaceable" by a quantifier Q_2, denoted to by $Q_1 \rightarrow Q_2$, iff Q_2 is "reachable" from Q_1 according to the hierarchy of quantifiers given in (3). Clearly, this is a transitive relation. More formally,

(5) *Quantifier Replacement Rule (QRR)*
Given background knowledge indicating a Q_1Q_2 relationship between two concepts X and Y, a $Q'_1Q''_2$ relationship is allowed iff $Q_1 \rightarrow Q'$ and $Q_2 \rightarrow Q''$ according to (3).

4.2 Role of Background Knowledge

In addition to a hierarchical organization of quantifiers, we also assume that cardinality information regarding relationships between various concepts is part of our background knowledge. For example, we assume the fact that the binary relation $LocatedOn(x,y)$, between houses and streets, is a many-to-one relationship is part of the KB. That is, we assume knowing that houses are typically located on streets, must involve knowing the (physical) fact that a house can not be located on more than one street. Moreover, we believe that we not only know a relation such as $Love(x,y)$ is a many-to-many relationship, but that the number of those who love something is typically much bigger than the number of all those who love the same y. The two possible readings for (6) are given is (6a) and (6b).

(6) $\qquad$ *Every man loves a woman.*
(6a) $\qquad \forall x \exists y [Man(x) \wedge Woman(y) \rightarrow Loves(x,y)]$
(6b) $\qquad \exists y \forall x [Man(x) \wedge Woman(y) \rightarrow Loves(x,y)]$

Although neither the syntactic structure nor the underlying semantic relationship give us any clue as to which of the two is the preferred reading, most readers would interpret (6) as (6a). Informally, the reason for this has to do with knowing the relative ratio of m to n in an *m-to-n* relationship. While example (6) will not be discussed further, the strategy discussed below will suggest an approach towards formalizing this line of reasoning.

4.3 Rules for Quantifier Scoping

To illustrate the significance of the assumptions given in the previous two sections, consider the relations shown in Figure 1. It is assumed here that these relations exist in the KB along with the cardinality information, as indicated above.

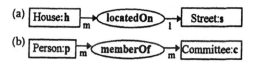

Figure 1. Cardinality information in the KB.

The relations shown in Figure 1 suggest that a house determines a street, i.e., a street is a function of a house (figure 1a), and that both a person and a committee determine a set of the other (figure 1b). We represent these semantic dependencies as ∀h∃s and ∀p∀c respectively. According to the quantifier replacement rule (QRR) given in (5), the possible replacements allowed are shown in Figure 2. Bold circles denote a reading that is not allowed according to the rules[2]. However, if a syntactic construction dictates this combination of quantifiers, the scope of quantifiers is reversed in the final translation.

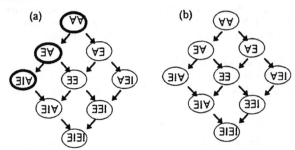

Figure 2. The possible quantifier scopings for the relations in Figure 1.

For example, since the relation shown in Figure 1(b) is many-to-many, all possible quantifier "branchings" are allowed as shown in Figure 2(b). Thus, we can speak of:

(8)   *Q member of Q committee, for all Q* ∈ { *a(specific), some, every* }

In Figure 2(b) this is indicated by the fact that all possible scopings are allowed. However, the relation in Figure 1(a) is more restrictive. For one thing, we can not speak of *"a house that is on every street."* That is, the (intuitively) correct reading of (9) is (9a) and not (9b):

(9)   *John visited a house on every street.*
(9a) $∀s∃h[House(h) ∧ Street(s) ∧ LocatedOn(h,s) → Visited(John,h)]$
(9b) $∃h∀s[House(h) ∧ Street(s) ∧ LocatedOn(h,s) → Visited(John,h)]$

Since the combination of quantifiers that is needed for (9) is ∃s∀h, and since this combination of scoping is indicated in a bold circle in Figure 2(a), the reverse scoping is chosen.

4.4 Disambiguation of Quantifiers

Disambiguation of quantifiers in our opinion falls under the general problem of "lexical disambiguation", which is essentially an inferencing problem (Corriveau, 1995). For example, the disambiguation of "a" in (1a) and (1b) is determined in an interactive manner by considering all possible inferences between the underlying concepts. What we suggest is that the inferencing involved in the disambiguation of "a" in (1a) proceeds as follows:

1. A path from grade and student in addition to disambiguating grade, determines that grade is a feature of student.
2. We establish that the relationship is ∀s∃g (i.e., grade is a function of student).

---

[2] Note that $∀x∃y(.. x .. y ..) ≡ ∃y∀x(.. x .. y ..)$, and, $∃x∀y(.. x .. y ..) ≡ ∃x∀y(.. x .. y ..)$.

3. In (1a), *a grade* refers to *a student grade*, and there is *a grade* for *every student*.

This process is shown in Figure 3(a). What is important to note here is that by discovering that grade is a feature of student, we essentially determined that "grade" is a (Skolem) function of "student", which is the effect of having "a" fall under the scope of "every".

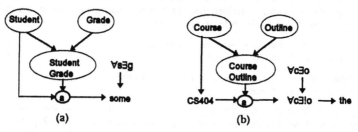

Figure 3. The disambiguation of "a grade" and "a course outline".

However, in contrast to syntactic approaches that rely on devising *ad hoc* rules, such a relation is discovered here by performing inferences using the properties that hold between the underlying concepts.

The inferencing involved in the disambiguation of "a" in (1b), graphically depicted in Figure 3(b), proceeds as follows:

1. A path from course and outline disambiguates outline, and determines outline to be a feature of course.
2. The relationship is $\forall c \exists o$ (i.e., a course outline is a function of course).
3. A path from course to CS404 determines that CS404 is a course.
4. Since there is one course (CS404), "*a course outline*" refers to "*the*" course outline.

This inference is allowed, since $\forall c \exists ! o$ can be inferred from $\forall c \exists o$ (recall (5) and Figure 2b). Note that if (1b) was replaced by

(10)   *Every student received a course outline.*

that is, if we were not speaking of any course in particular, then "a" is again interpreted as "some" as shown in Figure 3a, which is what we would expect, since the more plausible reading of (10) is "every student received a course outline for every course s/he is in."

5 Time and Memory Constraints

Beyond the *conceptual* (or *knowledge*) *level*, where the linguistic context must be considered, the analysis of quantification at the *implementation level* is a process that is highly dependent on time and memory constraints. In order to justify the role of time and memory constraints, consider the following examples:

(11a)   *Cubans prefer rum over vodka.*
(11b)   *Students in CS404 work in groups.*

Our intuitive reading of (11a) suggests that we have an implicit "most", while in (11b) we have an implicit "all". We argue that such inferences are dependent on time constraints and constraints on working memory. For example, since the set of students in CS404 is a much smaller set than the set of "Cubans", it is conceivable that we are able to perform an exhaustive search over the set of all students in CS404 to verify the proposition in (11b) within some time and memory constraints. In (11a), however, we are most likely performing a "generalization" based on few examples that are currently activated in short-term memory (STM). The basic idea here is that a quantifier is essentially a complex inferencing procedure that is dependent, not only on the linguistic context, but also on time and memory constraints. In order to further argue this point, consider the following examples, where an additional complexity is added due to the role of discourse:

(12a)   *This room is full of over ambitious accountants.*
        Everyone works at least 14 hours.

(12b)   *John's report on Japanese professionals is remarkable.*
        Everyone works at least 14 hours.

It seems probable that, through a combination of disambiguation and reference resolution, "everyone" will be interpreted as "each accountant" in (12a), but as "most accountants" in (12b), since the set of Japanese professionals has an indeterminate cardinality for most readers.

6   Logical Basis of a Cognitively Plausible Model

Our suggestion that time and memory constraints are part of the overall context that determines the meaning of quantifiers is related to theories of default reasoning. To show this consider a 1-place property P. There are three ways to conceive of verifying the truth (or falsity) of a property (or its negation), as shown in Figure 4 below.

P	¬P		P	¬P		P	¬P
1	0		1	0		1	0
0	1		0	1		0	1
-	-		-	1		-	0

(a)   (b)   (c)

Figure 4. Three models of negation.

In (a), we take the view that if we have no information regarding $P(x)$, then, we cannot decide on $\neg P(x)$. In (b), we take the view that if P can not be confirmed of some entity x, then $P(x)$ is assumed to be false[3]. In (c), however, we take the view that if there is no evidence to negate $P(x)$, then assume $P(x)$. While such a view might seem unjustifiable at first, in reality such situations arise quite frequently. For example, suppose a person were to visit the jungles of the Amazon. Given that we "know" several wild animals typically roam around the jungle, it is most likely that one would attribute "wild" and "dangerous" to any animal that fits some stereotype, even if she has never seen the animal, which could very well be a harmless animal. Note that model (c) essentially allows one to "generalize", given no evidence to the contrary - or, given an overwhelming positive evidence (the relevance of this point to quantification over infinite domains will be made clear shortly).

Of course, formally speaking, we are interested in defining the exact circumstances under which models (a) through (c) might be appropriate. We believe that the three models are used, depending on the context, time, and memory constraints (to

---

[3] Note that this is the *Closed World Assumption* typically assumed in database systems.

mention a few). For example, model (a) is more appropriate if one is trying to verify that all cables have been connected properly, when one is interested in diagnosing a failure in a certain device, for example, since otherwise no decision can be made as to what the cause of the failure is. However, when trying to verify if a seat is available on some flight, it is usually more appropriate to assume the negative in the absence of any information.

The model in (c), however, is of a particular interest to us here, since it is related to the notion of stereotyped generalization that we tend to make when reasoning about infinite (or relatively large) domains. In this model, we believe the truth (or falsity) of a certain property $P(x)$ is a function of the following:

$np(P,x)$ *number of positive instances satisfying $P(x)$*
$nn(P,x)$ *number of negative instances satisfying $P(x)$*
$cf(P,x)$ *a certainty factor denoting the degree to which P is "generally" believed of x.*

It is assumed here that cf is a value $v \in \{\perp\} \cup [0,1]$. That is, a value that is either undefined, or a real value between 0 and 1. We also suggest that this value is constantly modified (re-enforced) through a feedback mechanism, as more examples are experienced. This is similar to what has been suggested by Wang (1995), where the system is allowed to dynamically revise its beliefs.

7 Role of Time and Memory Constraints

In this section we consider the problem is one of interpreting statements of the form *every C P*, where C has an indeterminate (potentially infinite) extension in more detail. Verifying *every C P* is depicted graphically in Figure 5 below. It is assumed that the property P is generally attributed to members of the concept C with certainty $cf(C,P)$, where $cf(C,P)=0$ represents the fact that P is not generally assumed of objects in C. On the other hand, a value of cf near 1, represents a strong bias towards believing P of C at face value (i.e., without actual verification of the fact). In the former case, the processing will depend little, if at all, on our general belief, but more on the actual instances. In the latter case, and especially when faced with time and memory constraints, more weight might be given to prior *stereotyped* knowledge that we might have accumulated. More precisely, verifying *every C P* could proceed as follows:

1. An attempt at an exhaustive verification of all the elements in the set C is first made (this is the default meaning of "every").
2. If time and memory capacity allow the processing of all the elements in C, then the result is 1, if $np = |C|$ (that is, if *every C P*).
3. If time and/or memory constraints do not allow an exhaustive verification, then we will attempt making a decision based on the evidence at hand, where the evidence is based on cf, nn, np (a suggested function is given below).
4. If 3 applies, then cf is computed from any available C elements that are currently active in short-term memory (if any), otherwise cf is the current value associated with C in the knowledge base. (this allows us to put more weight on the currently activated instances (examples) when making a generalization).
5. The final output is used to update our certainty factor, cf[4].

In 3, the final output is determined as a function F, that could be defined as follows:

(13) $F_{(C,P)}(nn,np,\varepsilon,cf,\omega) = (np \,\cdot\, \varepsilon.nn) \wedge (cf(C,P) \,\cdot= \omega)$

---

[4] The nature of this feedback mechanism is quite involved, and will not be discussed here.

where ε and ω are quantifier-specific parameters. In the case of the quantifier "every", the function in (13) states that, in the absence of time and memory resources to process *every C P* exhaustively, the result of the process is "true" if there is an overwhelming positive evidence (high value for ε), and if the there is some prior stereotyped belief supporting this inference (i.e., if *cf* › ω › 0). Note that processing *every C P* using the above function, amounts to interpreting "every" as "most" (recall examples (11a) and (11b), and the hierarchy of quantifiers discussed in section 4.1). If "most" was the quantifier we started with, then the function in (13) and the above procedure can be applied, although smaller values for ε and ω will be assigned.

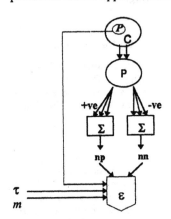

Figure 5. Quantification in a time and memory constrained model.

Figure 6. The *standard* quantifiers using (13).

	np	nn	ε
every	$np = |C|$	$nn = 0$	$ε › 0$
some	$|C| › np › 0$	$|C| › nn › 0$	$ε › 0$
no	$np = 0$	$nn = |C|$	$ε ‹ 0$

At this point it should be noted that the function in (13) is a generalization of the theory of generalized quantifiers, where quantifiers can be interpreted using this function as shown in the table in figure 6. However, it should be noted that in the theory of generalized quantifiers *cf* and ω, discussed above, are irrelevant. In this regard we agree with the argument made by Faccounier (1994) that logic usually abstracts a solution that could work rather well in some idealized and controlled situation (referred to as a model in formal logic), but fails in modeling the idiosyncratic nature of human languages.

8 Concluding Remarks

Gurevich (1988) has shown that the problem of branching quantifiers is an NP problem. Therefore, the only hope of a computationally tractable model of quantification is one that relies on some "heuristics." We believe that such heuristics must be "semantic" in nature, and must be based on a model that reflects our apparent ability to quantify over infinite domains and resolve references rapidly and effortlessly, given limited time and memory resources. In this paper we have argued that quantifiers in natural language do not have a fixed truth functional meaning. Instead, we argued for a more cognitively plausible model where quantifiers are generally assumed to be ambiguous, and where their meaning is modeled as a complex inference procedure that is dependent on the linguistic context, as well as time and memory constraints.

Acknowledgments

The authors would like to thank three anonymous reviewers for their valuable suggestions and comments on an earlier draft of this paper.

References

1. Alshawi, H.(1990). Resolving Quasi Logical Forms, *Computational Linguistics*, 6(13).
2. Barwise, J. and Cooper, R. (1981). Generalized Quantifiers and Natural Language, *Linguistics and Philosophy*, 4, pp. 159-219.
3. Cooper, R. (1995), The Role of Situations in Generalized Quantifiers, In L. Shalom (Ed.), *Handbook of Contemporary Semantic Theory*, Blackwell.
4. Cooper, R. (1983). *Quantification and Syntactic Theory*, D. Reidel, Netherlands.
5. Corriveau, J.-P. (1995). *Time-Constrained Memory*, Lawrence Erlbaum: NJ.
6. Dummet, M. (1973). *Frege- Philosophy of Language*, Harvard University Press.
7. Fauconnier, G. (1994). *Mental Spaces*, Cambridge University Press.
8. Flach, P. A. (1992), An Analysis of Various Forms of 'Jumping to Conclusions', In K. P. Jantke (Ed.), *LNAI, No. 642*, Springer, pp. 170-186.
9. Forbes, G. (1989). Indexicals, In D. Gabby and F. Guenthner (Eds.), *Handbook of Philosophical Logic*, Volume IV, D. Reidel. pp. 463-490.
10. Goertzel, B. (1993), *The Structure of Intelligence*, Springer-Verlag.
11. Gurevich, Y. (1988), Logic and the Challenge of Computer Science, In E. Borger (Ed.), *Trends in Theoretical Computer Science*, Computer Science Press, pp. 1-58.
12. Harper, M. P. (1992). Ambiguous Noun Phrases in Logical Form, *Computational Linguistics*, 18(4), pp. 419-465.
13. Johnson-Laird, P. (1994).Mental Models and Probabilistic Thinking, *Cognition*, 50.
14. Kamp, H. (1981), A Theory of Truth and Semantic Representation, In Groenendijk, et al (Eds.), *Formal Methods in the Study of Language*, Mathematisch Centrum, Amsterdam.
15. Kuipers, B. (1979), On Representing Common Sense Knowledge, In Findler, N. (Ed.), *Associative Networks*, Academic Press, pp. 393-408.
16. Le Pore, E. and Garson, J. (1983). Pronouns and Quantifier-Scope in English, *Journal of Philosophical Logic*, 12, pp. 327-358.
17. McCarthy, J. (1987), Generality in Artificial Intelligence, *CACM*, 30(8).
18. Montague, R. (1974). *Formal Philosophy: Selected Papers of Richard Montague*, edited with an introduction by Richard Thomason. Yale University Press.
19. Moran, D. B. (1988). Quantifier Scoping in the SRI Core Language, *In Proceedings of 26th Annual Meeting of the ACL*, pp. 33-40.
20. Newell, A. (1980), Physical Symbol Systems, *Cognitive Science*, 2, pp. 135-184.
21. Partee, B. (1984). Quantification, Pronouns, and VP-Anaphora, In J. Groenedijk et al (Eds.), *Truth, Interpretation and Information*, Dordrecht: Foris.
22. Pereira, F. C. N. and Pollack, M. E. (1991). Incremental Interpretation, *Artificial Intelligence*, 50, pp. 37-82.
23. Shastri, L. and Ajjanagadde, V. (1993). From Simple Associations to Systematic Reasoning, *Behavioral & Brain Sciences*, 16.
24. Wang, P. (1994), From Inheritance Relation to Non-Axiomatic Logic, *International Journal of Approximate Reasoning*, (to appear).
25. Zeevat, H. (1989). A Compositional Approach to Discourse Representation theory, *Linguistics and Philosophy*, 12, pp. 95-131.

Lecture Notes in Artificial Intelligence (LNAI)

Vol. 827: D. M. Gabbay, H. J. Ohlbach (Eds.), Temporal Logic. Proceedings, 1994. XI, 546 pages. 1994.

Vol. 830: C. Castelfranchi, E. Werner (Eds.), Artificial Social Systems. Proceedings, 1992. XVIII, 337 pages. 1994.

Vol. 833: D. Driankov, P. W. Eklund, A. Ralescu (Eds.), Fuzzy Logic and Fuzzy Control. Proceedings, 1991. XII, 157 pages. 1994.

Vol. 835: W. M. Tepfenhart, J. P. Dick, J. F. Sowa (Eds.), Conceptual Structures: Current Practices. Proceedings, 1994. VIII, 331 pages. 1994.

Vol. 837: S. Wess, K.-D. Althoff, M. M. Richter (Eds.), Topics in Case-Based Reasoning. Proceedings, 1993. IX, 471 pages. 1994.

Vol. 838: C. MacNish, D. Pearce, L. M. Pereira (Eds.), Logics in Artificial Intelligence. Proceedings, 1994. IX, 413 pages. 1994.

Vol. 847: A. Ralescu (Ed.) Fuzzy Logic in Artificial Intelligence. Proceedings, 1993. VII, 128 pages. 1994.

Vol: 861: B. Nebel, L. Dreschler-Fischer (Eds.), KI-94: Advances in Artificial Intelligence. Proceedings, 1994. IX, 401 pages. 1994.

Vol. 862: R. C. Carrasco, J. Oncina (Eds.), Grammatical Inference and Applications. Proceedings, 1994. VIII, 290 pages. 1994.

Vol 867: L. Steels, G. Schreiber, W. Van de Velde (Eds.), A Future for Knowledge Acquisition. Proceedings, 1994. XII, 414 pages. 1994.

Vol. 869: Z. W. Raś, M. Zemankova (Eds.), Methodologies for Intelligent Systems. Proceedings, 1994. X, 613 pages. 1994.

Vol. 872: S Arikawa, K. P. Jantke (Eds.), Algorithmic Learning Theory. Proceedings, 1994. XIV, 575 pages. 1994.

Vol. 878: T. Ishida, Parallel, Distributed and Multiagent Production Systems. XVII, 166 pages. 1994.

Vol. 886: M. M. Veloso, Planning and Learning by Analogical Reasoning. XIII, 181 pages. 1994.

Vol. 890: M. J. Wooldridge, N. R. Jennings (Eds.), Intelligent Agents. Proceedings, 1994. VIII, 407 pages. 1995.

Vol. 897: M. Fisher, R. Owens (Eds.), Executable Modal and Temporal Logics. Proceedings, 1993. VII, 180 pages. 1995.

Vol. 898: P. Steffens (Ed.), Machine Translation and the Lexicon. Proceedings, 1993. X, 251 pages. 1995.

Vol. 904: P. Vitányi (Ed.), Computational Learning Theory. EuroCOLT'95. Proceedings, 1995. XVII, 415 pages. 1995.

Vol. 912: N. Lavrač S. Wrobel (Eds.), Machine Learning: ECML – 95. Proceedings, 1995. XI, 370 pages. 1995.

Vol. 918: P. Baumgartner, R. Hähnle, J. Posegga (Eds.), Theorem Proving with Analytic Tableaux and Related Methods. Proceedings, 1995. X, 352 pages. 1995.

Vol. 927: J. Dix, L. Moniz Pereira, T.C. Przymusinski (Eds.), Non-Monotonic Extensions of Logic Programming. Proceedings, 1994. IX, 229 pages. 1995.

Vol. 928: V.W. Marek, A. Nerode, M. Truszczynski (Eds.), Logic Programming and Nonmonotonic Reasoning. Proceedings, 1995. VIII, 417 pages. 1995.

Vol. 929: F. Morán, A. Moreno, J.J. Merelo, P.Chacón (Eds.), Advances in Artificial Life. Proceedings, 1995. XIII, 960 pages. 1995.

Vol. 934: P. Barahona, M. Stefanelli, J. Wyatt (Eds.), Artificial Intelligence in Medicine. Proceedings, 1995. XI, 449 pages. 1995.

Vol. 941: M. Cadoli, Tractable Reasoning in Artificial Intelligence. XVII, 247 pages. 1995.

Vol. 946: C. Froidevaux, J. Kohlas (Eds.), Symbolic Quantitative and Approaches to Reasoning under Uncertainty. Proceedings, 1995. X, 430 pages. 1995.

Vol. 954: G. Ellis, R. Levinson, W. Rich. J.F. Sowa (Eds.), Conceptual Structures: Applications, Implementation and Theory. Proceedings, 1995. IX, 353 pages. 1995.

Vol. 956: X. Yao (Ed.), Progress in Evolutionary Computation. Proceedings, 1993, 1994. VIII, 314 pages. 1995.

Vol. 957: C. Castelfranchi, J.-P. Müller (Eds.), From Reaction to Cognition. Proceedings, 1993. VI, 252 pages. 1995.

Vol. 961: K.P. Jantke. S. Lange (Eds.), Algorithmic Learning for Knowledge-Based Systems. X, 511 pages. 1995.

Vol. 981: I. Wachsmuth, C.-R. Rollinger, W. Brauer (Eds.), KI-95: Advances in Artificial Intelligence. Proceedings, 1995. XII, 269 pages. 1995.

Vol. 984: J.-M. Haton, M. Keane, M. Manago (Eds.), Advances in Case-Based Reasoning. Proceedings, 1994. VIII, 307 pages. 1995.

Vol. 990: C. Pinto-Ferreira, N.J. Mamede (Eds.), Progress in Artificial Intelligence. Proceedings, 1995. XIV, 487 pages. 1995.

Vol. 991: J. Wainer, A. Carvalho (Eds.), Advances in Artificial Intelligence. Proceedings, 1995. XII, 342 pages. 1995.

Vol. 992: M. Gori, G. Soda (Eds.), Topics in Artificial Intelligence. Proceedings, 1995. XII, 451 pages. 1995.

Vol. 997: K. P. Jantke, T. Shinohara, T. Zeugmann (Eds.), Algorithmic Learning Theory. Proceedings, 1995. XV, 319 pages. 1995.

Lecture Notes in Computer Science

Vol. 961: K.P. Jantke, S. Lange (Eds.), Algorithmic Learning for Knowledge-Based Systems. X, 511 pages. 1995. (Subseries LNAI).

Vol. 962: I. Lee, S.A. Smolka (Eds.), CONCUR '95: Concurrency Theory. Proceedings, 1995. X, 547 pages. 1995.

Vol. 963: D. Coppersmith (Ed.), Advances in Cryptology - CRYPTO '95. Proceedings, 1995. XII, 467 pages. 1995.

Vol. 964: V. Malyshkin (Ed.), Parallel Computing Technologies. Proceedings, 1995. XII, 497 pages. 1995.

Vol. 965: H. Reichel (Ed.), Fundamentals of Computation Theory. Proceedings, 1995. IX, 433 pages. 1995.

Vol. 966: S. Haridi, K. Ali, P. Magnusson (Eds.), EURO-PAR '95 Parallel Processing. Proceedings, 1995. XV, 734 pages. 1995.

Vol. 967: J.P. Bowen, M.G. Hinchey (Eds.), ZUM '95: The Z Formal Specification Notation. Proceedings, 1995. XI, 571 pages. 1995.

Vol. 968: N. Dershowitz, N. Lindenstrauss (Eds.), Conditional and Typed Rewriting Systems. Proceedings, 1994. VIII, 375 pages. 1995.

Vol. 969: J. Wiedermann, P. Hájek (Eds.), Mathematical Foundations of Computer Science 1995. Proceedings, 1995. XIII, 588 pages. 1995.

Vol. 970: V. Hlaváč, R. Šára (Eds.), Computer Analysis of Images and Patterns. Proceedings, 1995. XVIII, 960 pages. 1995.

Vol. 971: E.T. Schubert, P.J. Windley, J. Alves-Foss (Eds.), Higher Order Logic Theorem Proving and Its Applications. Proceedings, 1995. VIII, 400 pages. 1995.

Vol. 972: J.-M. Hélary, M. Raynal (Eds.), Distributed Algorithms. Proceedings, 1995. XI, 333 pages. 1995.

Vol. 973: H.H. Adelsberger, J. Lažanský, V. Mařík (Eds.), Information Management in Computer Integrated Manufacturing. IX, 665 pages. 1995.

Vol. 974: C. Braccini, L. DeFloriani, G. Vernazza (Eds.), Image Analysis and Processing. Proceedings, 1995. XIX, 757 pages. 1995.

Vol. 975: W. Moore, W. Luk (Eds.), Field-Programmable Logic and Applications. Proceedings, 1995. XI, 448 pages. 1995.

Vol. 976: U. Montanari, F. Rossi (Eds.), Principles and Practice of Constraint Programming — CP '95. Proceedings, 1995. XIII, 651 pages. 1995.

Vol. 977: H. Beilner, F. Bause (Eds.), Quantitative Evaluation of Computing and Communication Systems. Proceedings, 1995. X, 415 pages. 1995.

Vol. 978: N. Revell, A M. Tjoa (Eds.), Database and Expert Systems Applications. Proceedings, 1995. XV, 654 pages. 1995.

Vol. 979: P. Spirakis (Ed.), Algorithms — ESA '95. Proceedings, 1995. XII, 598 pages. 1995.

Vol. 980: A. Ferreira, J. Rolim (Eds.), Parallel Algorithms for Irregularly Structured Problems. Proceedings, 1995. IX, 409 pages. 1995.

Vol. 981: I. Wachsmuth, C.-R. Rollinger, W. Brauer (Eds.), KI-95: Advances in Artificial Intelligence. Proceedings, 1995. XII, 269 pages. (Subseries LNAI).

Vol. 982: S. Doaitse Swierstra, M. Hermenegildo (Eds.), Programming Languages: Implementations, Logics and Programs. Proceedings, 1995. XI, 467 pages. 1995.

Vol. 983: A. Mycroft (Ed.), Static Analysis. Proceedings, 1995. VIII, 423 pages. 1995.

Vol. 984: J.-P. Haton, M. Keane, M. Manago (Eds.), Advances in Case-Based Reasoning. Proceedings, 1994. VIII, 307 pages. 1994. (Subseries LNAI).

Vol. 985: T. Sellis (Ed.), Rules in Database Systems. Proceedings, 1995. VIII, 373 pages. 1995.

Vol. 986: Henry G. Baker (Ed.), Memory Management. Proceedings, 1995. XII, 417 pages. 1995.

Vol. 987: P.E. Camurati, H. Eveking (Eds.), Correct Hardware Design and Verification Methods. Proceedings, 1995. VIII, 342 pages. 1995.

Vol. 988: A.U. Frank, W. Kuhn (Eds.), Spatial Information Theory. Proceedings, 1995. XIII, 571 pages. 1995.

Vol. 989: W. Schäfer, P. Botella (Eds.), Software Engineering — ESEC '95. Proceedings, 1995. XII, 519 pages. 1995.

Vol. 990: C. Pinto-Ferreira, N.J. Mamede (Eds.), Progress in Artificial Intelligence. Proceedings, 1995. XIV, 487 pages. 1995. (Subseries LNAI).

Vol. 991: J. Wainer, A. Carvalho (Eds.), Advances in Artificial Intelligence. Proceedings, 1995. XII, 342 pages. 1995. (Subseries LNAI).

Vol. 992: M. Gori, G. Soda (Eds.), Topics in Artificial Intelligence. Proceedings, 1995. XII, 451 pages. 1995. (Subseries LNAI).

Vol. 993: T.C. Fogarty (Ed.), Evolutionary Computing. Proceedings, 1995. VIII, 264 pages. 1995.

Vol. 994: M. Hebert, J. Ponce, T. Boult, A. Gross (Eds.), Object Representation in Computer Vision. Proceedings, 1994. VIII, 359 pages. 1995.

Vol. 997: K.P. Jantke, T. Shinohara, T. Zeugmann (Eds.), Algorithmic Learning Theory. Proceedings, 1995. XV, 319 pages. 1995. (Subseries LNAI).

Vol. 998: A. Clarke, M. Campolargo, N. Karatzas (Eds.), Bringing Telecommunication Services to the People – IS&N '95. Proceedings, 1995. XII, 510 pages. 1995.

Vol. 999: P. Antsaklis, W. Kohn, A. Nerode, S. Sastry (Eds.), Hybrid Systems II. VIII, 569 pages. 1995.